CITIES

CITIES

———

JOHN READER

GROVE PRESS
New York

First published in the United Kingdom in 2004
by William Heinemann, a division of Random House, London

Printed in the United States of America

Library of Congress Cataloging-in-Publication Data
Reader, John.
　　Cities / John Reader.
　　　p. cm.
　　Originally published: London : William Heinemann, 2004.
　　Includes bibliographical references and index.
　　ISBN: 978-0-8021-4273-3
　　eISBN: 978-0-8021-9573-9
　　1. Cities and towns. 2. Cities and towns—History. I. Title.
HT111.R42 2005
307.76—dc22   2005040999

Design by SX Composing DTP, Rayleigh, Essex

Grove Press
an imprint of Grove/Atlantic, Inc.
154 West 14th Street
New York, NY 10011

Distributed by Publishers Group West

www.groveatlantic.com

Contents

Foreword

The world is not short of books about cities. Thousands of titles adorn the bookshops, libraries and coffee tables of every community. Take your pick from among works featuring the marvels and wonders of this or that city in pages of glossy photographs and exuberant prose; or choose one of the stouter and denser academic volumes that look beyond the marvels to define aspects of history and architecture that make one city more worthy of in-depth attention than another – in the author's view. Then there are the travel guides, the musings of footloose essayists, the pronouncements of influential commentators, the fine prose of novelists and the evocations of poets:

> Giotto's tower,
> The lily of Florence blossoming in stone.

That was Longfellow, just a scrap of many takes on the Renaissance city awaiting the unsatiated enthusiast. London? Try Rasmussen and Ackroyd. American cities? Look for Reps, and especially Riis on New York. Mesopotamia and the early history of cities? It has to be Adams, and Van de Mieroop. Chinese cities? Wheatley, Steinhardt, and don't overlook Marco Polo. Among more all-encompassing works, the erudition of Mumford, Vance and Hall is unmatched. Morris provides an engrossing history of urban form up to the Industrial Revolution, and Cobbett gives a pithy account of what the nineteenth-century industrial city did to Britain. Details of these books – and many more – appear in the bibliography on pages 326–341, which raises a pertinent question: if so many books on cities already exist, why burden the shelves with another? Well, I like to think this one is different. It commends the magnificence of great cities, as other admirers do; and deplores their failings no less than any polemicist might; but beyond that, it searches for the context – ecological and functional – that is common to the phenomenon of the city everywhere, in every era.

Ecology is the key factor here. Forty years ago, the word was hardly known outside research establishments studying the relationship between organisms and their environment. Now the word is in every-day use – though not always used correctly. An entrenched conviction that the science of ecology applies only to the so-called 'natural' world has developed, giving a gloss of authority to negative assumptions concerning the city. In this scheme of things, anything man-made is 'unnatural'. Nothing more so than a city. You can point out that a city is as much part of the world as a termites' mound or a beaver's dam; that the biological imperatives of existence (food, sex, shelter and security) apply as much to people living in cities as to monkeys living in trees, but the rural–urban dichotomy persists: one good, the other bad. We have all met people who profess to hate the city so much that only regular retreats to a second home in the country can preserve their sanity. If the rural environment is so good for you, their words and behaviour imply, then the city must be inherently bad.

Hope for a more reasoned and inclusive understanding of ecology in respect of urban environments has been raised by news that the United States' National Science Foundation is funding a long-term, multi-million dollar ecological study of two cities: Baltimore and Phoenix. What could be more ecological than studying humans and their environment, in cities, the studies ask. What indeed. Especially as cities are destined to become the most significant phenomena on the planet. Even now, the behaviour of cities, as ecological entities interacting with their environment, affects the entire globe, and all humanity.

But this is not an ecological textbook on cities. It is a book that tells *a story* of cities, from their earliest manifestation to the present day, and attempts to understand them from an ecological point of view – how they grow, how they sustain themselves, and the nature of their relationship with immediate and distant surroundings. Along the way, examples from specific cities around the world illuminate particular points: their needs, their problems, their achievements – and their failings. People of course feature prominently, as essential components of the city. After all, cities would not exist without us. The question of the moment is: could we exist without cities?

Acknowledgements

The final draft is finished, and the accumulated papers and books, notes, references, diaries, e-mails, letters, addresses and telephone numbers suddenly become forceful reminders of how much this project has relied upon other people – especially the authors of the works cited in the bibliography. Without them, the book simply would not exist. That is a humbling thought, and I am deeply grateful to them all. Thank you.

My research was facilitated by generous help and hospitality from many quarters. In some instances a stay of several days was involved; in others it was an hour or two, a conversation, or perhaps just an e-mailed reference to something I might otherwise have missed. All contributions were very much appreciated. My thanks to: Leslie Aiello, Alan Berkowitz, Gerald Blomeyer, Cristina Boelcke, Bill Brown, Bobbie Brown, Simonetta Cavaciocchi, Harvey Croze, George and June Duncan, Rob Foley, Peter Goldsbury, John and Diane Grabowski, Jörg Haspel, Peter and Jessie Hawthorne, Andrew Hill, Ian Hodder, Richard Hosking, Fumio Ikuta, Norioki Ishimaru, Sue and David John, Hugh and Peggy Jones, Kathy Homewood, Gerd Koch, Urs Kohlbrenner, Hiroshi Kurose, Marta Lahr, Hubert and Diana Martin, Nomura Masato, Neil Maybin, Sally McBrearty, Rod McIntosh, Susan Keech McIntosh, Fumihisa Miyoshi, A. E. J. Morris, Klaus Müschen, Mirko Novak, Francis Pickard, Steward T. A. Pickett, Tim Radford, Charles Redman, Johannes Renger, Arsenio Rodriguez, Alan Rowlin, Esho and Shoko Togashi, Kay Woods, Rita Wright, Mayumi Yamane, Toshiro Yuasa, the staff of the University College London libraries, the London Library, the Institute of Ecosystem Studies, Millbrook, and the Istituto Datini, Prato.

A fellowship from the Bogliasco Foundation facilitated my work on the final draft of the book, and thus I am also indebted to the Foundation and its staff in New York and Liguria – many thanks.

At Heinemann, I have a lot to thank Ravi Mirchandani for – not least his choice of Caroline Knight as editor. Caroline's contribution has been invaluable, and it has also been good to know that Emily Sweet and Mark Handsley were there. Pat Kavanagh and Carol MacArthur at PFD were always there too – warm and steadfast as ever. On the home front, Brigitte has been just wonderful, Alice was the perfect companion for a research trip to Japan, and Mark has been a source of stimulating conversation. I offer sincere thanks to all.

List of Illustrations
and Picture Credits

William Heinemann has made every effort to contact copyright-holders of the images reproduced in the plate sections of this book and would be grateful for any further information should any accidental infringement of copyright have taken place.

1. Barrage balloon
   credit: © Hulton Archive/Getty Images

2. A London Policeman in smog, 1950s
   credit: © Hulton Archive/Getty Images

3. Battersea Power Station, 1954
   credit: © Hulton Archive/Getty Images

4. Venice: 'Healing of Man Possessed by Devil' by Vittore Carpaccio (1465-1525)
   credit: The Art Archive/Accademia Venice/Dagli Orti

5. St Mark's Square during floods in Venice
   credit: Graham Tween/Lonely Planet Images

6. Manhattan and Brooklyn bridges, New York City
   credit: © Owaki-Kulla/CORBIS

7. Vancouver skyline
   credit: © John Reader

8. Caral, Peru
   credit: © George Steinmetz/KATZ

9. Çatal Hüyük, an artist's impression
   credit: John Gordon Swogger

10. Wall painting of Çatal Hüyük in plan
    credit: published in *Gardner's art through the ages*. 9th edn 1991. Horst de la Croix, Richard G. Tansey, Diane Kirkpatrick (eds.). San Diego: Harcourt Brace Jovanovich

11. Artist's impression of the buildings of Çatal Hüyük
    credit: published in Mellaart, James, 1967. *Çatal Hüyük: a neolithic town in Anatolia* London: Thames and Hudson.

12. 'Assyrian royal palace at Nineveh', Woodcut *c.* 1880, Ernst Hayn after a reconstruction by A. H. Layard
    credit: AKG-Images

13. Street map of Ur by Leonard Woolley
    credit: published in Woolley, Sir Leonard, 1982. *Ur 'of the Chaldees'* London, The Herbert Press

14. Irrigation canals around the Euphrates
    credit: published in Adams, Robert McCormick, 1981. *Heartland of cities: surveys of ancient settlement and land use on the central floodplain of the Euphrates* Chicago, London: University of Chicago Press

15. Panel from the Standard of Ur
    credit: © Bettmann/CORBIS

16. Ancient Sumerian tablet showing earliest writing
    credit: © RMN Images

17. Ur site, Mesopotamia
    credit: Ancient Art and Architecture Collection Ltd/TopFoto.co.uk

18. Victory stele of Naram-Sin *c.* 2230 BC
    credit: © Gianni Dagli Orti/CORBIS

19. Stele of the Vultures, dedicated by Eannatum, prince of the state of Lagash, celebrating his victory over city of Umma. Early Dynastic Period Sumerian *c.* 2450 BC.
credit: Art Archive/Musée du Louvre, Paris

20. Phoenician galleys, after A. Layard
credit: published in: Casson, Lionel, 1971. *Ships and seamanship in the ancient world* Princeton, N.J.: Princeton University Press

21. Forum Romanum, Rome, Italy: View from the Temple of Vespanian to the churches.
credit: AKG-Images/Pirozzi

22. The Acropolis, Athens, Greece
credit: Royalty-Free/CORBIS

23. Roman mosaic showing the activities of the estate of Seigneur Julius: hunting, olive harvesting, offering game and produce to the landowner, AD 100-400, Carthage.
credit: R. Sheridan/Ancient Art & Architecture Collection

24. Roman mosaic from Tunisia: sowing.
credit: Ronald Sheridan/Ancient Art & Architecture Collection

25. The amphitheatre at El Djem, Tunisia
credit: Roger Wood/Corbis

26. Large roman merchantmen mosaic, illustrating Rome's merchant fleet, AD 200: freighter with rounded bow and standard rig and another with projecting cutwater and three mastered rig, from an archeological excavation, Ostia, Lazio.
credit: Alinari

27. The Isis Giminana, barge ferrying produce from a Tiber estuary to the city docks, from a tomb painting found in Ostia but is now kept at the Museo del Vaticano in Rome.
credit: Alinari

28. Big Roman merchantman at the entrance to Portus, in the Torlonia Museum in Rome.
credit: Alinari

Joseph Bazalgette (standing top right)
credit: © Hulton-Deutsch Collection/CORBIS

52. Visiting the sewers of Paris – the ladies are conducted by a special
boat. 1870
credit: Mary Evans Picture Library

53. The market gardens over the gravel beds at Gennevilliers, where the
outfall of the sewers was used to grow fruit and vegetables and water
was purified by gravel filtration
credit: L'Illustration

54. Post-war Vienna, 1947
credit: © Hulton Archive/Getty Images

55. Back-to-back housing at Staithes, Yorkshire. Late 19th century
credit: Mary Evans Picture Library

56. Industrial Detroit
credit: © E. O. Hoppé/CORBIS

57. Nineteenth-century engraving of bicycles
credit: S. T. Dadd, published in: Ballantine, Richard, 1990. *Richard's
New Bicycle Book* London, Sydney & Auckland: Pan Books

58. Atlantic 4-4-2 and Mono-Plane
credit: © O.S. Nock; Milepost 92 ½/CORBIS

59. Berlin's elevated train
credit: Ullstein Bild Berlin

60. People waiting for soup in Berlin, 1916
credit: © Hulton Archive/Getty Images

61. A circus elephant pulls a coal cart, Berlin
credit: Ullstein Bild Berlin

62. Potsdamer Platz before the Wall, 1931.
credit: published in: Schneider, Richard (ed.) 1993/4. *Historic Places
in Berlin* Berlin: Nicholai

63. Potsdamer Platz after the Wall, 1963.
credit: published in: Schneider, Richard (ed.) 1993/4. *Historic Places in Berlin* Berlin: Nicholai

64. Potsdamer Platz in 2004
credit: published at www.gtz/berlin/english/postdamer platz.htm

65. Reichstag, Berlin
credit © Alamy Images

66. Ellis Island immigrants waiting for ferry, *c.* 1900
credit: © Bettmann/CORBIS

67. Aerial view of tip of Manhattan *c.* 1942
credit: CORBIS

68. Shacks in a New York Slum, early 1900s
credit: © Bettmann/CORBIS

69. Spanish woodcut of the plan of Tenochtitlan
credit: Ancient Art & Architecture Collection/Ronald Sheridan

70. Sixteenth-century Spanish illustration of a typical Aztec village
credit: Stockholm: Ethnological Museum of Sweden

71. Archaeological survey of Tenochtitlan
credit: published in: William T. Sanders, Jeffrey R. Parsons, and Robert S. Santley, *c.* 1979. *The basin of Mexico: the ecological processes in the evolution of a civilization* New York: Academic Press

72. Air pollution in Mexico City
credit: © Julio Etchart/Still Pictures

73. The cathedral in Mexico City after subsidence
credit: © Frank Nowikowski/South American Pictures

74. Homeless mother and child, Calcutta, India
credit: © Mark Edwards/Still Pictures

1

First Impressions

Cities are the defining artifacts of civilisation. All the achievements and failings of humanity are here. Civic buildings, monuments, archives and institutions are the touchstones by which our cultural heritage is passed from one generation to the next. We shape the city, then it shapes us. Today, almost half the global population lives in cities. By 2030, the proportion is likely to be two-thirds.

I was born in London. My earliest urban memories are of cuddly barrage balloons anchored to a skyline of roofs and chimney-pots, and of air-raids that sent us scuttling from the house in the middle of the night, down into the shelter at the bottom of the garden. Next morning, our street was littered with lumps of shrapnel which might still be hot if you went out to collect them early enough. I grew up in a city under reconstruction, much of it wrapped in a fascinating lattice of ladders and scaffolding and adorned with buckets dangling on pulley hoists. Buddleia flourished on the best bombsites – their flowers attracting lots of butterflies – red admirals, lesser and greater tortoiseshells, peacocks and, more rarely, painted ladies. We caught them in nets made from old muslin curtains, and a popular *How To . . .* book told us how to anaesthetise them in jam-jars half-filled with crushed laurel leaves, and how to prepare them for our collections with a pin through the thorax and the wings held outspread with thin strips of paper.

We took fruit from the trees of abandoned gardens (and some not so abandoned gardens – scrumping, we called it), built fires with matches illicitly obtained, experimented with Woodbines, baked potatoes we had pinched from the kitchen and ate them half-cooked. Sometimes, but rarely, we dared to venture at least a few stairs down into the frightening dark cellars of bombed-out houses. For an eight-year-old, post-war London was an adventure playground with minimal adult supervision.

Grown-ups used to joke that London would be a wonderful place when it was finished, but I could never understand what was so funny about that; it seemed perfectly possible that a time would come when all the building work would be over and done with and that would be that: London, finished. And though I don't recall giving the matter any thought, I imagine now that my vision of the finished city would have been more or less the same as the London I knew, only just a bit tidier.

There were electric-powered trolley buses and trams as well as diesel-engined buses and you could often sneak on and off them without paying, but bicycles offered an altogether free – and freer – means of getting around the city. We were adventurous, but quickly learned to avoid getting a wheel stuck in the tramlines at tricky junctions, and after just one fall you never forgot to ride cautiously along the woodblock surface of Borough High Street on rainy days, when it was as slippery as a sheet of glass.

London's main rail terminals were the grand grimy cathedrals of the steam age in which we congregated to collect engine numbers. At Waterloo station, Victoria, Charing Cross, Paddington, Saint Pancras, Euston and Liverpool Street we scampered from platform to platform as the trains pulled up to the buffers – engines hissing steam and smoke. The locals and the expresses disgorged their passengers from third class and first class, while we peered into the Pullman carriages with their little table lamps alight at the windows.

We all either owned or yearned for a Hornby-oo electric train set, and given the opportunity would spend hours sprawled on the living room carpet, devising complex routes around the furniture. I cannot recall that any of us ever seriously wanted to be an engine-driver, but boys generally were supposed to cherish such ambitions and certainly our respect for the men who clambered up onto the footplates of the huge Golden Arrow and Castle class locomotives was unbounded. With fire and steam at their command, in grimy overalls and greasy caps they drove those magnificent creations of bright painted steel and shining brass across the length and breadth of Britain: the Flying Scotsman, the Atlantic Coast Express. The driving wheels – taller than a man – always juddered and skidded on the rails as the pistons began to push, and the locomotives really did seem to pant with the effort – just like *Thomas the*

2

Tank Engine. Awesome is the word recollections of those engines bring to mind now, but at the time – well, they were impressive, yes, but no more than a part of everyday city life. For us, their main significance was as bearers of the numbers we ticked off in our books.

Smoke was another awesome fact of life that seemed commonplace then. My recollection is that everyone smoked – at home and at work, in trains, buses, cafés and cinemas. The entire country – not just the railways – ran on coal (though it was delivered to our houses by horse and cart). Smoke wafted from the chimneys of more than a million households. Every day, thousands of tons of coal were burned in London's fireplaces, boilers, and furnaces. Clouds of steam, smoke and soot spewed continuously from locomotives, gas works, power stations and industrial smokestacks – with either Young's brewery on Wandsworth High Street or the malodorous Battersea candle factory adding their own distinctive whiff to the air in our locality – depending on the direction of the wind.

Throughout the city, buildings were coated with a patina of soot which in some instances gave the impression that burnished black basalt, not white Portland stone, had been used in their construction. During most winters there would be occasions when a layer of cold air hung for days over London, trapping the smoke rising from the chimneys below. Soon a sulphurous mixture of smoke, soot and moisture would envelope the city – tinged green, and thick enough to become known as a pea-souper. When you opened the front door, skeins of fog would drift into the hallway – and threaten to fill the house if you left the door open. On days when visibility was down to a yard or less, getting lost on the way home from school became almost a matter of pride: 'couldn't see my hand in front of my face,' you'd say.

The pea-soupers killed hundreds of people every winter – anyone with asthma, or another respiratory problem, was at risk from inhaling the toxic mixture of fog, smoke and soot-laden air. The word smog entered the vocabulary as a definition of this very serious threat to public health in Britain's cities (London was not the only city affected. The problem was as bad in all industrial cities). Widespread public demands for action over the number of deaths forced the government to act and a succession of Clean Air Acts were introduced during the 1950s and '60s.

I left London before even the first Act of 1956 could begin to take effect, and went to live in Cape Town, on the southern tip of Africa, where a prevailing weather system of wet north-westerlies from the

Atlantic and powerful dry south-easterlies from the Indian Ocean alternately washed and swept the city clean. Later I was based in Nairobi for a number of years. Meanwhile, the London I had known was being transformed.

Oil, gas and electricity steadily replaced coal as the city's fuel for factories, power stations and domestic use. The widespread introduction of central heating rendered household fireplaces and chimneys obsolete. Slum clearance opened up the urban landscape, and by the time I moved back to London in 1978 the city had become a markedly cleaner place – even to the extent of inspiring property-owners to have the patina of black soot scrubbed from the facades of their buildings. Smog and pea-soupers were bad memories that old people tut-tutted about over tea. And London seemed reborn – especially in the spring, when the plane trees had just come into leaf and the sun was shining.

Living and working in Africa for all those years, with only occasional visits to London, was absorbing and valuable in itself but also delivered an unanticipated bonus – in that it delayed the occasion of my first visits to some of Europe's major cities until fairly late in life. And I believe that whatever I may have missed by not touring Europe at an earlier age has been made up for by the older eye through which I viewed Vienna on a first visit in 2001, for instance, or by an extended stay in Paris during 2000; and by going to Venice for the first time in 1997.

'The thing about Venice, is that it never fails to exceed expectations,' a friend remarked when I told him of plans for that first visit. 'Whether you're going for the first time or the tenth, however much you already know and have planned for in advance, you always come away feeling that Venice has given you something extra.'

In an age that regularly oversells its offerings, arousing the jaundiced expectation that the reality will be less than the hype, this seemed highly improbable. On the other hand, Francis did not have a reputation for needless exaggeration and, true to form, he was absolutely right. Venice did exceed my expectations. The city did give me something extra. But not just the mental image and recollection of novel experiences, nor even the roll of pleasing photographs. More than that, I came away from Venice with nagging questions about its status as a city, and about the phenomenon, function and ecology of cities in general. Why do they exist? How do they work? Why do some seem so much more alive than others?

Venice is crowded, smelly, decidedly dirty in places, and much of it appears to be in a state of imminent collapse: crumbling and sinking into the murky waters of the lagoon. It has magnificent churches and palaces, the four wonderful gilded bronze horses of San Marco, numerous splendid galleries and Harry's Bar. Venetian history is richly documented in literature, painting and music; the city prompts echoes in the mind of Gabrieli, Monteverdi and Vivaldi; it gives three-dimensional form to the familiar paintings of Canaletto and Turner, and awakens recollections of Shakespeare, Bryon, Henry James and Thomas Mann.

John Ruskin, Charles Dickens and Mark Twain wrote fond accounts of Venice. Goethe and Proust spent time in the city; Ezra Pound is there still, in the San Michele Cemetery on the island of San Giorgio Maggiore. This improbable assortment of palazzos and piazzas, both linked and divided by meandering canals, was the setting for Visconti's lavish *Death in Venice* and Nicholas Roeg's haunting *Don't Look Now*. Even Woody Allen made a film here, in which he sits musing with Julia Roberts on steps beside the Grand Canal. There are comfortable hotels, good restaurants, an efficient water transportation system and it is a joy simply to wander about the city on foot – exploring, guidebook and map in hand.

As John Julius Norwich, an authority on the city, has remarked: 'Venice, for its size, made a greater contribution to Western civilisation than any other city in Europe or anywhere else.'[1]

There is no other city for which even the most casual visitor is so well prepared. Its influence touches every individual – whether it is absorbed by scholarly immersion in history, by enjoying music and the arts, or by simply frequenting the cinema, reading the papers, eating a Veneziana pizza, or drinking coffee in a Rialto or Lido café, everyone has some sense of what Venice is – not so much a *knowing,* as an unconscious *feeling* for the city. Venice gets under the skin in a way that no other city does. Which means that although the prospect of going to Venice seems no different from going anywhere else – in that the same kind of arrangements have to be made and the same trials of travel endured – the actual experience of being there evokes a unique sense of recognition, of belonging, even when in the company of several thousand other visitors. And the experience is accumulative. Venice is so stuffed with points of unanticipated recognition that its appeal never fades, just intensifies with each visit.

But is this what the city, a city, this city is *for*? Is it simply a reassuring touchstone at which to confirm our place in the centuries-long procession of Western civilisation? Where generations of Venetians once stood, we stand now, exposed to the history and the wonder of the place, and sensing the continuity of human endeavour which has kept the city going for hundreds of years. We are the latest cohort, but it is not just time that separates us from the generations that built and sustained Venice. We use the city differently too.

From its origin and for centuries, Venice existed primarily to serve the interests of its residents. But today Venice exists primarily to serve the interests of its visitors. In truth, Venice is a large, very fine museum which attracts over 12 million visitors per year – up to two-thirds of whom are day-trippers. The maximum tourist capacity of the historic centre has been calculated at 21,000 visitors per day, but numbers of up to 60,000 are not unusual and on some occasions over 100,000 people have flooded into the city – totally overwhelming the amenities and obliging the authorities to close the road bridge between Venice and the mainland.[2] And in February 2004 the city authorities decided that although Venice has always been free of cars it will no longer be a pedestrians' paradise, where people are free to walk wherever and however they like. The city's narrow streets and alleys become so congested during the tourist season that a system of one-way walking is to be introduced. Furthermore, anyone attempting to walk against the flow is liable to be fined – anything from €25 to €500, depending on the severity of the offence.[3]

Meanwhile, the permanent population of Venice appears to be in terminal decline after holding up well for centuries. There were about 200,000 people living in Venice when the city was at the height of its power in the sixteenth century, and probably not much less than that in the nineteenth century, when it first began to attract a significant number of visitors from foreign parts. The population was still as high as 170,000 in 1960, but since then the outflow of permanent residents has been as dramatic as the inflow of tourists. The resident population of Venice fell by nearly two-thirds during the forty years to 2000,[4] when it stood at around 60,000 and the city's simmering love–hate relationship with tourism had split the community into two conflicting and irreconcilable groups: one living from tourism, the other in spite of it.

So here's a paradox: because Venice awakens an empathetic sense of belonging in those who make a brief visit to the city, not many people want to live there permanently. The city has effectively abandoned the first duty of a viable and self-sustaining city, namely to generate the kind of environment and social ambience that will attract and retain residents.

Venice is one city among many – a very particular city, but nonetheless at root an expression in time and space of a phenomenon that is as old as civilisation. Indeed, it is hardly an exaggeration to say that the city is the defining artifact of civilisation. All the achievements and failings of humanity are encapsulated in its physical and social structures – in the buildings that give it substance, and in the cultures that give it life. From its inception, the city's concentration of physical and cultural power has broadened the scope of human activity and hastened the pace of everyday life. City buildings, monuments, archives and institutions are the accumulated cultural heritage of society and the touchstones by which that heritage is passed from one generation to the next.

Of course, the widespread distribution and growth of the world's great cities could not have occurred without a parallel growth and dispersal of the human population. Even so, the proportion of the global population living in urban communities remained low for a surprisingly long time. At the beginning of the nineteenth century, by which time cities in some shape or form had been around for over six thousand years, only about 10 per cent of the global population lived in cities. The other 90 per cent still lived and worked in small, largely self-sufficient communities – most of them of a predominantly agricultural nature. But the pace of urbanisation has accelerated dramatically rapidly since then. By 1900 city-dwellers comprised one-quarter of the global population, and now – at the beginning of the third millennium – almost half the world's population lives in urban communities. And the proportion is expected to increase still further, so that by the year 2030 two of every three people on Earth will be living in a city.

Fundamentally, the advent of the city as a centre of human activity freed ever-increasing numbers of people from the burden of finding food and shelter for themselves, directly from the land. Human ingenuity, tied for thousands of generations to the task of feeding and managing small groups of people, was now free to pursue its seemingly infinite potential. Cities provided food, security and a cultural environment in which select individuals like Michelangelo Buonarroti could paint and sculpt, Isaac Newton and Stephen Hawking could ponder the mysteries of the universe, and Adolf Hitler could hatch schemes to conquer the world. But for every genius or despot whose ambitions the city fostered there have been thousands to whom the city gave no favours at all.

Until comparatively recently, every large city was a potential death-trap (some still are), with death rates exceeding birth rates by a considerable margin. Indeed, it was only during the nineteenth century, as medical science and civic planners managed first to contain and later to conquer urban disease, that large cities could sustain numbers and actually begin to generate an increase in population from among their own inhabitants. Until then a city's survival was entirely dependent upon its ability to attract new residents.

Some people moved to the cities because they were surplus to requirements at home – and thus a drain on resources; others because they wanted to take advantage of the opportunities that cities appeared to offer, and doubtless some responded to both the push and the pull effect. In the cities of the ancient world, however, many newcomers had no say in the matter, having been brought in – or should we say bought in – as slaves. Without a steady stream of people coming to live within its boundaries, a city would shrink to insignificance. And only a very substantial influx of new residents would enable it to grow. Thus the city can be seen as a dynamic entity – not exactly a living organism, as the ancient Greeks believed, with recognisable cycles of birth, growth and death,[5] but certainly something that was nurtured by generations of people whose own life cycles kept the city functioning.

There is a tendency in the developed world for people to look upon cities as inherently bad, or at best necessary evils. They seem to exist in stark contrast to the countryside, one bad the other good. At its simplest, the dichotomy can be defined in terms of what is regarded as 'natural' and what is not. The countryside, fecund and brimming with a potential for growth, seems natural while the city, with its demands for maintenance constantly reminding us of decay, is labelled unnatural.

Bearing in mind that the term 'natural' itself is not wholly applicable to the modern countryside – most of which has been altered by human activity – and that decay is a natural process too, to what extent is a city 'unnatural'? After all, every bit of a city was originally a part of the earth, no less formed by a geophysical or biological process than the Grand Canyon or a ball of elephant dung.

Admittedly, the city is different in that it was assembled by the conscious direction and effort of people – but why should that make it unnatural? No one suggests that a termite mound is unnatural because it is a built structure. Of course, termites build their mounds by means of unconscious behaviour, each working instinctively for the good of the whole, but who is to say that the complex cooperative behaviour required of people as they construct, inhabit and maintain cities is not equally instinctive, equally directed to the good of the whole – which in this case means 'advancing civilisation'?

Clearly, the integral role of the city in human affairs runs deep – well beyond the streets and buildings and into the realms of conscious and sub-conscious awareness that make us who we are. To paraphrase Winston Churchill: 'We shape our cities, then they shape us.'[6]

2

How Did It Begin?

The first cities are said to have arisen from rural communities whose intensified farming practices produced surpluses large enough to free craftworkers and other specialists from working on the land. But it could have been the other way round. Compelling evidence suggests that the rise of cities actually preceded – and inspired – the intensification of agriculture.

Cities are such an all-pervasive aspect of modern life that their advent, and that of the civilisation they sustain, seems to have been inevitable. But was it? It is true that the domestication of crops and livestock provided both the means and an incentive for people to stay in one place longer than they might otherwise have done, but is that enough to explain the emergence of cities and civilisation in six widely separated places around the world – Mesopotamia, India, Egypt, China, Central America and Peru? The emergence was spontaneous in each location – none resulted from contact with another – but the dates of the emergence range over a considerable period of time. The earliest cities of Mesopotamia and the Indus valley civilisation in India date from around 6,000 years ago. Cities appeared in Egypt slightly later. The earliest Chinese city known so far (Her-li-t'on, south of the Yellow River in central Honan province) dates from about 4,500 years ago,[1] while those in Central and South America are a thousand years younger still. At each location the emergence of a city marked the beginnings of a distinct civilisation; it was as though once a set of preconditions had been established, cities and civilisation would inevitably follow. The question is: what were those preconditions, and what was the driving force that powered the rise of cities?

The traditional answer is that agriculture and warfare were responsible. The theory is simple: once farming had become a viable way of life, and people began living in settled communities, some would inevitably become richer than others. Successful farmers gathered together and built defensive compounds as protection from potentially aggressive neighbours; this in turn led to new ways of organising society. Powerful leaders emerged from among them, who eventually became pharaohs and kings with the authority to govern the community and order the construction of cities.

Experts who were convinced that complex society and cities had been born out of fear in this way pointed out that signs of battle were evident in every early civilisation, all around the world.[2] Each had had its generals and standing armies, they said; warriors had always occupied prominent positions in the social hierarchy; war had featured in the arts, and had influenced styles of architecture; where writing developed, warfare was a favourite subject.

South America was frequently cited as a prime example of war as a driving force in the development of cities and civilisation. Evidence of warfare was especially plentiful in the Maya, Aztec and Inca sites, for instance; but they were not very old. Then archaeologists discovered a site at Casma, on the Peruvian coast, that dates from about 3,500 years ago, and here the signs of battle were especially gruesome. Wall-carvings showed warriors standing over the decapitated and mutilated bodies of their vanquished foes; legs and hands had been cut off; blood flowed from eyes and mouths.

The evidence from Casma certainly confirmed that warfare had been a fundamental characteristic of early societies in South America for a very long time, and this seemed to make the case for warfare having provoked the development of cities and civilisation everywhere. But the case did not stand for long. Not long after the evidence from Casma had been published,[3] and before its wider implications had been given the gloss of general recognition, archaeologists working not a day's drive from Casma uncovered evidence of a large urban centre that was more than 1,000 years older and completely lacking in evidence of warfare.[4]

The new site was in a locality known as Caral, and radio-carbon dating of woven reed bags found at the base of the excavations showed that people had begun living there around 4,600 years ago. When it was most fully occupied Caral covered an area of just over 65 ha (which is the area covered by about thirty-six Manhattan city blocks[5]) and was dominated by a central zone containing six large platform mounds arranged around a huge open plaza. All six mounds appeared to have been built in only one or two phases, which indicates an exceptional capacity for complex planning, centralised decision-making and the mobilisation of sizeable labour forces. The largest mound, the 'Piramide Mayor', even now – after erosion has whittled at it for thousands of years – stands as high as a four-storey building and covers the area of a football pitch.[6]

The mounds are crowned with a maze of rooms, courtyards, stairs and other structures, which suggests they were used for administrative purposes, while three sunken circular plazas at the site testify to the regular occurrence of large, well-organised ceremonial events. The varied styles and quality of Caral's housing point to a distinctly stratified society, with grand stone-walled residences for the upper classes and more modest mud-brick homes for the rest. Gardens, irrigated by canals bringing water from the Supe river, produced a variety of crops, among which squash and beans have been identified, and there are signs that a lot of cotton was grown too – cotton for clothing, but also, it is believed, to trade for fish with communities on the coast, 23 km away. The fishermen needed cotton for their nets, the farmers needed protein, and the heaps of sardine and anchovy bones found at Caral indicate that fish was the community's prime source.

There can be little doubt that Caral was home to a large and complex society. Indeed, the social, political and ceremonial system founded at Caral probably provided the ancestral roots for the civilisation of the Incas, who ruled the Andes some 4,000 years later. It is the earliest known urban centre in the Americas; no other site is as large and as old. Caral, then, is a founding stone of civilisation. But there is no evidence that warfare provoked its development. Far from it. While the discovery of necklaces and body paint indicates a taste for personal adornment at Caral, while flutes, beautifully carved from the bones of condors, suggest an appreciation of music and song (and remains of the coca plant hint at an occasional use of stimulants), there is absolutely nothing to suggest that the Caral community went in for warfare. No weapons – not even a stone cudgel – no defensive fortifications, no city walls, no gory depictions of battle and victory. For a thousand years at the very beginnings of civilisation in South America the people of Caral knew nothing of war.

Caral is a distant outpost of human migration from Africa, where *Homo sapiens* had evolved over millions of years. Until about 100,000 years ago our species had existed only in Africa – nowhere else on earth. Then a small number left the continent across the Isthmus of Suez – in the footsteps, perhaps, of earlier members of the genus, *Homo erectus* and *Homo neandertalensis,* who had also evolved in Africa, migrated from the continent and subsequently become extinct. But our ancestors were destined to survive. Generation by generation, those pioneering populations multiplied and moved into every congenial environment that the globe had to offer. Their progress is illustrated by fossils found at locations where people had camped or settled briefly on the course of humanity's long journey around the world. The fossil evidence shows that after moving around the Mediterranean basin, bands of the migrants' descendants were well established in Europe by 40,000 years ago; others were present in China by 30,000 years ago, and some crossed the Bering Straits sometime before 15,000 years ago, when sea levels were low.

Once established in North America, the migrants moved steadily south along the coastal strip and had reached the tip of South America by 12,000 years ago. The American populations were small to begin with, and widely dispersed, which makes Caral a particularly important site, since it shows just how rapidly a human population can expand and establish an urban centre where conditions are suitable.

Meanwhile, the earliest descendants of the migrants from Africa had been living in the Middle East and around the Mediterranean for thousands of generations. Fossils dating back more than 90,000 years have been found in the Middle East. Such a long span of occupation means that people in these regions had a greater depth of experience in exploiting their environment than their counterparts in South America. Both populations were endowed with the same genetic inheritance and propensities of the ancestral human stock, but those in South America had had a shorter span of opportunity during which to exercise them – which might be one reason why the people who founded the cities of Mesopotamia were writing poetry at a time when the Caralians had yet to discover pottery.

Caral belongs to what is known as the Preceramic Period of South American archaeology. The continent's earliest pottery dates from about 3,750 years ago[7] – nearly 1,000 years after people first settled at Caral. Clearly the Caralians had managed very well indeed without pots, and must have found the available reeds, cotton, wood, leather, bone and stone adequate for their needs, but the advent of pottery is nonetheless an important marker when and wherever it occurs. Pots enabled people to keep larger supplies of water at hand; they could store harvested cereals more securely and cook a wide range of foodstuffs – either to enhance palatability or to preserve them. Even more significantly, pots enabled women to boil up a substitute for mother's milk and thereby hasten the weaning of their infants. This in turn led to shorter birth intervals, more babies and more people. Thus pottery is likely to have contributed significantly to an acceleration of the population growth rate,[8] with crucial implications for the development of cities and civilisation.

The existence of pottery at any archaeological site indicates that the people using it probably had been of a sedentary disposition; if not permanently settled, then at least staying in one place for lengthy periods (you would not expect to find nomadic hunter-gatherer populations carrying large quantities of pottery around with them). Pottery thus ties in with the origin of cities. As the evidence from Caral shows, it was not a prerequisite, but closely related. The potter's wheel, as Lewis Mumford puts it in his *The City in History,* was a foremost factor in humanity's transition from a wholly hunting and gathering or rural way of life to the stage at which the city first became a dominant aspect of human existence.

Along with the potter's wheel, Mumford cites the loom, the sailboat, metalworking, abstract mathematics, astronomical observations, the calendar, writing, the plough and grain cultivation as the developments and technological inventions that were essential requirements of what is known in the literature as the urban revolution. Of these, the plough and grain cultivation were far and away the most crucial, for without a surplus of storable food the community would be unable to support the specialists who were kept busy working full-time on all the other activities that define the urban revolution.

The earliest known evidence of people producing grain in quantities large enough to be considered a surplus, and thus capable of supporting a number of individuals who were not actively engaged in producing food for themselves, has been found on the alluvial plains of Mesopotamia, which lie between the Tigris and Euphrates rivers, in what is now Iraq. The evidence dates back to more than 6,000 years ago, and has been most definitively described from the south of Mesopotamia, in a region known to the ancients as Sumer.

The traditional view, deeply entrenched in academic literature and popular writing on the subject,[9] is that the development of grain cultivation on the fertile soils of Sumer, and the invention of the plough, enabled farmers to produce surpluses, which not only led to a rapid increase in population but also inspired village communities to coalesce and form cities. Thus the world's first cities are said to have arisen simply because farmers had discovered a way of producing more food than they needed for themselves. But there is an alternative view of the evidence, suggesting that the crucial developments occurred in reverse order – namely that the cities came first and advances in farming technology came only as a response to the demands of the cities.

The suggestion that cities came first can also be found in the literature, well-expressed but set tentatively against the bulk of received wisdom.[10] It deserves to be more widely known and considered. Pottery is the key.

In Sumer, the people who laid the foundations of a city directly on the virgin sand nearly 7,000 years ago were already using a sophisticated range of pottery, including beakers, round and oval plates, bowls, spouted vessels, large and small jars, goblets, thin cups and heavy cooking ware. Some of the items were very finely made, and elegantly decorated with patterns ranging from freely applied dots and strokes to intricate geometrical cross-hatching and depictions of animal-like and human figures.[11]

In fact, so much pottery was produced in the earliest permanent settlements of Mesopotamia, and the output was so standardised in terms of intended use, shape and decoration, that something approaching an industrial scale of production has been envisaged.[12] Highly skilled specialists were at work here,[13] but their skills had not evolved *in situ*. We can be sure of this because the ascending layers excavated at the sites contained no sign of early crude methods being refined, with practice, through time. So pottery production had arrived in Sumer fully fledged, at a highly advanced level of development. The essential skills must have originated elsewhere; but where, exactly? The most likely source was to the north and, indeed, equally refined but significantly older pottery has been found at sites further up the course of the Euphrates and Tigris rivers.

Farther north still, we come to the western horn of the fertile crescent that fostered the agricultural revolution, and here is a site, older than any in Sumer or the more northern regions of Mesopotamia, at which a scattering of very basic pottery has been found on the lowest living floors and increasingly sophisticated examples at higher levels. Here the evolution of the potter's craft can be traced from its beginnings to the advanced skills that were evident at Sumer. The earliest examples include crude box-shaped vessels that perfectly imitate the carved wooden boxes that were being made at the same time.[14] The most sophisticated are finely worked pots and decorative items.

The site at which this material has been found is called Çatal Hüyük. It is situated on the Anatolian Plateau of southern Turkey, about 100 km from the shores of the Mediterranean and 1,000 m above sea level. The most ancient levels date back more than 9,000 years; at times the site was home to a minimum of 2,000 extended families[15] – possibly as many as 10,000 people – living cheek-by-jowl in a sprawl of contiguous brick-walled houses covering an area of about 12 ha in total.[16] The site was discovered in 1958 by the British archaeologist James Mellaart, who introduces an account of the excavations he conducted there in the early 1960s with a claim that 'Çatal Hüyük ranks . . . as one of man's first known essays in the development of town-life. Before 6000 BC Çatal Hüyük was a town, or even a city, of a remarkable kind.'[17]

Çatal Hüyük is still often described as 'the world's first city',[18] but the results of renewed excavations at the site indicate that it was more of an overgrown village than a city – or a town – even though many modern urban centres have far smaller populations. The point is that for archaeologists and historians the most meaningful difference between a village and a city has nothing to do with size; it is instead a measure of social and economic differentiation within the communities. In this scheme of things, a place occupied exclusively by people who had left the land to become full-time craftsmen, merchants, priests and civil servants was a city, while anywhere occupied principally by farmers was a village. By and large, only farmers lived in villages, while 'a key defining feature of a town or city is that farmers *don't* live in them'.[19]

At Çatal Hüyük there was no evidence of full-time craftsmen, merchants, priests and civil servants living off the surplus of a rural hinterland. Each family produced its own food, and also made pottery (and other items) for themselves as required. There were no temple, or public buildings which could be interpreted as centres of communal activity; instead, each house was a discrete entity, and each group of two to four houses shared their own shrine.[20] Nor was there anything to indicate that the society at Çatal Hüyük was hierarchical, with lower and upper classes dominated by individuals of authority; no, the community consisted entirely of extended families grouped together in clusters of four or five houses, who carried on their daily activities more or less autonomously.[21] Overall, social and economic arrangements at Çatal Hüyük appear to have been remarkably homogeneous and egalitarian.

So Çatal Hüyük was something of a hybrid – large enough to be a town and possessing all the ingredients needed to become a city, but retaining the social organisation and features of a village. And the remarkable thing is that this state of affairs persisted uninterrupted and at more or less the same intensity for almost a thousand years up to 7,700 years ago, when the site was abandoned (for no obvious reason – there is no sign of violence or deliberate destruction) and a new site established a few hundred metres away. The new site appears to have been occupied continuously for at least another 700 years before it too was abandoned – again for no apparent reason.

But the puzzles of its history do not diminish the importance of what Çatal Hüyük does reveal. Indeed, the site is unique on two counts. First, it seems to document a move from the nomadic hunting and gathering lifestyle which had sustained humanity for most of its existence towards the sedentary life that was to be a formative characteristic of cities and civilisation. Second, it is the subject of a twenty-five-year programme of painstaking excavation and multi-disciplinary research which is applying the rigours of modern science and the latest technology to the search for an understanding of how people lived at Çatal Hüyük.[22] And thus Çatal Hüyük throws light on some of the puzzles surrounding the origins of settled life – and cities.

The most remarkable feature of Çatal Hüyük is that families lived in such close proximity to one another. A visitor arriving from across the marshy plain 9,000 years ago would have been confronted by the blank rectangular walls of the houses, joined to form a continuous perimeter. There were no approach roads leading into Çatal Hüyük, or lanes and alleys separating one mudbrick house from its neighbour. Indeed, with only a few open courtyards between them, the houses were so densely packed that access to the interiors was down a ladder through a hole in the roof (which also served as a vent for smoke rising from the hearth at which food was cooked in the room below). Yet each house had its own independent walls. There were very few houses that shared walls – party walls – with their neighbours. This suggests that a strong sense of ownership and independence governed human affairs at Çatal Hüyük, if only because separate walls allowed each family to follow its own cycle of use, maintenance and rebuilding.

The houses appear to have been regularly replastered and repaired for up to a century or so before they were pulled down, carefully filled in and levelled off, and a replacement built directly on top, following more or less the same floor plan (something that party walls would have made impossible). As house was built upon house during 1,000 years of occupation, the Çatal Hüyük mound grew to the height of 20 m – as high as a modern six-storey building.

It is clear that while Çatal Hüyük was rising, century by century, from the Anatolian Plain, its residents were no longer nomadic hunter-gatherers – nor yet exclusively farmers. In fact, they were the highly successful exponents of an intermediate way of life – exploiting an environment that provided them with a range of options. The woodlands and marshy plains surrounding the settlement were a hunting and gathering paradise, for example, amply stocked with game and wild foods, but they were also ideally suited for farming and raising domestic livestock. And the settlers made the best of both worlds. The bones of domesticated sheep and goats have been found on the site, along with bones of deer, gazelle, wolf and leopard, and those of the yet-to-be-domesticated wild pig and aurochs (the wild ancestor of cattle). Like-wise, there was plenty of evidence that the settlers gathered edible wild plants on a regular basis, including tubers, rhizomes, grasses, vetches, hackberries, acorns and pistachios; there is also evidence that they cultivated peas and lentils, and grew cereals such as barley, einkorn and emmer wheat (but no grind-stones, which suggests that the technology for baking bread had yet to be developed).

The benefits of the mixed food supply strategy adopted by the residents of Çatal Hüyük are unequivocal. By neither relying entirely on hunting and gathering, nor abandoning them totally in favour of farming, they got the best of both worlds – and a more secure food supply than either could provide alone. People everywhere were combining strategies in this way long before settlement began at Çatal Hüyük, and the act of gathering inevitably leads to an understanding of what promotes greater production of a plant food. In South Africa, for example, people were deliberately burning off vegetation to speed up the growth of edible rhizomes 70,000 years ago,[23] and it is well known that the Paiute Indians of eastern California regularly dammed rivers to create the swampy meadows in which nut grass, wild hyacinths and other edible roots thrived.[24]

The same sort of practices must have preceded the settlement at Çatal Hüyük – but here they led to an abrupt break with the past. At Çatal Hüyük a large number of people began living together in permanent houses at a single site. Why? It makes no sense. As at Caral in South America, there is nothing at Çatal Hüyük to suggest that warfare provoked the development. No less significantly, the rich potential of the surrounding environment could have been more readily exploited by people living in small settlements spread out across the landscape, rather than by thousands packed so closely together at Çatal Hüyük. But perhaps the incongruity of people living so closely together that they entered their houses through holes in the roofs, with no apparent benefit in terms of food supply and no need in terms of security, is a clue to how the transition from nomadic hunting and gathering to farming might have affected the minds and the worldview of the people involved.

Some authorities have suggested that the shift from a nomadic hunter-gatherer way of life to one that was increasingly dependent on growing crops and caring for domesticated animals was so profound that it induced a psychological shift too: a radical change of outlook. The idea here is that as people began exploiting their environment more purposefully and selectively, they began to look upon it very differently too. Fundamental beliefs in the sanctity of the landscape were at first thrown into doubt by the economic transformation their way of life had undergone, and then reconfigured to fit their new relationship with the environment. This implies that a shift in food acquisition practices (the agricultural revolution) is likely to have been accompanied by a shift in belief systems, symbolism and ritual (the cultural revolution). Çatal Hüyük is a source of primary evidence for this idea.[25]

That symbolism was a defining element of life at Çatal Hüyük is clear from the large number of spectacular artworks unearthed at the site – ranging from small statuettes fashioned in clay and blue limestone to wall paintings more than two metres across – many of which are open to interpretation as being of a symbolic nature, with religious connotations.

Cave and rock-shelter painting is an ancient art, developed to high levels of sophistication long before people began moving away from nomadic hunting and gathering towards farming as a way of life – the work of San Bushmen in southern Africa comes to mind, and the huge murals made by hunters in the Lascaux caves of France – but the decorative art at Çatal Hüyük adds unexpected dimensions of technique and perception to the overall picture. They used a far wider range of colours than is seen anywhere else, making their pigments mainly from minerals: red and brown, pink, orange, buff and yellow from iron oxides; vivid blues and greens from copper ores; very deep reds from mercury oxides; mauve and purple from manganese, and grey from galena; in at least one instance finely ground mica was added to the paint to give a glittering effect.[26]

Painting is a ubiquitous feature of Çatal Hüyük, appearing throughout the site at every stage of its development. James Mellaart has claimed that the people of Çatal Hüyük painted what they could when they could, applying paint not only to walls but also to plaster reliefs, clay statuettes, skeletons, wood, baskets and pottery. He assumed that textiles were dyed and believed that people painted their faces and bodies too. 'Cosmetic sets' containing a small spoon, a fork and a palette have been found; also shells filled with red ochre. These items, along with quantities of jewellery, including rings, bracelets, brooches, bead necklaces, amulets and pendants, testify to a liking for personal adornment at Çatal Hüyük[27] and, furthermore, there is also evidence that people liked to see how they looked. A number of mirrors have been found – slabs of a black volcanic glass, obsidian, ground flat and polished until you can see your face in them.

The mirrors are a convincing token of the cultural revolution mentioned above. Here, for the first time in human history, is evidence of people pursuing a reflection of the world that was both exact and capable of being repeated over and over again. Cave and rock shelter paintings from the sites in Africa and France – though evidence of considerable creative talent and technical skill – were never exact depictions of the real world, but rather seem specifically designed to invite interpretations that went beyond the practical and into the realm of the spiritual. Çatal Hüyük represents a break with this tradition – not only in the mirrors, but among the wall paintings too. Preserved in a room on one of the lowest levels, dating back to more than 8,000 years ago, there is a painting which all major art history textbooks (as well as the *Guinness Book of Records*) recognise as the earliest known picture of humanity's presence in an identifiable landscape.

This unique fresco brilliantly expresses an emerging awareness of individual space in the urban environment.[28] In the foreground, there is what amounts to a map of Çatal Hüyük, impressively detailed yet abstractly perceived, with the floorplans of about seventy-five separate rectangular houses shown on the rising terraces of the town. In the background loom the unmistakable twin cones of Hasan Dag, a volcano standing about 120 km to the east of Çatal Hüyük. The volcano is painted in shades of vermilion, with incandescent volcanic bombs rolling down its slopes and a cloud of smoke and ash hovering above the peaks.[29]

It is certain that the obsidian which Çatal Hüyük's craftsmen and women had used to make their mirrors, knives, arrowheads and other practical items had been collected from the flanks of the volcanoes, and there can be little doubt that this picture of Çatal Hüyük with the erupting volcano in the background is not only the world's earliest known painting of a town and its surrounding landscape, but also reflects the importance of the volcano to the economic well-being of the town.

Similarly, while the painting of the town and the volcano is a measure of Çatal Hüyük's functional and economic development, other artwork found at the site clearly has a symbolic or even spiritual significance. The representations of various animals suggest that the move from nomadic hunting and gathering to a settled way of life required not simply the domestication of plants and animals but also the symbolic domestication of the wild by bringing it into the house and controlling it.[30] This is especially true of the bulls' heads – those most splendid descendants of the wild aurochs – which feature prominently among the images of the wild that people built into their homes at Çatal Hüyük.

Of the 139 living spaces that Mellaart excavated fully, more than a quarter appeared to have been used for some religious or ritual purpose. These areas were distinguished by a platform or low walls marking off a corner or an end of a room, in which representations of bulls were given reverential prominence. In several instances bull skulls and horns were set on pillars or in rows on raised mud-brick benches; elsewhere they featured as elaborate wall paintings; or as moulded clay heads protruding from the walls. Some of the heads were massive, with a wide span of curving horns; others were of a more natural size. Many were painted with intricate geometric patterns, and set with real horns. Mellaart noted that in the lower levels dating from nearly 9,000 to just under 8,000 years ago the decoration of shrines (as he called them) followed certain rules: bulls were found only on the north walls – which faced the Taurus Mountains,[31] primeval home of the wild aurochs.

The prevalence of bulls among the images that adorn specific corners of the houses at Çatal Hüyük confirms their significance as a symbolic domestication of the wild brought into the urban environment – but that is not all these carefully ordered spaces represent. People were buried there too (up to sixty-four in one sequence of graves that archaeologists traced down through the site), the bodies tightly flexed and often wrapped in a cloth or shroud. Preliminary examination of the skeletons suggests that the burials customarily spanned several generations of an extended family, and it is hoped that DNA analysis will answer important questions about the social order at Çatal Hüyük: for instance, if the DNA identifies daughters of daughters of daughters in the sequence of burials, this would show that the society was matrilocal, and probably led by women. If the sons of sons of sons are identified it must have been patrilocal, with women marrying in from other families.[32]

By burying the dead in their houses, under platforms adorned with symbols representing the domestication of the wild, the people of Çatal Hüyük surely were expressing a profound sense of affiliation with previous generations. After all, conditions were cramped in those houses; people lived, ate and slept with their ancestors just an arm's length away beneath the floor. It has been suggested that such proximity may have served to protect the living from malevolent spirits; alternatively, rituals performed among the bulls on the platforms above could have been a means of appealing to the positive and regenerative powers of the dead.[33] So far, these are matters of speculation. What is certain, though, is that ancestors buried beneath the living floor gave the occupants a powerful claim to territorial ownership. Cemeteries are hallowed ground. In a very real sense, only the dead have a permanent residence. Here, perhaps, lie the origins of landownership — no one could contest a family's proprietorial claim to the land in which their ancestors were buried.

But however strong a person's rights to live at Çatal Hüyük, it is also certain that not everybody who was born there died there. Generation by generation, the community that thrived for 1,000 years inevitably produced more people than it could feed and accommodate at any one time. The excess population — individuals and whole families — had no choice but to move on. Some would have established or joined other villages (of which there is plenty of archaeological evidence in the region, though the settlements were all much smaller than Çatal Hüyük), others doubtless went back to the full-time nomadic hunter-gatherer way of life; but some will have left Çatal Hüyük with an ability to make a living without having to either catch or grow their own food.

And here we begin to touch on issues that give Çatal Hüyük — while not a city in itself — a supporting role in the contention that cities preceded agricultural intensification.

First we must remember that for the greater part of its existence, Çatal Hüyük was home to a large number of highly skilled artists, craft-workers, manufacturers (and probably merchants too). These included the earliest known weavers of cloth and tapestry, the first pottery-makers and carvers of elaborate wooden bowls, the first metalworkers, and a flint and obsidian knapping industry that was capable of producing fine blades, sickles and arrowheads — and mirrors. The most talented of these workers were developing highly specialised skills and making goods of a quality that the average villager could never match – but would be pleased to obtain as required – in exchange for food.

It is surely reasonable to suppose that although no single village could produce a food surplus large enough to support full-time craftwork specialists all year round (nor could they have used a year's craft production), a group of villages probably could have accumulated enough between them to give a range of specialists a short spell of board and lodging at each village in turn. Thus, before long there could have been a constant stream of itinerant craft specialists hawking their various skills around the villages.

Since the itinerant craft specialists had effectively abandoned the security of home and kin, we can imagine that analogous arrangements would have evolved to ensure their well-being – something like craft clans, perhaps. Children doubtless assisted their parents, picking up the skills and secrets of the respective crafts from an early age; in this way, distinct castes emerged – of potters, metalworkers, weavers, builders, carpenters, traders, merchants and so on – for whom economic independence not only became a viable substitute for the kinship and security of the village, but also freed them from the obligations of food production which had shackled humanity to the natural environment for millions of years.

At the same time, farmers who no longer needed to make their own tools and craft goods could devote more energy to farming, becoming highly skilled specialists in their own right, and constantly striving to produce enough of a surplus to pay for the craft goods they needed.

A new and revolutionary social order was emerging – one that would ultimately lead to the founding of cities. Once demand for the craftworkers' output had passed a critical point, they could afford to abandon the itinerant way of life. Rather than each craftworker travelling to the villages independently, they could instead gather together in permanent settlements where their full range of crafts was available to anyone at all times. And the villagers would come to them. Clearly, if a farmer wanted a hoe and a pot, he would prefer to get them from one place at one time rather than wait for the individual craftworkers to come to him. Conversely, the craftworkers could offer a larger variety of goods, and build up larger stocks, than the itinerant way of doing business had allowed.

Once set in motion, these arrangements would become self-perpetuating as more specialists joined the craft community, as merchants emerged to make a speciality of trading in craftwork, and as people with managerial talents began suggesting ways in which the society could be organised for the greater benefit of all. Add to this the ever-present requirements of symbolism, belief and ritual, and the sprawling conglomeration of workshops, houses, temples and public buildings would very soon have become a city.

The conclusion reached in this scenario[34] is that the first cities did not grow *directly* from agricultural communities which produced surpluses large enough to support craftworkers and other non-productive individuals. Contrary to this widely held view,[35] although cities have always been *sustained* by an agricultural surplus from surrounding regions, they were not *created* by it. In fact, the impetus was reversed: it was the establishment of cities that stimulated the production of agricultural surpluses. It was not farmers, but relatively egalitarian clans of craftworkers, merchants and managers who laid the foundations of the city and urban life – in terms of both the concept and its physical manifestation. Complex agrarian societies and the intensive farming that regularly produces surpluses came later, a consequence rather than a cause of cities.

In this scheme of things, Çatal Hüyük marks a significant point in the developments that led humanity from a nomadic hunting and gathering way of life to the creation of cities and the adoption of urbanism. It is the beginning. Where does the story go from here? Well, although it would be stretching credibility to suggest a direct link, through time and the geography of the Fertile Crescent, between Çatal Hüyük and the world's first true cities in Sumer, a process of diffusion, by which trends that had begun in Çatal Hüyük percolated gradually through the region, century by century, is surely feasible. After all, the social, economic and environmental circumstances of Sumer were uniquely predisposed for the rise of cities. A foremost authority has written: 'It is difficult to imagine a set of conditions more conducive to the precocious development of urbanism . . . than those that obtained on the ancient Mesopotamian plain.'[36]

3

Where Did It Begin?

Mesopotamia's fertile alluvial soils, and rivers from which to draw irrigation waters, sustained the rise of the world's first true cities. As the natural environment was shaped to serve their needs, cities grew prodigiously. The economic and social order developed accordingly, placing the city at the heart of human affairs. In due time, cities dominated the social, cultural, and natural landscapes.

Lying between the ancient water courses of the Euphrates and Tigris rivers, in what is now Iraq, Mesopotamia was home to the world's first predominantly urbanised society. It was a 'land of cities',[1] known to its inhabitants as Sumer. The trend to urbanisation began more than 7,000 years ago. One thousand years later there were literally dozens of what are unambiguously recognisable as cities – some quite small, but many covering areas of more than 40 ha. Population figures are notoriously difficult to extrapolate from the archaeological evidence, but it has been convincingly estimated[2] that by 4,000 years ago 90 per cent of people in Sumer were living in cities. Babylon was one of them, and by 2,500 years ago this was the world's largest metropolis. Alexander the Great planned to make Babylon the capital of his vast empire, but died in the city before his dream was entirely fulfilled.

Sumer lies on the eastern horn of the Fertile Crescent, and here even the land itself is a creation of the Euphrates (and the Tigris). For millions of years these rivers (and their earlier incarnations) have been steadily filling the deep trench that lay between the Arabian shield and the sharp folds of the Zagros mountains with silts eroded from the highlands. The resulting landscape is endowed with deep fertile soils, and is so flat that even 500 km from the coast the Euphrates is still less than 20 m above sea level.[3] The rivers flow slowly down this gentle incline, meandering and sinuous, creating new channels whenever the spring flood is particularly high and the rivers overflow their banks. The land is easily worked; digging irrigation canals to direct water from the rivers to the fields has never required excessive amounts of effort.

The opportunities for agriculture and settlement that the waters of the Euphrates brought to the flood plains of southern Mesopotamia were the foundations upon which the world's first urban civilisation was built. No river, regardless of size, has played such an important role in human history. The reliability of a food supply large and nutritious enough to support many more people than were needed to work on the land – year after year – fuelled a surge in numbers. Humanity's innate adaptability responded creatively with the development of effective ways to exploit and manage the new situation. It is hardly an exaggeration to say that the Euphrates watered the roots of the economic practices, social mores, politics, religion, administration, literature and art which define Western culture.

> . . . A city had not been made, a living creature had not
>   been placed therein.
> All the lands were sea.
> Then Eridu was made, Esagila was built,
> The gods, the Annunnaki he created equal.
> The holy city, the dwelling of their hearts' delight, they call
>   it solemnly.
> Marduk constructed a reed frame on the face of the waters.
> He created earth and poured it out by the reed frame.
> In order to settle the gods in the dwelling of their hearts'
>   delight,
> He created mankind.[4]

To the ancient Sumerians the city was the centre of the world. The creator, Marduk, had set the first city, Eridu, and the temples of Babylon, Esagila, on hillocks standing dry above the seasonal lagoons and shifting water courses of the alluvial plain. Cities were fixed points of stability in an inherently unstable natural environment, and the home of the gods whom humanity had been created to serve. Without the city, nothing could exist. Here, amid the temples, the houses and the gardens, people found shelter from the hazards of the wilderness, adequate food and drink, and the comforts of kin and friendship. City life was civilised life. In Sumerian beliefs, Eden was not a garden, it was a city, but unlike the biblical version from which humanity had been for ever banished, this Eden had been created specifically to give people a reason for existing. And so long as the citizens ensured that relations between their city and its gods were in harmony, they would live in prosperity and happiness.

The earliest inhabitants of the Mesopotamian flood plains are known to have been scattered groups of nomadic hunters and gatherers, but by around 7,500 years ago significant numbers of people were already planting crops and irrigating their fields.[5] The settlements were small at this time, and clustered in the south, where the plains merge into the marshes and provided ready access to fish and game. Like the residents of Çatal Hüyük to the north, these people were getting the best of both worlds, exercising their traditional hunting and gathering skills while exploiting the new opportunities that farming presented. For centuries, natural forces continued to direct the disposition of settlements and canals. As alternating regimes of dry season and flood shifted the course of the meandering Euphrates progressively to the south-west (today the river lies about 25 km from its ancient course[6]), people moved too.

But human endeavour gradually began to dominate the landscape. Deep and permanent canals were built to carry water farther away from the main streams, to areas that were safe from flooding. A remarkable map, reconstructed in the early 1980s from satellite imagery and land surveys, shows a dense web of ancient canals laid across the entire length and breadth of Sumer – bringing irrigation to nearly 17,000 km^2 of cultivable land.[7] Some canals are close together, like minor roads in a heavily populated landscape; others run like major highways for tens of kilometres, straight as an arrow, with large settlements dotted at intervals along their length.

Of course, not all the canals on the map were in use simultaneously. Some are much older than others and probably went out of use as new ones were dug, but an overwhelming impression of prodigious human activity is inescapable. More than 2,000 settlements have been located in the region;[8] most were quite small, some large enough to be called cities, and still more destined to achieve that status during the world's first flowering of civilisation, among them Ur, Larsa, Uruk, Umma, Adab, Shuruppak, Isin, Nippur, Kish, Ninevah and Babylon.

Urban society had by now moved on some way beyond the loose association of craft workers and traders which marked the origins of cities as outlined at the conclusion of the previous chapter. Many generations had come and gone; the economic and social developments that were little short of revolutionary 1,000 years before were now the norms of everyday life. The family remained the basic social unit, but affiliations within the broader community determined everyone's status and fate. Individuals (and families) fulfilled mutually complementary roles and thus contributed to the well-being of all. Indeed, as a leading commentator wrote, 'the earliest cities illustrate a first approximation to an organic solidarity based upon a functional complementarity and interdependence between all its members such as subsist between the constituent cells of an organism'.[9] In other words, cities thrived because their residents worked together. Cooperative effort was obviously the glue that held the earliest known cities together – and is no less essential today.

But although the city offers individuals greater security in return for cooperation with the joint effort, city-dwellers often have been obliged to suffer a loss of free choice as well. Some more than others. Sumerian society, for instance, was structurally divided – on a sliding scale of reward and obligation, with religious leaders and administrators at one end, craft workers, merchants and farmers jostling together in the middle, and slaves at the other end. Slavery was a fundamental feature of the Sumerian economy and society. All households had one or more slaves, and some large estates had as many as ten or twenty in a single household – both males and female. Any children they might have had became the property of the slave-owner. Slaves were listed along with other property in documents such as wills and household accounts; they are mentioned time and again in tablets recording property holdings, bills of sale, legal matters and even in the form of notes that neighbours might exchange:

> . . . about our slave on which I gave you instructions – Ibi might come and let that slave out without asking me. Put a halter on [him], and put the copper band which I left with you on him. Call on Beletum, the barmaid of Ibi and say: 'the slave is entrusted to you until Etirum comes. The slave must not go out of the gate. Keep an eye on him, and don't let him get upset.'[10]

There are records of slaves attempting to escape, and the law codes stipulated that the loss of a slave should be announced by the public herald, with citizens obliged to hand runaways over to the authorities.

Slaves were acquired by war and plunder, or from merchants specialising in the slave trade (at one time slaves brought from the mountains to the east of Mesopotamia were especially popular), and doubtless their numbers contributed significantly to the 'extraordinarily rapid, massive process of growth' and permanent settlement in two key regions – Uruk and Nippur – that occurred around 6,000 years ago. It seems likely that the population of Sumer grew tenfold in less than 200 years around that time[11] – and continued to grow during the centuries that followed. Significantly, most of this growth occurred in urban centres, so that by about 4,500 years ago, almost 80 per cent of the region's population was crowded into large cities.[12]

The total amount of food consumed each day by people living in the Sumerian cities was huge. A combination of statistics from different sources indicates that a city with a population of 40,000 would have needed to arrange for the supply and distribution of just over three tonnes of barley a day.[13] But of course barley was not the only food (nor was barley consumed only as bread – beer was made from the malted grain). There were also dates from the palm groves; apricots and grapes from the orchards, and vegetables from the cities' gardens, including beans, chick-peas, and onions – lots of onions. Among thousands of clay tablets revealing the scale and complexity of food provisioning arrangements throughout Sumer, the records of a prominent merchant include an order for 150,000 bunches of onions.[14] No wonder the Sumerian term for a garden – ki-sum-ma – literally means 'the place of onions'.[15]

The Sumerians were highly accomplished farmers, though from a climatic point of view the regions they cultivated were entirely unsuited to the production of food crops. Then as now, rainfall was meagre and fell principally during the winter months, when killing frosts were not infrequent and even heavy showers could do little to promote growth if the prevailing temperatures were low. No more than a trace of rain falls during the summer months, when average afternoon temperatures often exceed 40°C and highs of 50°C are not unknown.[16] It was a harsh environment, verging on desert. The indigenous vegetation was sparse, but the Sumerians brought the waters of the Euphrates to the land via their canals, and transformed the desert into a bread basket.

A Sumerian text, dating from nearly 4,000 years ago, gives an evocative insight into the paramount importance of cereals in Mesopotamia. Called 'The farmer's instructions', the tract is addressed by a father to his son for the purpose of guiding him through the annual round of agricultural activity, beginning with the flooding of the fields in May and June, and ending with the winnowing of the freshly harvested crops in the following April and May. In their detail, the instructions are an impressive indication of Sumerian efficiency. Here are some extracts:

> After you cut the weeds and establish the limits of the field, level it repeatedly with a thin hoe . . . Let a flat hoe erase the oxen tracks,
>
> Your implements should be ready . . .
>
> The plough oxen will have back-up oxen . . . each plough will have a back-up plough. The assigned task for one plough is [approximately 65 ha], but if you build the implement at [approximately 52 ha], the work will be pleasantly performed for you . . .
>
> Make eight furrows per *ninda* of width [approximately 6 m]; the barley will lodge in more closely spaced furrows. When you have to work the field with the seeder-plough, keep your eye on the man who drops the seed. The grain should fall two fingers deep. You should put one *gij* of seed per *ninda* [approximately 3 ml/m][17]

Thus the seed grain was not broadcast, as in Europe and elsewhere until relatively recent times, but was dropped, seed by seed, in regularly spaced furrows through a funnel fitted to the back of the plough. Farmers knew precisely how large their fields were, and on the basis of how many furrows would be ploughed and the distance between seeds regularly calculated in advance exactly how much seed, labour and time would be required to sow a given field. The cost of food for the labourers and fodder for the oxen was generally included in these calculations too.

Farmers sometimes varied the seeding rate and the distance between rows – perhaps because time or labour or seed was limited – but always aimed for the best yield in relation to the amount of seed sown, not the maximum per surface area of field.[18] And with such attention to detail.

Sumerian farmers achieved impressive results. Harvests amounting to 76 times the weight of seed sown are quoted (by comparison, yields in feudal Europe were commonly as low as twice the weight sown).[19] Getting the grain to the citizens called for yet more invention and organisational efficiency. Chariots and pack animals were used to a limited extent, but the waters of the Euphrates provided the most effective means of transport. After the harvest, capacious sailing vessels and barges brought vast quantities of grain from the rural threshing floors to the cities, where it was carefully stored. In the city of Shuruppak, for instance, brick-lined underground silos 4 m wide and 8 m deep could have held enough grain to feed 20,000 people for six months.

Then came the challenge of distribution, which was handled by the city authorities to begin with – and again the quantities involved were substantial. In Babylon 4,000 years ago, for instance, when the city was at the peak of its achievements, every eligible adult man could expect to receive a ration of 60 litres of barley per month from the city, and every eligible woman 30 litres. Throughout Sumer, thousands of urban-dwellers were the beneficiaries of these arrangements. The barley was free, but this was no free lunch. In return for rations, people had to be available for work as determined by the city, and they probably worked hard. Subsequently, however, the ration system broke down and was abandoned as a cash-based economy gained favour. Rather than working for food, people now exercised more independence: they could work as they chose and bought provisions from their wages.[20]

Meanwhile there were always some people who were provided with meals rather than rations, and there were some outstanding occasions when everyone was treated to a feast. Imagine, when Assurnasirpal II celebrated the inauguration of his new capital, Kalhu, he fed 69,574 men and women for ten days. There is no indication of how the logistics of this stupendous event were handled, but the ingredients are listed at length: oxen, calves, sheep, lambs, deer, ducks, geese, pigeons, birds, fish, jerboa, eggs, bread, beer, wine, sesame, greens, grains, pome-granates, grapes, onions, garlic, turnips, honey, ghee, seeds, mustard, milk, cheese, nuts, dates, spices, oils and olives.[21]

4

Common Threads

The earliest cities were founded several thousand years ago. It might be expected that such an expanse of time would have left an unbridgeable gulf between the life experiences of ancient and modern city-dwellers. In fact, the fundamentals of city life – and human nature – have hardly changed at all. The similarities are striking, and the differences are mainly a result of the way technology has made many aspects of life easier.

. . . wash well a large pot and add water, milk and heat. Wipe dry birds . . . sprinkle with salt and put in the pot. Add fat . . . *fines herbes* to choice, and de-leafed rue. When boiling add onion . . . leeks and garlic crushed together, and a little clear water.

. . . soak properly cleaned semolina in milk, and when it is damp enough, knead in [a spicy fish sauce] and, all the time watching to ensure it stays supple, add to the kneading . . . crushed leek and garlic, milk, and fat residue from the cooking. Make this mixture into two parts. Leave one to rise in a pot. Cook the other in small breads . . .

Continue kneading the semolina dampened with milk, adding oil, crushed leek and garlic . . . Take a flat round vessel large enough to hold the birds and their garnish. Line it with the pastry which must exceed the height of the rim.

Take up the dough already kneaded and placed to one side in a pot and spread it on another dish the same shape, chosen to cover the space with the birds and garnish. Sprinkle first with mint and then cover with the pastry to form the shape of a thin cover. [Place in] the front of the oven . . .

When cooked, remove the cover from its cooking vessel . . .

When the birds and their bouillon are done, crush and add leek [and] garlic . . . take the dish with pastry and place in the birds . . . leaving aside the . . . bouillon. Cover it all with the pastry cover and send to table.[1]

This is a recipe from a city in southern Mesopotamia, inscribed on a tablet of clay some 3,700 years ago. It could have featured at the feast Assurnasirpal II hosted to celebrate the inauguration of his new capital city around 870 BC. Equally, it could be an idiosyncratic version of game pie offered to modern gastronomes by a celebrity cook. What is striking, though, is how familar it seems.

The quantities of onions, leeks and garlic in the dish do indicate a predilection for the *alliacae* that ought not to be indulged before travelling on a crowded tube train, it is true, but otherwise this scrap of evidence from the kitchen suggests that we have much in common with the citizens of ancient Mesopotamia. They had no gas or electricity, no stainless steel utensils, no running water or paper napkins, but clearly they shared our concern with cleanliness in the kitchen and enjoyed a tasty dish, attractively garnished and brought steaming to the table, just as much as we do. Sumer offers many such glimpses into the lives of ordinary people thousands of years ago, and accumulatively they evoke a sense of how little the fundamentals of life have changed. Our lives and theirs could have been interchangeable. Only time separates us; we could have functioned there, and they could have functioned here.

That this might seem at all surprising is a consequence of the way history is told. Accounts of ancient cities and societies have for generations tended to concentrate on the higher rungs of society, implicitly stressing the presence and overwhelming importance of kings and conquerors. To a degree, this is inevitable, since temples, palaces and treasure-trove burials have always been the prime target of anyone digging up ancient remains. Even archaeologists have looked first for the treasure that signifies high status and hardly looked any further once they found it. At least that was the tendency until comparatively recent times. Nowadays far greater attention is paid to evidence from lower down the social ladder. Which makes eminently good sense to anyone seeking a picture of life for the majority in the ancient world. After all, stratified societies are generally pyramidical in shape, with large numbers below supporting a small elite above. And the lifestyle of the majority is unlikely to match the extravagant lives of the elite. No one would present the British royal family's daily round as typical of British life as a whole.

Archaeology was still deeply set in the traditional treasure-hunting mode during the 1920s and '30s, when Leonard Woolley began his excavations at the ancient Sumerian city of Ur. And true to form he discovered the burial chamber of King Meskalamdug and his Queen, Puabi, who had died sometime between 4,600 and 4,450 years ago. But even while calling for stories of ordinary people and their everyday lives, it would be a hard heart that denied Woolley the praise his discovery deserves. And in any case, he redeemed himself by subsequently moving on to uncover a whole city filled with the evidence of everyday lives. But first a brief account of the royal tombs.

Sealed chambers on the floor of the deeply dug tombs contained the King and Queen themselves, together with the remains of attendants in court dress, quantities of jewellery and numerous gold and silver vessels (which presumably had contained food and drink). The sealed chambers were guarded by armed men; chariots drawn by oxen stood in attendance; a procession of officers with insignias of rank; musicians bearing harps or lyres; women with head-dresses of carnelian and lapis lazuli, silver and gold lined the sloping approach to the tombs; in another part, sixty-four ladies of the court were laid out in orderly rows, each wearing ceremonial dress and jewellery of gold, silver, lapis lazuli and carnelian. It was apparent that all these people had given up their lives so that their rulers might be appropriately accompanied on the journey to the afterlife. A great copper pot found in the burial chamber is believed to have contained the lethal potion that was drunk by these sacrificial victims before they lay down, composed themselves for death and the grave was filled.[2]

The exquisite artifacts that Woolley recovered from the royal tombs of Ur are displayed for all to admire in museum collections. The gold head of a bull, with eyes, horn tips and beard of lapis lazuli is in the Museum of the University of Pennsylvania; a helmet of beaten gold worn by the dead king (fashioned in the form of a wig, with the locks of hair hammered up in relief, and the individual hairs delicately engraved) is in the Museum of Iraq, Baghdad. At the British Museum, Queen Puabi's head-dress of delicate gold leaves and flowers adorns a lifelike reconstruction of the Queen herself . . . There is much here to admire – but little to empathise with. A thought for the jeweller who carved the lapis lazuli so beautifully seems equally deserving, or for the goldsmith whose work gleams today much as it must have done on the day it left his workshop. And what of the dozens who were obliged to give up their lives for the dead king and queen?

Fortunately, there is plenty of evidence from Sumer to redress the balance. As with the recipe quoted above, all we need is the object, the word, the image that bridges the distance between our two worlds. Something that touches upon the fundamental imperatives of life, striking the chords which have been common to all society and culture. The ancient cities of Sumer are replete with images that speak eloquently of these things, across the millennia:

> His chant, the sweet, he sang for us,
> In sweet rejoicing he whiled away the time for us;
> While we by the moonlight take our fill of love,
> I will prepare for you a bed pure, sweet, and noble,
> The sweet day will bring you joyful fulfilment.[3]

The city of Ur at which Leonard Woolley had excavated the royal tombs was built on the inside bank of a bend in the Euphrates. Two harbours gave river traffic access to the city – one on the northern arm of the bend and another on the western arm. The northern harbour was largest, with a wide entrance opening onto nearly 2 ha of water where over 500 m of walled docks were available for the loading and unloading of goods and passengers. The western harbour was about half the size of its northern counterpart.

The oldest part of the city stood diagonally between the two harbours on high ground, safe from flooding, and it was here that Woolley had excavated the royal tombs. This sacred area, as Woolley called it, with its temples and ziggurat, was relatively small. Not much else was standing above ground, but there were remnants of a wall over 2 km long to the east and south of the sacred area, and this, together with river frontage of another kilometre, enclosed a total area of 89 ha – the size of about fifty north American city blocks – a large city by any reckoning. In fact, Ur was probably home to 35,000 people when the city was fully occupied about 4,000 years ago,[5] and the evidence of their lives was awaiting discovery in and under the numerous mounds of eroded rubble and brick that distinguished the site.

Moving away from the glories of the royal tombs, in 1930–31 Woolley began extensive excavations about halfway between the sacred area and the city wall, in what proved to be a large and densely populated residential area. As Woolley noted in an account of these excavations, 'there was no such thing as town-planning at Ur'; the residential area had grown organically, as houses were constructed first along approach roads, then filled the spaces in between to create a tangle of lanes and cul-de-sacs amidst an irregular pattern of tightly packed dwellings and courtyards. There probably had been a processional way leading to the sacred area at one time, but there was nothing so grand and predetermined about the rest of the city. Here the layout was dictated by happenstance and issues of landownership. Some blocks of property were neat and regular, but others were so large that only blind alleys could give access to houses in the middle of the block.[6]

Woolley's map of ancient Ur could as well depict sections of old cities which have survived more or less untouched to the present day, such as Jodhpur in India for instance – though perhaps the cities of medieval England would be a better analogy since Woolley chose to mark the throughways, alleys and prominent features on his map with names such as 'Paternoster Row', 'Broad Street', 'Church Lane', 'Old Street', 'Baker's Square' and so forth.

The streets were unpaved, but appeared to have been regularly littered with house sweepings and domestic rubbish, so that as these were trodden underfoot the level of the street gradually rose. This phenomenon is common to all old cities, but the process must have been exceptionally rapid at Ur. Woolley found, for example, that during the time the houses on Pasternoster Row were inhabited, the street level rose more than a metre. At a house he designated no. 15, a flight of six steps led from the street level down to the original house floor. Eventually, of course, this state of affairs would become intolerable, at which point the owner would demolish the house and build anew at the existing street level. It was in this way that the tells, or mounds, which hold the secrets of the ancient Sumerian cities were formed.

Woolley's site plans show that no two houses were exactly alike – in every case builders were obliged to adjust their ground plans to fit plots of varying size and often irregular shape. But construction methods were consistent. Exterior walls were built of baked clay bricks; interior walls had several courses of damp-proof baked brick at the base, with cheaper unfired mud bricks above. The walls could be one metre thick, so that in some instances they occupied nearly half the total floor space of a living area; there was an advantage to this, however, in that thick walls helped to moderate extremes of temperature. A single doorway led from the public throughways to each house, leaving exterior walls otherwise unbroken. Windows, such as they were, faced inwards, onto private courtyards – an arrangement that in addition to limiting the influx of direct sunlight also gave a measure of protection against windblown dust and sand from the street.

In a typical house, the front door opened inwards onto a small brick-paved lobby with a drain in one corner, which was probably where people washed their feet before entering the house proper. From the lobby, steps led down to a paved central court, where doors on all sides opened into a number of separate rooms. At no. 3 Gay Street there were seven such rooms of varying dimensions; one was large enough to have been a reception room; two were so small that they can only have been a latrine and washroom; another, which had two fireplaces and an adjacent store-room, was clearly the kitchen.

On the evidence of tablets found in many of the houses, Woolley concluded that the residents of this crowded area had been the middle class of Ur – the city's merchants, scribes, shopkeepers and so on. There were shops as well as residential houses. No. 14 Paternoster Row, for instance, was a private house that had been turned into a cook-shop, with a window cut into the street-facing wall at waist level opening onto the kitchen which now occupied the front room. At no. 1 Baker's Square the entire house had been turned into a metalworking shop, with stoke-hole and kilns, while no. 1 Broad Street had become a school, where Igmil-Sin held classes in the courtyard and reception room while the remaining quarters were reserved for domestic use.

Nearly 2,000 tablets were found in Igmil-Sin's school – some were mathematical tablets and multiplication tables, others were religious and historical texts of the kind that could have been used for dictation, or learning by heart, and a palpable sense of the rituals that link schooldays everywhere, in every age, is evoked by the hundreds of tablets which had obviously served the purpose that exercise books do today – they were covered with fair copies of given texts and essays. Not exactly in the vein of 'what I did in the holidays', but that sort of thing.

Some researchers have cast doubts on the validity of Woolley's conclusions regarding Igmil-Sin's school on Broad Street,[7] but that does not diminish its relevance so far as the importance attached to education in ancient Sumer is concerned. Thousands of tablets relating to all aspects of education have been recovered from all stages of the region's history, throughout Sumer. These include hundreds of practice-tablets filled with all sorts of exercises, the scripts ranging from the nervous scratches of the first-grade pupil to the elegantly made signs of the advanced student about to graduate.[8] Accumulatively, the material gives a full picture of the aims and methods of Sumerian education. Results were what mattered most. The curriculum was demanding, and pupils had to endure drab teaching methods and harsh discipline.[9] All in all, the experience of going to school seems to have been distinctly dreary and uninviting. No wonder then, that truancy and badly behaved teenagers were prevalent enough to earn a place among the texts – no less, perhaps, than they feature in newspapers today.

More than 3,700 years ago, for instance, a father was so outraged that his son spent so much time loitering about the streets instead of working diligently at school, and was so lacking in gratitude for the privileged life he led, that he just had to set his feelings down on a tablet addressed to the boy.

> I, never in all my life, did I make you carry reeds to the canebrake . . . I never said to you 'Follow my caravans'. I never sent you to work, to plow my field. I never sent you to work and dig up my field. I never sent you to work as a labourer. 'Go, work and support me', I never in my life said to you.[10]

In particular, the father was deeply disappointed by his son's lack of enthusiasm for the idea of becoming a scribe, like himself:

> Perverse one with whom I am furious, night and day am I tortured because of you. Night and day you waste in pleasures. You have accumulated such wealth, have expanded far and wide, have become fat, big, broad, powerful and puffed. But your kin waits expectantly for your misfortune . . .

But no father who cares enough to be worried can wish misfortune on a son; his anger is tempered with love and what began as a tirade of complaints ends with a series of blessings:

> May you find favour before your god,
> May your humanity exalt you . . .
> May you be the head of your city's sages,
> May your city utter your name in favoured places,
> May your god call you by a good name.

We take the written word so much for granted that it is perhaps only when a message recorded thousands of years before tells us so intimately of a father's concern for his son that we may pause to consider the wonder of it. Writing preserved the father's sentiments far longer than he could have imagined, and similarly provides insights into every aspect of life throughout the millennia. When and where did this now indispensable adjunct of civilisation begin? Clearly, the practice was well-established when the angry father was writing to his wayward son around 1700 BC; in fact, the earliest known evidence of writing goes back another sixteen hundred years – to 3300 BC and the city of Uruk, which stood close by the Euphrates, about 100 km upstream and to the north-west of Ur.

Both Ur and Uruk date back to the very beginnings of urbanisation, but Uruk blossomed sooner and steadily outstripped its nearest large neighbour. Indeed, Uruk was 'probably the largest settlement in the entire world'[11] around 5,000 years ago. Best estimates suggest that up to 80,000 people were living in the city by then,[12] their homes and temples and places of work ringed around by a massive baked-brick wall that was nearly 10 km long and studded with nearly a thousand semi-circular bastions.[13]

At its height, Uruk covered an area of over 5 km^2 – twice the size of Athens in the fifth century BC; even Rome, as capital of an enormous empire under Hadrian in AD 100 was only twice as large as Uruk had been more than 3,000 years before.[14] But the importance of Uruk was not limited to the size of the city – nor even to Mesopotamia. Between about 5,500 and 5,000 years ago, the cultural influence of the Uruk spread over a huge geographic area, leaving its mark on the early histories of what is now Iran and Syria and even as far west as Egypt's Nile delta. Long-distance trade in commodities of one sort or another was doubtless the stimulus for this extensive cultural diffusion, but its medium was literacy – the written word. In the beginning, literacy was simply a series of recognisable labels, numbers and lists inscribed on damp clay tablets as a record of commercial holdings and transactions. It is rooted in economics, but literacy quickly blossomed into the potent form of communication and expression that it is today. The clay tablets declare that literacy was the prime mover of civilisation. The poet writes of where it all began – Uruk:

> Touch the threshold-stone – it dates from ancient times.
> Go up on the wall and walk around,
> Examine its foundation, inspect its brickwork thoroughly.
> Is not its masonry of baked brick,
> Did not the Seven Sages themselves lay out its plans?

One square mile city,
One square mile palm groves,
One square mile brick pits,
Three square miles . . . of Uruk it encloses.[15]

The thin elongated wedge-shaped signs of the script (called cuneiform – from the latin *cuneus*, meaning wedge) that expressed these words were made with a sharpened reed on a tablet of damp clay. The tablets were left to dry, or baked, and thousands upon thousands of them have been recovered from Uruk and other cities, from all periods of Sumer's history. They give us invaluable information on the times during which they were made but, quite apart from this, the tablets are the unique record of how a system of writing evolved over a span of 3,000 years – from the simple dots of numerical reckoning on the oldest tablets to the intricate patterns of fine impressions on the most recent. In the earliest scripts the representations were distinctly pictorial – the sign for a fish was recognisably a fish, likewise a plough, a man's head and a loaf of bread – but over time the signs became more abstract, and a more formalised style of single strokes was adopted, thick at one end and thin at the other. These developments eliminated the confusion that could arise in the interpretation of curved and freely drawn signs, while the introduction of symbols denoting grammatical structure permitted the fuller and more accurate expression of the spoken word and any implied sentiment.

Over time, the steadily increasing sophistication of the script endowed it with a remarkable capacity for recording and communicating complex information – as indeed it had to in an increasingly sophisticated and complex society. All aspects of Sumerian life and culture are recorded in the tablets – history, beliefs and legend; law; building methods; farming practices; business conduct; wages; taxation; education; and the training of craftsmen. The various materials and quantities required to build a house, a temple or a boat are all here.

In the harbour at Ur sometime around 4,000 years ago, for instance, the construction of a sea-going vessel was ordered, requiring the purchase of 178 mature date palms; 1,400 large pines; 36 tamarisks; 310 measures of palm-fibre rope and 418 of rushes; 17,644 bundles of fresh and dried reeds; 951,000 litres of purified bitumen and sundry other items.[16] A ship like that would have had a capacity of around 90 t and probably sailed down the Gulf to buy copper from the mineral-rich mountains of what is now Oman. It could also have sailed across to the

Indian sub-continent, where luxuries such as spices and precious stones, as well as more utilitarian items, were obtainable from traders on the Indus river valley.

These were large-scale, expensive operations, requiring careful preparation and watchful management. The merchant Eanasir ensured that the details of his business were set in clay and stored on shelves in his house at no. 1 Old Street, where Leonard Woolley found them four millennia later[17] – a far more permanent record than the merchant could have imagined.

Enumeration featured prominently in the business records, as might be expected, but the use of mathematics in Sumer went far beyond mere arithmetic. School texts provided tables of reciprocals, multiplications, squares and square roots, cubes and cube roots; the sum of squares and cubes needed for the solution of complex equations; exponential functions, coefficients giving numbers used in practical computation (such as the approximate value of the square root of 2), and numerous calculations giving the areas of rectangles, circles, irregular figures and so forth.[18] Indeed, the mathematics course at a Sumerian school was requiring students to learn the principles of the Pythagorean theorem some 2,000 years before Pythagoras was born.[19]

Knowing that in a right-angle triangle the square on the hypotenuse is equal to the sum of the squares on the two other sides, as Pythagoras famously showed, helped Sumerian surveyors to calculate areas of land; with this knowledge farmers could work out how much seed to sow, and from that information the size of harvest to be expected. Similarly, maths enabled irrigation officials to put figures on the volume of earth to be excavated from the course of a proposed canal, the amount of labour required for the job, and the rations that would need to be provided for the workers.

One memorable school exercise presented students with the problem facing a commander ordered to capture a city; he planned to build a ramp up against the city wall, over which the army would invade: how big must the ramp be? A transcription of the problem and its solution appears in an authoritative text. The problem is easy enough to understand, but the solution is something that would confound even a mathematics graduate today.[20] One can only guess at how well the students to whom the problem was presented got on with it. At least they would have been familar with the Sumerians' sexagesimal system of numeration (i.e. one based on sixes, rather than tens as in our decimal system) and would not have been confused by the absence of a zero (the

Sumerians knew nothing of the concept). Even so, it must have set gloom and despair in the hearts of ill-prepared students, 4,000 years ago:

> From the foot of the earth-ramp I went forward 32 lengths. The height of the earth-ramp is 36: what is the length I have to advance in order to capture the city . . . ?
> You take the reciprocal of 32, you find 1.52.30. Multiply 1.52.30 by 36, the height, and you find 1.7.30. Take the reciprocal of 6, the base of the earth-ramp, you find 10, multiply 1.30 (the volume of the earth) by 10 and you find 15. Double 15, you find 30. Multiply 30 by 1.7.30 and you find 33.45. Of what is 33.45 the square? It is 45 squared.
> 45 is the height of the wall. By how much does 45, the height of the wall, exceed 36, the height of the earth-ramp? It exceeds it by 9. Take the reciprocal of 1.7.30, and you find 53.20. Multiply 53.20 by 9, and you find 8.8 is the length you advance forward.[21]

Crafts are also well documented in the Sumerian tablets. At this pre-industrial stage of manufacture, component parts were not made separately at distinct locations and then brought together for assembly. Instead, anything from a royal chariot to a piece of jewellery, a door or a pair of boots was made from scratch in a single workshop, where the various specialists worked together – metalworkers, carpenters, stone-cutters, goldsmiths, jewellers, leather-workers . . . Subsequently, however, arrangements similar to the guild system of medieval Europe developed, with craftsmen occupying distinct quarters of various cities and their professional designations being used as the equivalents of family names, such as Tanner, Smith, Potter and so on.[22]

A skilled craftsman occupied a distinct and prominent position in Sumerian society, and had to qualify by serving an appropriate period of apprenticeship – anything from sixteen months for a cook to eight years for a builder. Fathers passed their skills on to their sons, and in some instances a family might even apprentice their servant's child to a trade. A tablet reveals, for example, that Atkal-ana-Marduk, the servant of Itti-Marduk-Balätu, was given to Bël-etir to learn the weaver's trade for five years. The contract stipulated that Itti-Marduk-Balätu was to provide the apprentice's food and clothing throughout and if Bël-etir failed to make him a competent weaver then a quit-rent of 6 litres of grain would be due. Furthermore, breaking the contract would render the guilty party liable to a fine of one-third of a pound of silver.[23]

2

A personal view. For the author's generation of Londoners, first impressions of city life were conditioned by the exigencies of war. Barrage balloons (1) were friendly airborne neighbours. Pollution and smog (2 and 3) were recurrent aspects of everyday life.

1

3

4

Venice was a thriving mercantile city in the Middle Ages (4), with a population of about 200,000 people. Today the city thrives on tourism, attracting millions of visitors each year. But while tourist facilities include duckboards across the flooded St Mark's Square (5), Venice has become less attractive to permanent residents. The present population is around 60,000.

6

In contrast to Venice, New York (6) and Vancouver (7) are highly rated for the quality of life they offer permanent residents.

8

The world's earliest urban settlements, such as Caral (8) in Peru and Çatal Hüyük (9) in Turkey, were founded where residents could irrigate domesticated crops while continuing to hunt and gather natural resources.

9

Çatal Hüyük was occupied for almost 1000 years up to 5700 BC. Access to the
densely packed houses (11) was via holes in the roofs. A wall painting (10) shows
Çatal Hüyük in plan, with an erupting volcano behind. Dating from 8000 years ago,
this is the earliest known representation of a town and landscape.

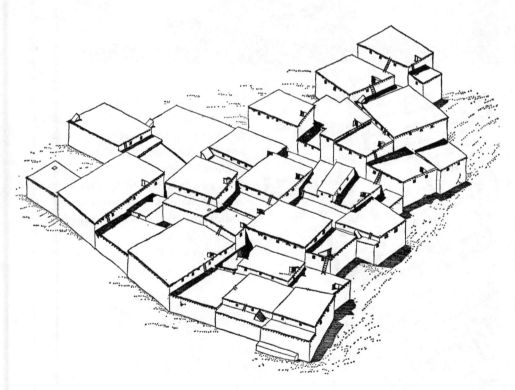

12

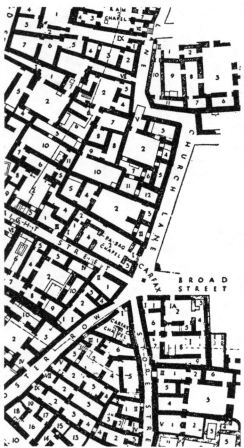

With agricultural economies supported by the extensive network of irrigation canals that modern surveys (14) have revealed, the world's first true cities arose in Mesopotamia around six thousand years ago. Nineteenth century reports inspired dramatic reconstructions (12), while 20th century excavations revealed street plans reminiscent of a medieval European town – and named accordingly (13).

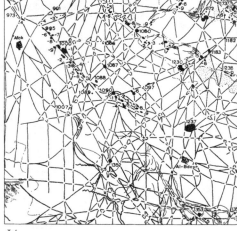

13

14

15

16

Inscribed clay tablets (16) have been an invaluable source of information on all aspects of life in ancient Mesopotamia. The cuneiform script dates back more than 5000 years and is the world's earliest known form of writing. A delicate mosaic of shell, stone and lapis lazuli (15) shows a peaceful scene of attendants bringing provisions to a royal feast. In 2003, Mesopotamia, the cradle-land of cities, became a war-zone (17).

Though warfare did not provoke the initial establishment of cities, it subsequently became a feature of their history everywhere. Sumerian rulers maintained armies of professional soldiers 5000 years ago. A commemorative stele praise victory (18), and portrays the defeated as food for vultures (19).

18

19

Weaving was a favoured occupation. Woollen textiles – light in weight, and therefore relatively easy to transport; always in demand, and therefore of a fairly constant value – were a major item of Sumer's local and long-distance trade. The records of the royal wool office at Ur speak of an organisation handling about 2,000 tonnes of new wool each year, plucked (not sheared) from a total of over 2 million sheep. Most of the sheep were raised on pastures that lay beyond the city's agricultural lands in flocks under the care of individual shepherds; though the texts also record the feeding of barley to as many as 52,553 sheep that were kept in stalls over a three-month period.[24]

The wool industry employed an enormous labour force. Quite apart from the shepherds who looked after the animals, and the thousands who plucked, cleaned, packed and transported the wool, there were over 13,000 weavers operating in Ur alone at the height of the city's prosperity around 4,000 years ago, with similar numbers engaged in the region's other urban centres.

The weavers were mostly women, employed full-time and paid in rations of food and clothing; it seems they did not work at home, as was the case with Europe's pre-mechanised textile industry, but commuted each day to what might be called weaving workshops. Children accompanied their mothers, and older children were often engaged on tasks which required keener eyesight than their mothers possessed – such as threading the loom. Cloth was woven to order, to specific grades of quality, and the length of time spent on each piece varied accordingly. Three women could weave about 25 cm of third-grade cloth in one day, for instance, or about 36 cm of a fourth-grade cloth. Such rates of production are well below the norm for even the most primitive of manually operated looms in medieval Europe. This suggests a lack of technical expertise, inefficiency or bad management but perhaps it should be regarded as a revealing indication of what time counted for, 4,000 years ago. Certainly, as the example quoted below suggests, there seems to have been plenty of time available for work at the top end of the range. In this case, 400 workdays went into the production of a second-quality garment weighing 3.5 kg:

three months and six days: twisting
two days: cleaning
two days: trimming
one month: sewing up
two days: pressing

one month and twenty days: teaselling
four days: scraping and levelling
one month: sewing, teaselling, and finishing
six days: beating
two months: picking the threads from the front
twenty days: picking the threads from the back
ten days: stretching and pressing
one month and eighteen days: untwisting
one month and ten days: blowing.[25]

But lest it is thought that life in the cities of Sumer 4,000 years ago was a Utopian idyll, with weavers, craftsmen and all members of the community striving joyfully for perfection in all things, a letter from a complaining customer to a goldsmith brings us back to the real world. It recounts an all too familiar state of affairs:

To Ili-idinnam say, thus speaks Bahlatum: You have acted towards me as if you and I have never talked, and you are not solving my problem. Earlier, I had given you grain in order to buy stones for my necklace! It is four years ago that I paid you! . . . Now, if you really are like a brother to me, for the sake of all gods, send me that piece at once. Do not hold it back! If that piece does not reach me at once, this commission will no longer be in effect . . .[26]

Pause for a moment. To convey this message to the goldsmith, the customer first had to prepare a tablet of wet clay and cut a reed, or call in a scribe to take dictation (as was more likely, since the customer was a lady of standing in the community); the tablet was then left to harden before being delivered. From our perspective this cumbersome and lengthy procedure might seem guaranteed to ensure that the message would be drained of all but its central message. And yet the lady's outrage and frustration – moderated between the lines by a sense of sympathy for the wayward goldsmith – comes winging down through the millennia as clearly as if it had been delivered by telephone.

But whether Sumer was a utopian idyll or a familiar round of humdrum everyday life, it did not last. For all their achievements and the civilised world they built on the Mesopotamian plain 4,000 years ago, with its glories and grandeur and generations of ordinary people with whom we might have shared a meal and a joke, the Sumerians were destined to leave us a message that no city or civilisation can dare to ignore: entropy rules.

No natural system, be it a lawn or a rainforest, can remain the same for ever. And no matter how robust they seem, or how long they have existed, cities and their support systems are just as prone to the natural cycle of growth and decay as a tree or a blade of grass. It is true that, having constructed a city in the first place, people can instigate maintenance programmes to forestall decay. But the process inevitably extends beyond the physical structure of the city itself, touching the surrounding countryside and affecting the way people behave – sometimes perversely.

> In former days the vast plains [of Mesopotamia] were nourished by a complicated system of canals and watercourses, which spread over the surface of the country like net-work . . . Like islands, rising from a golden sea of waving corn, stood frequent groves of palms and pleasant gardens, affording to the idler or the traveller their grateful and highly-valued shade. Crowds of passengers hurried along the dusty roads to and from the busy city. The land was rich in corn and wine. How changed is the aspect of that region at the present day! Long lines of mounds, it is true, mark the courses of those main arteries which formerly diffused life and vegetation along their banks, but their channels are now bereft of moisture and choked with drifted sand; the smaller offshoots are wholly effaced . . . All that remains of that ancient civilisation – that 'glory of kingdoms,' 'the praise of the whole earth' – is recognizable in the numerous mouldering heaps of brick and rubbish which overspread the surface of the plain. Instead of the luxuriant fields, the groves and gardens, nothing now meets the eye but an arid waste – the dense population of former times is vanished, and no man dwells there. Instead of the hum of many voices, silence reigns profound . . . Destruction has swept the land . . .

These were the words of William Kennet Loftus, one of the earliest European travellers with an interest in relics of the ancient world, who visited Mesopotamia in the 1840s and '50s.[27] In the century following the early investigations of Loftus and others, archaeologists unearthed plenty of evidence to confirm the glories of the past, but were forever baffled by the collapse and destruction that eventually ensued. And as the accumulating evidence made it abundantly clear that Mesopotamia was the cradle of Western civilisation, the fate of those who had thronged the streets of Ur and Uruk assumed a significance of more than just academic interest. These were people we could relate to as individuals; they had lived at the very beginnings of a progression on which we are the latest manifestation. You could not help but empathise with people whose personal letters you have read, and whose meals you would have enjoyed to share. What had happened to them?

In the 1950s there were grounds for expecting that answers would be forthcoming. Under the terms of a far-sighted statute, the Iraqi Government had allocated 70 per cent of the country's oil revenues to a programme of capital investment which would transform many aspects of the national economy. The programme acknowledged that central and southern Iraq – Mesopotamia – was a unique repository of evidence concerning the past effectiveness of irrigation agriculture in the region, and thus an indispensable background for the formulation of development plans. Accordingly, multidisciplinary investigations of the entire 6,000-year record of irrigation agriculture in the Tigris–Euphrates flood plain were initiated.[28]

The programme included the study of ancient textual sources from Mesopotamia, which were widely scattered in the world's libraries and museums, climatic and ecological investigations, and extensive archaeological fieldwork designed to elucidate the history of irrigation and settlement on the floodplain. The studies were on-going and had already amassed a considerable amount of valuable data when political upheaval and revolution engulfed Iraq in the late 1960s and into the 1970s. Investigations had effectively ceased when Saddam Hussein took power in 1979. The new regime had other uses for the country's oil revenues; but at least there was some comfort in the fact that, although the work was suspended, the archaeological sites remained more or less inviolate. Sadly, however, the region became a war zone in March 2003. The fate of Mesopotamia's ancient inhabitants does not begin to measure against the plight of its present residents. Few scholars would dare to hope that more archaeological information will be forthcoming for many years yet.

The curtailment of archaeological and other investigations in Iraq itself notwithstanding, the evidence previously known has been enough to stimulate theory and voluminous discussion concerning the final years and ultimate demise of the Mesopotamian civilisations. At the broadest level, the collapse seems to have been a final turn in the cycles of prosperity and destitution which characterised the early history of the region. War, famine, flood, pestilence and political upheaval repeatedly occurred, and the clay tablets reflect the population's keen awareness of the disaster that ensues from a breakdown in social order. But of course the documentary and archaeological evidence comes principally from the periods of settled peace and prosperity. Descriptions of the intervening 'Dark Ages' do not present a picture of cause and effect, but are rather couched in terms of admonishment, warning people of the activities which are likely to anger the gods and bring about another round of disaster. Hence the gods' apparent determination to destroy humanity is blamed upon the size and clamour of the cities:

> Twelve hundred years had not yet passed
> When the land extended and the people multiplied.
> The land was bellowing like a bull,
> The god got disturbed with their uproar.
> Enlil heard their noise
> And addressed the great gods:
> 'The noise of mankind has become too much for me,
> With their noise I am deprived of sleep.
> Let there be a pestilence [upon mankind].'[29]

This and other tablets suggest that it was not so much the noise of the cities that angered the gods, but the sheer number of people. In other words: Mesopotamia had become over-populated, and the gods had variously employed war, pestilence, drought, flood and famine as a means of keeping the size of the human population under control. But there were other ways of doing this. By adopting practices that limited population growth, the people could avoid provoking the gods to take action; and thus brith control becomes a feature of the tablets:

> O Lady of Birth, Creatress of the Fates,
> [Let there be] among the people [child-]bearing women and
>   barren women,
> Let there be among the people a . . . demon,
> Let it seize the baby from the mother's lap.
> Establish [several classes of] priestesses,
> They shall be taboo-ed, and thus cut off child-bearing.[30]

Infanticide, chastity, celibacy and methods of intercourse that avoid pregnancy are advocated: 'the high priestess will permit intercourse *per anum* . . .'[31] – but ultimately none of this could save Mesopotamia from becoming the victim of its own success. Having developed a highly productive agricultural system that kept the cities fed and functioning for thousands of years, that success brought them face to face with an intractable problem: a well-fed population inevitably grows to the limits of available space and resources.

It is unlikely that people as worldly as the Sumerians were unaware of the dangers of allowing population size to outstrip food supply. But even while they identified the problem, their attempts to avert the dangers of over-population ultimately made matters worse. As the cities grew, Sumerian farmers were subject to the repeated – if not constant – pressure of rising demand. The evidence mounts with the passing centuries as the tablets reveal more and more instances of fields kept in continuous production, rather than fallowed for alternate years; of lower yields from given quantities of seed; and – most ominously – of the land's rising salinity.

It is a sombre truth of farming in Mesopotamia that while it is easy enough to direct water from the river to the fields, the shallow incline of the plain makes it exceedingly difficult to drain the water off again. And when water lies on the surface, or soaks the land excessively, deep-lying soluble salts are brought to the surface, rendering the land increasingly saline and poisonous to crops. This salinisation of the land can be traced to the waters of the Tigris and the Euphrates, which contain very small quantities of salts derived from the sedimentary rocks through which they flow in their northern reaches. Over the millennia these salts have accumulated in the groundwaters of southern Mesopotamia, making it highly saline. This becomes a problem when the water table rises with repeated irrigation, floods or heavy rain. At that point, the salts rise through capillary action and accumulate in the upper layers of the soil, gradually rendering the land useless to farmers.[32] As water dries from the land the salts left on the surface gleam like snow, and even in modern times have been collected and marketed for culinary use by rural families as an extra source of income.

The case for salinisation having been responsible for a catastrophic fall in productivity and urban populations in the south of the region – in Sumer, that is – about 3,700 years ago, has been convincingly made.[33] Tablets from the time reveal returns on labour input which had fallen to about one-fifth of the yields expected from a similar magnitude of effort 800 years before. The number of occupied sites in the region fell by 40 per cent, and many major urban centres were abandoned.[34] There appears to have been a shift from wheat cultivation to barley – which can tolerate higher levels of salinity – and in the eighteenth to seventeenth centuries BC the major urban centres in the south were almost completely abandoned. 'The whiteness of the fields' appears in Sumerian poetry from around this time as a description of famine.[35] And famine was seen as the gods' ultimate censure against the continuing demands of an expanding human population:

> He let milled foods be insufficient for the people,
> vegetable food grew scant in their bellies,
> Above Adad made scarce his rain.
> Scarce became below the flood, it rose not from the source.
> The field decreased its yield,
> repulsed the grain,
> (from being) black the tilth turned white,
> the broad plain gave birth to wet–salt,
> the womb of the Earth revolted,
> no plants came up, the ewe conceived not.[36]

The theory that progressive salinisation of the soil undermined the economy of ancient Sumer was published in 1958, and has remained the most commonly accepted explanation of the region's ultimate political and cultural demise. But the theory remains unproven. The study of Sumerian agriculture has made considerable progress since then, and further examination of the original evidence fails to substantiate the theory in detail.[37] There are problems of interpretation and incomplete analysis of the texts (the preliminary nature of the report did not permit thorough analysis of the texts and associated evidence at the time), and the treatment of statistics is questioned; all of which raises doubts as to whether soil salinity was widespread enough to cause a general collapse. On the other hand, failing to substantiate the theory does not disprove it.

Unproven, but not disproved, the salinisation theory must await further investigation. There is no doubt that saline fields were a problem at a local level, of which the farmers were well aware and probably knew how to deal with, but the experts want to know much more about the relationships between water supply and land used, the reversibility of salinity, and the social and technical feasibility of large-scale shifts in areas of cultivation before deciding whether or not local salinity problems would have converged into a long-term deterioration of the entire south.[38]

Such information may not be available for some time. Meanwhile, the rise and fall of Sumer warns of the fragility of cities and institutions, and here and there speaks tenderly of the individual joys and fears that have sustained humanity through countless generations. We live, and we die:

> Seizing me, he led me down to the House of Darkness, the
>   dwelling of Irkalla,
> to the House where those who enter do not come out,
> along the road of no return,
> to the House where those who dwell do without light,
> where dirt is their drink, their food is of clay,
> where, like a bird, they wear garments of feathers,
> and light cannot be seen, they dwell in the dark,
> and upon the door and bolt lies dust.[39]

5

War, Greece and Rome

An adequate and reliable food supply is the first priority of
every city – a priority handled so efficiently in the modern
world that we take it for granted. Ancient cities, contending
with the vagaries of climate and problems of transport, were
not so fortunate. Securing the food supply pushed cities into
war and conquest, but also inspired significant advances in
farming, transport and government.

Sumer can claim a number of important firsts in world history – the first
cities, the first irrigated agriculture, the first civilisations, the first written
language – and the influence of these is with us still (not least in that
every passing minute, every hour acknowledges the Sumerians'
sexagesimal system of numeration), but there is one first that humanity
might have preferred to do without: warfare.

Warfare itself did not provoke the establishment of cities generally
(see pp. 11–12), and there is certainly nothing to suggest that warfare
inspired the foundation of Sumer's earliest cities, but there is plenty of
evidence indicating that, once established, cities and the fruits of
civilisation became important factors in the development of military
power. The story of Sumer persuasively suggests that the advent of
organised warfare probably began as the growing populations and falling
agricultural production described at the end of the last chapter combined
to create severe food shortages on the plains of Mesopotamia, and one
desperate city attempted to seize the reserves of another. Furthermore,
as Sumer water engineering approached its geographical and technological limits, as irrigation canals became larger and longer, every new
withdrawal from the rivers began to affect the water supply of cities

51

downstream. Water rights could become a matter of life or death in the dry season – even more pressing than the problems of salinisation. When disputes could no longer be resolved peacefully, war between neighbouring cities, and ultimately between rival coalitions, became a terrible and recurring feature of life in Sumer.[1]

The human propensity for killing people predates the Mesopotamian civilisations by thousands of years,[2] but cities and the newly acquired skills of working in bronze added another dimension to the undertaking – one of scale. Bronze weapons and protective shields rendered stone axes and clubs and flint-tipped arrows obsolete. Furthermore, the new military equipment could be produced on an industrial scale. With such technology and administrative experience at their disposal, the Sumerians were the first to apply method and efficiency to the conduct of warfare.

There is evidence of fighting between warrior castes in Sumer more than 6,000 years ago, but it was with the development of cities and their centralised administrative institutions that humanity's belligerent tendencies were first organised to create an instrument of ruling authority and ambition. Administrative records show that cities maintained armies of 600–700 men from an early stage; these were full-time soldiers, with their equipment, training and upkeep provided for. By just less than 5,000 years ago there was a comprehensive military presence throughout Sumer, organised along modern lines. The standing army of professional soldiers had become a permanent feature of society, accorded the respect and privileges of special status. And it has been with us ever since.[3]

War appears to have been an almost annual event in the Ur region,[4] and although explicit explanation is sparse, it can be assumed that boundary disputes over agricultural land and water rights were the primary cause of war throughout Mesopotamia:[5]

I behave to you like a father and a brother and you behave to me like an ill-wisher and enemy. What requital is this for the fact that the weapons of Adad and Yarim-Lim rescued the city of Babylon, and gave life to you and your land? . . . Indeed, Sin-gamil, the King of Diniktum, like you is rewarding me with hostility and obstructions. I have moored 500 boats in the quay of Diniktum, and for 12 years I have supported his land and himself. Now you are rewarding me with hostility and obstructions like him. I swear to you, by Addu, the god of my city, and Sin my personal god, I shall not rest until I have destroyed your land and yourself! Now I shall come at the beginning of spring, and I shall advance to the doors of your city gate, and I shall acquaint you with the bitterness of the weapons of Adad and Yarim-Lim.[6]

As might be expected, while a few inscriptions (such as the one above) tell of the circumstances that lead to war, the Sumerian epics concern themselves almost entirely with the heroics of battle and victory. The texts proclaim that in 2525 BC, for instance, Eannatum of Lagash attacked and defeated armies from the city of Umma. He 'hurled the great net [his army] upon them and heaped up piles of their bodies in the plain . . . The survivors turned to Eannatum, they prostrated themselves, for life they wept.'[7] In commemoration of the victory Eannatum commissioned a stele, complete with grisly depictions of vultures and lions tearing at the corpses of the defeated as they lay dead on the desert plain. It is known as the Stele of Vultures, and can be seen in the Louvre, Paris.

Two hundred years and many wars later, Sargon, a ruler from Akkad in the north, led his army into Sumer, defeating all before him. The inscriptions claim that he had an army of 5,400 men, fought thirty-four battles, and destroyed many city walls. Ur, Lagash, Umma, Uruk and many other cities of lesser size fell to Sargon. By force of arms he conquered all Sumer, the entire basin of the Euphrates and Tigris rivers, and created an empire that stretched from the Taurus mountains to the Persian Gulf, and possibly even to the Mediterranean – the world's first military dictatorship.

Aristotle, whose reflections on civilisation and the behaviour of ideal citizens were to become a founding component of Western philosophy, thought it entirely proper for one group of people to subjugate another in the manner of Sargon. But then he lived in a society that ran on slave labour. Though the word 'democracy' comes from the Greek *demos,* meaning common people, and the concept of democratic rights for all is now a central tenet of mainstream political beliefs, the people enjoying the privileges of democracy along with Aristotle in fourth-century BC Athens were exclusively male, outnumbered by women and other free residents of the city, and owned an average of 2.5 slaves each. The free and civilised activities of this minority were utterly dependent on the economic surplus produced by a captive majority.

Slaves were very cheap in classical Greece. In the late fifth century BC, for example, two good strong slaves could be bought outright for the cost of hiring one artisan for a year (by comparison, one slave generally cost at least four times an artisan's annual wage in mid-nineteenth century America).[8] Most of the slaves were barbarians – barbarian being the Greek term for anyone who did not speak Greek – brought back by the boatload from plundering expeditions around the eastern Mediterranean. Thirty thousand are said to have been sold in bulk to slave-dealers following the sack of Thebes by Alexander in 335 BC. One source writes of large-scale expeditions that captured 50,000 slaves in 240 BC, and another reports that the price of Jews to be captured on an expedition in 165 BC was fixed even before the campaign had begun.

Human beings featured prominently in the trading economy of classical Greece, but the greater part of what is known of Greek trading concerns a far more crucial commodity – namely the fuel required to operate both slaves and the urban-based society they sustained: grain.

As the settled communities scattered about the Aegean Sea coalesced during the eight century BC into the city-states of the classical Greek era, they soon strained the agricultural resources of their immediate environment. If anything, the Greek city-rulers faced an even more serious situation than the Sumerians had confronted. Deep alluvial soils had made Mesopotamia a fertile location for the initial founding of cities. By contrast, the soils of Greece were generally shallow and light; there were few large rivers and so widespread irrigation was not feasible. Farmers did the best they could, producing good crops of fruit and olives, and raising ample flocks of sheep and goats, but they could grow only limited amounts of the staple food – grain.

As their populations grew, the city-states were obliged to look further and further afield for their grain supply. Those with limited wealth, or situated inland, had precious little chance to alleviate their plight and succumbed to more powerful states, while those on the coast, with access to timber and shipbuilding expertise, looked across the sea for alternative supplies, and the interacting agencies of need, ingenuity and initiative soon created a network of trade routes across the Aegean and beyond. This was a critical point in the development of the city as a functioning entity. It was beginning to reach out on a grander scale than ever before – though certainly not as a source of benevolent influence, simply to secure whatever it needed to survive.

During the fifth century BC, Athens was bringing grain from the shores of the Black Sea, tapping into the western end of Russia's great wheat lands. By the fourth century, the city controlled the grain trade of the entire eastern Mediterranean. During the third century Alexander the Great extended the power of Greece down the Nile, across south-east Asia and into India.

Grain supply was an obligatory subject on the regular agenda for the main meetings of the Assembly in Athens, ranking with defence as issues of highest importance.[9] Indeed, a substantial naval force was constructed and maintained at sea for the express purpose of keeping the grain routes open. With the Assembly devoting so much attention to ensuring that the staple food supply reached the country, one might reasonably suppose that it would also retain firm control over the wholesale purchase and retail distribution of this vital commodity. But no: the grain trade of ancient Greece, both the acquisition abroad and its local sale, was left entirely in the hands of private merchants. This is a revealing instance of private initiative being left to cater for the public good.

It could be, of course, that although the Assembly would have preferred to have control of the grain trade, few or none of its members were keen to take on the risk of being held responsible in the event of things going wrong. But whatever the case, there were important advantages to leaving the trade in the hands of private individuals. Firstly, it spared the Assembly from having to raise the large amounts of capital involved. Secondly, it broadened the pool of talent that could be applied to the trade. Rather than being handled by whatever talent was available within the adminstration, the grain trade attracted the most resourceful and able members of society. There was a lot of money to be made. Anyone who was rich enough and clever enough could earn a share. But they had to deliver.

With success being so richly rewarded and failure promising little but ruin, the drive to succeed in the grain trade had a knock-on effect of stimulating other private trading enterprise in Athens and beyond. To acquire grain abroad on a regular basis (rather than by one-off attack and pillage) traders had to offer something worthy of exchange. This inspired the manufacture and supply of goods for export and thus became the basis of a vigorous economy within the home cities. Landowners traded fruit, olives, oil and wine for grain; manufacturers developed new lines in pottery, cloth and metal goods – all of which contributed to the economic and cultural development of the city as well as fuelling the export trade.

Xenophon wrote around 400 BC:

So deep is their love of grain that on receiving a report that it is abundant anywhere, merchants will voyage in quest of it; they will cross the Aegean, the Euxine [Black Sea], the Sicilian Sea; and when they have got as much as possible, they will carry it over the sea, and they will stow it in the very ship in which they sail themselves. And when they want money, they don't throw the grain away anywhere haphazardly, but they will carry it to the place where they hear that it is most valued and the people prize it most highly . . .[10]

By the second century BC, the flower of Greek civilisation was fading, and Rome was blossoming to succeed Athens as the greatest power in the Mediterranean. The influence of Rome in Western civilisation is itself founded on the cultural heritage of Greece, and the architecture of our cities – with their columned civic buildings and squares, adorned with statues of rulers and conquering heroes – makes enough reference to the classical mode for us never to forget the glories of either Rome or Greece. The skills and resources they applied to ensuring that their citizens were adequately fed are rarely brought to our attention, even though the fundamental importance of grain is evocatively illustrated by the ears of wheat or barley depicted on some of its coinage.[11]

Famine, or the threat of famine, was a permanent fact of life for most people in the ancient world – especially in the cities. Powerful communities, such as Athens, had depended upon private enterprise to secure continuous and adequate supplies of grain, with minimal state involvement. But for Rome, the sheer size of the population multiplied the scale of the problem many times over. As in Greece, private enterprise was a core component of Rome's provisioning arrangements, but as the city became home to more and more people, its rulers and governing authorities became convinced that feeding the capital could not be left to merchants who stood to become rich when things went well, but could not be held accountable if they failed to deliver. The Senate became increasingly involved. Grain supply became an issue of intense political importance. Indeed, as the historian Geoffrey Rickman points out in his study of Rome's grain supply:

If there is a single thread which deserves to be emphasized in the story it is the slow but over-growing involvement by the state in the wide range of activities which supported the supply of corn to Rome. In this sphere, as in so many others, the history of Rome saw a fundamental change in the relationship of the state to the individual, whether he was a farmer, a shipper, a baker, or metropolitan corn recipient. The feeding of Rome was always a political as well as an economic problem and it involved much more than simply putting food into the stomachs of the inhabitants.[12]

Rome is located on an extensive plain of fertile volcanic soils well suited to the cultivation of grain crops, and was thus inherently better able than its Greek counterparts to support large numbers of people. Indeed, the construction of aqueducts towards the end of the fourth century BC suggests that water rather than food was the most pressing of the city's provisioning problems during the early stages of its development. Inevitably, however, the problems of food supply increased with the growing population, and the city's location then proved to be less advantageous. It is estimated that by the middle of the second century BC there were at least half a million people living in Rome; keeping them fed was the city's foremost concern.

In 123 BC, under the tribunate of Gaius Gracchus, laws were introduced establishing the basic right of every Roman citizen to a monthly ration of grain at a fixed rate that undercut prevailing market prices. The intention here was to even out the price fluctuations resulting from variations in supply, but the taxes imposed to pay the subsidies needed to gain the suppliers' support for the scheme made it a hot political issue for the next sixty years. A law extending the number of grain distribution recipients was passed in 62 BC, and when Clodius became tribune four years later he abolished payment for the grain ration altogether. From then on, supplying a monthly ration of grain – free – to every eligible citizen became the responsibility of Rome's governing authority (private merchants would continue to supply the needs of non-eligible residents and the city's substantial slave population). Moreover, Clodius' law appears to have extended beyond the mere distribution of grain to cover all matters concerning both public and private supplies, the grain fields, the contractors and the grain stores. Clearly, Clodius intended that public control would prevent private traders profiting in grain speculation at the expense of citizens and the state, but his action marked an unprecedented interference by the state in the private rights of individuals.[13]

Clodius' law was popular with the Roman citizenry in general, but had some expensive consequences; not least in that the prospect of free grain increased demand. Large numbers of the rural poor drifted into Rome hoping for some benefit, and the city suddenly became especially attractive to people in surrounding communities who held or could invent the qualifications needed to claim Roman citizenship. Whole families moved from country to city to take advantage of the distribution. Furthermore, many of the city's wealthy householders began to make free men of their slaves, so as to transfer the expense of upkeep from themselves to the state. This was doubly beneficial to the former slave-owners: by legal devices that bound the slaves, at the moment of manumission, to continue rendering various services and labour, former owners retained the profits of the slaves' productivity while shifting a large part of the cost of their maintenance onto the state.[14]

Cicero claimed that the abolition of the charge for the grain distribution in 58 BC cost Rome more than one-fifth of all its revenues.[15] Scholars caution that this could be mere rhetoric, but there is no doubt that a great deal of the city's resources and energy was devoted to securing enough grain and distributing it to eligible citizens. The system was struggling to meet the ever-increasing demand. Trouble flared whenever the distribution faltered and succeeding governments were deeply conscious that their power was inextricably tied to the provision of free grain for the citizens of Rome.

But there was no escape. In AD 22, the Emperor Tiberius in a letter to the Senate sombrely stated the gravity of the problem and the Emperor's ultimate responsibilty: '*Hanc, patres conscripti, curam sustinet princeps; haec omissa funditus rem publicam trahet*' – 'This duty, senators, devolves upon the [Emperor]; if it is neglected, the utter ruin of the state will follow.'[16]

Naturally enough, the grain distribution, its cost and management, were always powerful factors in the political machinations of the city. In 46 BC, Julius Caesar attempted to cut the costs by limiting the number of eligible recipients, but disputes over who was eligible and who was not rendered his scheme difficult to implement. Caesar was assassinated three years later, and his scheme died with him, but the widespread free distribution of grain continued for centuries – ultimately becoming even more generous than in Caesar's day. Septimius, who was emperor from AD 193 to 211, gave out quantities of free oil along with the free grain; Aurelian (270–275) added pork and wine to the distribution.[17]

So far as has been ascertained, the ration of free grain stood at about 45 kg for every eligible recipient, every month, throughout the history of the grain distribution. This was enough to provide recipients with between 3,000 and 4,000 calories a day,[18] which is comfortably in accord with the modern recommended daily allowance of 2,900 calories for an adult male. Forty-five kilograms a month, less than 2 kg a day, does not seem an unmanageable quantity to acquire and handle at the individual level, but multiply it by tens and hundreds of thousands as the population of Rome increased through the centuries and the scale of the task that Clodius had burdened the state authorities with becomes starkly apparent. The total quantities of grain that had to be acquired and distributed – without fail, month by month, year after year – were gigantic.

Scholars believe that the growth of Rome's population started in the third century BC and accelerated rapidly in following centuries. The growing wealth of the upper classes was the principal factor, with the import of household slaves, the number of craftsmen, shopkeepers and labourers catering for their needs, and the continual drift of the rural poor into the city all contributing to its rapid growth. The mounting number of public and utilitarian buildings, porticoes, markets and docks all attest to this growth – as do repeated demands for greater supplies of cleaner water – but in no sense had the reconstruction of the city been planned after its occupation by the Gauls in 390 BC, or its growth controlled.[19]

By the time Augustus became emperor (27–14 BC), Rome was a crowded, jerry-built muddle of house-blocks too high for their own safety, vulnerable to both fire and flood, with one or two public areas of some architectural distinction, and a population of around one million – all of whom had to be fed; many at the expense of the state. In records dating from 5 BC, Augustus himself reports that he distributed free grain to 320,000 eligible citizens that year, which implies that the remainder (consisting of 480,000 women and children, plus 200,000 slaves and other residents) bought their supplies on the open market. Assuming that non-eligible residents bought slightly less per person than was distributed free, and that slaves received the same amount as was detailed in accounts from other periods, it is estimated that Rome was consuming about 272,800 t of grain a year at that time – over 5,000 t a week.[20] Today, 5,000 t of grain would barely cover the bottom of a bulk carrier. A century ago it would have filled perhaps 100 goods train wagons. In Roman times, maintaining that volume of supply, week after week, with only muscle and the most basic of mechanical power, was an outstanding achievement. Nothing else matches it. Indeed, neither Rome, nor its adminstration and empire would have lasted for long if the city's grain supply had been anything less than secure and sustainable.

The Romans were extremely good at planning and building roads. From the fourth century BC, first Italy and then the provinces of the empire were connected to Rome by a network of roads which were so shrewdly surveyed and magnificently constructed that the course and sometimes the structure of many Roman roads has endured until modern times. Their purpose was originally military – providing fast and direct routes for the legions and their support divisions. Trade generally follows the flag, but although the armies, forts and fortresses of the far-flung Roman endeavours certainly did attract trade locally, the road system did not generate high and steady levels of trade all along its length. With Rome requiring 5,000 t of grain a week (and much else besides), one might imagine that all roads leading to the city would have been constantly full of traffic. But although some local grain and other produce certainly did reach the city by road, feeding Rome by that means was simply impossible. The stark truth is that however well-made the roads were, transporting goods along them – especially heavy and bulky goods – was slow and prohibitively expensive.

There were several factors. First, though brilliantly surveyed and constructed, Roman roads generally were not wide enough for two wagons to pass abreast. Thus, single file was the only option, with traffic from one direction having to leave the road and wait for traffic from the other direction to pass. Second, the heavy four-wheeled Roman ox-wagon carried about only half a tonne of grain and travelled at little more than 3 km an hour (slow and steady oxen were the draught animals of the ancient world, until the invention of a suitable collar harnessed the power of horses). Third, each wagon required two oxen to pull it, a man to drive it, daily supplies of food and water for men and beasts, and overnight lodgings along the route. This meant that since Rome would have required a minimum of 10,000 wagonloads a week, the costs involved would have been greater than the value of the grain they carried. Furthermore, there were no grain-growing regions of sufficient size within reasonable distance from the city. And finally, Rome would have been obliged to devote much of its energies and resources to building and maintaining roads, rather than building an empire.

In point of fact, water transport was the only practical means of supplying Rome with enough of its vital foodstuff. The Tiber helped to some degree, with barges delivering grain to the city from locations upstream, but the quantities were small. The city had to look further afield and, to all intents and purposes, was fed from abroad throughout the centuries that its regime dominated Europe and the Mediterranean.

Roman forces conquered Carthage in 146 BC, giving the city access to the agricultural output of not only the north African territories, but also that of the lands Carthage had controlled in Sicily, Sardinia and Spain. With the express purpose of boosting grain supplies, 6,000 Roman citizens were settled on generous allotments of farmland in north Africa, and eventually Rome was receiving at least 200,000 t of grain each year from the north African colonies. Meanwhile, the rich grainfields of the Nile delta came under the control of Rome with the conquest of Egypt in 30 BC and within decades they were shipping over 100,000 t a year to Rome.

The production of such vast quantities of grain in foreign lands, regularly and reliably, year after year, called for a massive administrative organisation. Arranging for the cultivation and harvesting of the grain was challenging enough, and transporting it to the harbours by wagon, donkey and camel train was also a formidable task. Furthermore, the grain ripened in summer, so that no matter how promptly the crops were harvested and transported to the ports, not all of it could be shipped out in the same year. Substantial amounts had to be stored over winter for shipment the following year.

Storing grain in bulk presents its own problems. Quite apart from the obvious need to guard it against the depredations of rodents and thieves, in silos big enough to hold the volume, and stout enough to withstand the considerable pressure that bulk grain exerts in all directions, temperature and humidity control are critical. If the temperature rises above 15°C there is a risk of weevil and beetle infestation; if the moisture content is more than 15 per cent the grain is likely to germinate and rot.[21] At Alexandria the grain was stored in huge granaries, under the control of Roman officials, until the moment came for shipment to Rome.

At every phase of the operation – from field to threshing floor, to transport, storage and final shipment to Rome – responsible officials issued and demanded receipts to protect themselves from liability and prevent fraud. In the case of shipments down the Nile to Alexandria (and probably on the long voyage to Rome as well), it was customary to send sealed samples of the grain cargoes along with the boats. These so-called *digmata,* sometimes in the form of small pots and sometimes leather wallets, were labelled with details of the shipment and the people responsible for it. In his study of the Roman granaries, Geoffrey Rickman cites the instance of a pot used as a *digma* in 2 BC, which had written on its side not only the names of the two skippers, the emblem of their boats, and the name, rank, and unit of the soldiers acting as guards, but also states that the pot contained a sample of a cargo of grain of a specified kind of a certain year, which had been measured out by granary officials of a certain district, and which constituted the tax due for a certain period. The statement ends with the declaration that the cargo had been sealed with the seals of both men, and a witness confirms the sealing of the *digmata* and the date.[22]

But the efforts of production and getting the grain to the ships in good condition would be wasted if the ships failed to reach Rome. The fleets of ships that traversed the Mediterranean were the crowning achievement of the provisioning enterprise. Think of it: simply keeping the grain dry (without the benefit of modern packaging) in wooden ships was a challenging proposition, and the voyage itself (without the benefit of engines) was by no means the kind of Mediterranean cruise that people enjoy these days.

Some ships had capacities of over 1,000 t; others carried less than 100. The average appears to have been between 340 and 400 t, which means that a minimum of 800 shiploads would have been required to feed Rome in 5 BC, though the actual number is likely to have been considerably higher. It was a challenging voyage. Shipwreck, pirates and spoilage all took their toll,[23] but the supply of grain to Rome had to be maintained. The story is told of Pompey, who in 57 BC was given complete command of the grain supply throughout the entire Roman world, urging reluctant captains to set out from Africa in the face of a great storm. He personally led the way on board, and gave the order to set sail for Rome with the inspiring phrase: '*Navigare necesse est, vivere non necesse*' – 'To sail is essential, to live is not.' These of all Pompey's words were long remembered. In the Middle Ages the phrase was carved on the buildings of great Hanseatic trading firms in Bremen.[24]

A voyage from the mouth of the Tiber to Africa is on record as having taken just two days – the fastest known. And it was possible to sail nearly as fast in the opposite direction. Cato the Elder once showed the Senate at Rome a fig that had been picked in Carthage just three days before; all of which indicates that grain from Africa was readily available to Rome, so far as the journey by sea was concerned. At worst perhaps no more than a week away. Voyages between Italy and the eastern Mediterranean were an entirely different matter. The Egyptian port, Alexandria, was over 1,500 km from Rome and, although the Mediterranean's prevailing north to north-westerly winds could make for a relatively easy week's outward voyage, tacking back against the wind, heavily loaded, in square-rigged ships that could head within no more than seven points of the wind, was an arduous and frequently dangerous exercise which could take up to ten weeks – or even longer, as St Paul found when he boarded an Alexandrian ship bound for Rome in AD 62.[25]

With a cargo of wheat and 276 crew and passengers, the ship took a northerly route to Myra on the Turkish coast, then sailed slowly west along the southern shores of Crete. Here the captain and navigator decided to spend the winter in a small harbour, since it was already late in the season. Before they could put this plan in operation, however, a favourable breeze sprang up and persuaded them to try for a better harbour. This proved to be a bad mistake. Between harbours, the ship was caught in a fierce east-north-east gale and forced to ride helplessly before it, bare-masted, for fourteen days. 'And when neither sun nor stars in many days appeared, and no small tempest lay on us, all hope that we should be saved was then taken away.'[26]

The crew cut away the rigging, passed ropes around the hull to stop the seams of the ship opening, and finally jettisoned the grain cargo to lighten the ship.The storm raged on; the ship ran before it; then, at midnight on the fourteenth day, the sound of breakers heralded land nearby. Four anchors were cast to hold the ship off the rocks. At daybreak, they decided their only hope of salvation was to cut the anchors and try to run the ship aground. With Paul's encouragement, the strategy worked, and although the ship broke in two, everyone on board survived. The land turned out to be Malta, from where Paul sailed on to Italy three months later – in a ship which had prudently wintered in the island harbour.

Overall, bad weather during the winter months, when navigation by sun and stars was hindered by cloudy skies, restricted sailings to high summer for the cautious, and to the months from spring to autumn for the more adventurous, so that, at the very most, there were only eight months of the year (early March to early November) in which sailings were feasible, and only four months (late May to September) during which prospects of a safe voyage were good. No wonder Seneca writes (around AD 64) with such excitement of the arrival of the grain ships from Egypt: 'The Alexandria clippers . . . suddenly hove in sight today. Campania welcomes the sight of them: all the population of Puteoli posts itself on the pier . . . all around me were scurrying in hot haste to the watersides . . .'[27]

The voyage was over; the grain ships had arrived safely, often in large flotillas – dozens at a time. But now the importers were faced with all the problems of handling and transportation which had confronted the exporters. If anything, the problems for Rome were greater than in Alexandria and north Africa, for Rome lacked a suitable and accessible harbour.

Rome nestled nicely among its seven hills, and while still a small city was easily served by small craft plying the Tiber. They could load and unload at docks on the river no distance from the city centre. But large grain ships could not. Their only option was to anchor in the open roadstead at the mouth of the Tiber and have their cargoes transshipped to Rome by barge. Dionysius of Halicarnassus wrote of the advantages, and disadvantages, of the Tiber mouth roadstead at the end of the first century BC:

> The river widens considerably as it reaches the sea and forms large bays, like the best sea harbours. And, most surprising of all, it is not cut off from its mouth by a barrier of sea sand, which is the fate even of many large rivers. It does not wander into changing marshes and swamps, thereby exhausting itself before its stream reaches the sea, but is always navigable and flows into the sea through a single natural mouth, driving back (with the force of its current) the waves of the sea, though the wind frequently blows from the west and can be dangerous. Ships with oars, however large, and merchantmen with sails of up to 3,000 [amphorae, equal to about 78 tons] capacity enter the mouth itself and row or are towed up to Rome; but larger ships ride at anchor outside the mouth and unload and reload with the help of river vessels.[28]

The town of Ostia, situated on a bend of the Tiber a short distance inland from the river mouth, provided some protection for small vessels, and from the time that the introduction of cheap grain in 123 BC brought a surge in supplies, the facilities at Ostia became increasingly important to the city of Rome. Hundreds of metres of riverside were declared to be state property; docks and warehouses were constructed. But these were of limited use to the large vessels serving the grain trade in later times. The Tiber was only some 100 m wide as it flowed past Ostia – not wide enough for large ships to manoeuvre safely on a fast-flowing river when powered only by sail or oars.[29]

The grain ships from Alexandria were the largest then afloat, with capacities of up to 1,000 t. Their cargoes were for Rome, but their options for delivery were limited: they could either anchor in the exposed Tiber roadstead, and have their cargoes transferred to barges for conveyance to Ostia and then Rome, or they could sail to Puteoli on the Bay of Naples, where excellent harbour facilities awaited them. Most chose the latter option, which excited Seneca but left the responsible authorities with the problem of then getting the grain to Rome – more than 250 km away. Some doubtless was carried in trundling ox-wagons or on the backs of pack-animals, but the greater proportion was transshipped and sent in smaller vessels up the coast to the mouth of the Tiber, and Ostia.

Clearly, both the facilities at the Tiber mouth and the alternative transshipment of cargoes in Puteoli were highly unsatisfactory, but only major public works – such as a new harbour for Rome – could rectify matters. Plutarch reports that Julius Caesar had something of this sort in mind:

> He . . . proposed to divert the Tiber immediately below Rome by a deep canal which was to run round to the Circaean promontory and be led to the sea at Terracina. By this means he would provide a safe and easy passage for traders bound for Rome. In addition he proposed to drain the marshes by Pometia and Setia and so provide productive land for thousands of men. In the sea nearest to Rome he intended to enclose the sea by building moles, and to dredge the hidden shoals off the coasts of Ostia, which were dangerous. So he would provide harbours and anchorages to match the great volume of shipping. These schemes were being prepared.[30]

Being prepared, yes, but shelved when Caesar was assassinated, to be resurrected nearly a century later by the emperor Claudius. According to Seneca, Rome had only an eight-day supply of grain in reserve when Claudius became emperor in AD 41.[31] Thus, although he may have been influenced by what was known of Caesar's project, the threat of famine was a far more compelling incentive to solve the problems of getting grain from the ships to Rome. The immediate crisis could be met with emergency measures, but Claudius took a long-term view, ordering a new harbour for Ostia. At a site some 3 km north of the Tiber, two massive curving moles were built out into the sea, enclosing a roughly circular basin of about 81 ha; short canals connected the basin to the Tiber. The scheme in its initial form was only a partial success. Unfortunately, the coastal currents and prevailing winds swept not only sand but also considerable amounts of silt northwards from the Tiber, so that the Claudian harbour was almost as vulnerable to silting as if it had been built at the river mouth.[32] Furthermore, the enclosed basin was too big to provide shelter for all the ships it could accommodate – indeed, Tacitus reports that 200 vessels loaded with grain for Rome sank in the basin when it was struck by a violent storm in AD 62, creating shortages which can only have been exacerbated by a fire that in the same year destroyed 100 barges full of grain at the docks in Rome itself.[33]

So the new harbour at Ostia did not improve conditions for arriving ships to the extent that Claudius had hoped. There was still considerable danger, and, as Seneca noted, the large grain ships from Alexandria continued to dock and unload their cargoes at Puteoli. Trajan finally rectified matters in the decade after he became emperor in AD 98, with the excavation of a new and smaller inner harbour, hexagonal in form, and about 33 ha in area. This was one-third the size of the Claudian harbour, but that comparison speaks more of Claudius' unrealistic ambitions than of any lack of foresight on Trajan's part. The new harbour was quite large enough, and beautifully proportioned (as can be seen today in its excavated and restored form at Portus); each side of the hexagon was 357.77 m long, and the maximum diameter 715.54 m.[34] At last, a practical and completely safe harbour was available to even the largest ships of the day. During the second century AD, the grain fleets from Africa and Alexandria ceased to use the facilities at Puteoli, but sailed direct to Ostia instead.

But even when the grain was brought directly and safely to Ostia, the problem of getting it to Rome remained. This had never eased. Throughout, the grain was transferred to barges and towed up the Tiber to docks at the city's market district, just downstream from the first of the city bridges. Though arduous in the extreme, towing was the only option, since although the river was navigable between Ostia and Rome for even quite large vessels, the strong currents and tortuous meanderings of the river made sailing upstream impractical.

Towing a barge the 35 km up the winding river to Rome took three days (compared with two or three hours by road). Teams of men and oxen trudged continuously along towpaths on either side of the Tiber . . . and now the logistics of the operation become particularly impressive. If, as seems likely, the average capacity of the barges was about 68 t, then more than 4,500 bargeloads would have been needed to bring Rome its annual grain supply. But of course grain was not all that Rome imported. For much of its history, Rome was the world's largest centre of consumption. Besides grain, the city imported massive quantities of wine, oil, timber, cloth and luxury items – not to mention the marble brought in for public building works.

Given that it took three days to tow a barge from Ostia to Rome, it is clear that even if the traffic was controlled and spread through the year (with grain in particular stored in Ostia for shipment as required), an enormous number of barges must have been available. The Tiber and its towpaths must have heaved with traffic, day after day, week after week, month after month, year after year. And the logistical challenge of Rome's grain supply did not cease at the docks; the grain then had to be offloaded and stored for distribution. At least 6 million individual loads were carried down the gangplanks from ship to shore each year.[35]

At the height of its power, the Roman Empire controlled the entire Mediterranean and the rest of the known world, from Hadrian's Wall to the Euphrates. An army of over 600,000 men was stationed among its 119 provinces; 30,000 civil servants administered affairs abroad. The citizens of Rome continued to be fed courtesy of the state. But from the beginning of the fourth century AD Rome was merely one of the empire's capital cities, and in Constantinople had a rival that would outlast it. As one city grew and the other shrank in significance on the changing geopolitical stage, the grain from Egypt was allocated to Constantinople and Rome became entirely dependant on supplies from north Africa. But there were fewer people in the city now, its importance was diminishing, and the imperatives of a grain supply system which had fed the city for centuries were slipping away . . . just one factor in the decline and fall that Edward Gibbon summarises so well:

> The decline of Rome was the natural and inevitable effect of immoderate greatness. Prosperity ripened the principle of decay; the causes of destruction multiplied with the extent of conquest; and, as soon as time or accident had removed the artificial supports, the stupendous fabric yielded to the pressure of its own weight. The story of its ruin is simple and obvious; and instead of inquiring why the Roman Empire was destroyed, we should rather be surprised that it had subsisted so long.[36]

6

The Works of Giants Mouldereth Away

Cities are built to last, but many have vanished and none survives today in exactly the form of its initial construction. A genius for regeneration distinguishes the most ancient of existing cities, fostered by the political ambitions, or economic might, of leading citizens. In China, an idealised concept of the city transcended and survived its physical realities. In Europe, ruins evoke images of past glory.

More than 3,000 years separate Imperial Rome from the Sumerian cities on the plains of Mesopotamia – Ur, Uruk and Eridu. They had much in common. They were home to thousands of people. It is not difficult to imagine that the citizens of each could easily have adapted to the ways of life followed in another. Even today, setting aside the tales of kings and conquering heroes, there is much in the recorded evidence of everyday lives 2,500 years ago that dovetails perfectly with our own sympathies and concerns. There are big differences too, of course, but mainly of a technological nature, while at the level of ordinary human existence there is more that joins than divides us.

But here's an interesting point: while we live in cities that for the most part seem destined to last for ever, neither Ur, Uruk, Eridu nor even Athens or Rome did. Despite their talents and achievements, they rose, then fell. The Sumerian cities collapsed to the extent of leaving only the scars on the landscape that archaeologists may later investigate; Rome shrank to become a ruined shell of its former self. As Edward Gibbon put it in his definitive *Decline and Fall of the Roman Empire*, 'the private and public edifices that were founded for eternity, lie prostrate'. It was the failures of food supply that brought city life in Sumer to an end; in the case of Rome, an overstretched economy and administration was largely to blame, hastening the invasions of avaricious neighbours from the East.

Rise and fall. The cycle of growth and decay was rapid in some instances, in others it covered many human lifespans. Some have flourished and collapsed completely, as in Sumer. Others have collapsed, then subsequently have risen afresh, like Rome. This has been the pattern, across the millennia and around the world. Indeed, the pattern has been so prevalent that the history of great cities has a discomforting effervescence about it. Cities appear to rise like bubbles from the surface of the earth, swelling, bursting – some dying altogether, others healing themselves and rising again. At the beginning, the world's large cities seem almost to have replaced one another, as though compelled to maintain a degree of equilibrium, but since the turn of the nineteenth century cities have been growing in unison – and at an accelerating rate, like metastasing cancers.

In a pioneering work,[1] the geographer Tertius Chandler has traced the rise and fall of cities around the world. The story begins, of course, in Mesopotamia, then moves to the Nile in Egypt. Thereafter, the location of the world's largest city moves about the landscape in a remarkable manner, first exclusively in Egypt and the Middle East, then to India, China and finally to Europe, America and the Far East.

According to Chandler, Memphis on the Nile in Egypt (to the south of present-day Cairo) already had a population of around 40,000 people more than 5,000 years ago, and so was then ahead of the Sumerian cities. But Uruk soon caught up, and with up to 80,000 inhabitants 4,800 years ago[2] is said to have been 'probably the largest settlement in the entire world'[3] at that time. Within a thousand years, however, Babylon, on the Euphrates to the north of Uruk, had taken the lead with 100,000 inhabitants. When Babylon fell to invaders in 1595 BC the mantle returned to Memphis, which remained the world's largest city for nearly a thousand years. Then the Assyrian city of Nineveh took over, then Babylon again, reaching new heights of civic splendour in the sixth century BC under Nebuchadnezzar, when it had a population of about 200,000.

Sravasti and Rajagriha in India vied with Babylon for the title during the fifth century BC, but when Alexander the Great founded a new capital in Egypt that city, Alexandria, raced ahead of all others, becoming the world's largest by 320 BC and eventually home to over 300,000 inhabitants. Less than a century later, however, Alexandria was outstripped by Patna, an Indian city with even more people living within its 30 km circumference.

Meanwhile, the growth of cities was proceeding apace in China too. The process had started later, but records show that the city of Hsienyang (present-day Xianyang, nearly 1,000 km south-west of Beijing) was founded around 220 BC with 120,000 households. At a conservative estimate of four individuals per house, this gives Hsienyang a population of close to half a million – comfortably ahead of all others. The Chinese empire had a total population of around 60 million at the time, and its leadership in terms of great cities was not challenged until the rise of the Roman empire. Rome itself had 486,000 inhabitants in 57 BC; 800,000 by AD 180. With the move of the Roman capital to Constantinople in 330, however, Rome declined rapidly while the new capital took the lead. Patna, from whose palaces the Gupta dynasty now ruled half of India, reigned supreme – if briefly – from 410 to 450, then it was Constantinople's turn again, with a population of half a million from 450 to 650, after which it too began to decline.

The title of world's largest city now moved back to China, where Changan under the Tang dynasty between 618 and 907 probably had a peak population in excess of one million, according to Chandler's research. But Baghdad was now rising as the capital of the Muslims and appears to have acquired a population of more than a million before shrinking again around 935. By then Changan – no longer the capital of China – was also shrinking, while Córdoba in Spain was expanding with the expansion of trade that followed the Muslim invasions. Córdoba and Constantinople shared the title of the world's largest city from 935, with populations of around 450,000, but dramatic changes in their fortunes during the eleventh century precipitated rapid decline. Kaifeng had now become the capital of China, and by 1102 it was the largest city in the world, with 442,000 inhabitants.

Morocco enjoyed a spell of prosperity during the twelfth century and Fez could have been the world's largest city from about 1160 to 1180 (when a change of capitals in China caused its largest cities to shrink), though it may have had only about 250,000 inhabitants. Similarly, Polonnaruwa in what is now Sri Lanka was large enough to have had a moment of glory between 1180 and 1200, when the world's existing great cities were in either stasis or decline. But one hundred years later the world's largest city was most certainly in China. On the basis of extended visits between 1276 and 1292, Marco Polo reported that Hangchow and its environs had a population of several millions.

Chinese census figures show that Hangchow's urban population alone stood at 432,000 in 1273.

Hangchow was then the busiest port and trading centre in the world. It and Peking were capitals of the Mongol empire, which stretched across Asia and into Europe. This was the largest continuous land empire the world has ever seen – too large, in fact, to be sustained for long. When it split the capitals shrank, leaving Cairo to become top-ranking city with a population of half a million around 1325. But the Chinese cities soon recovered. Nanking and Peking alternated as leading cities for over 250 years until 1635, when Agra, capital of Mogul India, took the title with a population of 660,000. Next it was Constantinople's turn again, with 700,000; then Delhi, which held the title until 1684, when the Mogul emperor Aurangzeb moved the capital and its people to a site in south-central India. It was a move from which neither the emperor nor the cities recovered.

Chandler's research shows that Paris was next in line, but forfeited its chances in 1685 when Louis XIV expelled the Huguenots from France and substantial numbers left the city. Now Constantinople was in front yet again, but only to be eclipsed (in 1700) by Peking and the Chinese capital, with a population soaring to more than one million during its reign, retained the title until 1825 – when London took over.

The industrial revolution had now concentrated the focus of city growth on Europe and the pace was accelerating. Less than twenty years after becoming the world's largest city, London became the first city with more than 2 million inhabitants, when the census of 1841 recorded a population of 2,235,344. By 1900 more than 6 million lived in London, but New York was growing even faster and became the world's largest city in 1925, when its population stood at about 8 million. New York was still leading in 1950, with 12.3 million inhabitants; and again in 1960, with 14.2 million; but by 1970 the greatest growth had moved to the other side of the globe, putting Tokyo with 16.5 million just ahead of New York with 16.2 million; New York was still in second place in 1980, but slipped to fourth place in 1995 and to fifth in 2000.[4]

By the year 2000, phenomenal growth had taken Tokyo's population to 26.4 million, well ahead of all others and ensuring that Tokyo would remain the world's largest city for some time to come. Second place was taken by Mexico City with 18.1 million, an ascendancy which indicated that economic dominance was no longer a primary determinant of city growth. Huge cities were appearing in all parts of the world now – in poor countries as well as in the regions of greatest wealth. In 1970 only three cities – Tokyo, New York and Shanghai – had 10 million or more inhabitants; thirty years later there were nineteen of them, fourteen in the developing world. And the trend is set to continue: by 2015 twenty-three cities will have passed the 10 million mark, all but four in developing countries. By then, Mumbai, Dhaka, Lagos and São Paulo each will have populations of more than 20 million. Furthermore, it is expected that 564 cities around the world will have a million or more inhabitants by 2015. Of these, 425 will be in developing countries.[5]

The welter of statistics that Chandler presents is interesting in its own right, as a dazzling miscellany of facts, but its subliminal effect is surely to stimulate further enquiry. And the first question it raises is: why? What are the factors that determine the rise and fall of great cities? Their origins, we can safely assume, lie with the kind of social and economic developments that were described in previous chapters. But beyond origin, what factors determine their continuing existence; their success – or failure?

At a basic level, the original choice of location is the most obvious factor. The elevated mounds of Sumer provided the river access that stimulated economic and social interaction and – no less important – gave people a substantial measure of safety from the floods to which the Euphrates and the Tigris were prone. Memphis, though founded later than the Sumerian cities, was supremely well-located, right at the head of the Nile delta. Here the river became shallower, and spread out over the alluvial plain and flowed to the Mediterranean via a tangle of waterways. The river provided abundant water, and each year its floods deposited a fresh layer of fertile soil over the low-lying farmlands. Memphis itself stood a short distance upstream, where firm high ground provided a solid and floodproof foundation for the city.

Deserts extending to east and west constituted major difficulties for any forces that might contemplate attacking the city from its landward flanks, while its position 150 km from the open sea gave it at least the benefit of distance (and advance warning) from the landing of invaders from overseas.

If Chandler's extrapolations are correct, then Memphis was the world's largest city for 1,000 years – longer than any city in history. But although its location at the head of the Nile delta was fundamental to the longstanding pre-eminence of Memphis, it was not enough to keep the city in the front rank when the ambitions of Alexander the Great began to influence events in the region.

The citizens of Memphis actually welcomed Alexander when he arrived at the city in 331 BC, and even crowned him Pharaoh of Egypt twelve months later. One year after that, however, their new ruler decided that the city of Alexandria should be built on the seaward edge of the Nile delta, and the fortunes of Memphis slipped into decline. The new city was founded to serve the political integration of Egypt and the Mediterranean, and thus it was primarily politics – rather than location – that fuelled Alexandria's rise to dominance. Memphis became a secondary place, and as it shrank in status, it shrank in size too. Today, only negligible archaeological traces remain.

The site on which Memphis once stood is close enough to the modern city of Cairo to suggest that the former must be the predecessor of the latter, but in fact there is no direct connection between the two. Surprisingly perhaps, Cairo is not an ancient city, but was founded as Misr El Kahira in AD 969, as the base from which Muslim forces began their drive west across Africa.[6] And so here in the vicinity of the Nile delta it is clear that while environmental advantages had stimulated the initial founding of a city (Memphis), the major centres of subsequent urban development were driven by political and economic factors (Alexandria) and religion (Cairo). Location in itself was not enough to guarantee growth and a sustained existence.

Indeed, as Jane Jacobs wrote in *The Economy of Cities* (1970), 'cities simply cannot be "explained" by their locations or other given resources. Their existence as cities and the source of their growth lie within themselves . . . Cities are not ordained; they are wholly existential.'[7] If location were the prime determinant, she points out, one might expect major cities to have grown around wonderful natural harbours such as King's Lynn, Shoreham and many others in Britain; or Sag Harbor (on Long Island) and Portsmouth (North Carolina) in the United States. Conversely, why do many very successful cities occupy such notably inferior sites? Tokyo, for instance, and Los Angeles.

Location provided plenty of clear sunny days for the nascent movie industry of Los Angeles at the beginning of the twentieth century (when films were shot in daylight), but it has been a serious hindrance in other respects of the city's development. A US senator succinctly defined the problem in the 1920s, when Los Angeles was appealing to the government for funds to build itself a port. 'You have made a big mistake in the location of your city,' he told the appellants, 'you should have put it at some point where a harbor already exists, instead of calling on the U.S. government to give you something which nature has refused!'[8] But Los Angeles has flourished anyway, despite the senator's objections, despite its location (and who is to say that the problems of location did not stimulate the citizens of Los Angeles to make more progress than might otherwise have been the case?).

Regarding the inadequacy of location as an explanation of why some cities flourish while others founder, the Greek poet Alcaeus wrote more than 2,500 years ago: 'Not houses finely roofed nor the stones of walls well built nor canals nor dockyards make the city, but men able to use their opportunity.'[9] And here, surely, is the nub of the issue. Far from being an end in themselves, cities have always been a means by which opportunists fulfil their ambitions: the craftsmen of Çatal Hüyük, for example; the kings of Sumer, Alexander the Great, the ruling assemblies of Athens and Rome and even the founding fathers of Los Angeles. Some ambitions have been more honorable than others, but all share the characteristic of having access to the power of economics, or politics or religion.

That these three factors − economics, politics and religion − have been the primary motivating forces of urban history is generally agreed, though opinion on their relative importance is sharply divided.[10] In point of fact, most cities contain elements of all three categories, and their relative significance is blurred. Even so, there are plenty of examples − both historical and contemporary − in which the pre-eminence of one particular category can be clearly seen. The fabric of a cathedral city is clearly religious, for example, a royal seat political and a free port economic.

But in the modern world, even where the determinant factors of a large city's origin and rise are quite obvious, their relevance has long since been rendered subservient to the practical expediencies of everyday life. Far from being driven by single determining factors, large modern cities thrive as a measure of their capacity to accommodate diverse and conflicting interests. We do not spend much time thinking about it, but city life really is a paradox. By my reckoning, we live in more private seclusion than the residents of a small village, but are regularly in much closer contact with many more people. Though we may be but vaguely aware of who lives next door, we mingle shoulder-to-shoulder with complete strangers on the tube, and in the supermarket. We know these people only insofar as their activities coincide with ours at that moment, and have little or no idea of what they do with the rest of their time. And yet their ambitions may affect our lives more forcefully than any villager's could. While I grow courgettes, for instance, Norman Foster plants his 'erotic gherkin' in my London skyline. So it is that cities can evoke gasps of amazement as the physical expression of individual ambition suddenly becomes evident; these experiences are sometimes pleasing, occasionally outrageous, but rarely boring.

Of course, every city has a planning department that is charged with the task of controlling its direction and progress. But the job was compromised from the start. So long as cities have been the means by which individual opportunists fulfil ambition, change has been the currency that sustains them – demolition and reconstruction, the recycling of investment – and change is virtually impossible to predict and accommodate in long-term urban planning. Thus our cities are a cluttered consequence of all the compromise and conflicting interest that has been acted out over the years. And we seem to like it that way. Perhaps because although we constantly seek permanence and security, our world view accepts the inevitability of change. With this in mind, the contrasting history of cities in China is especially interesting.

Urban development – and the civilisation that it fosters – got off to a slow start in China. While the cities of Mesopotamia flourished, China (like Europe) was still deep in the stone age. Bronze, which was already being used as tools and weapons in Mesopotamia before 3000 BC, appears in China only around 1600 BC, later than in Britain. Iron smelting, which was known throughout the Middle East and the Mediterranean by 1000 BC, was not developed in China until between the fifth and the third centuries BC. There are not many old buildings still standing in China – nothing as old as the Acropolis or the Parthenon, for instance, and surprisingly few that can match the age of Salisbury Cathedral. Even the original Great Wall is lost beneath successive rebuilding.

But what China lacks in antiquity is more than compensated for in continuity. As the architectural historian Andrew Boyd notes in his observations on Chinese urban development,[11] the rise of Chinese civilisation has been unbroken, highly distinctive and extremely sophisticated. From the advent of bronze technology around 1500 BC, right up to the modern era, this remarkable continuity led to the creation of one nation with one world view, one system of ethical concepts, one tradition in the arts and literature, one written language, one style of architecture and town planning.

This is not to suggest that China from the beginning has been a single unified national entity, pursuing a path towards moral and material perfection. Far from it. Early Chinese history is fraught with episodes of brutal conquest and counter-attack among the warlords who ruled the country's far-flung and disparate regions. But throughout, remarkably, crucial aspects of the culture's singular nature were nurtured, and their advantages consolidated at key points in the country's history. Eventually, a centralised monarchy that ruled all China was established under Shi Huangdi, or First Emperor, in 221 BC. Shi Huangdi ruled for less than two decades, but he founded an imperial system whose fundamental principles directed China's history for more than two millennia.

Shi Huangdi's most visible legacies today are China's best-known tourist attractions: the Great Wall and the subterranean tomb complex at Xian with its lifesize terracotta army of thousands, but his short reign also endowed China with more lastingly practical assets. He standardised the country's coinage, weights and measures, for example, and even stipulated that cart-axles should be of a standard width. A programme of road-building was instigated, inter-state boundaries were abolished and the empire was divided into a hierarchy of regional units, each administered by an appointed (and non-hereditary) bureaucracy that was ultimately answerable to the central government and the First Emperor himself. Perhaps most significant of all, however, the Chinese written script was standardised too, and subsequently became the universal instrument of administration throughout the empire.

China had a written script well over 1,000 years before Shi Huangdi's time – he just made it more useful. The script is conceptual in form, which means that it uses symbols to convey ideas (rather than letters to express sounds). The disadvantage of the system is the huge number of symbols (over 50,000 altogether, although 'only' about 2,500 are needed to make a daily newspaper intelligible), but the overriding advantage is that it does not attempt to communicate the spoken word. An item of Chinese script can be read and understood by people who speak mutually incomprehensible dialects or languages. They can communicate in writing even while not understanding a word that is spoken. This was an important – if not indispensable – component of making a unified empire of China and founding cities from which to rule its disparate regions and feuding factions. Add the principle of providing education for all promising candidates, along with the practice of employing graduates in a civil service that promotes ability before birthright, and the centralised control of a sprawling empire becomes a practical reality.

This did not happen overnight, of course. Indeed, it is doubtful whether many of Shi Huangdi's edicts were seen as beneficial even during his lifetime. China's Cultural Revolution of 1966–76 extolled him as a great progressive leader, but a more circumspect look[12] reveals a ferociously cruel, paranoically suspicious and prodigiously credulous man of but average ability. His chief minister, Li Ssu, is credited with being the principal architect of Chinese unification, but the process extended well beyond his lifetime too – through war and turmoil and a succession of dynasties. So where in all this were the fundamental principles of the imperial system that directed China's history for more than two millennia? Where was the world view, and the continuity that nurtured it? Answer: in the cities, where ambitious rulers could deploy the resources at their command to spectacular effect – but only within the constraints of pre-existing principles. There was a greater authority to which even rulers were beholden.

The interesting point here is that although the emperor was absolute ruler and the holder of divine status – regarded by his officials and subjects as an intermediary between human labour and heavenly favour whose virtue and proper performance ensured the stability of the state and guaranteed a pacified world – he was constantly being compared with the idealised examples of past rulers. Changes of any kind could be regarded as a challenge to established ideals. Better to stay with the tried and tested, and the form of a capital city was a primary means by which an emperor could legitimise his position as both ruler and guardian of tradition. This applied even to the First Emperor, Shi Huangdi, who was quick to acknowledge the achievements of pre-imperial rulers. 'I have heard of Wen Wang of Zhou's capital at Feng and of Wu Wang's capital of Hao. The likes of Feng and Hao are the imperial cities of emperors,' he declared,[13] and set about following their example. His imperial city and palace would be large enough to entertain 100,000 men 'who will come by cart to drink wine and on horseback to warm their hands by the fire', he boasted but its overall plans conformed with those of his predecessors. Shi Huangdi died before his city and palace were completed. What stood at the time of his death was destroyed in a fire which is said to have burned for three months.

Just look at the layout of the city walls —
On every side there opened three gates,
Each with a three-lane roadway level and straight.
Running parallel were chariot tracks, twelve in number,
Streets and thoroughfares crossed back and forth.
The residential plots and wards followed regular lines,
The tiled roofs were even and smooth.
The high-class residences of the Northern Watch-tower
Opened directly to the road.
They selected the most adept craftsmen to apply their skills,
And expected their dwellings never to crumble or collapse.
The timbers were garbed in pongee and brocade;
The ground was painted vermeil and purple.
The imperial arms of the Arsenal
Were placed in racks and crossbow frames . . .
They greatly expanded the Nine Markets,
Joined by encircling walls, girdled by gates.
From the flag pavilion, five stories high,
Officials looked down to inspect the countless shop rows . . .
Precious wares arrived from all quarters,
Gathered like birds, amassed like fish scales.
Sellers earned double profit,
But buyers were never lacking . . .
The palaces and lodges of the capital commanderies and kingdoms
Were one hundred forty-five in number . . .
The encircling walls stretched continuously
Four hundred *li* and more . . .[14]

The poet here was writing of Chang'an, the capital city built by the
emperors of the Han dynasty who succeeded Shi Huangdi. It was
located a few kilometres south-east of present day Xianyang; not far
from the site Shi Huangdi had chosen for his city, but nothing of
Chang'an is visible above ground now either. As remarked earlier, there
are very few buildings in China today that are more than a few hundred
years old. Even so, many city plans are available for scrutiny — in the
tangible results of archaeological excavations, and even more explicitly
in the form of pictorial and written representations.

The oldest such evidence of cities in China goes back almost to the
origins of Chinese writing itself. Oracle bones and bronze vessels dating
from about 1500 BC have been found bearing inscriptions of the symbol

denoting a city. The symbol is wonderfully explicit, and a very good example of how a concept is conveyed in an ideographic script: a square with simple roofed buildings top and bottom (next to pl. 30). In its romanised phonetic rendition, this symbol is written as *ch'eng*, and if *ch'eng* means city, then a clue to the most important feature of a city in terms of Chinese urban concepts is the fact that *ch'eng* also means wall.

One might suppose that, since the word and symbol for city and wall are synonomous in Chinese, the origin of cities in China must have been defensive – and indeed, the evidence of feuding communities is as ancient as that of cities. But the significance goes deeper than that. As Andrew Boyd notes,[15] a city was not merely walled; the principal internal parts of the city were walled too, as in Beijing, where the Imperial City was a walled enclosure within the Inner City and the Palace was a walled enclosure within that again. Every important ensemble of buildings and spaces was a walled enclosure in itself and if large enough would be composed of separate walled enclosures. The Palace was a labyrinth of walled enclosures. Not only a palace, a temple, a library or a tomb – even a family home would be a walled enclosure.

There was nothing arbitrary about any of this. Ancient texts and drawings (supported in some case by archaeological investigation) reveal that the ideal Chinese imperial city was planned in entirety from its inception, and construction began with the outer wall. At times building inside the outer wall occurred before the enclosure was complete, but the size and configuration of the wall, and thus the size of the city, were rarely accidental. Some imperial cities were enormous. Indeed, while they flourished, most Chinese capitals were the largest cities in the world in terms of area (as well as population, as Chandler has shown). The walls enclosing seventh-century Chang'an, for example,[16] added up to a total length of 36.7 km; Beijing in the seventeenth century encompassed an area of 62 km^2, the size of San Marino, the world's oldest and smallest republic, on the border of northern Italy.

Among the literature of China's classical age there are texts which clearly show that an ideology of capital-city building was formulated long before the country was unified under Shi Huangdi. A twelfth-century BC ruler, for example, is urged to assume the responsibility of God on high and serve at the centre of the land where, having constructed a great city, he shall be a counterpart of Heaven and govern as the central pivot. 'If you rule from this central place,' he is told, 'the myriad states will all enjoy peace and you, the King, will achieve complete success.'[17] Another text defines the procedure by which the city should be constructed:

> The *jiangren* [official responsible] constructs the state capitals. He makes a square nine *li* on each side; each side has three gates. Within the capital are nine north–south and nine east–west streets. The north–south streets are nine carriage tracks in width. On the left (as one faces south, or, to the east) is the Ancestral Temple, and to the right (west) are the Altars of Soil and Grain. In the front is the Hall of Audience and behind the markets.[18]

Here and elsewhere it is stated time and again that the city must be four-sided as a physical manifestation of the Chinese belief in a square-shaped universe that held the Son of Heaven at its centre, and bounded by walls which were oriented precisely on the north–south axis. Each wall (and quarter therein) was associated with the season that its angle to the sun exemplified: east was spring; south was summer; west autumn and north winter.

But while written advocations and pictorial representations of the ideal city were an unbroken strand of the Chinese world view, persisting and reiterated in virtually identical form through centuries – indeed, millennia – of considerable change and upheaval, their physical existence was not so enduring. The fact that some early emperors decided to build their imperial city on another site, rather than occupy that of their predecessors, was an important aspect of this – but even then the principal reason that Chinese imperial cities were short-lived was a consequence of the materials with which they were constructed. China has always been short of stone. City walls (and even the first Great Wall) were made of pounded earth; the buildings within them were built principally with wood. Fire was a constant threat and frequent occurrence; many cities were razed to the ground, leaving the eroding effects of the weather to work on the heaps of pounded earth left standing.

So we find that while the Chinese world view regarding the nature and form of cities was established over 3,000 years ago, and persisted virtually unchanged for millennia, its most enduring representations have been writings and drawings on pieces of parchment, silk and rice paper, or simply in the minds of the responsible authorities. It is an intriguing thought: the ideal outlives the reality. Indeed, there is a revealing instance in which plans dating from the early days of a city's prominence are an idealised version of the reality: Hangchow. The city was founded as an imperial capital in the twelfth century, and is renowned for the accounts that Marco Polo has left of his visits there (he called the city Quinsai, or Kinsai, which is thought to be a corruption of the Chinese term *jingshi,* meaning 'capital').

Hangchow was beautifully situated, on undulating ground with a fresh-water lake immediately adjacent to the west, and a large river on its eastern flank. Marco Polo writes extravagantly of a city with hundreds of miles of wide streets and canals and 12,000 bridges. He says the lake skirting the city 'commands a distant view of all its grandeur and loveliness, its temples, palaces, monasteries, and gardens with their towering trees running down to the water's edge. On the lake itself is an endless procession of barges thronged with pleasure-seekers.'[19]

The city was large in Marco Polo's day, and certainly fulfilled its role as imperial capital; but Hangchow was a planted capital, set in a pre-existing commerical town, not a city designed and built to the stipulated imperial pattern. Furthermore, the lie of the land made it impossible to fit a proper four-sided walled city on the site. Consequently, the city was squeezed onto the strip of land that lies between the lake and the river – nowhere more than 2 km wide. The main thoroughfares were in the required north–south and east–west orientation, but the city wall was obliged to follow the twists and turns of the natural landscape, with hardly a straight and level stretch or square corner in its entire 25 km perimeter.

So the reality of Hangchow was far from ideal. But no matter. The heavenly approved and classically sanctioned plans for an imperial city transcended the pattern of walls, streets and buildings that mere mortals had assembled. The Chinese imperial city had to be geometrically perfect; the city's actual layout was therefore irrevelant to those charged with the task of recording its existence for posterity. And so the drawings they produced show a rectangular palace-city within a perfectly rectangular outer city, with the walls and customary buildings and thoroughfares laid out according to classical stipulation.

In the Chinese world view regarding cities, expressions of the ideal were more important than exact depictions of reality; the drawings of Hangchow were made to ensure that even when the material remains of the city could no longer be found, the city plan, though fictitious, would ever after be recorded, perceived and certified as that of an ideal Chinese imperial city.[20]

★

Though the abstract ideal and the physical reality of a Chinese imperial city could be conveniently integrated in a two-dimensional representation – and thus perpetuate a point of faith, or world view – it was practical expediencies that held the empire together and kept it running for 2,000 years. Indeed, what we might see in the maps of Hangchow as a distortion of reality was in itself an example of practical expedience. And the Chinese were nothing if not practical. Continuity does not necessarily depend upon absolute uniformity throughout. Pictures and texts from any particular period during those 2,000 years give an impression of unchanging uniformity, but in fact the only constant was the repetition of content and style that artists, writers and draughtsmen were obliged to follow. The map of Hangchow is again a classic example of this.

Thus it would be wrong to think of Chinese society as 'static' simply because the surviving representations of its basic ideals and structure did not alter over such a long period. Even 'stable' seems inappropriate when the violence of the empire's vicissitudes and upheavals are taken into account. But it certainly 'worked', in the sense that during those 2,000 years the empire was able to develop technology that successively increased production and wealth which, in turn, supported rapidly growing numbers of people – comparatively large numbers of whom had a high standard of living.

Technology was the key factor here, and for fully three-quarters of its imperial history, China was technically and economically in advance of Europe and initiated most of the significant inventions of the period. These ranged from such basic adjuncts to human labour as the wheel-barrow, to the complexities of the iron chain suspension bridge and canal locks, aerodynamically efficient sails, the sternpost rudder, the magnetic compass, gunpowder and explosives, paper, movable type, printing and porcelain. There was also a parallel early ascendancy over Europe in the fields of medicine, surgery, pharmacology, astronomy and mathematics.[21]

All of this invites comparison with other empires that the world has known, and their cities. Rome is of course the first that comes to mind, and indeed the influence of the Roman Empire is still evident today throughout Europe, north Africa and the Middle East. But then the Romans had access to more stone than the Chinese. The stone has endured, but the Roman Empire was not so long-lasting – just a few centuries, as compared with China's two millennia.

The foundations of the Roman Empire date back to the third

century BC, but it was not until the second century AD, under Hadrian and his successors Antoninus Pius and Marcus Aurelius, that the empire reached its pinnacle of achievement. Their reigns crowned a long period of economic growth. The population had increased considerably; agriculture had penetrated the forests and wastelands. 'Cultivated fields have overcome the forests,' wrote Quintus Tertullian, 'the sands are being planted, the rocks hewn, the swamp drained; there are as many cities today as there were formerly huts.'[22]

The Roman Empire at this time extended from Hadrian's Wall in the north of Britain; through central Europe, France and Spain to the Atlantic coast of Portugal; south through Italy and Sicily to North Africa and Egypt, and east to Greece and Turkey. Best estimates of its population put the number at not less than 31 million (and possibly as high as 56 million). The subjects of the empire were enjoying a period of relative peace, after centuries of intermittent, even of continuous, war. Peace brought changes to much of Europe's outlook and culture. Many millions of people became 'romanised', which principally meant frequenting cities and enjoying urban entertainment – for the fact is that despite all their literary expressions of love for the simple country life, it was city life that the Romans desired most. In their view, urban living distinguished the civilised from the uncivilised. A Roman senator, Flavius Magnus Aurelius Cassiodorus, summarised the prevailing sentiment: 'Let the wild beasts live in fields and woods; men ought to draw together into cities.'[23]

Prior to the advent of the Roman Empire, the concept of a city was unknown in Europe to the north and west of Greece and Italy. In these as yet 'uncivilised' regions, the dominant settlement pattern was one of small villages and scattered farmsteads. In all probability, most settlements were no more than hamlets, consisting of only two or three farming families. Some were fortified (usually those built on a hilltop), but in most cases even the occasional surrounding palisade seems to have been designed as much to prevent animals wandering as to deter undesirables from entering.[24] But, of course, nothing could hold off the invading Romans.

Once the business of conquest was done with, the Romans imposed their authority through a patchwork of provinces and – in effect – city-states that were administered from an urban centre built specifically to house the government and military services. These urban centres were linked by an extensive network of well-engineered and surfaced roads, along which officials could travel up to 320 km in a day on important routes where changes of horse were provided.[25] All roads led to Rome, as the saying goes, but not in every sense. It is true that Rome was the ultimate centre of administrative authority; that the emperor controlled the movement and stationing of military forces, and that the emperor and Senate between them nominated senior provincial officials and thus dictated policy. Even so, the day-to-day government of regions away from Rome was essentially decentralised, and most were governed by the appointed provincial and local authorities. The empire was, in essence, an informal federation of city-states: 'a vast experiment in local self-government,' is how one authority describes it.[26]

The exact number of cities and towns established across Europe by the Romans is elusive – but there were certainly hundreds of them; the Roman historian Pliny enumerates 175 city-states in one province alone. Beyond Italy and the Mediterranean coastlands (where the Roman ideals of urban living were more or less bolted on to pre-existing towns), provincial governors usually had their cities built on virgin sites, with temple and forum, basilica, theatre and baths laid out according to an established grid pattern of regular blocks and streets. Evidence of the Roman grid-iron style of city planning survives today wherever there has been some continuity of occupation; it is recognisable in cities as widely separated as Córdoba and Ljubljana; Nîmes and York.[27]

But continuity of occupation was relatively rare once the decline of the Roman Empire became irreversible towards the end of the second century AD; as military forces were withdrawn, administrative functions closed down and institutions abandoned, the cities became empty shells, their streets and fine buildings neglected. With the end of urban living as the Romans had pursued it, the imperial cities lost the greater part of their purpose. There was no other group capable of moving in to take their place – not on the same scale. Some people doubtless attempted to carry on from where the Romans had left off, occupying empty houses and so forth, but very many Roman towns and cities were to all intents and purposes totally abandoned. All in all, the Romans left hundreds of cities, towns and other remnants of their culture scattered across Europe from Scotland to the Danube, but very little survived in the form of viable, self-sufficient urban centres after the collapse of the empire.

The Romans, it seems, were very good at ordering stones to be placed one on another in a manner that ensured they would remain standing for 2,000 years, but rather less good at establishing a style of urban living that would continue to flourish in their cities when the architects had left. We tend to think of the Romans as superb city-builders, but this is true only in an exact and limited sense. They were great engineers and architects, but when it came to sustaining the life of the cities they had designed, they were simply incompetent.

The problem was that the major cities of the empire parasitised the regions under their control to an unsustainable extent. All cities are parasites, feeding off their agricultural hinterlands, but the cities that thrive best develop a relationship with the hinterland which over time becomes distinctly more symbiotic than parasitic. They give something back, in other words, in the way of manufactured goods, services and so forth that the rural communities feeding them could not otherwise obtain. The Romans did very little of this. Attention to practical expediency such as the Chinese had demonstrated was not an important constituent of the Roman world view. Their roads, to cite just one instance, were beautifully engineered, but too narrow for the carts which could have been the basis of viable trade networks. In any case, trade was regarded as a demeaning occupation; wealthy Romans preferred to put their money in agricultural capitalism.

With grain supply so fundamental to Rome's existence, the economy of Roman cities was profoundly extractive. This was fine while the Empire was expanding, but inevitably became an intractable problem once the decline had set in. And it is here that the Romans' world view on cities and urban living was so shortsighted. They were a pioneering and ingenious people, inventive civil engineers, but seemingly incapable of making the technological advances in food production and the manufacture of tools and consumer goods that might have helped matters. In fact, although the political face of Europe had changed beyond all recognition under Roman rule, the practicalities of life for most people had not changed very much at all. Only a tiny minority actually lived in cities, and in rural areas life went on much as before. Farming techniques were little altered. The areas under cultivation had been expanded to supply growing populations, but there was little in the practice of agriculture in the second century AD that would have seemed strange to farmers of the fifth century BC. No serious attempt to economise on labour or improve output was made, partly because the people in charge apparently could not see the advantage of increasing productivity, and partly because an abundance of labour was available in the form of slaves.

So, as demands increased, the sweated labour of captured slaves kept the unimproved agricultural and manufacturing technology creaking along for a couple more centuries. Higher and higher taxes were imposed, but nothing could halt the inexorable decline to total collapse. The barbarians took over Rome itself, while over large areas of the former empire urban life wasted away. Many provincial cities became at best little more than villages, their much-reduced populations living among the relics of a great civilisation with little use for its civic buildings except as a convenient source of nicely dressed stone. During the succeeding centuries many were abandoned altogether – today, the stone ruins evoke images of the glory that had been, while an Anglo-Saxon poem speaks of what was left behind:

> the work of giants mouldereth away.
> Its roofs are breaking and falling; its towers crumble
> in ruin. Plundered those walls with grated doors –
> their mortar white with frost. Its battered ramparts
> are shorn away and ruined, all undermined
> by eating age.[28]

Europe's Dark Ages – dark from our perspective, in that it is difficult to see the detail of what was going on, but clearly quite well lit from within, since events were moving towards the establishment of political and economic systems which inspired the rise of powerful and viable cities throughout the region. Politically, the period was initially dominated by the machinations of Charlemagne's Holy Roman Empire and the eruption of Islam from its point of origin on the Arabian peninsula westward through north Africa and across the Mediterranean into Spain, but within these grand schemes there were significant developments at the local level. In the Christian domain, kings and princes were perfecting the mechanisms of government, aristocrats were building castles, and merchants were building walls around their developing cities and institutions. Cathedrals, monasteries and humble parish churches were rising from one end of Europe to the other.

Overall, it was a period of tremendous creativity – in the arts, and in technology. Agricultural innovations such as the heavy plough, the horseshoe and the horse collar combined with changes in land holding and farming organisation to intensify food production and thus generate regular and marketable surpluses. Increased food production fuelled population growth, and the drive to convert surpluses to profit encouraged a move away from an economic system based on self-sufficient food production towards a wider distribution of marketable goods.

Even so, difficult journeys, the insecurity of travel and scarce means of transport limited the number of venues at which goods could be bought and sold. Markets, such as they were, took place in the gateways of castles, or monasteries, and in the early days of this mercantile activity a chaotic diversity of weights and measures and currencies restricted the circulation of goods to a considerable degree. Barter was the tried-and-trusted means of acquiring goods, but getting what you wanted was no easy matter. A peasant might bring in his domestic surplus – eggs, perhaps a chicken, some wool or even a piece of cloth woven in the household – and leave with a stool. A more prosperous man 'would trade a horse for a sack of [grain], a piece of cloth for a measure of salt, a pound of pepper for a pair of boots'.[29] Money existed, artisans and workers were paid in cash, but the coinage was of limited use in the everyday life of most people. A servant could expect to earn a silver penny for a day's work in the early twelfth century, for instance, and could buy a quarter of a sheep carcass with it, but the coin would not help him to buy a pound of chops.[30]

Ultimately, though, marketing was simplified and an increasing demand for manufactured goods and better distribution opened new opportunities at all levels of society. Markets were often the nucleus around which a town and then a city developed. Bruges, for instance, originated in this way – as was described in a contemporary account:

In order to satisfy the needs of the castle folk, there began to throng before his [i.e. the prince's] gate near the castle bridge traders and merchants selling costly goods, then innkeepers to feed and house those doing business with the prince, who was often to be seen there; they built houses and set up inns where those who could not be put up at the castle were accommodated. The houses increased to such an extent that there soon grew up a large town which in the common speech of the lower classes is still called 'Bridge'.[31]

Ambitious people with talent and new ideas gathered in towns, creating centres of economic activity capable of serving all manner of needs. Even the most impoverished peasants went to the towns for cloth, salt, household utensils and tools they could not obtain locally, while the higher echelons of society had extravagant needs and wishes that only distant producers could satisfy – which in turn opened up the potential of long-distance trade for enterprising merchants. Nobles were eager to buy rich fabrics and rare spices.

Knights in isolated castles wanted armour and weapons, war-horses and harnesses.

Markets and trade developed a momentum of their own, fuelling the growth of market towns – and cities. As the trend became irresistible, perceptive rulers used their powers to secure a piece of the action. Between 1227 and 1350 the kings of England, for example, granted exclusive market rights to 1,200 urban communities[32] and, in return for the privilege, acquired an income in taxes and duties from each. Similar arrangements were made everywhere, as thousands of towns sprang up to service the trading requirements of communities on the coasts and rivers, farmland, forests and pastures of Europe. The shores of the Mediterranean sheltered an array of ports – Amalfi, Genoa, Narbonne among them. Urban revival was marked in France, England and Lombardy, where many towns grew on the sites of abandoned Roman settlements; the Moorish cities of southern Spain were large and prosperous. Flanders too was becoming increasingly urbanised, particularly in areas where the cloth industry was developing.[33]

By 1200 a network of genuine cities was in place, carrying most of Europe's industry and a substantial portion of its trade. The principal centres of urban growth – and certainly of the city's independence from the territorial rule of the old order – were northern Italy, Flanders and the adjacent portion of north-western France. Germany too had cities poised to grow dramatically in the thirteenth century, and the provincial cities of England were expanding with their increasingly profitable role as suppliers of high-quality wool to the Flemish cloth trade.[34]

Economics were obviously the primary determinant of urban development as Europe emerged from the Dark Ages, but there was another important contributing factor that should not be overlooked: religion. The monotheistic belief systems formulated in the Middle East grew into unifying umbrellas of faith that protected their adherents from the conflicts that diverse ethnic and cultural origins might all too often precipitate. Well, that is not altogether true; the adherents often fought anyway – among themselves as well as between groups – but the point here is that despite these secular lapses from grace, the practice of religion interacted with economics to move the development of cities along faster than either would have done alone.

Monasteries were the most deeply set aspect of religious involvement with the economic development of Europe. Initially founded as self-sufficient religious farming communities, the dedication of their constantly available (and often large) labour forces rendered them more likely to succeed than fail when times were difficult, and more successful than lay communities when times were good. In short, monastic estates exercised a profound influence on land use, settlement and the course of regional events. As they grew and consolidated their properties, acquiring land in bequests from the laity, and exchanging or selling remote or less valuable parcels for more conveniently located lands, they became Europe's largest and most firmly entrenched landowners. Immensely wealthy in many cases, they were also politically influential as interpreters (if not always exact followers) of the divine message. And, of course, the influence of individual monasteries was reinforced by the all-seeing, all-powerful authority of the Church.

By the year 1100 most of Christian Europe had been divided into units of ecclesiastical organisation, of which the diocese and the parish were the essential components. The parish was an area of land deemed capable both of supporting a church and of being ministered to by its priest, and a dense network of parishes spanned central and western Europe by this time. The parish church, as the focus of the ecclesiastical organisation, was founded most often in the principal village or hamlet – and its influence was all-pervasive. Few parishioners, if any, could avoid the obligations of attending church and contributing to the expense of maintaining the building and its minister. Each parish was in turn obliged to contribute to the expense of maintaining the next level of ecclesiastical authority – the diocese – and it is here that the Church played a crucial role in making cities a core feature of Europe's world view. Drawing upon the secular authority of classical glories, the largest and most powerful dioceses were established in the ruined shells of cities the Romans had built.

As noted above, the Roman cities served little or no practical function after the fall of the empire. The Church was probably the only institution that saw any use for them at all, and the reason is not hard to deduce. The Church was, after all, founded in Rome; it was rich, and the former imperial Roman cities symbolised an established authority the Church could reclaim in the process of rebuilding them. Furthermore, and perhaps most crucially in terms of ecclesiastical authority, the language of imperial Rome was also the language of the Church: Latin. As in China, and the Roman Empire itself, language conveyed the message; with, as ever, an emphasis on the ideal vision colouring its view of reality.

So, from mouldering ruins the cities rose again. Cologne, Trier, Tours, Narbonne, Lyon and a number of smaller Roman cities and towns became the seats of powerful bishops who, aside from the influence they wielded in the Church, also became increasingly involved with secular affairs – even to the extent of sometimes becoming lords of the cities themselves – and commerce. Indeed, as the most universal institution of its time, the Church itself generated an immense volume of trade. Moreover, the practices of relic worship and pilgrimage encouraged travel, which in turn led to the growth of towns as the site of way stations along the pilgrim routes. Thus, overall, the Church established an economic function for towns that transcended their village or castle gate origins and would ultimately lead to the creation of great cities.[35]

As a measure of the Church's contribution to both the world view of Europe at this time, and its physical expression, we could hardly do better than consider the cathedrals. Here, the determinants of religion, political will and economics combined to produce the most sublime symbols of an age. In the introduction to his book *The Cathedral Builders* Jean Gimpel gives an indication of the effort – and faith – that was employed:

In three centuries – from 1050 to 1350 – several million tons of stone were quarried in France for the building of 80 cathedrals, 500 large churches and some tens of thousands of parish churches. More stone was excavated in France during these three centuries than at any time in Ancient Egypt, although the volume of the Great Pyramid alone is 2,500,000 cubic metres. The foundations of the cathedrals are laid as deep as 10 metres (the average depth of a Paris underground station) and in some cases there is as much stone underground as can be seen above.

The size of the cathedral at Amiens, which covered 7,700 square metres, made it possible for the entire population of the city – some ten thousand people – to attend one ceremony . . .

The height of naves, towers and spires is startling. A fourteen-floor building could be erected in the choir of Beauvais Cathedral without reaching the vaulting, which is 48 metres high. In order to compete with the people of twelfth-century Chartres who built their spire 105 metres high, the present municipality would have to build a thirty-floor skyscraper; and a forty-floor skyscraper would be needed to equal the spire at Strasbourg, which reaches to 142 metres.[36]

But despite the boost that the Church and commerce gave to the spread of towns and cities during the twelfth and thirteenth centuries, most of Europe's population still lived on the land and most urban centres were still very small at the beginning of the fourteenth century. Indeed, an authoritative survey[37] of the available evidence indicates that no more than about 3.5 per cent of Europe's entire population lived and worked exclusively in the urban centres – the remainder lived and worked on the land. Of the 3,267 cities and towns covered in the survey, only nine had more than 25,000 inhabitants; thirty-eight had between 10,000 and 25,000; 220 had between 2,000 and 10,000 inhabitants, and the rest of Europe's urban centres – 3,000 in all, nearly 90 per cent of the total – were home to fewer than 2,000 people. Little more than a village in modern terms. But the following 200 years were to see a tremendous spurt in the growth of cities.

By 1500, Europe's urban network included 101 cities with more than 20,000 inhabitants, twenty-one of which had populations of between 50,000 and 100,000.[38] In all, Europe now had between 5,000 and 6,000 cities and towns wherein the interacting dynamics of economics, politics and religion were in operation, but their distribution was increasingly determined by manufacturing and distribution considerations. They were spread thickly in the Low Countries, the Rhineland, central Germany and northern Italy – all regions where manufacturing and commercial activity was greatest, and an element of continuity was evident: indeed, by the mid fourteenth century an urban map of Europe had been established that in its core features remained virtually unchanged until the nineteenth century.[39]

The number of cities established during the fourteenth and fifteenth centuries, the magnitude of their population increases and the speed at which these developments occurred were remarkable enough – but consider, too, that this was a period during which between one-quarter and one-third of Europe's population died of plague – most of them in the cities. Clearly, the phenomenon of the city exerted a more powerful grip on the social and economic life of Europe during those terrible years than even the threat of the Black Death could loosen.

These were cities with complex administrative, religious, educational and economic functions. Many had cathedrals; some had universities too. Their economies were diverse, including a wide range of artisans, service workers and merchants. Indeed, the large cities owed their size and potential prosperity to the multiplicity of functions which they fostered – and which the merchants orchestrated to an increasing extent. Where the ebb and flow of a city's fortunes had once been determined by the whim or strategic manoeuvres of secular and religious rulers, merchants were now essential participants in urban affairs. With their involvement a city could acquire both wealth and grandeur; without them it foundered. By variously exploiting, reconfiguring and building upon the old order of authority, merchants created a social and economic dynamic that valued future prospects as much – if not more – than it respected the inherited practices of the past. The princes of Church and state still maintained a determining influence on the course of events, but the merchant's city was poised to carry humanity from the marketplace to the market economy.

7

In the Name of God and for Profit

In the changing world order of the Middle Ages commerce
became an arena in which material success was a measure of
talent – not just of influence or birthright. Merchants profited
from their commercial dealings with the Church, but learned
to be cautious of covetous prelates. Great cities rose with
either the power of the Church or commerce; the two forces
might coexist, but neither could assume that the mere
presence of the other would further its interests.

Marco di Datino was one of thousands who died when the Black Death
struck the Italian city of Prato, near Florence, in 1347–8. His wife,
Monna Vermiglia, died in the plague too, as did two of their four
children. Very little more is known of Marco – only that he was an
innkeeper who owned some land in the vicinity of Prato which had
been in the family since at least 1218. There is also an account of him
selling meat from his cattle at a stall in the Prato marketplace, with his
son, Francesco, helping to serve the customers. That is all. Three fleeting
glimpses – innkeeper, smallholder and part-time butcher – and even
these references would have lain unnoticed in the city archives were it
not for the achievements of his eldest surviving son, Francesco di Marco
Datini, which subsequently inspired researchers to find and record every
detail of his family history.[1]

Francesco di Marco Datini is credited with having created the
economic environment that made Prato one of the richest cities of
medieval Italy. He became very wealthy in the process, but bequeathed
his entire fortune, plus his worldly goods and the grand house he had
built in Prato, to the poor of the city – 'because I loved my city above

all other things'.[2] Francesco di Marco Datini was an exceptionally successful merchant. A statue of him stands today in the city square, clothed in the round biretta and sweeping robes of the fourteenth century, clutching a sheaf of business documents. On the walls of the house he bequeathed to the poor, faint traces remain of frescoes telling the story of his life which were painted after his death. This was a high honour, and an important break with the past. Until then, it was customary for only princes, saints and popes to be commemorated in this way – but a new concept of heroism had emerged during Francesco's lifetime – for which even an innkeeper's son might qualify, and that a city should choose to depict the saga of a merchant's life rather than a saint's pilgrimage or a prince's progress, speaks eloquently of the changing times.

Francesco was born in 1335 and lived until 1410. Seventy-five years spanning a tumultuous period of war, plague and famine, when a lack of producers and customers following the massive depopulation of Europe led to economic slump and stagnation. The old despotic order was under threat. The hitherto unquestioned religious and feudal authority which had suffused all aspects of social, cultural and economic behaviour was yielding to the need for something new – a rebirth, a renaissance. And trade – the dispassionate arbiter between the ideal and the practical – was the current that carried the greatest force of change. Authority based on religious and hereditary status was no longer enough – especially when wielded by inadequate men. As the fortunes of princes and popes waxed and waned with their wildly varying talents, the currents of trade flowed on, strongly and dependably, giving the greatest rewards to the most enterprising and efficient operators. After all, once the presumptions of birth or status had been set aside, the peasant was as good as the prince in the marketplace of the new world order; and the innkeeper's son as good as the pope.

But however sceptical of worldly authority they may have become, the merchants responsible for creating the new economic environment still believed in the transcendental authority which would determine their fate in the afterlife. Belief was a powerful force, which the insecurities of strife and civil war, famine, and the haunting menace of the Black Death could only strengthen – even while they weakened the grip of the old order. For ages past, Christian faith had marked the route from cradle to grave with a series of comforting devotional acts which offered at least a chance of divine protection in this world, and God's mercy in the next. No one questioned them.

Francesco was not, and did not consider himself, a wholly virtuous man. His natural temperament was sceptical rather than pious, but even a merchant who was inclined to look for the flaws in every proposition never doubted the necessity or the efficacy of the devotions that Christian doctrine required him to perform. In common with most people, he prayed morning and evening, attended Mass and went to confession regularly; as a man of means he built shrines and chapels, gave alms freely and paid his tithes promptly. A painting of St Christopher guarded the Datini front door; during Lent, Francesco and his wife fasted so strictly that friends declined their social invitations.

In the fashion of the times, Francesco's letters – both personal and business – began and ended with a reverent salutation. The Ten Commandments were written on the flyleaf of the Datini ledgers, and the pages were headed with the words: 'In the name of God and for Profit'. To modern eyes, this conjunction of piety and profit motive looks questionable. Certainly it offends our insistence that religion should not influence the conduct of political or commercial affairs. But while a belief in divine authority has become little more than a sideshow in Western everyday life, in the fourteenth century such belief was all-pervasive, obligatory, and unquestioned. So, dedicating ledger pages to both God and the profit motive was simply an acknowledgement of God as the all-seeing and final arbiter of human affairs – including commerce. Every merchant, every commercial enterprise, prefaced the record of their business dealings in this way. It was customary, and beyond that its purpose would come into question only if it was left out. That would be subversive.

But faith was not blind, and there was a distinction to be made between God and his representatives on Earth – the clergy. The divine authority of the former was never in doubt, but the motives and behaviour of the latter could be open to question. This too was a fourteenth-century fact of life, and something that is hinted at in a painting by Filippo Lippi which shows Francesco kneeling at the feet of the Blessed Virgin. The painting was completed more than forty years after Francesco's death, and although it depicts an act of true Christian devotion, it also alludes to the distinction he made between the unblemished purity of the divine and the inherent baseness of human affairs. The four good men of Prato kneeling with him are bareheaded, their hands held in prayer at their chests, and their eyes gazing upward in benign reverence. Francesco is gazing upward too, but with brow furrowed and a worried rather than a reverential look. His head is covered and his hands are not clasped in prayer but instead are protectively holding the group of four men (who are drawn at a smaller scale). God is one thing, he might be saying, the Church another.

God will be our salvation, but 'the earth and the sea are full of robbers', Francesco once advised a partner, 'and the greater part of mankind is evilly disposed'.[3] Nor did he exclude God's representatives on earth from this damning assessment. Indeed, he often scoffed at the behaviour of priests and monks, and only a lifetime of experience can have led him to stipulate, in his will, that the clergy should be denied any opportunity of becoming involved with the charitable foundation that was to be established after his death.

This foundation – the Ceppo di Francesco di Marcho – Mercatante dei Poveri di X[4] – was to inherit not only his fortune and the income from his business enterprises so long as they remained in operation, but also his house in Prato, the Palazzo Datini. The bequest was intended 'for the love of God, so as to give back to His Poor what has been received from Him, as His gracious gift'. But although the bequest was a gift of God being returned for the benefit of the poor, Francesco's will firmly stipulated that it should be 'in no respect under the authority of the Church or of officials or prelates or any other member of the clergy'. Moreover, 'no altar or oratory or chapel' should ever be set up within the walls of the house 'by means of which [the foundation] might be considered a place belonging to [the clergy] and evilly disposed men might come in and occupy it, saying it was a benefice; all of which is against the testator's intentions'.

The testator's intentions could hardly have been more clearly expressed, and the Ceppo di Francesco di Marcho has been functioning most satisfactorily without the involvement of the Church ever since.

Historians write of two hearths of economic activity from which the growth of large cities in Europe was kindled during the early medieval period: Flanders and northern Italy.[5] In each region, towns which had been important in the old order grew with the increased output of their manufacturers and artisans, and prospered on the sheer volume of trade generated by merchants supplying the demands of markets all over Europe. Francesco di Marco Datini was not the first, the foremost, the most famous or the richest of these medieval merchants; but he holds a prominent position in the history of Europe's early economic development by virtue of two unique features, which together reveal a great deal about his life and times.

First, Datini's career was one of uninterrupted success. Daring on occasion, but more often cautiously prudent, his deals generally succeeded in making a profit. Unlike the Bardi and Peruzzi family firms before him, who went spectacularly bankrupt in the 1340s with combined debts of 1.5 million gold florins (debts which are often attributed to Edward III's failure to repay the loans he had taken to finance the opening phases of the Hundred Years War – though this is disputed[6]), and the famous Medici family business after him, which also suffered ignominious collapse, Francesco di Marco Datini's fortune increased steadily throughout his life. The reason for this was not a lucky succession of good deals, high profit margins or even a talent for operating in the right place and right time – no; although Datini certainly did benefit from some instances of gratuitous good fortune, his success accrued primarily from an assiduous attention to detail and close personal control of every aspect of his business.

Datini had partners, but no family relations in the business who might feel entitled to claim privileged status, or expect rewards beyond those specified in the carefully worded legal agreements he drew up with all his partners. No brothers; no cousins; not even children that he could nurture and coach to take over the business as he grew older. Indeed, although such a prosperous man might have expected his name and fortune to be carried forward and enhanced by future generations, Datini was denied that gratification – his wife bore no children. And so his life's work – 'in the name of God and for Profit' – survives only in the Ceppo di Francesco di Marcho – Mercatante dei Poveri di X, which brings us to the second unique feature of his life and success as a merchant.

During his lifetime Francesco di Marco Datini collected every letter and business document he received; he made copies of those he sent out and instructed his branch managers to be equally fastidious – all correspondence and business records were to be carefully preserved. In his will he left instructions for the papers to be collected together and stored in his house in Prato. And indeed they were, and lay forgotten until 1870, when foundation staff hauled a pile of sacks from a dark and dusty recess under the stairs and found the papers bundled inside. A few pages had been nibbled by mice and insects during the 460 years since Datini's death but otherwise the neglect was not entirely unfortunate for, as Iris Origo points out in her book *The Merchant of Prato,* at least thieves and fools had remained unaware of their existence. And the hoard was astonishing, in both its quantity and the depth of information it contained: 150,000 letters, over 500 account books and ledgers, 300 deeds of partnership, 400 insurance policies and several thousand bills of lading, letters of advice, bills of exchange and cheques.[7]

There is a personal history here, which is beautifully told in Iris Origo's book. Husband and wife, the family and friends, the house, their clothes; the food and drink they served and the medicines they resorted to in times of illness; their escape from the plague. Francesco was thirty-five years old when he married Margherita, she was sixteen. Childlessness gnawed at their marriage, and Iris Origo believes this could account for the irascible tone of some letters that Francesco wrote home to his wife during lengthy absences on business; Margherita was at first defensive, petulant, feisty even, but ultimately a resigned sadness characterised her side of the correspondence. She agreed to adopt and bring up the daughter, Ginerva, whom Francesco had fathered with a servant. (This is not as surprising as it sounds. That a man should have relations with a servant was commonplace in medieval times, and not frowned upon. Also it was customary for the children to be raised as part of the family household.[8]) When Ginerva married in 1406 he gave her a dowry of 1,000 florins. She wore a wedding gown of crimson silk interwoven with gold thread, with a long train and a collar of white ermine, and a head-dress embroidered in gold and adorned with golden leaves and flowers of enamel. Most of Prato's high society attended the wedding banquet.

The correspondence reveals that Francesco could be generous to the point of arousing complaints from his friends: 'You will not leave me alone with your partridges,' one wrote on receiving yet another consignment of the expensive delicacy, '. . . by God, wipe me from the page on which you have writ down the friends on whom these birds must be bestowed'. Margherita protested about a surfeit of what seems to be penny-wise, pound-foolish behaviour: 'At one time you count the wicks, and at another you let a whole torch blaze without need.' He could be eccentric, ordering marmosets, porcupines and peacocks (presumably for household amusement), and pestering the agent for instructions as to 'how they should be kept, from their birth until they are great, and what food it is meet to give them'.

He entertained princes and gave extravagant gifts: stained glass and paintings, vestments adorned with costly embroidery, and silver candlesticks for the Church; a very fine mastiff for the Cardinal of Bologna, dressed up with a collar of gilded silver engraved in enamel with the Cardinal's arms, and a chain of gilded copper with a tassel, a coat of scarlet cloth, 'like a race-horse's, to wear upon the mountains', and a breast-strap lined with chamois-leather and covered with red velvet 'to defend him against wild boars'. The accoutrements alone cost more than 50 florins, and a sapphire ring for the wife of the intermediary who had undertaken to deliver the dog to the Cardinal cost as much again. Francesco had hoped the gift would persuade the Cardinal to officiate at Ginerva's wedding, but it elicited only a warm letter of thanks addressed to 'the noble and illustrious Francesco di Marco di Prato, our good friend'. And at the age of seventy-one, even a wealthy and sceptical man who had devoted considerably more energy to the pursuit of profit than to the veneration of God could believe that kind words from a cardinal were worth the price of an expensively equipped hunting dog.

The biblical maxim 'gifts blind the eyes of the wise and alter the words of the just'[9] could describe the motive behind much of Francesco's generosity during his career as a merchant. Conversely, the suspicion that others might be attempting to pull the wool over his eyes, or twisting his words, was fundamental to his dealings with anyone that he did not know well. 'When you have lived as long as I and have traded with many folk,' he wrote in later life to a young agent, 'you will know that man is a dangerous thing, and that danger lies in dealing with him.' Francesco believed in neither the honesty of men nor the stability of governments. Though confident that God promised salvation in the afterlife, the failings of human institutions – secular and religious – made caution and constant vigilance the hallmark of his behaviour in this life. He deliberately spread his interests as widely as possible, never putting too much in any single company, never entrusting too much respon-sibility to any one partner; always ready to pull out at a moment's notice if a reversal of fortune seemed likely.

With an acute, nose-twitching, nimble and entrepreneurial sensitivity to the flow of events and their likely outcome, Francesco would have been a commercial success in any age – trading wheat in Mesopotamia, selling slaves in ancient Greece, dealing on the modern stock exchange – except that he lived in especially tumultuous times, in daily dread of bad news: war, pestilence, famine or insurrection. Increasingly, though, trade and commerce were creating a tough and resilient network of mutual interest on which all sections of society depended regardless of their afflictions, affiliations or antagonisms. With nodes of activity based in the cities, commerce was pushing political allegiances into second place as merchants responded to the pressures of supply and demand.

Few new cities were founded simply on the whim or strategic resolve of state or Church as the 'tidal wave of medieval urbanisation' was superseded by the powerful and sustained currents of commercial incentive.[10] Merchants went where there was money to be made. Cities rose and fell according to their location in the economic landscape rather than by their status in the political environment. As the twelfth-century poet and philosopher Allain of Lille had presciently noted: 'Not Caesar now, but money, is all.'[11] And Francisco di Marco Datini was one among thousands who capitalised on this development – exceptional only in that he left such a complete record of his personal and business life.

Francesco di Marco Datini was thirteen years old when his father and mother and two siblings died. Before he was sixteen he had served a brief apprenticeship with merchants in Florence, sold a piece of land inherited from his father for 150 florins, and set off for Avignon to trade as a merchant on his own account.

Situated on the Rhône – a natural artery joining northern and southern Europe – Avignon was supremely well-placed to serve the two hearths of economic activity which had kindled the growth of large cities – Flanders and northern Italy. Down the Rhône valley came the wool and cloth of Flanders and England; from over the Alps came the wheat, barley, linen and armour of Lombardy; Spanish wool, oil, leather and fruit was brought in from across the Pyrenees; spices, dyes and silks from the Levant and further afield reached Avignon via the ports of Provence and Languedoc.

So much commercial activity attracted religious as well as secular attention. When Francesco travelled to Avignon in 1350, the city was the capital of Christendom, with Clement VI on the papal throne commanding one of the richest courts in Europe. The previously small provincial capital was swollen to bursting point by the papal presence. A census made in 1376 lists nearly 4,000 officials and attendants, including the pope's thirty chaplains, sundry knights and squires, grooms, body-guards and jailers, servants and tradesmen. In addition, each cardinal at the palace had a large court of his own that had to be accommodated.[12] Beyond the grandeur of the papal palace and its environs, however, conditions were appallingly crowded, malodorous and dangerous. Ambassadors complained. The poet Petrarch found the city unbearable: 'From this impious Babylon, from which all shame has fled . . . I, too, have fled away, to save my life.'[13]

Impious, shame – words indicating that worship and godly behaviour were not the most distinctive features of life in fourteenth-century Avignon. And indeed they were not. Though the pope was ostensibly Christ's representative on Earth, avarice was as commonplace as devotion in the capital of Christendom as artists and craftsmen, tradesmen and merchants, scrabbled for a portion of the wealth that the papal presence attracted and dispensed. The banqueting and audience halls of the palace were hung with woollen and silk tapestries from Italy, Spain and Flanders; the table services were of silver or gold; sumptuous banquets were frequent. Twice a year – every spring and autumn – new clothes were distributed to all members of the papal court – at an annual cost of no less than seven or eight thousand florins. Yet more fabulous sums were spent on furs – though only for the upper echelons of the papal hierarchy. Palace accounts reveal that on one occasion Clement VI bought no fewer than 1,080 skins of ermine for his personal wardrobe alone; a successor, John XXII, had even the pillows on his bed trimmed with ermine.

Italians were prominent among the artisans and craftsmen working in Avignon. Indeed, a list made in 1376 records 1,100 Italians among a fraternity of 1,224 assorted masons and sculptors, carpenters, jewellers and goldsmiths, weavers, leather-workers and armourers. Italian merchants and tradesmen were no less ubiquitous, with a community of some 600 families dominating the city's trade in luxury items and dealing widely in commodities such as wheat and cloth, timber, cheese and wine. Most were from Tuscany and those from Prato enjoyed the favoured attention of their very own cardinal, Niccolò da Prato, whose role in securing the election of Pope Clement VI had ensured that he became one of the most powerful men in the papal administration.

Francesco di Marco Datini lived and worked in Avignon for thirty-two years after his arrival there in 1350. The early progress of the fifteen-year-old innkeeper's son with meagre capital resources is largely unrecorded – surviving letters are few – but the Datini archive reveals that by 1361 he was in partnership with two other Tuscans and their trading profits were such that two years later they were able to invest more than 1,200 florins in another shop. The partnership was renewed in 1367, with each contributing 2,500 florins to the business. Now they owned three shops, all providing a handsome return on the investment, which encouraged Francesco to set up yet another trading partnership with a joint investment of 800 florins which – over a period of eight years – brought him and his partner no less than 10,000 florins.

Arms and armour were a mainstay of trade during the early years of the Datini business career – with no qualms about supplying both sides in a conflict, and an astute eye for the advantageous turn of events: when a round of hostilities in Liguria ended in 1382, Francesco promptly instructed his agent in Genoa to buy up all the military equipment he could lay hands on. 'For, when peace is made, they are wont to sell all their armour,' and Francesco knew that sooner or later they, or some other party, would need it again. Sentiment had no place in Francesco's business dealings. As the Datini network expanded, branch offices were opened in Barcelona and Valencia, Florence, Pisa, and finally in Majorca and Ibiza, all managed by resident partners, but all controlled by Francesco's enquiring eye and indefatigable pen.

Despite the difficulties and limitations of transport in the fourteenth century, communications were remarkably fast and reliable. The Venetian Republic, for example, maintained a postal service between Venice and Bruges which took just seven days to deliver a package from door to door. Small companies entrusted their mail to the post-bags of large companies, or used the services of professional couriers who were to be found in every trading city, ready to set off in any direction.[14] The Datini offices in Barcelona and Valencia exchanged letters with the Majorcan branches and agents in other Spanish cities on an almost daily basis, and there was also frequent correspondence with Paris, London and Bruges, Nice, Lisbon, Rhodes, Alexandria, Tunis and Fez. There were letters written in Latin, French and Italian, in English, Flemish, Catalonian, Provençal, Greek – and even a few in Arabic and Hebrew.

As Iris Origo notes, whenever the letters reported on matters other than business, such as a battle or a truce, a rumour of plague, famine or flood, it was always with a view to the likely effect on trade. When Tuscany was invaded just before the harvest, and it was certain that famine must ensue, Tuscan traders did not concern themselves with the likely outcome but swiftly began buying up Genoese wheat. When peace was signed, letters conveying the good news did not so much rejoice at deliverance from what would have been a ruthless rule so much as they cheered the fact that 'God be thanked, journeying will be safe again.' Likewise, when the Hundred Years War was interrupted by a three-year truce, Datini's agents in Bruges were quick to report: 'Now many English merchants will tarry here, and we shall trade more with them.' The truce did not hold, though. Hostilities broke out again two years later with a calamitous effect on trade. 'The fair here took place on the seventh, but never was there so sad a one; and all for the default of the English, who ever spend most at this fair and who may not journey here, because of their war with the French.'[15]

The efficiency with which the Datini companies handled the complexities of their trading operations – checked over by Francesco himself at every stage – is little short of staggering when compared to modern procedures that entrust the detail of sales and purchases to automated systems. Francesco and his partners lacked even the convenience of a ballpoint pen – let alone the typewriter and the telephone – but nonetheless recorded every detail of every transaction and kept such complete accounts of money spent and received that – for instance – a profit of 8.92 per cent could be reported on a venture which bought twenty-nine sacks of wool in Majorca, sold half to a client in Florence, spun and wove the remainder into six cloths (of about 33 metres each) in Prato, which were sold in Valencia, Barbary and Palma. From ordering the wool to final sale the operation spanned three and a half years. Every item of expenditure relating to this single venture was independently recorded, from the purchase of the raw wool, to the shipping and insurance costs, mule transport, taxes, tolls and duties, wages for the ninety-six women who picked, washed, combed, carded and spun the wool, and payments to the specialist weavers, fullers, dyers and finishers who prepared it for sale. And this was just one venture among dozens that were proceeding simultaneously.

Often, more than one Datini company was involved in the transaction – though each was an independent enterprise, charging interest and commission on all their dealings. Iris Origo cites an instance in which cloth from the Datini company in Prato was consigned to the company in Florence for sale in Venice. Instead of selling it, however, the Venetian agents took it upon themselves to exchange the cloth for pearls (108 strings of 74 pearls each) which were then sent (appropriately insured) to the Datini company in Valencia for sale to a customer in Catalonia. When the sale was completed the company in Florence credited the sum due to its counterpart in Prato. Thus three of Francesco's companies and an agent in Venice were involved in a single transaction, each taking their commission as goods flowed in one direction and proceeds in the other.[16]

The motive behind all this activity was of course the prospect of money to be made at every stage, which then became available to individuals for spending howsoever they wished. But if the transport and conversion of wool shorn in Majorca to cloth woven in Prato and sold in Valencia and elsewhere was challenging, the movement of hard cash in the opposite direction was close to impossible. Weight alone, never mind security and tricky matters of currency values, ruled against it. Hence the bills of exchange, and cheques as we know them today. Francesco has been credited with the invention of this vital device – his statue in Prato's main square shows him with a sheaf of such bills in his hand. Wider investigations have discounted this claim, but the Datini archive certainly confirms that he made extensive use of these convenient alternatives to actual money – there are more than five thousand of them among his papers. A typical example reads:

> In the name of God, the 12th of February 1399 Pay at usance [the time allowed for payment, usually twenty days], by this first of exchange, to Giovanni Asopardo £306 13s 4d. *Barcelonesi,* which are for 400 florins received here from Bartolomeo Garzoni, at 15s 4d. per florin. Pay and charge to our account there and reply. God keep you. Francesco and Andrea, greetings from Genoa. Accepted March 13.[17]

For a man inclined to suspect the worst of people, the operation of international businesses that obliged him to entrust so much wealth and responsibility to others called for an unflagging attention to detail. The fourteenth-century businessman with interests abroad faced the same basic problem as his modern counterparts – he had to find competent, trustworthy staff and keep them motivated enough to stay in his employ – but regulatory measures were far less rigorous. Embezzlement and costly mistakes were a constant risk and evidence of the consequences was hard to miss: 350 large companies failed in Florence alone during the thirteen years immediately prior to Francesco's merchant apprenticeship in the city.[18] But help was at hand for managers on the lookout for deceitful, erring or undermotivated personnel – an ingenious accounting procedure which Goethe placed 'among the finest inventions of the human mind':[19] double-entry bookkeeping – the practice of entering every transaction twice, in both the credit and the debit columns of the ledger, thus creating a record of assets and liabilities which should always balance and would reveal some error or impropriety if it did not.

Previously, entries had been made transaction by transaction in a single column, in paragraphs giving the details of customer, sales and purchases with credits appearing below the related debits; in the new system, accounts were opened for each customer, with debits and credits entered in opposing columns either on the same page or on opposite pages of the ledger.[20]

In sympathy with the sentiment Goethe had expressed, double-entry bookkeeping has been described[21] as a response to the needs of burgeoning capitalism as business became increasingly complex in the early medieval period, and the need for a sound and efficient system of bookkeeping became apparent. A treatise on the subject published in 1494[22] indicates that Venetians had been using a system of this sort for over 200 years,[23] and some authorities have argued that it was double-entry bookkeeping which gave Italian merchants a head start in the early stages of Europe's economic development – the theory being that the system allowed them to delegate more authority and make larger deals, further afield and with less risk than their northern counterparts, whose ventures were restricted by the limitations and opacity of the old single-entry system.[24]

This traditional view of double-entry as a prerequisite for the growth of capitalism and the administration of distant agencies has been discounted,[25] but it is worth noting that after operating a kind of 'halfway-house' bilateral system for a number of years, Francesco di Marco Datini converted first his main office to a double-entry system in 1386, and then all branches – Florence, Prato, Genoa, Avignon, Barcelona, Valencia and Majorca – during the 1390s. Along with the introduction of double-entry bookkeeping, managers were expected to send a copy of their balance sheets to Francesco on a regular basis, many of which are preserved in the Datini archive. The books balanced, and analysis of the entries has shown 'beyond any doubt that the books were kept according to the most exacting standards of double entry.'[26]

It is impossible to know whether or not double-entry bookkeeping alone actually contributed to the overall success of the Datini enterprises, but there can be little doubt that the system made it easier for Francesco to monitor and assess the performance of his managers in distant offices.

Towards the end of 1382, after thirty-three years in Avignon, Francesco decided to move his household and main office back to his home city – Prato – while leaving his Avignon business in the care of two partners who had been working with him for several years. The deed of partnership drawn up between them stated that while the capital of 3,866 florins remained Francesco's, the partners may trade with it 'as they think best', with half the profits going to Francesco and the partners sharing the rest. The Datini household goods were packed and dispatched by ship via Arles and Pisa, while Francesco, Margherita and their servants rode across the Alps – a party of eleven in all. They travelled in the depth of winter, and the journey took just over a month – two weeks crossing the Alps to Milan, where they rested for a week, then ten days by way of Cremona to Prato, where they arrived on 10 January 1383.[27]

An experienced and widely respected merchant, astute, wealthy – and without an heir – Francesco was now forty-seven years old, a good age in a century which had seen so many in Europe die of plague or from the ill-effects of civil unrest and famine. In the spring of 1386 he made Florence the hub of his operations. Thereafter, if he did not exactly commute between his home in Prato and his office in Florence (a distance of only 20 km), he adopted a lifestyle that maintained his dominant influence in both places. He wrote letters to Margherita almost daily – loving or chiding by times; occasionally irascible, frequently demanding: 'Remember to wash the mule's feet with hot water, down to her hoofs, and have her well-fed and cared for . . . and speed the sale of the two barrels of wine in Belli's cellar . . . Remember, as you lie abed in the mornings . . . to send to the mill the sack of grain that was left over . . . and remember to water the orange-trees . . . and remember to keep the kitchen windows shut, so that the flour does not get hot . . .'[28]

Margherita complained of being treated 'as an inn-keeper's wife!' but she unfailingly attended to Francesco's needs, laundering the clothes and linen he sent back to Prato, and keeping him supplied with food from the Prato farm and gardens. They were a good team. Oil and wine, flour, eggs, vegetables, fruit, poultry and meat; even the bread was baked in Prato and sent to Florence by mule-back – sometimes thirty loaves at a time – and Margherita herself would make special treats occasionally, and send them carefully packed so that they would not spoil on the road.

Business, though, continued to occupy the greater part of Francesco's attention – even in his twilight years, as he thought more and more about exactly how the profits he had received as the gift of God could be returned without exposing them to the avarice of men. For God and for Profit: Francesco's maxim, and the two motives of human endeavour which did most to formulate the history and urban network of Europe. Either the Church or commerce was responsible for the growth of every great city during the medieval period; often they coexisted, but neither could assume that the presence of the other would further its interests. Mutual support was often short-lived and when discord arose, commerce was the more rigorous arbiter. An aspect of Francesco's career makes the point. He had gone to Avignon in 1350, seeking a share of

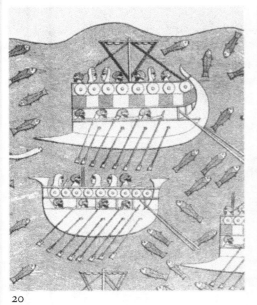

20

21

The Mediterranean spawned and sustained empires. An early mosaic (20) applauds the achievements of Phoenician fishing and naval vessels. At the height of their power, both classical Athens (22) and Rome (21) were crucially dependent on resources shipped in from abroad.

22

23

Rome could not have survived without the grain produced on estates in Africa following its conquest of Carthage in 146BC, and Egypt in 30BC. The seasonal round is shown in mosaics from villas in Tunisia (23 & 24). The amphitheatre at El Djem in central Tunisia (25) is almost as big as Rome's Colosseum.

24

25

26

27

28

A substantial merchant fleet kept Rome supplied with produce from across the Mediterranean (26). Barges (27) ferried produce from a Tiber estuary harbour to the city docks (28). With the fall of its empire, Rome foundered and had become a city of picturesque ruins (29) by the 18th century.

29

Marco Polo leaves Constantinople on his epic journey to China (30). The Chinese had an idealised concept of the city, exemplified by Beijing's Forbidden City (31) but quite different from the surroundings (34). Similarly, Marco Polo's map of Hangchow (32) is a good geo-

graphical representation, but a Chinese map of the same period shows the city in idealised form – walled and square (33). The Chinese pictograph (left) denotes a "walled city".

30

31

32

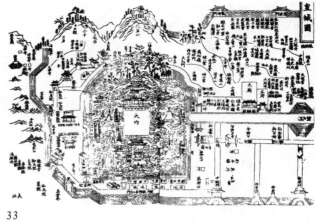

33

34

35

Though a famous 14th century fresco typically depicts Europe's ideal city as sensitively propor-tioned and well-governed (35), the realities of origin were often more basic. Bruges grew from markets held at the castle bridge (36).

36

37

The towers of San Gimignano (37) are
relics of fiercely independent enterprise.
Palma Nova in Mallorca was planned in
1593 with defence in mind (39), and
retained that configuration well into the
20th century (40). Copenhagen housing
estates (38) mimic the cartwheel layout.

38

39

40

41

The 14th century Italian merchant, Francesco di Marco Datini, is credited with having invented the bill of exchange, or cheque. A statue in Prato's main square (42) shows him brandishing a sheaf of such bills. From his palatial residence (41) his trading operations ranged across Europe and around the Mediterranean. Voluminous records of Datini's business and personal life are preserved in present-day Prato.

42

the luxury trade generated by the pope and his court, and left the city in 1382, largely because of political difficulties affecting him personally. Meanwhile, the pope and his court had moved to Rome in 1378. The move deprived Avignon of its luxury trade, which caused some upset but left the core trading assets of the city's location untouched. The Datini business in Avignon remained profitable and flourished under the partners Francesco had left in charge. The luxury trade which Avignon had enjoyed for decades followed the pope to Rome, but the city was nonetheless a 'wilderness among crumbling ruins' in 1450.[29] There was never a Datini company based in Rome.

8

Prince's Capital and Merchants' City

The interaction of economics and politics produced two kinds of cities: one the creation of powerful rulers, while the other grew to meet commercial and social imperatives. Conflict of interest was rife – a catalyst for violence within cities as well as between them. Where despotic rulers prevailed economic development was often curtailed. But for their prevalence the Industrial Revolution might have occurred much earlier.

Francesco di Marco Datini had returned to Prato in 1382 principally because the political situation in Avignon had made it difficult for citizens of Tuscany to continue trading as merchants in the city. In 1386 he moved the hub of his operations from Prato to Florence, and again the decision was politically motivated. But this time he was attracted by the political situation, not repelled, for the city had recently come under the rule of a few powerful families – bankers, merchants and professional men – whose laws and judgements he believed were likely to further the interests of men such as himself.

The strong government which Francesco welcomed had taken control of Florence after the city had suffered half a century of calamitous social and economic upheaval. Plague and famine, the depredations of intermittent warfare and the spectacular collapse of three great Florentine banking houses (which brought down many smaller concerns with them) had progressively heightened the insecurity of the city's wealthy elite – the *popolo grosso* – and deepened the misery of its poor – the *popolo minuto*. There was civil unrest too, as the unquestioning respect for authority which had kept workers at their allotted tasks despite harsh conditions and minimal reward had vanished along with the city's affluence – to be replaced by increasingly strident calls for better conditions of employment. They were bleak times. Employers struggled to maintain viability (and their wealth); workers formed craft associations in the hope of using their numerical superiority as a bargaining chip, though probably investing as much faith in the words of a covertly distributed prophecy which told that one day: 'the worms of the earth will most cruelly devour the lions, leopards and wolves; and the blackbirds and small fowl swallow up the greedy vultures. And at the same time the common and little folk will destroy all tyrants and false traitors . . .'

The worm may turn – one day; meanwhile, the threat of starvation left the workers with little choice but to accept whatever work and wages were on offer. Their simmering discontent frequently erupted into unruly protest and riots but it was not until 1378 that the issue of work and wages finally came to a head in Florence. In that year, a massive and violent uprising – led by the poorest of the poor – presented the city authorities with uncompromising demands for the right to representation, and guaranteed minimum levels of production which would guarantee them a reasonable wage.

The uprising was swiftly subdued. Reprisals were unforgiving, but events had finally persuaded the city leaders that the grievances of the *popolo minuto* must be addressed. Three craft associations were legitimised and became part of a coalition government – 'the most genuinely "democratic" that Florence had ever known' is how Iris Origo describes it in her biography of Francesco di Marco Datini.[1] But although the newly democratised government was more sympathetically disposed to the *popolo minuto,* it was unable to restore the city's prosperity – not least because many wealthy merchants saw the change of government as a threat to trade and profits and responded by closing down their operations in Florence. The coalition struggled on for nearly four years, until 1382, when a counter-revolution put the *popolo grosso* back in power.

And four years after that, Francesco di Marco Datini decided that his business interests would flourish in the political climate created by the small reactionary oligarchy which was to govern Florence for the next forty-two years.

The evidence Iris Origo has drawn from the Datini archive reveals that Francesco took no interest in politics and government except insofar as they affected his business. In an earlier age, when the citizens of Florence were also its part-time soldiers, he might have found himself expected to bear arms on the city's behalf, but since its battles were now fought by foreign mercenaries, taxes and compulsory loans were all he was obliged to contribute towards the defence and civic expenditure of Florence. Of course, then as ever, taxes and loan levies were an irritation. But although every merchant no doubt believed he could manage the city's finances and taxes more advantageously than the current incumbents, only a select few ever acquired the high status that gave them a chance to do so. Most were disdainful of politics and public office. Indeed, the less important government posts were so hard to fill that names were drawn by lot, and large fines imposed upon those who dared to refuse the appointment. It seems that Francesco was never called upon. He was chief member of the council of magistrates in Prato for a time, it is true, but in Florence – the controlling base of his business operations – he remained completely aloof from government and politics at all levels.

Francesco's relationship with Florence – and with every other city in which he operated – was motivated by the extent to which he was left free to run his business and make a profit. As with most successful trading endeavours, pragmatism determined in which cities he would establish a base of operations. For their part, the cities, as providers of the location and security that made trading possible, regarded the merchants as a source of revenue to be drawn upon as required – in the form of taxes and compulsory loans. In 1401, for instance, when Tuscany was threatened with invasion by its neighbours and the German emperor had agreed to provide a defensive force, Florence turned to its merchant citizens for the emperor's fee of 500,000 florins. To raise this enormous sum, fifteen compulsory loans were levied in 1401 alone – in addition to the taxes imposed in previous years. 'Bethink you how merry I am,' Francesco wrote to a friend, 'forasmuch as since I became a citizen I have paid 6,000 florins in six years, and now [the taxes] are doubled . . . I have reached such a point that methinks, if a man stabbed me, no blood would issue forth!'[2]

In time-honoured fashion, Francesco did whatever he could to avoid giving the city all that it demanded by way of loans and taxes. And it seems he did not mind if avoidance occasionally strayed beyond what was legally permissible into the illegality of deliberate evasion. For instance, he lingered in Bologna while one round of taxes was being assessed, thus evading the call to submit account books to the revenue officials in person and discuss the full extent of his taxable wealth with them. Francesco's notary undertook to negotiate the assessment on his behalf, writing that he would be 'saying and unsaying, promising and vowing and preaching, and living in Hell, a devil among devils'. Suspending honesty in favour of a client's financial interests, the notary drafted a letter stating that Francesco's foreign business was so unprofitable that he was thinking of withdrawing from Avignon and Catalonia, and that all his moveable property was worth less than 2,500 florins. But then, owning a palatial residence and more than twenty smaller houses rather contradicted these pleas of impoverishment. A levy of 775 florins was imposed, and another 106 florins were demanded the following spring.[3]

It hardly needs to be pointed out that what Datini and his notary were doing in the fourteenth century huge companies such as Enron and their accountants, Andersen, were doing at the beginning of the twenty-first. Both Datini and Enron sought to enhance their financial position by illegal means, with the connivance of notary and accountants respectively. The only difference is the massive scale of the Enron scam compared with Datini's – plus the fact that Enron and Andersen were caught and indicted. Otherwise the morality – or lack of it – is identical and its persistence across seven centuries of cultural and economic experience suggests that the relationship between merchants and cities, between business and government, is inherently combative – even antagonistic. Each needs the other to further its own ends; but their motives are not always compatible.

And cities themselves play a fundamental and contributory role here, for while providing the stage for action and fostering humanity's innate propensity to exploit advantageous opportunities, the sheer size of a city weakens the constraints of proximity that otherwise control wayward behaviour. In small communities, a web of personal interactions and shared views makes it difficult to offend with impunity, whereas the rules and regulations of city life are so impersonal that they virtually invite defiance – especially if the chances of getting away with it seem good. In other words: evading taxes is easier on the conscience than cheating a neighbour. Indeed, entire communities will acquiesce in – if not actually condone – the behaviour of people who succeed in getting the better of any large faceless organisation, while at the same time vilifying the person who abuses a minor aspect of neighbourly trust.

Since earliest times, some form of local pressure has served to keep social behaviour under control in small communities. In England the frankpledge,[4] by which men were compulsorily organised into groups of ten neighbours and obliged to stand surety for each other, has a history dating back to King Alfred's reign (871–99) at least and was still widespread in the thirteenth century. The essence of the frankpledge was that if any one member of the group broke the law, the other nine would be jointly responsible for bringing him to court. Similar systems doubtless existed everywhere, but their efficacy was steadily eroded by the growth of cities, where for centuries trade had been presenting the nefariously inclined with a multitude of opportunities for gaining an unfair advantage over their fellow citizens under the cloak of anonymity. Here is the nub of city government. When regulation by consensus no longer works, how does a community ensure fair play?

The phrase 'horse-trading' doubtless acquired its pejorative connotation many, many years ago – perhaps even before cities existed, and from ancient Mesopotamia to modern Houston (home of Enron) the historical record is littered with instances of unscrupulous dealings and society's efforts to uncover, control and punish the perpetrators. A few examples: there was a 'rule' in ancient Greece declaring that an unfamiliar person buying up the best fish was liable to arrest and even immediate execution if unable to prove the money being spent had been honestly earned;[5] in Roman times, jurists were much exercised by consignments of wine which had tasted good at the vineyard but were more like vinegar at the point of delivery;[6] in pre-Columbian Mexico, the criminally inclined had ingenious ways of counterfeiting the cacao beans used as a form of money by the Aztecs;[7] and in medieval London, the reputation of wholesale spice merchants became so debased by some who bulked up the product with less expensive substances that in 1393 an ordinance was issued decreeing that every batch had to be checked and cleared by an official 'garbler' before sale. One merchant found guilty of contravention was put in the pillory and had the offending product burnt under him; another paid a fine of £50 – the equivalent of more than £85,000 today.[8]

The 1393 ordinance under which this unhappy merchant was tried and punished had been drawn up by the London Guild of Grocers, following a pattern of developments in trade which was first documented in the twelfth century and became commonplace throughout Europe by the fourteenth and fifteenth centuries: the guilds. Thus, via the guilds, it was economics that established the ground rules for city government. Princes and prelates of despotic tendency probably would have preferred to retain control of every aspect of life in their spheres of influence, but their dependency upon the cities for manufactured goods (especially weapons), banking facilities and much else besides left them no choice but to negotiate arrangements of mutual accord with the city guilds and authorities.[9] London, for instance, had guilds before even the city itself was granted a charter by William I in 1067.[10] Paris had 101 guilds in 1260; in Nuremberg, the metalworkers alone had already divided into several dozen independent craft and trade guilds by the end of the thirteenth century.[11]

A similar proliferation of guilds occurred in cities across Europe as merchant trade expanded and the division of labour created more groups of like-minded individuals anxious to preserve the integrity and exclusivity of their livelihoods. Venice had 130 guilds in the seventeenth century; Rome had at least seventy-five;[12] Florence had a similar number, though nearby Prato had just fifteen guilds during Francesco di Marco Datini's lifetime – judges and notaries, money-changers and goldsmiths, doctors and apothecaries, wool-merchants, wool-workers, grocers, blacksmiths, cobblers, butchers, vintners, tailors, bakers, millers, barbers and carpenters.

In Prato, as elsewhere, the influence of the guilds was all-pervasive. On reaching adulthood, every man who could afford the fee enrolled himself in an appropriate guild, swearing to obey its laws and stand by his fellow members. Only via the guilds could a man hope either to make his fortune or participate in running the city. Indeed, to be a citizen a man had to belong to a guild.[13]

The purpose of the guilds had been to bring together the members of a single trade, whose interests they defended collectively. Their attention was concentrated especially on activities in the city markets where, naturally enough, every trader wished to gain and retain a fair share of the available business. Devious practices were banned. Fourteenth-century Exeter, for instance, waged a continuous battle against 'forestallers', who intercepted goods before they reached the city and sold them in the market at a higher price; and 'regrators', who bought up large quantities of goods available in the market early in the day and resold them later when shortages had driven the prices up.[14] Attempts to control these quite common practices met with limited success however, mainly because the profits to be made on them far exceeded the cost of being charged and fined; indeed, the same names appear repeatedly in the court records – which suggests that offenders regarded the fines they paid as more of a tax on their activities than a deterrent.

And inevitably, while the guilds struggled to maintain good standards of honesty among their own members, the greedy tendencies they had been formed to control eventually began to erupt between the guilds themselves. Some guilds – and their members – became more powerful than others; especially in the broader arena of city government.

From its beginnings, the guild movement had soon evolved into a hierarchy of social standing and influence. The richest, oldest and most prestigious were the merchant guilds, such as Francesco di Marco Datini belonged to. Collectively, they specialised in the long-distance whole-sale trade; the Guild of Grocers (whose name refers simply to merchants who dealt in gross lots), best exemplifies the nature of their business: with large amounts of capital at their disposal, they bought and sold whatever they could reckon to make a profit from. Next came the guilds of the local tradesmen, retailers – the bakers, butchers, coopers, wagoners and shopkeepers – who bought their supplies from the grocers. And finally there were the craft guilds – the weavers, dyers, blacksmiths, saddlers, carpenters, painters, potters, tailors and so forth.

Given the huge disparity in the value attached to a man's labour and the value of imported merchandise – in Datini's time, for instance, an artist was paid one florin a day, while the same florin would buy only a single ounce of the pigments he worked with; and receipts in the Datini archive show that Francesco himself once paid a tailor just one florin to make a gown from silks and velvets that had cost more than a hundred florins[15] – it is hardly surprising that the merchant guilds should have steadily accumulated greater power, as well as greater wealth, than the guilds who worked with their labour and manual skills rather than with financial capital. Exeter is a case in point.

There was a merchant guild in Exeter by the twelfth century, ruling that only its members could trade in the city and its immediate environs. Furthermore, reciprocal arrangements rendered Exeter's merchants exempt from tolls and custom duties throughout England and Normandy. During the thirteenth century, as Exeter became the foremost commercial centre in south-west England, the functions of the merchant guild and the city's expanding administration effectively merged into a single civic institution – with merchants steadily gaining control. The office of mayor was introduced in 1205, and before long the merchant guild's control of trade and city government was being exercised through what was called the 'freedom' of the city.[16]

Soon the circle was closed. The freedom of the city became a self-serving institution, controlled by merchant guild members, for merchant guild members. Only those who had been admitted to the freedom of the city could stand for civic office, and those civic officers in turn decreed that only persons with the freedom of the city should enjoy the privileges at its disposal: trading monopolies, tax and custom duty exemptions, contracts to provide city services, first call on city properties for sale, and even lenient treatment in the courts. Thus the mercantile elite gained control of the city's political affairs as well as its economic activity. No wonder, as Maryanne Kowaleski shows in her study of trade in medieval Exeter, there was a 'high correlation between political office, wealth and commercial privilege . . . more often than not, political power, economic privilege and personal wealth went hand-in-hand in late fourteenth-century Exeter'.[17]

Exeter was the centre of England's fastest growing regional economy in the fourteenth and fifteenth centuries. No other provincial city in England grew so fast – with its population rising from a mere 3,100 in 1377 to 7,000 in the 1520s[18] – but if the size and number of a country's large cities are taken as the measure of economic and urban development, it is clear that differences were emerging among the trading nations of Europe. England had four cities with populations of more than 10,000 in the early 1500s, the Netherlands had twelve and France had thirteen; Italy, however, had no fewer than twenty-nine such major cities at that time and by the early 1700s that number had increased to forty-five – while the combined number of major cities in the Netherlands, England and France actually had declined to twenty-two. Thus, even though London, Paris and Amsterdam had grown into very large cities by then (with populations of 575,000, 510,000 and 200,000 respectively), Italy was by far the most widely urbanised country in Europe[19] – with a greater preponderance of the largest, richest and most splendid cities.

The French essayist Michel de Montaigne had noticed the trend on a tour through Italy in 1580–81, when he visited most of the grand cities of Italy's north and central regions, and wrote of their large populations and numerous very wealthy citizens (in contrast to those of his home country).[20] Wealth and conspicuous consumption were a feature of the Italian cities, with architects defending (naturally enough) the morality of lavishly expensive buildings, and merchants occasionally feeling obliged to offer some justification for their extravagance: 'I think I have done myself more honour by having spent money well than by having earned it,' the Florentine merchant Giovanni Rucellai explained, 'Spending gave me deeper satisfaction, especially in the money I spent on my house in Florence.' And Michelangelo held similar views, once remarking that 'A noble house in the city brings considerable honour, being more visible than all one's possessions.'[21]

Honour, social visibility and possessions were central themes of urban and political development in Italy during the fifteenth and sixteenth centuries. As exemplified by events in Florence (see pages 108–9), the *popolo grosso* were in the ascendancy; the elite guilds were becoming increasingly exclusive, protectionist and conservative – and more concerned with social and political status than with the grubby business of making money. Indeed, many top-ranking guilds lost their economic functions completely. In his book on the social history of early modern Italy, Christopher Black writes of 'the aristocratising top families' of Perugia, for instance, amongst whom membership of the merchant and banking guilds was granted only to those deemed suitably noble – a status which clearly had more to do with the city's social and political affairs than with its commerce and banking activities.[22]

Broadly speaking, families deemed suitably noble were those which owned sufficient property to support themselves from its revenue alone. They included titled landowners with country estates – princes, counts and dukes – but many were city-based families which had originally acquired their wealth from commerce or banking. But money was not an automatic passport to noble status – and certainly not new money. In Milan, for instance, anyone directly or indirectly involved in commerce was expressly barred:

> One must consider . . . only those who derive their origin from an ancient family and one of ancient nobility; a family is considered ancient if it is over a hundred years (both of nobility and residence in Milan), and if furthermore it has abstained from trading, from business, and from sordid profits of all kinds, whether exercised personally or through intermediaries . . .[23]

Thus, aristocratic government was formally established in the major cities of northern Italy – Venice, Genoa, Florence, Milan and so forth – privileged, powerful and controlled by a wealthy minority. Notably, Venice adopted the practice of listing precisely which families were eligible to provide members of its governing Grand Council. The city's famous Golden Book was opened in 1297, and is remarkable for the continuity it reveals: the same family names appear again and again through the centuries. In fact, hardly any fresh blood was admitted for nearly 400 years, until 1646, when the Council decided to admit a broader spectrum of the community to the list. The decision was not willingly taken, but rather forced upon the Council by a lack of candidates from the noble families.

The plight of Venice in 1646, when entry qualifications for the Golden Book were eased, highlights a fundamental problem of hereditary aristocratic rule: time takes its toll of the available talent. Not every family produced a legitimate male heir. The plague eliminated entire family lines. Some individuals disqualified their families by marrying beneath their standing or entering ignoble professions, and the pool was further drained when members of eligible families emigrated or chose to spend long periods abroad. Consequently, a city's privilege and power was inherited – generation by generation – by a diminishing number of families and individuals. Genoa, for instance, had 289 noble families in 1621, but only 127 in 1797. In Venice, the total of about 2,500 nobles eligible for the Grand Council in the mid sixteenth century had shrunk to 1,660 a hundred years later, when the Golden Book was opened to replenish the stock.[24] In Florence, the *benefiziati* numbered 3,000 or more in the fifteenth century, but only 800–1,000 in the eighteenth century, so that when the Habsburg-Lorraines became grand-dukes of Tuscany in 1737 (following the demise of the Medici family), they were obliged to create new nobles.[25]

The social historian Fernand Braudel asks if there is not 'an insidious law' at work here, constantly ensuring that as regions and cities grow more populous, and economies more prosperous, those enjoying privilege and prosperity will always be disproportionately few in number, whatever the society and whatever the period. As an example, he quotes from a letter written by a resident of Sienna in 1531:

> In every republic, even a great one, in every State, even a popular one, it is unusual for more than fifty citizens to rise to the posts of command. Neither in ancient Athens nor in Rome, neither in Venice nor in Lucca, are any citizens called to govern the State, although these States govern themselves under the name of republic.[26]

Whether or not there is an insidious socio-economic law ensuring that a privileged few will enjoy the greater part of a community's power and prosperity, there is certainly a socio-biological principle ensuring that within any such exclusive and privileged community there will be competition – competition for enhanced hierarchical status, for a greater share of the available material resources and even for the preservation of an unsullied breeding stock. Shakespeare's romantic tragedy *Romeo and Juliet* dramatises the point. The Capulets and Montagues of Verona may be theatrical invention, but vendettas and feuding families were a common enough feature of Renaissance Italy to give the play a sound basis of historical fact. Indeed, the prevalence of blood-feuds and vendettas in Italian cities had been remarked upon in the eleventh century by chroniclers of Milan, who observed that when citizens of that powerful but representative city '. . . lack external adversaries [they] turn their hatred against each other'.[27] By Francesco di Marco Datini's day, vengeance by bloodshed was considered not only a sacred duty but also a source of pleasure – Francesco's contemporary, Paolo da Certaldo, listing the five main griefs and pleasures of life in his *Book of Good Manners,* wrote: 'The first grief is to receive injury; the first pleasure, to wreak vengeance.'[28]

Given that when obliged to choose between just and effective government there was a strong inclination to be effective rather than just, the virtually institutionalised prevalence of violence in Italian society during the Renaissance period is perhaps not surprising. Some scholars have described it as an unavoidable consequence of coercive government – the only means by which political change could be achieved. Politics made no sense without violence, writes the social historian Lauro Martines as he arrives at what he calls 'the surprising conclusion that violence had the potential for being a constructive force in politics'.[29]

In the nineteenth century, Jacob Burckhardt took a more psychological view, pre-empting Nietzsche's reverence for strength as he wrote of the 'unbridled egoism' of the Italian individualist that goaded every passion towards violence. 'There is violence which cannot control itself because it is born of weakness,' he wrote, 'but in Italy what we find is the corruption of powerful natures. Sometimes this corruption assumes a colossal shape, and crime seems to acquire almost a personal existence of its own.'[30]

In his book on the social history of early modern Italy published in 2001, Christopher Black stresses the significance of geography as a contributing factor in the prevalence of violence. The high density of many Italian cities – on hilltops, or climbing up the cliffside as in Genoa – made keeping order within cities very difficult, he suggests, while the ruggedness and remoteness of much terrain provided retreats and bases for fugitives and again put the forces of law and order at a considerable disadvantage. In fact, the countryside was infested with bandits, he writes, many of whom were available for hire as participants in the blood-feuds and vendettas of leading families. In some instances, powerful local figures from among the nobility and merchant fraternities actually went so far as to support the activities of bandits who made a practice of attacking mule-trains on the trade routes. Thus banditry was connected with both feuding and commerce, lawful and unlawful.[31]

Another historian, David Herlihy, has looked among the social attitudes and age structure of city populations[32] for the roots of what Renaissance Italians themselves called 'the *furori* and the *rumori* of the Tuscan city – the violent temperaments of many of its citizens and the frequent disruptions of its social peace through riots and factional battles'. He found a clue in the vastly differents ages at which men and women married. The sons of wealthy families often did not marry until in their thirties, for instance, while the daughters married very young; many before they were fifteen and nearly 85 per cent by the age of twenty. Girls who lacked an adequate dowry or were physically unattractive (in either case they had slight hope of finding a husband) were hastily packed off to a convent. All of which skewed the sex ratio, leaving the cities with an excess of unattached and wealthy young males with lots of time on their hands.

Among the wealthiest families of Florence in 1427, unmarried young men aged between fifteen and thirty constituted more than 50 per cent of adult males. With urban society flooded with large numbers of such young men, unable or unwilling to marry for two decades after puberty, free from household responsibilities but responsive to fierce family affiliations (and poorly restrained by the much older and rapidly thinning generation of their own fathers), heightened levels of tension among them were to be expected and there can be little wonder that it so often found release in the perpetration of violent deeds, writes Herlihy.[33]

The cities, then, were veritable stews of conflicting interest – with feuding families and antagonistic factions living cheek-by-jowl in what James E. Vance Jr has described as a 'state of bristling accommodation'.[34] Animosity among elite families was constantly on the point of eruption, merchants were competing for power as well as wealth, and the *popolo minuto* resorted to violence and rioting when the exploitations of the *popolo grosso* became too much to bear. Thus the cities became clusters of self-serving minorities, obliged to associate and interact in order for the city to function as a viable administrative and economic entity, but otherwise jealously preserving their independence – in a manner which gave Italian Renaissance cities a unique form and identity.

The most powerful families established enclaves within the city, consisting of houses or palaces for the senior branches of the family (where perhaps as many as fifty close relatives lived together), with more distant and poorer relatives living on adjacent streets. The enclave might be a group of connected buildings along a street or it could surround a square, but whatever the form it ideally included everything the family required to sustain its independent existence – living accommodation of course, but also shops and warehouses, common bathing facilities, a church or chapel, gardens and possibly even a market for the exclusive use of the family and retainers. Such enclaves were powerful and defensible social units, based on wealthy and established family lines, supporting – and supported by – dependants ranging from lesser family members to skilled artisans, shopkeepers and retainers.[35]

That the enclaves should be defensible – more from potential enemies within the city than from without – encouraged the wealthier families to construct fortified buildings, with strategically sited towers into which the vulnerable could retreat when danger threatened, and from which potential attackers could be seen in advance and a suitable reception prepared. Most cities in upper Italy 'bristled with towers', Vance reports, quoting a twelfth-century traveller who described Pisa as 'a very great city, with about 10,000 turreted houses for battles at times of strife'.[36] Ten thousand was probably an exaggeration, but towers still stand in Pisa (one leaning) and elsewhere as testimony to the enclaves and factional nature of city layout at the time – in Florence, Bologna, Mantua and Verona to name but a few. The most impressive surviving example is probably San Gimignano, 56 km south of Florence, where fourteen tall towers dominate the beautiful skyline view of the city. San Gimignano, with a population of about 7,000, is today more of a town than a city, but in its heyday, enriched by a strategic position on important trading and pilgrim routes and its exclusive control of the saffron harvested in the nearby Valle d'Elsa, it had a population of 13,000 or more and the aristocratic families who controlled the city built seventy-two tower-houses – some up to 50 m high.[37]

But there came a time when there were more than enough fortifications to preserve the integrity of the jealously independent enclaves, when an era of political stability consigned the feuds and vendettas of jealous families to the background of civic relationships; then a rigid social formality took control, and the families' smouldering differences were expressed not so much in outbursts of violence as in the ostentatious display of wealth. Thus, as the need for physical protection declined, the tower and associated buildings were redesigned to become more opulent (though still forbidding enough to deter any who might wish to harm the family and its retinue). It was at this stage that the Renaissance palace was born, James E. Vance Jr declares, preserving the large modular size of the family enclave with its accommodation for numerous retainers, but becoming more gracious in its apartments and more carefully conceived as an architectural creation. 'The *palazzi* of Florence clearly demonstrate this transformation,' says Vance, 'combining a rather formidable grace with the reminder of ancient and arbitrary power present in the tall tower'.[38]

Meanwhile though, the economy was faltering. While elite families, the Church and city authorities were spending fortunes on the exquisite buildings, paintings and sculpture for which Renaissance Italy is justly renowned, the axis of commerce which had brought the region such magnitudes of wealth was shifting. The cities of northern Europe were in the ascendant – Amsterdam, London and Paris foremost among them. Florence and Milan, Venice and Genoa, lost their supremacy in many markets – such as the international trade in pepper and other spices, in shipbuilding and capital investment – as the cities of northern Europe grew and expanded their economic influence. Dutch and English merchants arrived in the Mediterranean with grain from the Baltic when Italy's harvests failed and thereafter made profitable use of the contacts they had established in the region.

The English in particular took over the shipping of goods in and out of Italy, especially via the port of Livorno, but Italian exports of manufactured goods, such as woollen textiles and metal goods, declined as manufacturers lost their customers to cheaper Dutch and English products. At the same time, merchants shipping in counterfeit goods undermined the market for high-quality Italian cloth, glass and soap. The French attempted to deceive the world with imitation Venetian glass when their efforts to bribe or cajole Venetian glass-blowers to emigrate failed.[39]

The cities which Michel de Montaigne had praised for their wealth and vitality in the late sixteenth century drew less complimentary remarks from the Grand Tour travellers of the eighteenth century. Rome, Venice and Florence were still pleasant cities to visit, but Italy by then no longer qualified as a dynamic urban manufacturing economy.[40] In considerable measure this eclipse of the Italian city as the urban leader in Europe stemmed from its internalised conflicts, James E. Vance Jr declares, likening the effect to that of 'an internal cancer that saps the body's basic vitality'. Thus, he says, the despotic popes had beautified Rome in the sixteenth and seventeenth centuries, while their highly undemocratic practices had left it a pathetic shell of a city.[41]

The interplay between economics and politics produced two distinct patterns of city development in Europe during the sixteenth century, a dichotomous process that led to what Vance describes as the 'polar extremes' of the 'Prince's Capital and the Merchants' City'. The former was the creation of powerful elites who wanted the city to be a physical expression of their absolute power. The latter simply grew to meet the needs of commerce, industry and citizens. Rome and London are prime examples of the difference. Popes rebuilt Rome in the style of the classical city that had graced the seven hills in antiquity, recreating a grand urban design of monumental buildings, elegant squares and sweeping vistas. But their Rome was a feeble place economically, constructed and sustained only by the tributes flowing in from its ecclesiastical empire. London, by contrast, became the capital of an economic empire long before there was anything remotely imperial in the design and buildings of the city itself.

But although London served Mammon it had not abandoned Christ. By the thirteenth and fourteenth centuries there were already more churches within the city walls of London than in any other European city, 126 in all – of which sixteen were devoted to St Mary, the mother of Christ – along with several monasteries and convents.[42] Thus the piety of Londoners was never in doubt, and their readiness to support religious institutions was demonstrably apparent, but it was commerce that built and sustained the city. London was never the seat of ecclesiastical power. The symbolic heart of the English Church was the cathedral in Canterbury, a market-town nearly 100 km south-east of the city. Its leader, the Archbishop of Canterbury, directed church affairs from Lambeth Palace, a few kilometres upriver from London, and his influence on the city was limited to the location of its churches and the words emanating from their pulpits.

Royal influence was similarly excluded from the city of London. Even the Tower of London – that symbol of royal authority wherein traitors and others who displeased the monarch were imprisoned (and some executed) – was essentially a defensive bastion built on the city wall by William the Conqueror, not a centre from which royalty could aggressively interfere with the development of the city itself. Indeed, the royal seat was eventually established at the Palace of Westminster, across the Thames from the Archbishop of Canterbury's Lambeth Palace, and monarchs were allowed to enter London only with special permission. Elizabeth I made a well-meaning attempt to limit the growth of London in 1580, with a Proclamation commanding:

> all manner of persons, of what quality soever they be, to desist and forbear from [building any new] house or tenement within three miles of any of the gates of the said city of London . . .[43]

This might have been Britain's first legally established city green belt, but the directive failed, however, simply because commercial interests insisted that buildings associated with the functions and operation of the port should be excluded from the embargo – thus facilitating the expansion of London's commercial enterprise and leading directly to the urban sprawl which the Proclamation had been intended to restrain.

London, neither regally controlled nor ecclesiastically ordained, grew with the wealth that its enterprises generated until the boundaries of Greater London now lie not three but up to twenty miles in every direction from where the city gates had stood in 1580. The Royal Palace of Westminster eventually became the seat of parliament, while the court has moved to Buckingham Palace and the present monarch lives for much of the time in Windsor Castle and sundry other royal properties around the United Kingdom. The City of London remains a discrete entity – both in the abstract sense of its world domination in the financial markets, and in the down-to-earth reality of its geographic location. The city's independence has been rigorously preserved. Even in the twenty-first century, on an occasion celebrating her fifty years of reign, Queen Elizabeth II was obliged to step down from her gilded coach at the site of the old city gates and formally ask the Lord Mayor of London for permission to enter the city – the only British citizen who is required to do so.

As with London, so other cities have prospered and grown in the absence of (or relief from) the rule of princes, popes or bishops. Amsterdam was allowed to flourish as a free commercial centre, while the Dutch monarchy established its permanent residence at The Hague. Paris prospered until the Bourbon kings – aided and abetted by Cardinal Richelieu – imposed their rigorous centralised control. *'L'état, c'est moi'* – the state, that's me, Louis XIV insisted and although his move to rural

Versailles in the seventeenth century relieved Paris of the royal presence, only the revolution of 1798 could free the city and France from the monarchy's stultifying influence on commerce.

Madrid, on the other hand, was founded as a royal capital and although it became the hub of a worldwide political and administrative structure, controlling and taxing a vast network of commercial activity, it was never an important commercial centre. Similarly, in the modern era, Washington DC has the layout and monumental buildings of a city devoted to political machinations, and lacks entirely the vitality (and soaring monuments) that commerce brought to New York. Canberra is the capital of Australia, but enterprise gravitates to Sydney; Brasilia lags behind Rio de Janeiro, and in Africa government determination to make Dodoma the capital of Tanzania and Abuja the capital of Nigeria will remain little more than extravagant political gestures while Dar es Salaam and Lagos continue to dominate the economies of their respective countries.

The 'polar extremes' of the Prince's Capital and the Merchants' City epitomise a recurring theme of political and economic studies – namely the proposition that despotic rule inhibits economic development and thus restrains the growth of cities. The French philosopher Charles-Louis de Secondat Montesquieu, for instance, compared the booming economies of republican Holland and constitutional England with the stagnant economy of France under the absolutist rule of the Bourbons and concluded that:

> Great enterprises in commerce are not found in monarchical, but in republican governments . . . greater certainty as to the possession of property in these states [encourages merchants to] undertake every-thing . . . sure of what they have already acquired, they boldly expose it in order to acquire more . . . A general rule: A nation in slavery labours more to preserve than to acquire; a free nation, more to acquire than to preserve.[44]

Montesquieu was writing in 1748. Adam Smith wrote in similar vein in 1776:

> in all countries where there is tolerable security, every man of common understanding will endeavour to employ whatever stock he can command . . . In those unfortunate countries where men are continually afraid of the violence of their superiors, they frequently

bury and conceal a great part of their stock . . . in case of their being threatened with any of those disasters to which they consider themselves as at all times exposed.[45]

The phenomenon that Montesquieu and Adam Smith were describing can be readily explained: despotic princes (and governments) believed only they could guarantee the prosperity of the realm; maintaining their status was a primary concern and a disproportionate amount of the resources they controlled was spent on dealing with opposition to their absolute rule. They restricted freedom within the realm and waged wars beyond it; they built ostentatious palaces, adopted extravagant lifestyles and paid the bills by taxing their long-suffering subjects to the hilt. Though merchants like Francesco di Marco Datini evaded payment whenever they could, continuous levels of excessive taxation inevitably discouraged commercial enterprise (why bother with a risky venture if the profit would be punitively taxed?), and thus dampened the fires of economic growth.

Where liberal governments were in control, however, they were either led by men of a mercantile middle-class origin (who were far more interested in maintaining the flow of commerce than in stately power and the splendours of the court), or they were beholden to an independent parliament. Either way, liberal governments recognised that prosperity was a consequence of economic vitality, not the guaranteed outcome of absolute rule, and aimed to minimise state intervention and the deleterious effect of taxes on the economy.

In the early 1990s, the economists J. Bradford De Long from the United States National Bureau of Economic Research and Andrei Shleifer from Harvard University added some hard statistical data to the proposition that despotic and absolute rule inhibits economic development, with an analysis of absolutist rule, prosperity and the growth of cities in Europe during the 800 years prior to the Industrial Revolution.[46]

Hitherto, historians had been inclined to celebrate the establishment of princely authority – praising Louis XIV, 'the Sun King', of France, Frederick II, 'the Great', of Prussia, and Ferdinand and Isabella of Spain for creating the core of absolutist states around which the nation-states of the nineteenth century were to form. But the findings of De Long and Shleifer invite a contrary conclusion. They show that from a perspective which values the welfare of citizens, or the long-term growth of the economy, 'The rise of an absolutist government and the establishment of princely authority are events to be mourned . . . not celebrated.'[47]

Taking France under the Bourbons as the classic example of an absolutist regime, and the constitutional governments of England and the Netherlands as their non-absolutist models, De Long and Shleifer plotted changes in the size and growth rates of Europe's major cities against the position of their governments on the absolutist-to-non-absolutist continuum.

By 1800, western Europe had fifty-six cities of more than 40,000 inhabitants, and sixteen with more than 100,000; London and Paris each had populations of more than half a million. But the nodes of commerce and city development had shifted during the preceding centuries, and De Long and Shleifer's analysis showed that the ebb and flow of economic prosperity had been directly related to the form of government. The 'incidence of absolutist rule is significantly and negatively related to urban growth,' they concluded. In other words: where an absolutist regime had a controlling interest in commerce, cities had grown slowly, simply because merchants responded to restrictive practices by moving their centres of operation to regions where trade and commerce flowed more freely (viz. Datini and his move from Avignon). The cities they moved to had grown more quickly as a result.

Overall, where princes ruled, economies faltered; where merchants thrived, cities flourished. So, the persistence of absolute rule in regions like Italy and Spain and its failure to become entrenched in Holland and England were decisive factors in making the Europe of 1800 an urban civilisation focused on the English Channel and the Atlantic rather than on the Mediterranean.

Furthermore, the economists' extrapolations showed that, if all Europe had been under absolutist rule for an additional 150 years, the urban population would have been two million less than it was. Conversely, if all Europe had been free of absolutist rule throughout, it would have had an additional forty cities with 30,000 or more inhabitants and a total urban population of nearly eight million, say De Long and Shleifer, and this level of commerce and urban civilisation could have been enough to set the Industrial Revolution in motion considerably earlier.[48]

9

By What Complicated Wheels

The Industrial Revolution enhanced the positive aspects of city life for some, and intensified its negative effect on others. Industry and manufacture generated immense wealth, but spawned great poverty too. Amidst the fact and fiction of social commentary and Utopian ideals, the self-perpetuating interdependence of rich and poor is starkly obvious.

In 1800 the world was poised on the cusp of the Industrial Revolution and, fortunately for the cities that were to bear the brunt of the forthcoming upheavals – economic, social and cultural – food supply for the growing urban masses was not a problem. Vitally important, of course, but by then so well provided for and conducted by commercial interests that it was virtually an industry itself – the agricultural industry – which got on with the business of feeding the cities and left the manufacturers and civic administrators free to manage their factories and keep the cities working.

More than 5,000 years had passed since the world's first cities had coaxed Mesopotamian farmers away from the simple life of self-sufficiency and into the business of producing surpluses. With plough and irrigation – and not a little enterprise – farmers had discovered how to grow and harvest far more food than they needed to feed themselves. That was the Agricultural Revolution.

Five thousand years. From Agricultural Revolution to Industrial Revolution. Cities had been growing through all that time, in terms of both their total number and the number of people they accommodated. And the remarkable thing is that the farmers kept pace – producing more and more food for more and more cities. Such has been the efficiency of the agricultural industry that only in times of stress have cities felt the pinch. Food supply, while never something that a city could take for granted, has rarely been an issue of urgent concern. But of course it was not an altruistic humanitarian concern to ensure that everyone had enough to eat that drove the process – it was the profit motive. There was money to be made here. Keeping people fed was a business for which there would never be a shortage of customers.

By the time of the Industrial Revolution, the huge quantities of food being produced in the countryside surrounding the cities was perhaps the least remarkable aspect of the food industry. The scale of the purchasing, packing, transporting and distribution network was even more impressive. Getting the food to the cities, fresh, day after day, called for the deployment of manpower and equipment on a military scale. But this was not run by generals and staff officers with well-trained and obedient foot-soldiers to call up at a moment's notice. No, a city's food supply was managed by people keen to see a profit on the ledger at the end of each week, and also keen to ensure that their relationship with suppliers and customers remained good enough to keep them all in business next week – and the week after.

London had a population of over 800,000 by the year 1800. By 1850, the population had more than doubled. In terms of carbohydrates, a city that size needed at least 4 billion calories a day. If, for argument's sake, that were to be consumed in the form of bread alone, the city's daily requirement was over seven million one-kilogram loaves. And beyond all that making the bread entailed – the grain, the millers, the bakers, the ovens and fuel for the fires, the delivery men, their horses and carts – beyond the carbohydrate requirement there were the proteins, fresh fruit and vegetables that people must have to stay healthy. Plus all the beer, gin, whisky and wine they were drinking principally because they enjoyed it.

Keeping the city fed was a huge undertaking – but not one that was centrally controlled, or pre-planned, or growing at a predictable rate. It was growing organically, powered by the economic dynamics of the city itself, regulated by the mechanism of supply and demand, driven by the entrepreneurial instincts of businessmen with an eye on the profit margin. And remember, though steam power was carrying the Industrial Revolution forward, it was manpower, and horsepower, that got most of the work done. Steam trains simplified issues of high-volume transportation – both long distance and local – but there were no lorries to carry produce to and from the railway stations. Porters at Billingsgate rushed about with stacks of fish boxes on their heads (they wore flat-topped wooden hats), at Covent Garden with sacks of potatoes, at Smithfield with sides of beef . . . and so on.

The grain supply of ancient Rome, when the city provided all eligible citizens with free bread, was impressive indeed, but the food supply of London in the 1850s is little short of stupendous. Certainly the anonymous author of a long article in *The Quarterly Review* was lifted to heights of eloquence by the scale and complexities of simply feeding the city:

If, early on a summer morning before the smoke of countless fires has narrowed the horizon of the metropolis, a spectator were to ascend to the top of St Paul's, and take his stand upon the balcony . . . he would see sleeping beneath his feet the greatest camp of men upon which the sun has ever risen . . .

In the space swept by his vision would lie the congregated habitations of two millions and a half of his species – but how vain are figures to convey an idea of so immense a multitude . . . Switzerland, in her thousand valleys, could not muster such an army; and even busy Holland, within her mast-thronged harbours, humming cities, and populous plains, could barely overmatch the close-packed millions within the sound of the great bell at his feet. As the spectator gazed upon this extraordinary prospect, the first stir of the awakening city would gradually steal upon his ear. The rumbling of wheels, the clang of hammers, the clear call of the human voice . . . would proclaim that the mighty city was once more rousing to the labour of the day, and the blue columns of smoke climbing up to heaven that the morning meal was at hand. At such a moment the thought would naturally arise in his mind . . . By what complicated wheels does all the machinery move by which two millions and a half of human beings sit down day by day to their meals . . .? As thus he mused respecting the means by which the supply and demand of so vast a multitude is brought to agree . . . thin lines of steam, sharply marked for the moment as they advanced one after another from the horizon and converged towards him would indicate the arrival of the great commissariat trains, stored with produce . . . Could his eye distinguish in addition the fine threads of that far-spreading web which makes London the most sensitive spot on the earth, he would be enabled to take in at a glance the two agents – steam and electricity – which keep the balance true between the wants and the supply of London.[1]

This paean to the smooth functioning of London goes on to describe the quantities of meat, fish, vegetables, fruit, bread and beer that the city consumed, and the means by which it was brought to the city and distributed. Between December and May, for instance, a fleet of 240 clippers brought 60 million oranges and 15 million lemons to the city from Portugal and the Azores; 200,000 pineapples arrived each year from the Bahamas. Less exotically, 1,200 cattle and 12,000 sheep were slaughtered in the vicinity of Smithfield market each Friday night to provide for Sunday dinners across the city. Fresh herring, cod, sole, haddock, plaice and sundry other fish as available came into Billingsgate market daily, by the ton. Each year 200 million kippers and bloaters were consumed, over a million lobsters and 500 million oysters.

At Greenwich, Chelsea, Battersea, Putney, Brentford and elsewhere, 17,000 acres of market gardens supplied the city with vegetables and fruit, the gardens laid out with such precision that 'the furrows seem finished rather with the pencil than the plough'. Whole acres were covered in glass. Flocks of chickens were deployed to combat insect pests, their feet dressed in socks to prevent them scratching out the crops; toads were bought in at six shillings a dozen to take care of slugs and snails; and 200,000 gherkins were cut in a morning for the pickle-merchants. Each day, wagon-trains transported tons of produce to Covent Garden market and the 'same wagon that in the morning brings a load of cabbages, is seen returning a few hours later filled with manure'. The land was so generously composted and deeply dug that it produced four and sometimes five crops a year.

The review concludes with an attempt 'to convey an adequate impression to the mind of the . . . enormous supplies of food required to victual the capital for a single year'. The figures themselves are impressive enough, but 'let us try', the writer suggests, 'to fill the eye with a prospect that would satisfy the appetite':

If we fix upon Hyde Park as our exhibition ground, and pile together all the barrels of beer consumed in London, they would form a thousand columns not far short of a mile in perpendicular height. Let us imagine ourselves on the top of this tower, and we shall have a look-out worthy of the feast we are about to summon to our feet. Herefrom we might discover the Great North road stretching far away into the length and breadth of the land. Lo! as we look, a mighty herd of oxen, with loud bellowing, are beheld approaching from the north. For miles and miles the mass of horns is conspicuous winding along the road, ten abreast, and even thus the last animal of the herd would be 72 miles away, and the drover goading his shrinking flank considerably beyond Peterborough. On the other side of the park, as the clouds of dust clear away, we see the Great Western road, as far as the eye can reach, thronged with a bleating mass of wool, and the shepherd at the end of the flock (ten abreast) and the dog that is worrying the last sheep are just leaving the environs of Bristol, 121 miles from our beer-built pillar. Along Piccadilly, Regent-street, the Strand, Fleet-street, Cheapside and the eastward Mile-end-road line, for seven-and-a-half miles, street and causeway are thronged with calves, still ten abreast; and in the great parallel thoroughfares of Bayswater-road, Oxford-street, and Holborn, we see nothing for nine long miles but a slowly-pacing, deeply-grunting herd of swine. As we watch this moving mass approaching from all points of the horizon, the air suddenly becomes dark – a black pall seems drawn over the sky – it is a great flock of birds – game, poultry, and wild fowl . . . as they fly wing to wing and tail to beak they form a square whose superficiaries is not much less than the whole enclosed portion of St. James's Park, or 51 acres. No sooner does this huge flight clear away than we behold the park at our feet inundated with hares and rabbits. Feeding 2000 abreast, they extend from the marble arch to the round pond in Kensington Gardens – at least a mile. Let us now pile up all the half-quartern loaves consumed in the metropolis in the year, and we shall find they form a pyramid which measures 200 feet square at its base, and extends into the air a height of 1293 feet, or nearly three times that of St. Paul's. Turning now to the sound of rushing waters, we find that the seven water companies are filling the mains for the day. If they were allowed to flow into the area of the adjacent St. James's Park, they would in the course of the 24 hours flood its entire space with a depth of 30 inches of water, and the whole annual supply would be quite sufficient to submerge the city (one mile square) 90 feet. Of the fish we confess we are able to say nothing: when numbers mount to billions, the calculations become too trying to our patience. We have little doubt, however, that they would be quite sufficient to make the Serpentine one solid mass. Of ham and bacon again, preserved meats, and all the countless comestibles we have taken no account, and in truth they are little more to the great mass than . . . the skimmings of the pot.

From details given in the census of 1851, the author of this evocative piece calculated that an army of not less than half a million people was directly or indirectly employed in feeding the city. And what kept them all working together so efficiently? The author declares:

> The smooth working of this great distributive machine is due to the principle of competitions, which so nicely adjusts all the varying conditions of life, and which, in serving itself, does the best possible service to the community at large, and accomplishes more than the cleverest system of centralization which any individual mind could devise.

London was then the largest city in the world, its web of diversity sustaining the greatest concentration of people ever seen. The machinations of competition, applauded by *The Quarterly Review*, variously enriched, impoverished or simply entrapped the millions whose diverse energies had constructed the web – and a majority view condoned the massive degree of social differentiation that competition had produced among London inhabitants. Some people were very rich, some reasonably well-off, but the majority were either poor, extremely poor or totally destitute.

This was a time of tremendous social upheaval in Britain (and throughout the developing world). The beginnings of the Industrial Revolution had hastened the growth of urban areas and created a new order. Invention and finance were replacing landownership as the mainstay of the nation's economy. While industrial towns sprouted in the Midlands, where coal and iron ore were readily accessible, London flourished as the capital of financial affairs. Paper money replaced the physical possession of gold or land as the measure of wealth. Speculators trading in stocks and bonds and insurance could make (or lose) fortunes overnight. The wealthy found lending money to the government (in the form of War Loans) a highly remunerative exercise while British forces were pursuing the French across Europe but left the government virtually bankrupt at the end of it.

National assets were traded off against the debts. Prime real estate belonging to the nation (London's Marlborough House, for example) passed into the ownership of private individuals. Novel concepts of taxation were introduced to alleviate the debt, but the load was spread disproportionately – not everyone paid as much as they should, while many paid more than they could afford. Direct taxation on the incomes and property of the wealthy, for instance, brought in little by comparison with the indirect taxes on goods and services that everyone had to pay. Furthermore, the wealthy had access to ways and means of evading the tax burden. And so the poor paid far more than the rich.

Poverty was rife in the cities, but it was even more widespread among people in the countryside – and no less crippling. The mechanisation made possible by the Industrial Revolution brought huge changes in farming methods. In the long term the Agricultural Revolution led to a greater abundance of more varied crops, and the production of larger and more useful livestock. These developments brought significant benefits – indeed, the nation could not have survived twenty-two years of war and the ensuing blockade on imports without them. In the short term, however, the changes inflicted unsustainable hardship on farm labourers thrown out of work; on villagers whose common grazing lands were enclosed, and on tenant farmers whose holdings were repossessed by landowners converting their properties into single large farms. Many independent farmers who could not keep up with the trend simply went bankrupt. The social commentator William Cobbett reported that of 260 debtors held in the Fleet prison in June 1823, 120 were farmers who had lost everything.[2]

William Cobbett was born of farming stock in 1763, at a time when life was measured more by the passage of the sun and the seasons than by the clock. He died in 1835, having lived through the first flush of the Industrial Revolution. Cobbett had spent his early years working on the land. He had learnt the three Rs at his father's knee, and grew up with an unquenchable conviction that he knew best what was right and what was wrong with the world. He remained a farmer at heart all his life, but became a writer too – with a flair for the vituperative phrase and a fearless, even reckless, determination to expose the failings and misconduct he saw among people in high places.

With publishing interests in London, and farms in Hampshire, Surrey and Kensington, Cobbett had a foot firmly planted in both the urban and the rural camps. But there was never any doubt where his sympathies lay. He was deeply concerned about the effect the growth of large cities was having on the lives of country people. While Dickens, Hugo and Zola wrote on the subject of urban deprivation, creating powerful novels of great literary merit that were also unforgettable evocations of a period when immense wealth and grinding poverty existed side by side in the cities of Europe, Cobbett has left us a unique record of what was going on in the countryside – where people might lack even the flicker of hope that encourages a beggar on city streets to hold out his (or her) cap yet again. He wrote of the countryside and its people knowledgeably and with feeling, but had nothing good to say about the cities – and reserved his greatest ire for London. His passion on the subject inflames the page (often in capital letters): 'This monstrous WEN,' he wrote in 1823, 'this corrupt and all-devouring WEN [which is] sucking up the vitals of the country.'[3]

'[Cities] devoured market towns and villages, and shops devoured markets and fairs . . .' Cobbett claimed, adding that, among the urban community, 'Scarcely anyone thought of providing for his own wants . . . to buy the thing ready-made was the taste of the day. Housekeepers bought their dinners ready cooked: nothing was so common as to rent breasts for children to suck . . .'[4] Even the pleasant Cotswold spa town of Cheltenham aroused Cobbett's displeasure:

> . . . they call [it] a 'watering place'; that is to say, a place, to which East India plunderers, West India floggers, English tax-gorgers, together with gluttons, drunkards, and debauchees of all descriptions, female as well as male, resort, at the suggestion of silently laughing quacks, in the hope of getting rid of the bodily consequences of their manifold sins and iniquities.[5]

The government was not unaware of problems on the land and, although its concerns were almost certainly more to do with increasing production than with improving standards of welfare, a commission on agriculture was appointed to investigate the state of affairs. Cobbett, distrusting the motives and abilities of the commissioners, set out to see things for himself. Over a period of ten years in the early 1800s he covered the whole of southern England – on horseback. Reports on these tours of inspection appeared periodically in the columns of his publication *Cobbett's Weekly Register,* and in 1830 were published in book form as *Rural Rides* – Cobbett's masterpiece.

Though *Rural Rides* leaves the reader in no doubt that Cobbett loved the countryside and detested cities, it is first and foremost a social record of outstanding vigour, volume and exactitude. Cobbett writes in detail of land holdings, soil quality, farm management, crops sown and harvested, livestock reared and slaughtered – in fact he gives enough detail to show that in terms of energy inputs and outputs a typical pre-industrial farm of Cobbett's day was almost twenty times more efficient than its modern counterpart.[6]

Cobbett was a stickler for facts and accuracy, but not above weaving a thread of nostalgia through his accounts of early nineteenth-century farming life. He mourned the passing of an era in which gentlemen landowners accepted responsibility for the land and people entrusted to their care:

> Here was *education*. Here were early rising, industry, good hours, sobriety, decency of language, cleanliness of person, due obedience . . . This was *England* . . . From this arose the finest race of people that the world ever saw. To this the nation owed its excellent habits . . . These were the breeding places of sober and able workmen. This supplied the cities, occasionally with their most active and successful tradesmen and merchants; and it supplied the fleet and army with *hardy* men, fashioned to due subordination from their infancy.[7]

By the 1820s that England was already vanishing. Forced from the land, some found work on the roads being built to speed up transport around the country – not least the movement of produce from farm to city. Wages were abysmal. 'How do you live on half a crown a week?' Cobbett asked a young man cracking stones at a Surrey roadside. 'I don't live upon it,' the man replied, 'I poach; it is better to be hanged than be starved to death.'[8] Poverty had forced many into poaching and the government had responded with a cruel range of penalties for anyone caught in the act. A man could be transported to Australia for seven years if he was caught and convicted taking a hare or even a partridge; he could be hanged for attacking a gamekeeper.

Some landowners set mantraps in their grounds (even after they were outlawed in 1827). On a ride through Kent, Cobbett came across a property called Paradise Place with a notice on the fence warning: 'Spring guns and steel traps are set here.' 'A pretty idea it must give us of Paradise,' he fumed:

> to know that spring guns and steel traps are set in it! This is doubtless some stockjobbers place . . . whenever any of them go into the country, they look upon it that they are to begin a sort of warfare against everything around them. They invariably look upon every labourer as a thief.[9]

With painful awareness of how the countryside was impoverished as the city grew rich, Cobbett wrote in September 1826:

For my own part, I am really ashamed to ride a fat horse, to have a full belly, and to have a clean shirt upon my back, while I look at these wretched countrymen of mine; while I actually see them reeling with weakness; when I see their poor faces present to me nothing but skin and bone . . . I am ashamed to look at these poor souls, and to reflect that they are my countrymen.

A few days later Cobbett was admiring a herd of oxen fattening on a Hampshire field, but found the pleasant sight tarnished by the certainty that:

these fine oxen, this primest of human food, was, aye, every mouthful of it, destined to be devoured in the Wen, and that, too, for the greater part, by the Jews, loan-jobbers, tax-eaters, and their base and prostituted followers . . . who, if suffered to live at all, ought to partake of nothing but the offal, and ought to come, but one cut, before the dogs and cats!

In Cobbett's view, the city's upstart financiers had conspired with politicians, aristocrats and clergymen to overthrow long-established traditional practices and grow rich at the expense of people who for generations had earned an honest living from the land. And he noticed another interesting trend: as city-dwellers grew wealthy they developed an urge to live in the country. Cobbett remarked on this and its consequences in his report on a ride from Kensington to the south coast in May 1823:

The town of Brighton, in Sussex, 50 miles from the Wen, is on the sea-side, and is thought by the stock-jobbers, to afford a *salubrious air* . . . Great parcels of stock-jobbers stay at Brighton with the women and children. They skip backward and forward on the coaches, and actually *carry on stock-jobbing,* in 'Change Alley, though they reside at Brighton . . . There are not less than about *twenty coaches* that leave the WEN *every day* for this place; and, there being three or four different roads, there is a great *rivalship* for the custom. This sets the people to work to *shorten* and to *level* the roads; and here you see *hundreds of men* and horses constantly at work to make pleasant and quick travelling for the jews and jobbers. The jews and jobbers *pay* the turnpikes, to be sure; but, they get the money from the *land and labourer.* They drain these, from John-a-Groat's House to the

Land's End, and they lay out some of the money on the Brighton roads![10]

Rural Rides is so imbued with Cobbett's love for the countryside that the harsh realities of country life he described have been consistently overlooked. The book is a unique account of major changes in British society, recording with deep feeling and a journalist's acumen the effects of the inexorable shift from an agricultural and market economy to one based on industry and manufacture, but it is Cobbett's rants against the evils of the city that are most often quoted. By comparison it is inferred that the countryside in Cobbett's day must have been a good and pretty place. In places it surely was, as John Constable's paintings so beautifully reveal. For the greater part, though, it was even harder for ordinary working people to make a living in the countryside than in the cities during those times of economic uncertainty. Which of course is why so many of them gave up the attempt and went to look for a job, a bed and a crust in the cities. And from the cities' point of view it was a good thing they did. For without this constant flow of migrants from the countryside, the cities could not have kept growing.

From what one reads about the growth of cities, one might be inclined to suppose that the human capacity for reproduction has contributed significantly to their constantly increasing populations. Even if the inflow of migrants had stopped completely, surely there would have been enough natural increase within the city population itself. Not true. The fact is that until recently (and then only in the developed world) more people died in cities than were born in them. So here is another way in which the city parasitises the countryside. As with the food supply, so with the population. Both these cornerstones of city growth and survival have come from the surrounding rural areas. Just as city-dwellers could not produce their own food, nor could they raise enough children to replace the citizens who died. And the truly astonishing thing is that rural birth rates managed to keep up with the urban demand for people. In fact, the Agricultural Revolution had not only powered the Industrial Revolution – it had also fuelled the Demographic Revolution that filled the cities.

Take London as an example of this remarkable phenomenon. In 1551 the population of the city was about 80,000. In 1801, 250 years later, it stood at 865,000 – a more than tenfold increase. Where did all those people come from? Some of course had been born in the city, but most were a consequence of the fact that the rural areas were much better at producing and raising children to adulthood than the cities were. Over that 250-year period, London's average birth rate was 13 per cent lower than that of rural England, and its death rate 50 per cent higher.[11] The net effect of this was that since birth and survival rates consistently exceeded deaths in the countryside, a rural surplus was available to make up the urban deficit. Just as well for London.

These facts seem to suggest that country life has always been the better option, but it is not as simple as that. The fundamental problems of cities – poverty, disease, vice and crime have always been social, and cannot be attributed to urban or rural environmental circumstance. People create problems, not the environment. But the tendency to make a qualitative distinction between the urban and the rural is always with us. Whether promoting the countryside or deploring the cities, William Cobbett and others of that ilk strike a chord that resonates deeply in the modern psyche. When the joint towns of Brighton and Hove petitioned to become a city in the millennium year 2000, for instance, the columnist (and Brighton resident) Julie Burchill shouted from her high-horse that 'Wanting to be a city is about as sensible as wanting to be a wart. There should a word for such wanton self-immolation – Citycide.'[12] But at an instinctive level perhaps, countryside and city do seem diametrically opposed – the former inherently good with its continuous round of growth and renewal, and the latter inherently bad with its never-ending demands for maintenance and reconstruction.

Evolutionary biologists might suggest that there is a genetic basis to such instincts, given that by far the greater part of our species' evolutionary history was spent living directly off the land, in hunter-gatherer mode. Living in settled communities is a very a recent phenomenon, so perhaps the genes are telling us that the individual and collective ills of the city could be most effectively cured by a return to the countryside.

On the other hand, adaptability is also a genetically endowed characteristic of the species. After all, the capacity to adapt has been humanity's greatest asset, whether expressed in the evolutionary process of adapting the ancestral form and behaviour to the environment (as happened on the African savannas more than 3 million years ago) or in adapting the environment to suit human needs (as has occurred since the advent of farming 10,000 years ago). Civilisation has been a consequence of that process and from a purely biological point of view it has been a tremendous success – more people are alive now than ever before.

★

That it would be interesting – and possibly even useful – to learn as much as possible about how cities are founded and grow, and how society organises its affairs in the urban environment, is a self-evident truth which has engaged learned minds from the ancient Greeks to the postmodernists. The shelves are packed with books on the subject. There are journals, publishing scores of articles each year, and even a science: ekistics – the study of human settlements and how they develop. But the search has not been straightforward; quantity has not produced clarity.

During the nineteenth century, as technology hastened the pace of urbanisation around the world, science applied a gloss to the study of human affairs which not only was misleading in itself, but has also taken a long time to wear off.

In a gloomy *Essay on Population* published in 1798, the English clergyman and economist Thomas Malthus had declared that since, according to his deductions, populations increased by geometric progression while food supplies increased arithmetically, the former must inevitably outstrip the latter. Only warfare, or misery (i.e. starvation and disease), or 'moral restraint' (i.e. birth control), could control the growth of numbers and deprivation which was so evident in the cities of the day. While this proposition caused many heads to nod sagely in agreement, its emphasis on reducing the breeding potential of the more numerous poor people so outraged William Cobbett that he addressed an open letter to Malthus, proclaiming: 'Parson, I have during my life, detested many men, but never anyone so much as you!'[13]

Others again took a more discerning view of the parson's essay. Charles Darwin, for instance, was roused to consider that whatever the case as regards human populations, it was demonstrably true that wild animals and plants lived in balance with the 'natural' world. Some innate mechanism must be controlling their population size, he deduced, and from this insight went on to develop the concept of natural selection as the keystone of his theory of evolution.

It is often assumed that the term 'survival of the fittest' was coined by Darwin as a means of explaining how natural selection works. This is not true. The term came from the pen of Herbert Spencer and was published in 1852, six years before Darwin's *On the Origin of Species*. But for Spencer and others so inclined, the 'survival of the fittest' melded neatly with Darwin's more rigorous science to produce a concept of social evolution – the idea that society had 'advanced' from primitive origins to Victorian drawing-rooms by a selection process that allowed only the 'fittest' to survive and reproduce their kind. Thus the odious social darwinism was born. Here the 'fittest' were in fact the richest – and now they had a 'science' of sorts to support their lack of sympathy for the masses of poor people crowding into the cities. The poor were unfit for a world order in which wealth ruled and power was centred in financial and industrial centres. Unable to compete, they could not survive and would eventually die out: that was the gist of the social darwinists' argument.

And while the emerging social sciences interpreted the social failings of the nineteenth-century city with misplaced confidence, and novelists described it in graphic terms, a select band of thinkers followed the Utopian tradition of not simply describing how bad things were, but of telling instead how good they ought to be. The word 'Utopia' was invented by Thomas More as the title (and subject) of his book published in 1516, but the concept of an ideal world goes back further than that (examples from ancient Egypt are nearly 4,000 years old), and is more widespread than might be supposed. In one form or another, visions of Paradise, or a Garden of Eden, place the ideal world concept firmly at the core of beliefs which ease the burden of everyday life.

Religious faith of all kinds promises the blesséd and well-behaved an afterlife of Utopian bliss – most commonly in a heavenly Paradise of eternal fine weather, orchards and babbling brooks. Medieval peasants dreamt of the Land of Cockaigne, where they would find relief from poor food and backbreaking labour. Also known as *Schlarraffenland*, or 'land of milk and honey' by the Germans, and *Luilekkerland* or 'lazy luscious land' by the Dutch, the Land of Cockaigne promised a life of feasting, sleeping, and pleasure – and the more you slept the more you earned.

A painting by Brueghel the Elder shows residents of the Land of Cockaigne in various states of over-indulgence. An imaginative fifteenth-century map shows Cockaigne with mountains of grated cheese floating on a sea of wine; with roasted birds falling from the sky like rain; with trees producing fruit ripe for the plucking all year round; owls distributing fur coats and people being arrested for working.[14]

No one has returned from the dead to confirm the existence of a heavenly paradise, and there can be few peasants who truly believed that the Land of Cockaigne was anything more than fantasy. (Though it did inspire the Cuccagna feast days in eighteenth-century Naples, when an arch of meats, cheese, bread, fruit and vegetables was erected as a gift of the king. When the king gave the signal, people scrambled to destroy the arch, grabbing as much food as they could and providing an entertaining spectacle for the king and his court.[15]

Putting fantasy aside, the city Plato describes in the *Republic,* written about 360 BC, is the earliest surviving Western attempt to devise a Utopia that tackles the problems of humanity and the existing world head-on, rather than dreaming up unrealistic alternatives. Indeed, Plato's scheme deals so thoroughly with the realities of human need, ambition and behaviour that it not only qualifies as Utopian in its own right, but also has become a foundation stone of Western intellectual history.[16]

Plato's version of Utopia is brutally realistic about the strengths and frailties of humanity. He is an uncompromising advocate of law and order, rigidly enforced; indeed, much that he proposes is repugnant to modern readers: slaves outnumber citizens three to one; society is rigidly divided into three classes, and ruled by guardians, to whom private property and families are banned. Wives are held in common; breeding is strictly controlled and designed to produce strong intelligent children; warfare is an honourable pursuit. But Plato's aim is not so much to create the 'ideal' city, as to describe the 'just' city, and in this he is more concerned with addressing the realities of human relationships than with dreams of coercing people towards a state of perfection. Thus it is the principles he identifies, rather than the solutions he proposes, that makes Plato's Utopia especially interesting.

Seeking to define the conditions under which a city can be described as 'just', Plato begins by acknowledging that a city exists principally because different men have found it advantageous to practise their different crafts, trades and pursuits in close proximity. Diversity then, is a founding and indispensable characteristic of the city in Plato's view, and he believed a city would be just so long as citizens fulfil their designated tasks − only then could diversity be unified and the city thrive. Of course, the city's essential diversity may range across the whole scale of values, from the most noble to the most vile, from the most privileged to the most deprived − but that's all right; Plato's scheme does not expect that every individual will be just − he demands only that the group of citizens authorised to apprehend the unjust and safeguard the common good should do their job.[17]

It is interesting that Plato should have stressed diversity as the characteristic that enables a city to thrive. More than 2,000 years later, Charles Darwin similarly noted that a plot of ground sown with a diversity of plants produces a substantially greater weight of herbage than an identical plot sown with a single species,[18] and since then ecologists have described the importance of diversity in all living systems. Plato was ahead of them all. He had, in effect, noted that the fundamentals of ecology apply to human systems too: a city thrives on diversity. It is, one might say, a single multipli*city* of mutually supportive activities and interactions.

The city is central to Plato's propositions. In fact, proposed Utopias seem always to have been set in urban environments. It is as though the cities themselves indicate humanity's domination of the forces of nature, with their geometric buildings and street patterns subliminally reiterating the design of their social and political organisation.

Thomas More creates fifty-four cities on his *Utopia* (it is an island, 500 miles in circumference, lying somewhere beyond the known world), spaced out regularly across the territory 'none of them distant from the next above one day's journey afoot.'[19] The capital city is Amaurote, but it differs in no distinctive characteristics from the other fifty-three, since they are all the same size and built to an identical plan. 'Whoso knowth one of them knowth them all, they be all so like to one another,' says More's informant. 'The houses be of fair and gorgeous building, and on the street side they stand joined together in a long row through the whole street, without any partition or separation. The streets be twenty foot broad.' Every ten years the householders must draw lots and change houses accordingly.[20]

Everyone has a trade (carpenter, mason, blacksmith, tailor) and, since a given number of city residents must change places with an equal number of people in the countryside each year, everyone is an experienced farmer too. A six-hour working day is the rule, and sufficient to provide enough of everything for everyone. Food and all necessities are kept in storehouses from which the designated officials of each district may freely collect supplies. Families are allowed to eat at home, but usually prefer to eat in the communal halls, where the food is excellent (prepared by women on a rota system) and accompanied by music and educational reading. Leisure time is devoted to gardening, attending lectures, or exercising the mind with board games. There are no wine-taverns or ale-houses; 'no lurking corners, nor any places of wicked councils or unlawful assemblies'. Everyone goes to bed at eight o'clock.[21]

There is no such thing as money in Utopia – nor even a concept of goods as value. The pearls that the Utopians gather from the seashore and the diamonds they pluck from certain rocks are used to adorn infants, and discarded by the children themselves as they grow up. Precious metals are valued only for their utility: 'Of gold and silver they make commonly chamber-pots and other vessels that serve for most vile uses not only in their common halls but in every man's private house.' Privacy, however, is a relative term. In the countryside no household or farm has fewer than forty persons, living communally 'under the rule and order of the goodman and the goodwife of the house, being both very sage, discreet, and ancient persons'. In the cities, every house has a door front and back but they are never locked or bolted, and are so easy to open that the touch of a finger will suffice. Anyone may go into any house without embarrassment or fear of being accused of theft, 'for there is nothing within the houses that is private or any man's own'.[22]

More's Utopia is a land of happy, healthy, well-behaved and public-spirited people who share everything, and are all absolutely committed to the rules that govern their lives. Everyone surrenders their personal interests to the common good. This proposition is common to every Utopia that has been devised – from Plato to Marx. Everyone conforming happily to strict rules of conduct; no competition; equality in all things, for everyone. If only it could be so, the problems of humanity and the city would vanish at a stroke. But of course there is a paradox at the heart of the Utopian ideal: strict rules and imposed equality require an authority to judge what is equal and what is not. As Orwell pointed out, some are likely to consider themselves more equal than others.

Given the modern state of knowledge regarding evolution, human biology, sociology and politics, the sense of unreality that pervades virtually all Utopian tales is hard to miss. They are interesting and can be entertaining, but totally unrealistic. And besides, with everything so organised, perfect and predictable, wouldn't life in Utopia become extremely boring? Can people take so much of a good thing? Surely someone, somewhere, sometime is bound to sleep late, steal a gold chamberpot or otherwise step out of line – if only to relieve the monotony of perfection. As the Victorian romantic William Morris permits a disgruntled grandfather to remark in his Utopian fable, *News from Nowhere* (first published in 1890): 'I think one may do more with one's life than sitting on a damp cloud and singing hymns.'[23]

10

The City Found Wanting

The rapid growth of late-nineteenth-century cities was due to the employment opportunities they offered. Food production generally kept pace with the growing urban populations. But demand outstripped supply in a key instance where pre-industrial farming and marketing practices persisted. Germany and its cities became increasingly dependent upon supplies of essential commodities from abroad – with calamitous consequences during the First World War.

The open sandy plains of what is now northern Germany, with their lakes and heathland and forests of pine and birch, would have been an improbable location for Thomas More's Utopia or Plato's Just City – or any other city for that matter – but it was here that a Hohenzollern prince known as 'Irontooth' took over a pair of twelfth–century villages on the banks of the River Spree in 1443 and laid the foundation of one of Europe's greatest cities. The villagers themselves were not at all happy about the prince's arrival. They objected, violently. But Irontooth was not to be defied. He built a castle and established a base for his exploits – which were largely of an acquisitive and expansionist nature. And henceforward this small and obscure rural centre – which possessed neither natural resources nor a location that might otherwise have made it important – gained mounting status from the fact that it was the administrative base of a state that gained control of a progressively larger and larger expanse of east and central Europe. It grew to become the capital of Brandenburg in 1450; capital of Prussia from 1701; capital of a German state in 1871; capital of a reunited Germany in 1990, and the geographical capital of Europe in 2004, when the European Union expanded eastward to embrace former Soviet countries: Berlin.

Berlin is very much an artificial political creation. Under the Hohenzollerns, Frederick the Great and the Kaisers it ranks high among cities that merit the title 'Prince's Capital', as described at the conclusion of Chapter 8. It was the seat of an absolutist government and the nucleus around which the nation-state of Germany was established. With the might that the Industrial Revolution brought to Germany, Berlin was a force to reckon with on any measure of assessment at the end of the nineteenth century: size, population, economy, wealth, culture. But ambition proved to be Berlin's most potent force. The ambitions of princes – imperial ambitions.

In 1870, the Prussians invaded France. By January 1871 they were besieging Paris and their King, Wilhelm I, was solemnly proclaimed German Emperor in the palace Louis XIV had built at Versailles.[1] Thus began the Second Reich[2] – with its illusions of grandeur reflected not only in the Hall of Mirrors, where the ceremony took place, but also in the title given to Wilhelm. Hitherto he had been known as König, a term that comes from the Old High German 'chunig' meaning 'kin' or 'race'. In the Hall of Mirrors they dubbed him Kaiser, a title derived from the name of the most famous Roman emperor, Julius Caesar.

History leaves little doubt that Kaiser Wilhelm I and his government regarded the Kaiserreich as a reincarnation for the industrial age of the imperial might that Caesar had deployed. The imperial eagle was the emblem of state; Berlin, the capital city, was adorned with edifices in the classical style and German ambitions of empire assumed global dimensions with the acquisitions of colonies abroad.

But while the Roman Empire ruled for centuries, the Second Reich lasted only forty-seven years and ten months. Not because it lacked the manpower, the talent, the industrial capacity and the wealth to pursue its imperial ambitions, but ultimately because it entered and fought the First World War without paying sufficient regard to the obligations that the Emperor Tiberius had stressed in AD 22 when he told the Roman senate that 'the utter ruin of the state will follow' if it fails in its duty to feed Rome.[3] Ultimately, it was not military setbacks that brought the war to an end, but the plight of Germany's civilian population – starvation. Berlin suffered cruelly. It is a salutary tale.

When Berlin had become capital of a united Germany in 1871, the city was already benefitting from policies that Frederick the Great had instigated a century before, with education foremost among them. Frederick had ordained that Berlin should become a 'new Athens on the Spree'. But the aim was not to produce a host of philosophising Platos and Aristotles. It had a more pragmatic and down-to-earth purpose. Frederick wanted Germany to have advanced expertise in technical subjects, especially in those which would serve to build up Prussia's industrial and military power. Accordingly, the Mining Academy of Berlin was founded in 1778; the Technical University in 1799; and the University of Berlin in 1808.

From these beginnings, Berlin became one of Europe's great centres of learning, home to some of the most distinguished figures in all fields of science and the humanities. The geographer Alexander von Humboldt, pathologist Rudolf Virchow, Nobel Prize-winner Robert Koch (who made important discoveries in respect of tuberculosis and cholera), Kirchoff (who developed the spectroscope), Hertz (radio waves), Röntgen (x-rays), Justus von Liebig (chemistry) and numerous leading scholars in history, philosophy, linguistics, sociology and archaeology either worked in Berlin or influenced academic life there. Berlin inspired a remarkable period of intellectual and scientific achievement. By 1890 there were twice as many academic scientists in Germany as in Britain.[4] And, as Frederick had planned, Berlin's investment in education ultimately paid handsome dividends in the form of industrial development.

Werner von Siemens, for instance, was seventeen years old when he moved to Berlin from a town north of the city, Mecklenburg, in 1834. One of fourteen children born to a tenant farmer, he lacked the money required for enrolment on a technical course at university, so joined the army instead, under whose auspices he gained the equivalent of a university education at the United Artillery-Engineers School. In 1846 the army introduced him to the intricacies of the newly invented electric telegraph, then of great interest to the Prussian General Staff. But Werner von Siemens looked beyond the military applications of the telegraph, and could see that it would enable industry, businesses and people to keep in touch everywhere. With a civilian colleague he formed a company to exploit its commercial potential.

The firm of Siemens and Halske was soon heavily engaged with work for the army, for the railways and for the Prussian Telegraph Commission – but not so busy that the company did not also commit substantial resources to research on the application of electricity to other areas of technology. A workable dynamo invented in 1866 solved the problem of running a machine on electricity; with further work and refinement this development led to the demonstration of a practical electric railway for Berlin in 1879, and in 1881, the city's first electric tram service.[5]

Meanwhile, a Berlin-born engineer, Emil Rathenau, was expanding his interest in electrical installation and supply into what was to become the Allgemeine Elektrizitäts Gesellschaft, AEG – the company responsible for the crucial innovations from which the world's dependence upon electric power has developed. It was AEG that solved the problem of converting direct current into alternating current; this – in conjunction with other crucial AEG inventions – made it possible for electricity to be generated in big central power stations and distributed to a widespread network of consumers. The first long-distance electric power cable was laid by AEG in 1891 between Lauffen and Frankfurt-am-Main, a distance of 175 kilometres.[6]

So, with AEG concentrating on the heavy side of electrical engineering, and Siemens & Halske taking the lead in communications technology, Berlin became the leading industrial city of Europe, and the electrical capital of the world. The ultimate example of the progressive city: 'Elektropolis', as Berliners called it.

But progressive is always a relative term. While Berlin's industrial development raced ahead, progress on the social front lagged far behind. As with cities throughout Europe during the nineteenth century, thousands of people were flooding into Berlin every year. Werner von Siemens was one of a fortunate minority whom the city needed and welcomed. Most immigrants were a liability, who had come to the city in search of relief from the mounting hardships that the Industrial Revolution had brought to the Prussian countryside. There had been half a million small linen and wool looms and tens of thousands of spinners in Prussia in the early nineteenth century, for instance, but as industrial-scale textile mills were established, life for the traditional cottage workers became a struggle for survival. Priced out of the market, they flocked to Berlin.

Huge encampments sprang up on the fringes of the city, which was already swarming with people hoping to find work. At first the city authorities attempted to ignore the troublesome hordes at its gates, in the hope that they would simply go away. But of course they did not, and eventually the Prussian government demanded that the city should prepare plans for new housing developments. James Hobrecht, a young architect and civil engineer, was assigned the task in 1858 with instructions to avoid grand or radical schemes and keep costs down by paying careful attention to topography and property boundaries.

Hobrecht delivered his development plan four years later. Describing the proposals as 'brilliant, meticulous, all-encompassing, and fundamentally flawed', the historian Alexandra Richie holds Hobrecht responsible for turning 'Athens on the Spree' into the 'biggest working-class slum on the continent'.[7] Some authorities go further, and accuse him of making Berlin 'the greatest city of tenements in the world'.[8]

Hobrecht had set out to create a socially 'integrated' city. He drew a ring around the designated urban area, and divided the available land within it into large 400 m² blocks separated by a grid of connecting roads. This was the extent of the city's contribution and influence. Then the speculators and developers took over. Hobrecht's plan had assumed they would break up the blocks with small airy side streets, parks, footpaths and gardens, then construct spacious apartment buildings with a socially appropriate mix of expensive flats at the front, and cheaper accommodation at the back: But the developers did nothing of the sort.

Rejecting all pleas for lawns and lanes, and in the absence of any enforceable restrictions, the developers proceeded to pack the blocks with massive rectangular seven-storey buildings, separated only by narrow, dark and dingy paved courtyards. Within a decade these red and ochre brick barracks had spread like cancer across the city. The rooms were tiny and badly lit, the air was poor and the facilities abysmal – but the places were always full. Official records from 1870 report an average occupation rate of five people per room, with some flats housing more than twenty. Over 60,000 people 'officially' inhabited the dank, airless underground rooms which the builders had provided for coal storage. And heightening international tensions frustrated hopes of improvement; there were more pressing priorities. The result was that by 1914 Berlin had too many people, too few jobs, a massive housing problem and with the outbreak of war faced a food supply problem of utterly intractable dimensions.

While Germany's industrialisation forged ahead, the population of the country grew from 40 million in 1872 to 67 million in 1914 (despite the emigration of more than 2 million Germans to the Americas[9]), and the demographic structure of the country changed dramatically – from two-thirds rural to two-thirds urban.[10] A single generation of Germans saw their country move from an agricultural to an industrial economy. Indeed, the proportion of total population living in cities increased faster in Germany during this period than in any other European country.[11]

In 1871 there had been just eight German cities with populations of more than 100,000 people; by 1910 there were forty-eight.[12] And no city grew as large and as fast as the capital of the Second Reich – Berlin. From 827,000 in 1871, Berlin's population grew to just over 2 million in 1910 (making its 63.4 km² the most densely populated in the world at that time) and had reached 4 million by the outbreak of war in 1914.[13]

Migration from countries to the east of Germany, improved standards of living and enhanced life expectancy accounted for the growth of the national population as a whole, but the growth of urban communities was the consequence of industrialisation itself. On the one hand, hopes of employment attracted people to the cities while, on the other, mechanisation had diminished the need for a full-time workforce on the land. But this demographic shift was not accompanied by the changes in food production that would keep everyone adequately fed. The sober fact is that while industry had built Berlin into the capital of the new-style nation-state, and had established the fortunes of other cities around the country – Essen, Bremen, Stuttgart and so forth – core elements of the nation's agriculture remained set in a pre-industrial mode of production.

Machinery, along with the growing use of fertilisers, had led to greater production of crops such as potatoes and sugar beet (pre-war Germany was one of the world's largest sugar producers), it is true, but the production of essential cereals and meat had hardly increased at all. To make up the deficit, the country imported supplies from abroad. By 1914, Germany was importing one-third of its total food supply – including 27 per cent of its protein requirement, 19 per cent of carbo-hydrates and 42 per cent of all fats consumed.[14] As a measure of how vitally important these imports had become, consider the following: between 1871 and 1914 the population of Germany grew by more than 60 per cent; food imports during the same period grew by 500 per cent.[15]

The problem was that despite having moved from an agricultural to an industrial economy with two-thirds of its population living in cities, Germany at the outbreak of war was still fed predominantly by small farms supplying local markets. One-third of the population remained on the land, but of the country's 5.7 million independent farmers recorded in the census of 1907,[16] 4.38 million held under 5 ha of land each – not much more than enough to support the family working it. Of the remainder, fewer than 300,000 held more than 20 ha, and of these only

24,000 farmed more than 100 ha. Not much had changed by 1914, and the situation after the outbreak of war was not helped by the slump in production on the large grain estates of eastern Germany, where the war brought the annual inflow of migrant farmworkers from Russian Poland to an abrupt halt.

The Allies instigated a naval blockade soon after the commencement of hostilities, but since military experts (on both sides) believed the war would be over in a matter of months, this might not have alarmed the German government too much – even though two-thirds of their merchant fleet of over 3,000 vessels, totalling about 5.5 million tonnes of shipping, was either at sea or in foreign ports at the outbreak of war. But the war dragged on, and apart from a continuing dribble of trade with neutral states around the Baltic, Germany's international maritime trade was effectively terminated by the end of August 1914.[17] For the duration of a terrible war, Germany lacked supplies of food and commodities which had been essential even in peacetime.

As the demands of fighting a war intensified, Germany's plight could only get worse. Indeed, the blockade became the Allies' most potent weapon. Analysing its effect immediately after the war, the British economist John Maynard Keynes concluded that the blockade 'was Whitehall's finest achievement; it had evoked the qualities of the English at their subtlest . . .' The two wartime prime ministers were more blunt. Herbert Asquith wrote: 'control of the sea by the British Navy . . . by successive stages drained the life-blood of the enemy and won the War'. Lloyd George told parliament: 'Germany has been broken almost as much by the blockade as by military means.'[18]

Needless to say, food was not all that Germany had imported before the blockade, and within three months the curtailment of saltpetre imports (an essential ingredient of explosives) had left German artillery on the western front with only a four-day supply of shells.[19] But German science (more winners of Nobel prizes in science had come from Berlin than anywhere else[20]) and the organisational efficiency of the military rapidly developed ways and means of ensuring that critical shortages and production crises were overcome. The abrupt drop in food supplies that the blockade inflicted proved more difficult to accommodate. Yields throughout the country dropped when fertilisers made from imported Chilean nitrates were no longer available – the grain harvest plummeted during the course of the war, from 30 million tonnes pre-war to only 16 million tonnes in 1918[21] – and livestock production was severely affected by the lack of the imported barley and clover, maize and oil cake which had previously supplemented the animals' diets.[22] Overall, the blockade led quickly to a drop of about 25 per cent in German agricultural production – and this in addition to the loss of food imports. Furthermore, the prevailing methods of farming, harvesting and distribution made it virtually impossible to ensure that everyone got a fair share of the inadequate amounts that were being produced.

A commission reporting in October 1914 on the state of Germany's food supply assessed the national shortage of calories at a quarter, and of protein at a third.[23] Clearly, a general tightening of belts was necessary if the country was to survive the war – and tighten them they did, but the effect was felt most severely by middle- and lower-class city-dwellers, while many others continued to enjoy pre-war levels of consumption.

The 8 million men under arms by 1915 were allocated full rations, for example, and a comparable number of older men, women and children working on the farms took advantage of immediate access to the product of their labours throughout the war. These two groups constituted no more than a quarter of the population, but they consumed at least half of all Germany's farm production, leaving the other three-quarters of the population to survive on what was left[24] – if they could get their hands on it.

With army procurement officers purchasing massive stocks of food, and troop movements blocking rail deliveries, supplies quickly ran short in the cities. Panic buying exacerbated the situation as people sensed a very real threat of starvation. Prices rose, and while those with the means could still afford to eat well, officials estimated that at least half of the urban population could not. In attempts to ensure that essential foods were available to all, city governments across the country set price ceilings on staples such as bread, milk and potatoes. But to little beneficial effect; if anything, the decrees made matters worse.

Farmers immediately began boycotting markets under official control and took their produce instead to outlets that offered higher prices. And when laws were passed to regulate prices at every outlet, farmers stopped producing supplies on which the price was fixed (thus worsening the shortages) and turned to products on which prices were still unregulated. Fixing the price of milk, for example, immediately heightened shortages as farmers switched to producing butter or cheese (still as yet unregulated), or sold their cattle for slaughter. Similarly, price controls on bread also created shortages, as farmers found it more profitable to feed their grain to livestock than sell it to flour mills.[25]

Within months it was clear that price controls merely distorted market forces and could not on their own regulate the food supply to beneficial effect. The only alternative, the government concluded, was to avoid market forces altogether and regulate everything from production to consumption by means of rationing. They started with bread. The Imperial Grain Corporation was established within the Ministry of the Interior with powers to purchase the country's entire grain crop at controlled prices. Local administrations throughout Germany were allocated supplies according to their population size; the administrations shared out the allocation among their registered bakers, from whom customers bought their daily ration of bread at a controlled price.[26]

The rationing of bread began in Berlin in January 1915 and was extended to the rest of the country six months later. The bureaucratic challenge of the undertaking was considerable – and only increased as the war ground on. To begin with, Berlin's Bread Supply Office sought to meet the basic dietary needs of the city's nearly 4 million inhabitants with a staff of twelve civil servants and sixty-five assistants. By the end of the war it employed twenty-two high-ranking civil servants, over 1,800 clerks, and 245 volunteers who checked the weight of flour sacks, distributed ration cards and inspected the purity of bread.[27]

Prior to the outbreak of war the average German family of two adults and three children, with an annual income of 1,000 marks, had spent nearly 12 per cent of its income on bread alone.[28] As in many countries, bread was not simply a filling and essential component of the diet. Bread – freshly baked and on the breakfast table while still warm from the oven; with cheese and cold meats at any time, and always accompanying the main meal of the day – confirmed that all was well with the world. Especially in Berlin, where virtually every street had several bakers, each serving a loyal band of discerning customers from the immediate neighbourhood. Bread was baked at least twice every day (except on Sunday), beginning no later than four in the morning. Every day, the appetising aroma of fresh baking drew customers into the shop; shelves were stacked with a dozen different kinds of bread; baskets were filled with crusty rolls, and a glass-fronted counter offered cakes, tarts and pastries.

It was the luxuries that disappeared first, and with little complaint since giving up cream cakes and the like was not too much of a sacrifice to make for the war effort. But when Berlin's Bread Supply Office proposed substituting a 'standard loaf' for all the varieties, shapes and sizes which previously had been available there was outrage. Berliners were being asked to give up even their *Brötchen* – their cherished white breakfast rolls – and this was too much. A letter to the authorities typifies widespread popular feeling:

> The intention of the city government to do away with the *Brötchen* horrifies me. For health reasons I have been a white-bread eater all of the 53 years of my life. If the city goes ahead with its plans for the introduction of a 'standard loaf', there is no way I will ever be able to satisfy my hunger pangs again.[29]

The authorities relented. Berliners continued to enjoy their *Brötchen* for a while, but soon any kind of bread would become yet another luxury that must be sacrificed for the war effort.

As supplies of wheat flour, heavily dependent on imports in the pre-war years, declined, the government issued directives requiring bakers to produce a patriotic *Kriegsbrot* – 'war-loaf' – made with 20 per cent potato flour. However, following the disastrous potato harvest of 1916 even this level of adulteration could not be sustained. By early 1917 the *Kriegsbrot* consisted of 55 per cent rye flour, 35 per cent wheat flour and 10 per cent unspecified substitutes, and as the supply situation worsened still further, powdered dried turnips replaced the rye flour. Meanwhile the daily ration of even this hard, unpalatable and often indigestible bread was cut from 225 g in 1915 to 160 g in 1917.[30] And the situation was no better in respect of other foodstuffs and essential commodities.

As soon as the Imperial Grain Corporation was seen to be running with reasonable efficiency, it became the model for rationing in virtually all sectors of German agriculture and consumer supplies. By 1916 there was even a War Corporation for Sauerkraut. Every aspect of the food industry was covered: from production to distribution and consumption. 'Meatless days' were stipulated, public eating-halls established, and supposedly wasteful cooking methods outlawed. Tens of thousands of directives were issued, ostensibly for the entire nation but often specifically intended to alleviate conditions in Berlin. The morass of regulations certainly nourished the government's bureaucratic tendency, but what it did to ease the problems of finding enough to eat is hard to say. There were endless queues, and serious riots.

From early 1916 on, police reports make clear that Berliners were more interested in getting something – anything – to eat than in news from the front.[31] By the winter of 1916–17, when turnips were the only freely available food in all Germany, the war had turned the families of soldiers at the front into scavengers. Berliners, with characteristic wry humour, joked about the *Hamsterfahrt* – the constant queuing and foraging like hamsters for something to supplement the totally inadequate official rations. In effect, the war had spawned a new front, held by the women against the police and civil administrators who were trying to enforce rationing.

> Every smuggled pound of butter, every sack of potatoes successfully spirited in by night, was celebrated in their homes with the same enthusiasm as the victories of the armies two years before . . . Soon a looted ham thrilled us more than the fall of Bucharest. And a bushel of potatoes seemed much more important than the capture of a whole English army in Mesopotamia.[32]

Evelyn Blücher, an English wife resident in Berlin throughout the war, wrote in her diary:

> We are all growing thinner every day, and the rounded contours of the German nation have become a legend of the past. We are all gaunt and bony now, and have dark shadows round our eyes, and our thoughts are chiefly taken up with wondering what our next meal will be, and dreaming of the good things that once existed.[33]

As potatoes – the one staple food in which pre-war Germany had been self-sufficient – became increasingly scarce and turnips the only take-it-or-leave-it substitute, the search for alternatives to items in short supply lent a pejorative meaning to the words *Ersatz* (substitute) and *strecken* (to stretch). Coffee made from tree bark and milk that was 'stretched' with water were but two of some 11,000 *Ersatz* products in general circulation during the course of the war – including over 800 varieties of meatless sausage.[34] But neither the official ration nor the alternatives on offer could provide Berliners and German civilians generally with even the semblance of an adequate diet.

In 1916 a professor of hygiene at the University of Bonn performed an experiment in which he limited himself to the official food ration for an average person. After six months he had lost a third of his body-weight and was no longer fit enough to work. Once recovered, the professor prepared a report of the experiment for publication but it was suppressed by the censors, probably because the government knew the truth of what the professor had shown, but could do nothing about it.[35] In any case, the inadequacies of the rations were starkly obvious to everyone.

To make the point, an American newspaper correspondent based in Berlin during the war searched the food queues for someone who did not show the ravages of hunger:

'Four long lines were inspected with the closest scrutiny,' he reported. 'But among the 300 applicants for food there was not one who had had enough to eat for weeks. In the case of the youngest women and children the skin was drawn hard to the bones and bloodless. Eyes had fallen deeper into the sockets. From the lips all color was gone, and the tufts of hair which fell over parchmented foreheads seemed dull and famished – a sign that the nervous vigor of the body was departing with the physical strength.[36]

The German authorities were fully aware that maintaining health and physical strength required a daily intake of about 3,000 calories for the average individual, but they could do little or nothing for the civilians who, by 1918, were surviving on a ration of only 1,000 calories per day. By contrast, an adult British male consumed a daily average of 3,400 calories throughout the war.[37] There were food shortages and price rises in Britain too, but nothing like in Germany, and no British food rationing of any kind until February 1918 (even then, bread was not rationed).[38] But calories were not the only essential nutrients in short supply in wartime Germany. The fat ration had fallen to barely a tenth of pre-war levels, and the meat ration was down to less than a fifth.[39]

The effect of such deprivation was nothing short of calamitous. While well-nourished men were dying at the front, the civilian population was worn out with starvation, sickness and disease – especially in the cities. The number of people capable of completing a day's work had fallen by more than half. Mortality had soared. The death rate of children between the ages of one and five had risen by 50 per cent, and for children between five and fifteen by 55 per cent. Furthermore, the health of Germany's surviving children was truly appalling. In one instance, 20 per cent of children applying for admission to school were unfit to attend. In another, barely one in three of juveniles seeking employment was found to be healthy enough for manual labour. Rickets, resulting from vitamin D deficiency, was widespread; advanced pulmonary tuberculosis was rife. A charity that was caring for 8,892 consumptives in 1913–14 was nursing 20,669 patients in 1917–18.[40]

While Germany's population – and Berliners in particular – suffered, there were two groups of people who remained well fed. One was the army, and the other consisted of civilians with the means or the influence to procure food through other than the official rationing and distribution system. Of the army it must be said that there was general agreement that the men at the front should always receive adequate supplies. But if Edwin Schuster of the Bavarian Engineering Company No. 8 is to be believed, the common foot soldier got considerably more food, especially bread, than he needed.

No difference is more glaring than the paucity of foodstuffs at home and their *waste here in the battlefield.* The squandering begins immediately. During the transport, men receive a number of warm meals, and upon arrival at the Front, each soldier obtains four pounds of bread, sausages, and an additional pound and a half of red meat. These provisions are fully superfluous, for *virtually every man receives in care packages from home enough foodstuffs to keep himself stuffed.* We have no idea what to do with all the bread we receive, the Home Front's most important foodstuff. As soon as we arrive at the battlefield, we also get an entire week's ration of bread. Many throw the rock-hard loaves away. Others feed them to the horses.[41]

The other well-fed group included the farmers and landed gentry with access to agricultural produce from the very moment it was harvested or slaughtered. They seldom went short – as Evelyn Blücher discovered in July 1916 when her father-in-law died in a fall from his horse and her husband inherited the family fortune and properties. After many years of estrangement, the death brought family reconciliation and an abrupt change of lifestyle to Evelyn Blücher, as her diary tells:

It is not easy to describe the difference which suddenly took place in our lives. After having existed for more than two years in a bed-sitting-room in a hotel, we all at once found ourselves in possession of several beautiful castles and estates, a palace in Berlin, and many rich acres of land in the country. In fact it all seems rather like some new phase of the *Arabian Nights,* as by reason of the unusual relations existing between members of the Blücher family, we had not until now in any way shared in all these desirable things, and it seemed almost magical to wake up one morning and find oneself the owner of them.

On moving to the Krieblowitz estate, 280 km south-east of Berlin, she wrote:

It is as if some invisible curtain had fallen, separating us for ever from our nomadic life of unrest in Berlin, with all its political perplexities and vexations . . . and the constant irritating absence of everyday needs. Here we are living on the fat of the land, as the monks of old themselves most probably did in this very same monastery. We are in fact self-supporting, which means that my husband and the keepers supply us with all manner of venison and game, such as wild duck, hares, partridges, and pheasants. We buy no butcher's meat; the farm supplies us with milk and butter, flour and bread, and the garden keeps us in vegetables and fruit. As elsewhere, these things are more or less 'beschlagnahmt', [embargoed] but after having experienced what it is to be starved, we can appreciate all these luxuries well enough.[42]

One can sympathise with Evelyn Blücher's appreciation of the good life she found awaiting her in the countryside while people starved in the cities, and her change in fortune clearly demonstrates that food was available to those with the means or the influence to procure it. Everyone knew that, and the knowledge served to heighten tensions between the urban and rural populations. With city-dwellers convinced the available food was not being distributed equitably, and farmers resenting the demands being put upon them, neither group had much sympathy for the other. Evelyn Blücher herself reported just six months before her *Arabian Nights* transformation: 'The peasants now jeer at the town-breds, who have to spread their bread with Kunsthonig [Ersatz-honey], while they, the peasants, have a thick layer of their own butter and a slab of ham on top!'[43]

But while such behaviour lays the well-provisioned rural communities open to accusations of lacking in patriotism, responsibility for the starving cities lay ultimately with a government which had not taken into account the likelihood and consequences of a blockade. A long war had seemed inconceivable, virtually no one expected the conflict to last even a year, much less two, three and four. Cut off by the blockade from essential supplies from abroad, they had managed to feed the military but proved incapable of getting a fair share of the country's own agricultural produce to the cities. No substitute existed to replace the intricate free-market network of producers, distributors, wholesalers and retailers by which bread and other essentials had reached the urban masses in peacetime, and government intervention (in the form of rationing) only exacerbated relations between the cities and the countryside. As the historian Roger Chickering has put it:

> The suppliers were too numerous and savvy. Peasants greeted the incursions of regulations into their lives with an arsenal of evasions, which ranged from simple hoarding to elaborate schemes to mis-represent the size of their crop yields . . . Farmers were responding rationally to a simple fact: the market for agricultural produce had not disappeared. Rationing had merely driven the free market under-ground and colored it black.[44]

In effect the black market functioned as a competitor to the officially administered food supply – paying more for supplies, offering more for sale. The forces of supply and demand prevailed, and practically anything could be obtained – at a price. 'It is . . . difficult to season one's cooking,' Evelyn Blücher reported in October 1917, 'for the price of pepper, cinnamon, and nutmeg is enormous. These spices are almost worth their weight in gold.'[45] But the black market supplied staple foods as well as luxuries, and as the war dragged on it became more than just an adjunct to the official rations – even the authorities estimated that by the end of the war Germans were buying fully a third of all food on the black market.[46] And landowners, farmers and market gardeners were all becoming very prosperous as a result. The Blücher's own gardener, with just one hectare allocated for his private use, made 10,000 marks in 1916 alone – ten times the annual income of an average German household in 1914.[47]

Germany mobilised a total of over 11 million men during the First World War, of whom 1,691,841 died in battle; 4,247,143 were wounded and 772,522 were either captured or declared missing in action.[48] From the time that United States' forces joined the Allies in 1917, hopes of a German victory faded fast, but the plight of the civilian population was a no less powerful incentive by October 1918 when Germany asked President Wilson for an armistice on the terms he had proposed. In a speech to the German Cabinet, a minister expressed the crux of the matter in a few words: 'It is a question of potatoes . . . [The] misery is so great that it is like asking a complete riddle when one asks oneself: what does North Berlin live on and how does East Berlin exist?'[49]

Germany was a sick and despairing country. A memorandum issued by the National Health Office in December 1918 showed that 763,000 civilians had died as a direct result of the wartime blockade.[50] In the cities especially, many of the survivors were malnourished, weak and susceptible to disease. The rates of tuberculosis infection had doubled, and when the worldwide influenza pandemic struck Germany, 1,700 people died on a single day (15 October 1918) in Berlin alone.[51]

The Armistice was signed on 11 November 1918, but as the soldiers returned home they found the food supply situation in chaos. More than six months would pass before the blockade was lifted and supplies from abroad began to reach the country's sick and starving population. In Berlin meanwhile, minuscule amounts of flour and turnips were available, but deliveries of other essentials were less than a third of the quantities required.[52] By June 1919 the situation was even more catastrophic; virtually no produce was available in quantities even remotely approaching demand. It was precisely at this bleakest of times that the German delegation signed the Peace Treaty at the Palace of Versailles. The Kaiser had abdicated and fled to Holland and the heirs of the Second Reich were back in the Hall of Mirrors, their capital city starving, and their state in utter ruin.

11

The Impact of Numbers

The growth of cities during and immediately after the Industrial Revolution was directly related to economic growth. That trend has been reversed in recent times. The world's fastest-growing cities are in regions where economies are stagnant or in decline, and they struggle to provide even the most basic amenities. 'Urban farming' is not only a crucial source of food and income for many of their citizens – it is also a major industry.

By 1914, Berlin was Europe's fastest-growing city, and the world's most densely populated urban area, but the food crisis suffered by the city during the First World War was more a consequence of administrative ineptitude than numbers. Urban populations were growing massively throughout the developing world, and food supply was growing with them. The numbers were huge. In the forty years between 1880 and 1920, for example, Europe's population grew from 356 million to 487 million, giving the continent a yearly average of 3.27 million extra mouths to provide for[1] – which in effect was equivalent to burdening its provisioning budget with a city the size of present-day Berlin[2] every year.

People migrated from rural villages and towns to fill the cities, their growing numbers a result of the demographic transformation which occurred during the late nineteenth century as economies expanded and the acceptance of simple health measures brought about a fall in death rates while birth rates remained relatively high. Generation by generation, more babies survived to become adults; more people lived longer – more than enough to populate the cities as well as expand production and feed the city-dwellers (with the help of agricultural machinery the city-based industries were producing).

In the thirty years to 1910, Vienna's population trebled to more than 2 million; the population of Paris more than doubled from 2.25 million to 4.8 million between 1875 and 1925; London added 3.5 million inhabitants to its citizenry during the same period (an overall increase of 80 per cent) and across the Atlantic, New York grew from a city of 1.9 million in 1875 to become the home of nearly 8 million people by 1925, a more than fourfold increase which made New York the world's largest city.[3]

Demands on Europe's provisioning budget would have been greater still if a large proportion of the continent's burgeoning population had not chosen to emigrate, and seek a better life in North America. Over 20 million Europeans packed their bags and left Europe for the United States in the forty years between 1880 and 1920 – an average of 500,000 per year, nearly 10,000 a week, 1,400 a day (averages are misleading here – in some years as many as 1.5 million immigrants arrived, passing through Ellis Island in their thousands, every day). The immigrants contributed significantly to the growth of cities and settlement throughout the US – indeed, they constituted a large fraction of the nation's growth during that time, as the population more than doubled from just over 50 million to nearly 106 million.[4]

All over Europe and North America the additional people found places to live and work. Cities were fed. There were always some pockets of deprivation and hunger, it is true, but throughout a century of phenomenal population growth, with human numbers increasing year by year at an unprecedented rate, provisioning kept pace. In another age the gods would have been credited with this achievement, and certainly there is a touch of the miraculous about the fortuity of events as industrialisation boosted the production of food and other essentials just as more and more people required them. More people needed more of everything, which in turn required yet more people to produce and distribute the necessities. Thus the growing human population could not have been sustained without the Industrial Revolution, and the Industrial Revolution could not have been sustained without the massive growth of the human population. There was an elegant synergy at work here as the two interdependent forces enriched economies and sustained more people than ever before, and its most dynamic expression was in the rapid growth of cities.

The world had seen nothing like the proliferation of large and expanding cities that the Industrial Revolution brought about – in 1875 there were only five industrial cities in the world with populations in excess of a million, and between them they held a little more than 10 million inhabitants in total. By 1925, industrialisation had spread, there were thirty-one cities with more than a million inhabitants and their total population was just over 72 million.[5] Thus, the evidence suggests that the growth of large cities must be closely linked to the growth of industrial economies,[6] with the richest growing fastest – indeed, it seems likely that in the absence of a flourishing industrial economy the growth of cities would stagnate. But this is not so. In the latter half of the twentieth century most of the world's fastest-growing cities were located in the least developed regions. Here, some cities were expanding at rates far in excess of those the industrial revolution had generated – even though their national economies were hardly growing at all.

The result is that at the beginning of the twenty-first century there were twice as many city-dwellers in the less-developed world as there were in developed countries; furthermore, their numbers were growing nearly six times as fast. The sheer scale of this increase calls for pause and an historical comparison: during the fifty years between 1875 and 1925 the *entire population* of the developed world increased by just under 300 million. Between 1950 and 2000 the less-developed world's *urban population alone* increased by 1,682 million (while the developed world's urban population rose by little more than a quarter of that – 457 million).[7]

In Africa, the world's most impoverished continent, the number of city-dwellers multiplied nearly tenfold during those fifty years, rising from 32.7 million in 1950 to 309.6 million in 2000 and it is expected to double again by 2025, when more than half of Africa's entire population (which is predicted to have reached 1,495 million by then) will be living in the continent's cities.[8] In real terms, this means that a city such as Lusaka, the capital of Zambia, which had a population of about 26,000 in 1950 and 1.69 million in 2000, has been acquiring additional residents at the rate of 70,000 per year – which is more than double the entire population of Liechtenstein. It is doubtful whether Liechtenstein or any other civic administration in the developed world would be able (and willing) to provide adequate housing, infrastructure and services for so many extra people year by year for decades, and yet that is precisely what the cities of the developing world have been struggling to do.

Meanwhile, although Africa's gross national product has been rising slowly throughout, the per capita share of those earnings has been steadily shrinking since the early 1980s. On average, individual Africans have become poorer, and the poorest of them are in the continent's largest cities — the places least able to cope with the pressure to provide basic services, let alone health care and jobs.

People flock to the cities in the hope of better prospects — a job, an education, or any opportunity to generate some economic advancement. And a primary problem of developing countries is that their governments have tended to adopt the same view — looking upon cities as the centres from which economic growth will be generated. On the assumption that growth would be most readily fuelled by foreign investment, many national development plans focused their investment priorities on the built environment of their largest cities in an attempt to attract and impress multinational companies. Immense sums of money were spent on government buildings, conference centres, luxury hotels and other showpiece buildings while basic needs such as health care, shelter, water and power supply or proper sewage systems received minimal attention.

More than 50 per cent of Nairobi's population lives in settlements that lack even the most basic amenities, for example. These settlements (slums, in more honest terminology) are only an hour or so from the extravagances of the city centre, but do not qualify for a share of the city's amenities because they are deemed to be 'illegal'.[9] In Dar es Salaam a survey of civic amenities found that even in the city's 'legal' residential areas only 22.6 per cent of dwellings had piped water, and as another example of how far the residents of Dar es Salaam are removed from the expectations of ratepayers in the developed world, it may be noted that a survey in the 1990s found only one of the city's fifteen fire engines in working order.[10]

The quality of life for the majority of people in cities like Dar es Salaam, Nairobi, Addis Ababa, Kinshasa or Lagos and others in developing countries is desperately low, with squatter or slum housing being the norm rather than the exception. So why do people migrate to the cities in such numbers? The answer, contrary to the idealised Western view of the countryside as a haven to which city-dwellers yearn to escape, is that prospects are even worse in the rural areas. The cities may be poor, but the countryside is poorer still.

In Mozambique, for instance, it is true that 32 per cent of people in the cities live *below* the poverty line, but they count themselves lucky when compared with people in the rural areas — only 30 per cent of whom live *above* the poverty line. And similar ratios of urban to rural poverty are found in developing countries around the world: in the Philippines, where 40 per cent of urban and 54.1 per cent of rural people live below the poverty line; in Brazil, with 37.7 per cent urban to 65.9 per cent rural poverty; and also in Uganda, India, Pakistan, Mexico and Peru – to cite just a few.[11]

Indonesia bucks the trend, with 3.6 per cent more impoverished people in the cities than in the rural areas.[12] Indonesian cities share the familiar roster of chronic housing shortages; severely limited access to fresh water and other services; appalling levels of air, noise and water pollution; and few chances of finding a job – but even here an authoritative study of urbanisation concludes that 'the incidence of poverty notwithstanding, urban Indonesians on average are better off than their rural cousins, on almost every indicator of social and economic well-being'.[13]

'Well-being' is a highly relative term when applied to people living on or below the poverty line, but for those in the cities of the developing world it means first and foremost that starvation is unlikely. Famine and starvation occur principally in the rural areas (most frequently as a result of natural disaster, war or civil strife). When the last of their reserves have been eaten and famine beckons, rural families have no choice but to wait for aid relief – or trek to the nearest distribution centre, or join the millions in the cities.

They know there is always a good chance of finding something to eat in a city – not necessarily on a regular basis, or of a consistent or even acceptable quality, but something. As a last resort, every city has a substantial body of wealthy people from whom it may be worth trying to beg the price of a loaf. Charities, hotel kitchens and restaurants give handouts, and markets regularly have to dispose of produce which though no longer deemed fit to sell is still fit to eat. But begging and scavenging are the very last option. Most people want to earn their living – though for a majority of city-dwellers in the developing world it is more a matter of surviving than living.

Many households spend well over half their total income on food alone. A survey of low-income households in Harare, the capital of Zimbabwe, found that in more than a third of cases food and beverages accounted for over 70 per cent of household expenditure.[14] A London household on the average national income spends less than 7 per cent of its income on essential consumables.[15]

But people survive, even below the poverty line in the cities of the developing world. Despite the absence of any discernible planning, the cities have managed to feed themselves as they have grown. This has surprised some observers. In a tone of mild astonishment, a paper on the marketing and distribution of staple foods in African countries commends the 'success of the African distributive system, which transferred goods and services with unobtrusive efficiency', and remarks that 'If African markets for basic foodstuffs worked less well, we should probably know a great deal more about them. The truth of the matter is that they have done a remarkably good job of their first task, which is the provisioning of cities and towns . . .'[16]

So long as market forces continued to function with such unobtrusive efficiency, policymakers were rarely obliged to become involved with the provisioning of cities, and as time passed any inclination they might have felt was completely overwhelmed by all the other problems of rapidly accelerating city growth. Today, although finding enough to eat is the principal concern of most city-dwellers (i.e. those living below the poverty line) in the developing world, the issue is politically invisible, obscured from policymakers by the more strident demands of overcrowding, decaying infrastructure, unemployment and declining services.

A famine in the countryside provokes rapid response from the authorities because large numbers of people are affected simultaneously and political credibility is at stake, but policymakers respond to urban hunger only when major problems of supply or sudden price rises bring large numbers of angry urban residents out onto the streets, demanding action. Then the issue rises above the political horizon and receives some attention. But of course, in those instances it is the moderately well-off and outspoken urban middle class who are complaining. Political considerations oblige the authorities to pay some attention to what they are complaining about – though whether their response does anything to ease the day-to-day problems of the hungry urban poor is another matter.

The cruel fact is that although city-dwellers living on or below the poverty line constitute a majority that can be counted in their millions, they have no political clout. Ensuring that the poor have enough to eat is not a problem that policymakers feel obliged to deal with. The unstated supposition is that the city's food provisioning difficulties will be eased by the knock-on effect of the extra jobs, improved infrastructure and better services the authorities are battling to generate. Meanwhile, finding food is regarded as a personal matter that everyone – even the impoverished and destitute – is expected to deal with themselves at the individual or household level.

Left to their own devices in this way, neglected by the civic authorities, the poorest inhabitants of impoverished cities have responded by creating what is becoming the biggest employer in most of the world's developing cities: farming.[17]

Farming in cities – urban agriculture – sounds like a contradiction in terms, but while conventional wisdom might insist that cities are for industry (with a little gardening for recreation) and serious agriculture is a wholly rural activity, growing food has become a lifeline for many millions of people in cities, bringing a measure of self-sufficiency to even the poorest of families. No visitor to Nairobi can fail to notice the plots of carefully-tended maize, cassava, beans, cabbages, tomatoes, spinach and other food crops that flourish on roadside verges, roundabouts and sundry patches of open ground.

A survey[18] of 100 cities in thirty countries conducted during the 1990s concluded that one in three of the world's urban households grows food, either for the table, to sell or both, and the figures are rising. In Kenya and Tanzania three of every five families are engaged in urban agriculture, in Taiwan the figure is over one in two. Bamako, capital of Mali, is self-sufficient in horticultural products and even supplies regions beyond the metropolitan area: in Kathmandu, urban agriculture supplies all vegetable needs for a third of the households surveyed: in Lusaka, illegal squatters derive a third of their total food needs from agricultural plots in the city. Crops are grown on a full 60 per cent of Bangkok's land area.[19]

And such productive urban agriculture is not limited to the developing world: in Moscow, two-thirds of families grow significant amounts of their own food; London produces roughly 16,000 t of vegetables annually (and, interestingly, 10 per cent of its honey consumption – a bonus derived from the huge number of flowering plants in the city – urban hives generally are more productive than their rural counterparts).[20] Even the world's richest nation, the United States, produces more than a third of the dollar value of its agricultural output within urban metropolitan areas.[21]

Of course urban agriculture is not new. The world's most ancient written records from Sumer specifically mention the presence of gardens within the city walls of Ur, Uruk and Eridu nearly 5,000 years ago. And since the Sumerian word for 'garden' also means 'onion' (see page 29), it can be safely assumed that these gardens were not simply ornamental flowerbeds. China too has a long history of urban agriculture, and today virtually all the vegetable needs of China's eighteen largest cities and half their meat and poultry is produced in urban areas[22] – which is doubtless a consequence of the expansive city planning scheme that became the norm in the early history of Imperial China (see chapter 6).

The Chinese are justly renowned for their highly intensive cropping systems, but the key point is that food production takes precedence in Chinese urban planning; the total amount of land over which the cities have administrative control is vast, but built-up areas are intentionally compact, industry is deliberately restricted to specific parts of the city, so as to leave as much space as possible for farming. Beijing, now a city of over 12 million people, directly administers a farming area that is the size of Belgium. In Shanghai (14.2 million inhabitants), only 20 per cent of the land under city administration is actually built on; the remainder is farmed, making the city self-sufficient in vegetables and producing much of its rice, pork, poultry and pond fish.[23]

In effect, China has tackled the problem of provisioning cities by integrating rural and urban activities under the authority of a single administration. In the West, the growth of capitalism that accompanied the Industrial Revolution drove them apart, leaving city food supplies dependent solely upon market forces and thus the profit motive – to the point at which city-dwellers were encouraged to believe that growing food was literally none of their business and should be left to the farmers.

In Britain, as people flocked to the industrial cities during the nineteenth century, some politicians urged that local authorities should be compelled to make plots of land available for people wishing to grow their own vegetables, but the proposal was controversial and in some quarters even interpreted as a devious means of keeping down the cost of labour. John Stuart Mill, for instance, condemned the idea as 'a contrivance to compensate the labourer for the insufficiency of his wages . . . a method of making people grow their own poor rate'.[24]

Nevertheless, the provision of 'allotments', as they became known, was made mandatory in 1908 under the Small Holdings and Allotments Act. Many city-dwellers took on allotments during the First World War and – despite official reluctance to promote the idea because it was believed that advising people to grow food would be bad for morale – by 1918 (when the government finally launched a campaign) there were over 1.3 million allotments in Britain producing vegetables at a rate of 2 million tonnes annually.[25] Allotments have an even longer history in Germany, the earliest having been established in the nineteenth century. Berlin alone had 40,000 allotment holders at the outbreak of the First World War. They doubtless were able to make up something of the shortfall in official rations so far as their household vegetable requirements were concerned, and so helped to alleviate the city's provisioning problems, but their contributions could do little to ease the shortage of commodities which previously had been imported (see chapter 10).

When war broke out again in 1939, the German government was far more circumspect about maintaining food supplies, and the British government was far less concerned that people would be demoralised by the suggestion they should grow their own food. As hostilities commenced, a campaign was launched in Britain under the slogan 'Dig for Victory'. The Minister of Agriculture spoke to the nation via the radio:

Half a million more allotments properly worked will provide potatoes and vegetables that will feed another million adults and one and a half million children for eight months of the year, so let's get going and let 'Dig for Victory' be the matter for every . . . man and woman capable of digging an allotment in their spare time.

Local authorities turned public parks and wasteland into allotments – and even commandeered private garden lawns. Dig for Victory exhibitions were organised, demonstration plots were established and millions of information leaflets were distributed. The pros and cons of the allotment were discussed in talks on the radio; vicars were urged to stress the virtues of growing food in their sermons; and some authorities appealed to the competitive spirit of their communities with offers of prizes for the best vegetables – and even for the best compost heap.

The campaign was a huge success, with more than 50 per cent of those eligible keeping an allotment during the war, according to best estimates. Donors in the USA, Canada, New Zealand and Australia sent seed; fertilisers were subsidised; and in 1944, 120,000 ha of allotments and gardens produced 1.3 million tons of food – enough to supply half of Britain's vegetable and fruit needs, a quarter of the nation's eggs, and a significant amount of pork.[26]

Unlike Britain in 1939, Cuba was not at war in December 1989, but thirty years of US trade embargoes nonetheless meant that when presidents Bush and Gorbachev announced the end of the Cold War, Cuba and especially Havana, the capital city, faced massive food-provisioning problems.[27]

Until that fateful day, the Cuban government had been able to fulfil its avowed belief that having enough to eat was a basic human right by making guaranteed supplies of staple foods available to every citizen at subsidised prices. With its economy tied to the Soviet bloc for more than three decades, Cuba had developed a conventional, capital-intensive agricultural industry, using lots of artificial fertilisers and pesticides in order to achieve and maintain maximum production of sugar and other crops for export – and thus foreign exchange.

Meanwhile, growing food for home consumption was not seen as a national priority. By the mid-1980s, over 50 per cent of all food consumed in Cuba was imported – and the dangers of such dependence on external suppliers were exposed by the collapse of the Soviet Union. Virtually overnight, Cuba lost access to direct food imports, and the cheap fuel, tractors, fertilisers and pesticides upon which its intensive production systems had become heavily dependent. Export earnings fell drastically – thus denying Cuba the means of buying from other markets – and imports plummeted. As food supplies dwindled and rationing was introduced, the crisis was compounded by a further tightening of the US embargo, and the amount of food available in Havana is estimated to have fallen by as much as 60 per cent between 1991 and 1995.

With more than three-quarters of the country's 11 million population living in urban areas – 2.1 million in Havana alone – drastic action was called for. Previously there had been no need for even the poorest city-dwellers to grow food, but now gardens began springing up everywhere. Catching the mood, the government abandoned its restrictive control of agricultural production. Growing food, whether for personal consumption or for sale, was actively encouraged. Garden tools, seeds and advice were made available to everyone; street markets, previously banned, were welcomed. Fidel Castro declared that no piece of land – however small – should be left uncultivated (in due course the front lawn of the Ministry of Agriculture was given over to crops planted by employees).

Furthermore, because imported fertilisers and pesticides were no longer available, Cuba's urban agriculture was wholly organic – there was no alternative. 'Our problems must be solved without feedstocks, fertilisers or fuel,' Castro had declared in 1991 and so, making a virtue of necessity, Cuba's 'alternative model' has become the most impressive conversion to science-based, low-input urban agriculture in history – and certainly one of the most inventive. The aim is sustainability.

Education had been a first priority in Cuba since the revolution, and here was evidence that the policy pays dividends: Cuba has only 2 per cent of Latin America's total population, but 11 per cent of the region's scientists. As the food crisis loomed, and farmers were obliged to rediscover the sustainable techniques of their grandparents, replacing tractors with oxen, scientists were assigned to the cause of advancing sustainable agriculture. Newly graduated 'barefoot' agronomists (as they became known) went to work on the development of organic fertilisers and pesticides. Soon, more than 200 bio-tech centres were producing and distributing non-toxic bio-fertilisers and pesticides based on indigenous micro-organisms.

By 2000, over 40 per cent of Havana's 721 km^2 urban area was devoted to growing vegetables and fruit, supplying the city with 60 per cent of its needs. A 1996 city by-law allows only organic methods, and certainly nothing that grows in Ricardo Sanchez's garden needs anything from elsewhere. He feeds the vegetable plots with compost made from kitchen-waste, and protects the crops with a home-made natural pesticide. His catfish are fed on worms and larvae, and his rabbits on leaves and herbs. Tomatoes, guavas, avocados, mangoes and herbs jostle for space under the palm trees standing between his house and the neighbours.

This is intensive urban agriculture, demanding but highly productive, and only one of about 62,000 patio gardens – private plots of less than 800 m^2 – in Havana, all enjoying official support and abiding by the edicts of eco-organic production. Not all are as large as Ricardo Sanchez's – small backyards, verandahs, balconies and rooftops have all been put to use and officially recognised. In Cuba as a whole, more than a million patio gardens have been registered.

The patio garden functions at an individual or household level. Next in line are the market gardens organised by neighbourhood co-operatives, larger, and often employing a full-time staff as well as calling on the voluntary efforts of cooperative members. At the start of the urban agriculture movement, the government gave unused city land to any group that wanted to cultivate it. Now there are more than twenty 'organoponicus' gardens, as they are called, in the city. More than a hectare in size, all use an intensive raised-bed method of production; some are even situated on paved vacant lots and areas of poor or degraded soil that would be otherwise useless. The produce of the organoponicus gardens is generally sold on the spot – principally to members of the cooperative, but also to anyone who turns up. Prices are lower than in the city markets, though higher than in government-controlled outlets. But for cooperative members and casual customers alike it is the quality that is most appreciated – fresh and organic.

With Havana alone growing 60 per cent of its vegetable needs within the city boundary, the Cubans are justly proud of their urban agricultural revolution, and they see it as a beacon for the future. Some day, the US embargoes will be lifted. Cuba will be free to import artificial fertilisers and pesticides, tractors and fuel again; the economy will expand, and urban land will become too valuable for mere gardening. But Cubans engaged in urban agriculture are confident of maintaining the sustainable organic practices that necessity forced upon them. 'Americans want good food too,' says one. 'We'll export the stuff to them.' And an influential figure in government circles says: 'We've put an immense educational effort into sustainability. It simply isn't the policy of the government to have cheap imported goods. When the Americans lift the embargo, there will be tough negotiations. We want to attract investment rather than cheap goods. We fought the Americans for 40 years and they won't get the better of us now.'

Havana's achievements in urban agriculture are impressive, showing how much a city can do to feed itself and how quickly the benefits accrue once the need is recognised and the means facilitated. But Havana was helped by a factor which other cities in the developing world do not share: its food crisis was not compounded by a constant and massive influx of immigrants. Between 1990 and 2000, Havana's population grew from 2.1 to 2.3 million. Two hundred thousand is a substantial number of extra people, but a large proportion of them came from within the city population itself – from the increasing size of urban families as child mortality rates dropped and people lived longer.

Nairobi's population by contrast grew from 1.4 to 2.3 million during those same ten years; Mexico City added 3 million, growing from 15.1 to 18.1; Lagos had 10.2 million inhabitants in 1990, 13.5 million in 2000 – a massive 3.3 million increase that in itself was greater than the entire population of Lagos twenty-five years before.[28] Similar rates of growth occurred in cities throughout the developing world. Of course, some of it came from within the urban populations themselves – as in Havana – but most of the extra people were immigrants with little or no pre-existing means of support in the cities.

Furthermore, Havana was not the only city to suffer under the new world order that came with the end of the Cold War. The so-called Structural Adjustment Programmes imposed on developing and debt-ridden countries by the World Bank and the International Monetary Fund were intended to wean developing nations away from their aid and dependency cultures, into the realm of economic viability. The programmes made sense in terms of good financial management, but the reality of their application was harsh. Governments were required to balance their budgets, but could do so only by slashing what meagre funds they had been allocating to social needs and services – education, health, and the like. These moves may eventually establish a sound basis for economic growth that will benefit all; in the meantime, though, they have made life for most people even harder than it had been before. Just one example: while the population of Nairobi grew by 51 per cent between 1989 and 1997, wage employment in the formal sector grew by only 15 per cent. [29]

In all, only a third of Nairobi's working population has a regular job; the rest depend upon what has become known as the 'informal sector' for their livelihood. Now recognised as an integral part of the economies of large cities in the developing world,[30] the informal sector covers numerous activities, anything from scavenging on rubbish tips and shining shoes to offering a letter-writing service or repairing cars. It can represent a substantial fraction of a city's total economic activity, though it contributes absolutely nothing to city revenues in the way of taxes, licence fees or rates. In Kenya the informal sector has been christened *jua kali*, Kiswahili for 'fierce sun', in recognition of the fact that it typically operates in the open air, unprotected from the elements.

Jua kali is an appropriate term for one of Nairobi's most widespread informal activities – urban agriculture – and here the city has been remarkably (though unintentionally) generous. The city had lots of open space suitable for cultivation just when it was most needed. The origin of this happy paradox – a city bursting at the seams with people, but graced with abundant open space – lies with the reaction of planners to the squalor of industrial cities in Europe: new cities, especially colonial capitals, would be built to plans that eliminated the risk of squalor taking hold.

An awareness that something should be done about the wretched physical and social conditions of the world's industrial cities is almost as old as the cities themselves. One only has to think of Dickens and Zola, who were bringing to public attention the situations of which city-planners and architects were well aware. But what could be done? Not very much, so far as established cities were concerned, but at least their problems generated a lot of discussion on how a new city should be designed. The 'City Beautiful' movement emerged during the latter half of the nineteenth century. There was some resonance of classical concepts here, but also of late-Victorian gentility. 'Beautiful' was not a word that many would have been inclined to put alongside 'city', but the movement was given a unique opportunity for showing what it had in mind when central Chicago was rebuilt after the fire of 1871.

The Great Chicago Fire destroyed an area 6 km long and an average of 1.2 km wide – nearly 800 ha – including over 45 km of streets and 200 km of sidewalks (with over 2,000 lampposts). Eighteen thousand buildings and some $200 million in property were destroyed, about a third of the valuation of the entire city. The rebuilding of the city is a story in itself, most especially insofar as Chicago became the first city to which the ideals of the 'City Beautiful' were comprehensively applied. To commemorate its rebirth, Chicago was host to the World Exposition of 1893, and the 'White City', as it became known, attracted millions of visitors. Commentators with a professional interest in city planning admired the 'thrilling revelation of the powers of architects, landscape architects, sculptors and painters to evoke rapture and delight' in a city hitherto known principally for its slaughterhouses and grain-shipping facilities. Chicago's elaborate civic centres, treelined boulevards, waterfront plazas and parks, and overall design of balance and beauty showed the world 'what an ideal city might be,'[31]and inspired city planning everywhere.

In Europe, the ideals of the City Beautiful movement were carried forward by Ebenezer Howard in his 'Garden City' designs, which integrated thoughtful zoning of residential, industrial and commercial areas with large expanses of open space. Howard's book, *Tomorrow: A Peaceful Path to Real Reform,* published in 1899 (reissued as *Garden Cities of Tomorrow* in 1902), together with the founding of the Garden City Association in the same year, set the fashion for city planning in Britain and abroad during the twentieth century. Indeed, with colonies around the world, 'abroad' was virtually a laboratory for British city-planners. 'We want not only England but all parts of the Empire to be covered with Garden Cities,' an editorial in the journal *Garden City* declared in 1907.[32]

Certainly there was plenty of room – especially in Africa – as administrative centres were built, and railheads and ports were constructed to facilitate the extraction and export of produce from the colonies. Some of these centres were grafted onto pre-existing indigenous towns, such as Lagos and Kampala. And in at least one instance the ideals of the Garden City were applied even before the term had been invented, as when Sir Gerald Portal founded the British Mission to Uganda in 1893:

I moved the HQ from that close, unhealthy and altogether hateful spot Kampala to a lovely place on the Lake; two great grassy hills, like the Kingsclere Downs, rising almost straight out of the water; and a view over the Lake like a sea dotted with a dozen islands. I put the European quarters on the highest hill, and the Soudanese troops on the lower one, and we marked out all the streets and divisions giving each man a small compound, and established a market place, and cut great wide roads in every direction. Before I left there was already quite a neat town of about 1000 inhabitants, ten times more healthy than at Kampala.[33]

Elsewhere, the planners had *carte blanche*. The capital city and government centre of Northern Rhodesia (now Zambia) took its name from that of a local headman, Lusaakas, which in the Lenje language means 'thorn bush'[34] and accurately describes the site for which the British consultant (and ardent disciple of Ebenezer Howard), S. D. Adshead, was commissioned to design a city in 1931. 'It could hardly be described as a dramatic situation,' Adshead confessed, 'but covered with buildings it could be seen to advantage from a considerable distance, more especially along the line of the railway.'[35]

Salisbury (now Harare, the capital of Zimbabwe), Bulawayo and Blantyre (now Lilongwe, capital of Malawi) were similarly located for the convenience of colonial endeavours, but of all Britain's town-planning exploits in Africa it is Nairobi that best illustrates the Garden City dream of the mid twentieth century and the unimagined advantages it bequeathed to the city's impoverished residents fifty years later.

Sergeant Ellis of the Royal Engineers was the first white man to live in Nairobi. In 1896 he established a staging depot at the site, with stores and stables for the oxen and mules used as transport animals for the colonial administration. When construction of the railway from Mombasa to Uganda reached Nairobi three years later, the company decided to make its headquarters there and duly built a station, workshops and accommodation for its managers and employees.

Being just over halfway along the total length of the line, with a 40 km climb to the summit of the Kikuyu escarpment ahead, followed by a precipitous descent into the Rift Valley (and a long haul out again on the other side), Nairobi was a good place at which to base preparations for the difficult tasks ahead. But it was hardly the most suitable site for a city. In the words of an engineer in charge of track-laying operations, it was 'a bleak, swampy stretch of soppy landscape, devoid of human habitation of any sort, the resort of thousands of wild animals of every species'.[36]

'Uaso Nairobi', meaning 'cold water' in the vernacular, is the name the Maasai had given to the stream which flows from the hills onto the Athi plain at that point, and the name very accurately described the principal features of the site. Nairobi may be less than 200 km south of the equator but it is often miserably cool and damp. The stream, as it struck the plain in those days, spread out to create an elongated papyrus swamp which, at 2,000 m above sea level and with high ground to the north prone to trap rising moist air, was (and still is) frequently covered with a blanket of chilling cloud. 'The ground on which the town is built is low and swampy. The supply of water is indifferent, and the situation generally unhealthy,' Winston Churchill wrote following a visit to Nairobi in 1907, concluding that since 'It is now too late to change . . . lack of foresight and of a comprehensive view leaves its permanent imprint upon the countenance of a new country.'[37]

A census taken in the year before Churchill's visit recorded 559 Europeans, 3,582 Asians and 7,371 Africans living in Nairobi. By 1944 this total of 11,512 had swollen nearly tenfold to 108,900 – with 10,400 Europeans, 34,300 Asians and 64,200 Africans.[38] Nairobi was the largest urban centre in East Africa, and was expected to retain its premier position as Britain's three East African territories – Kenya, Tanganyika and Uganda – were nudged towards economic independence. Political independence, though in reality less than twenty years away, was not then on the agenda. The British aim was self-sufficiency (and minimal burden on the British taxpayer), which meant intensified development of the colonies' export potential – mainly agricultural, principally tea, coffee and sisal.

Suitable candidates were encouraged to emigrate from Britain to East Africa and become farmers. Sizeable sums of government money were made available for development schemes. The East African Groundnut Scheme began with an outlay of £25 million, for instance, and was cited as a model of the type of investment which would transform the Empire (the scheme was a disastrous failure). Meanwhile, experts were com-missioned to tackle the problem of how Nairobi, a 'frontier' town of railwaymen and pioneering settlers, could be transformed into a capital city worthy of the British Empire.

The *Nairobi Master Plan for a Colonial Capital* was published in 1948. Its three authors had come to the task with long experience of working in South Africa. Professor L. W. Thornton White was a practising architect and head of the Department of Architecture at Cape Town University; Mr L. Silberman was a lecturer in Social Studies at the University of the Witwatersrand in Johannesburg; and Mr P. Anderson was a town planning engineer responsible for the design of a steelworks town with 200,000 inhabitants at Vereeniging.

Though of course conscious that Nairobi, like every city in modern Africa, was built primarily for the benefit of Europeans and accommodated Africans only to the extent that they served European interests, the *Master Plan* claimed 'to be completely neutral on the subject of racial segregation'. But this was not easy to achieve. Racial segregation was a hot potato in Africa at that time. The British government had formally disowned it as a matter of policy but, if anything, this had hardened the opinion of those among Nairobi's white residents who were keen to see segregation made a reality in the city. Apartheid was about to become official policy in South Africa, and many whites in East Africa thought it was a good idea. They spoke forebodingly of instances where deliberate integration had led to 'racial and communal riots'.[39]

Adopting what its authors described as a 'humanistic bias' on the segregation issue, the *Master Plan* in effect concluded that the matter was best left to economic determinants, implying that when enough Asians and Africans had become sufficiently rich Nairobi would be a fully integrated city. Meanwhile, its zoning proposals stipulated that the existing densities of one house per acre should be retained in residential districts occupied by Europeans, two per acre where the residents were mostly Asian, and twelve per acre where most of the Africans lived.[40] Fortunately there was no shortage of space in which to accommodate this scheme.

The municipal area of Nairobi was about 85 km², giving an average population density of 12 persons per hectare – 'exceedingly low' in the words of the *Master Plan* and providing ample scope for the application of the Garden City concept of Ebenezer Howard to which its authors were firmly committed. '[The Garden City concept] conceives of town planning primarily as landscape gardening,' they wrote. 'It wishes to preserve as much of the rural atmosphere as possible in an urban area by restricting densities . . .'[41]

With its population growth predictions estimating that Nairobi would have a total of no more than about 250,000 inhabitants by 1975, after which it was thought unlikely to increase very much more (and undesirable that it should), the *Master Plan* was designed to ensure that Nairobi would always 'continue to afford that open-air life and sense of spaciousness which is the particular delight of the Kenya highlands.'[42] Indeed, an entire chapter was devoted to the subject of 'Open Spaces', emphasising that 'the importance of healthful, out-of-doors recreation grows steadily with the mounting intensity of modern industry and commercial life', and stressing that for the *Master Plan*:

'Open Spaces' means more than the preservation of tracts of land for vegetation, and the prevention of house building and the spread of industry. It means the conscious treatment of that preserved space, its landscaping and utilisation for enjoyment. What can be done with Open Space has been shown by many peoples and civilisations, each giving expression to a vital part of themselves, indeed contributing to that civilisation and summarising it to others.[43]

In pursuit of its Garden City ideal, the *Master Plan* called for the separate zoning of Nairobi's residential, commercial and industrial districts; for large areas of parkland and forest reserve to be preserved for public use; for broad grassy byways to be established along the Nairobi river and other natural water courses running through the city; for the exclusion of through traffic from residential areas, and the aesthetic as well as functional conversion of main roads into wide boulevards with grassed central islands, landscaped traffic roundabouts and wide verges. Spaciousness was the key concept, and to no small extent this was facilitated – if not fore-ordained – by an early colonial administrator, John Ainsworth, who had insisted that Nairobi's main thoroughfares should be broad enough to permit the turning of a wagon pulled by a full span of oxen.[44]

Nairobi's *Master Plan* still defines the layout of the city and its suburbs, even though its population in 2002 was more than ten times the maximum envisaged by the planners in 1948. Their estimate of a 250,000 maximum was reached in little more than ten years; by 1975 the population was 677,000; and by 2000 it stood at 2.3 million and is predicted to be nearly 3 million by 2005.[45]

But even while the population of Nairobi was growing so dramatically, urban poverty remained negligible for several decades; surveys in the mid-1970s found that only 2.9 per cent of households in Nairobi were living below the poverty line.[46] Since then, though, the economic downturn precipitated by the combined forces of the oil crisis, structural adjustment programmes and the end of the Cold War has made life much harder for the majority of people in Nairobi.

Many of Nairobi's impoverished citizens have taken to urban farming. For them, the open spaces that the *Master Plan* bequeathed to Nairobi are not venues for 'healthful, out-of-doors recreation', but patches of land which are vital for the maintenance of life itself. Most of Nairobi's urban farmers are crushingly poor; three-quarters of them cultivate land which is not theirs, and nearly half are using public land. Many possess no more than the most basic tools – a jembe (a traditional spade) and perhaps a machete; few own even a watering-can or a bucket; most describe their motivation in a single word: hunger.[47]

Inevitably, some of the open spaces created or preserved under the *Master Plan* have been re-zoned, and tracts of land that not long ago supported *jua kali* and urban farming enterprises are now given over to neat rows of middle-class townhouses. Furthermore, growing food in Nairobi is illegal. The Local Government Act empowers the City Commission to 'prohibit cultivation by unauthorised persons of any unenclosed and unoccupied land in private ownership and of any Government land and land reserved for any public road'.[48] As the land available for urban agriculture and *jua kali* has become more and more limited, and the activities more visible, calls for the law to be strictly enforced have become ever more strident.

In particular, some influential upper-income Kenyans and members of the expatriate business and diplomatic community have tended to regard urban farming and *jua kali* as an unsightly and embarrassing blot on the landscape – an unwelcome reminder that while the city is attempting to project an aura of progress and modernity, the basic needs of the poor are being neglected. At times city officials appeared to be acting as enthusiastic agents for this minority group, intensifying their crackdowns on unsightly *jua kali* enterprises and urban farming whenever international conferences brought large numbers of foreign visitors to the city. 'What is going on?' supporters of the informal sector asked, sensing that city officials seemed more concerned with presenting an illusion of modern sophistication than with confronting the realities that forced so many Nairobi residents to live in poverty. A Kenyan parliamentarian observed: 'do you hide your disabled child because a visitor is coming?'[49]

12

Cities Built on Water

No city can survive without an adequate and dependable source of water. The Aztec capital, Tenochtitlan, was located on an island in a large freshwater lake. Mexico City now occupies the site. The lake has gone; the city pumps in a substantial proportion of its water from elsewhere. Mexico City is an extreme example of environmental problems confronting the world's rapidly growing large cities.

Water, along with food, sunlight and air, is a vital resource without which life is impossible – indeed, water is life's solvent, essential for the transport of nutrients around the body (or plant) and the elimination of wastes. Some organisms require more water than others, and people need a great deal. The water content of a 65 kg human being, for instance, is nearly 50 litres, of which the average person loses and must replace about 2.5 litres every day in order to stay healthy. Thus people must have access to a good and dependable supply. These somewhat self-evident observations lead to the point that acquiring, designing and maintaining an adequate water supply is the biggest challenge that growing cities face, one that has inspired leading-edge feats of engineering.

The Roman aqueducts come to mind, remnants of which still stand solid nearly two millennia after their construction. At the dawn of the third millennium there is the unsung marvel of London's Ring Main – an 80-km-long water pipe, wide enough to take a London taxi – which encircles the city at a greater depth than most tube lines and is constantly full of water pure enough to drink. The Ring Main supplies London with over 1,300 million litres of water each day – enough to fill the

Albert Hall eight times over, the Thames Water website proudly reports, and has pump-out shafts capable of filling an average-sized swimming pool in under 50 seconds.[1]

But London's Ring Main, though of hugely impressive dimensions, is just the latest development in the city's history of keeping up with its citizens' water demands. Over the years since London began tackling its water supply requirements in an organised manner in the seventeenth century, the city has laid more than 80,000 km of mains pipelines under London's streets, with over 18 million connections. And like all urban residents, Londoners use lots of water. The 2.5 litres essential for bodily functions are but a fraction of daily consumption – showers and flush toilets, washing machines and dishwashers, garden sprinklers and car-washes bring the total up to an average of more than 250 litres per person, every day. And here perhaps it is worth noting that if you had to fetch that amount of water from the well, carrying two large bucketfuls at a time, you would have to make twelve or thirteen trips.

Even so, the average Londoner's water consumption is actually quite modest when compared with that of the United States, where 250 litres per day is about the minimum. Maximum US consumption is over 1,100 litres and the average consumption works out at 660 litres per person per day. South of the border, the residents of Mexico City each consume an average of 364 litres per day[2] – not unreasonable for a modern city, but already stretching the country's water resources and engineering ingenuity to its limits and posing serious problems for the future.

In 1950, Mexico City was home to just 2.8 million people. In the following fifty years, the population of the city soared to 18 million and is expected to exceed 19 million by 2015.[3] The water requirement figures are daunting: 19 million people, each using over 300 litres of water per day, works out to the equivalent of a lake one metre deep, one kilometre wide, and 5.7 km long – every day. Finding a source of that much water, and getting it to the consumers, is a challenge of dimensions that no city has ever faced. No wonder hydrologists and water supply engineers from around the world look upon Mexico City as a test case in the provision and management of urban water supplies.

Mexico City is built over the site of Tenochtitlan, capital of the Aztec empire, whose rulers controlled a vast territory and the destiny of millions during the fifteenth and early sixteenth centuries. The modern history of the city began in November 1519, when a contingent of Spanish conquistadors under the command of Hernán Cortés left Churultecal (present-day Cholula city), in the shadow of the then-active Popacatepetl and Iztaccihuatl volcanoes, and took the road to Tenochtitlan. Cortés intended to meet the Aztec ruler, Montezuma,[4] and persuade him to submit to the sovereignty of Spain and the church of Christ. His ambition was not only to conquer Mexico, however, but to colonise it as well, and to that end he had ordered the destruction of the ships which had brought his expedition to the shores of Mexico. There could be no turning back.

The heartland of the Aztec empire is a high mountain valley known as the Basin of Mexico. Lying some 2,250 m above sea level, the Basin is the highest valley in the region, surrounded by a succession of magnificent volcanic mountain ranges on three sides, and on the fourth by a series of hills and low ranges, making it a closed watershed and ecological unit of about 7,500 km^2 in area. Water cascaded from the mountains into the Basin, but none drained from it in Aztec times, and thus a chain of five shallow lakes filled about 1,500 km^2 of the Basin floor – lakes with many islands, and irregular shorelines of bays and promontories and marshland. Numerous villages and towns were located close to the lakes, and Tenochtitlan itself occupied a large island in the south-west corner of the largest lake, connected to the shore by causeways up to 8 km in length.

Archaeologists have estimated that by 1519 there were about 1.5 million people living in the Basin of Mexico, distributed among more than 100 towns – making it one of the world's most densely settled urbanised regions at that time[5] – comparable with parts of China, perhaps. At Tenochtitlan, the area of continuous urban habitation was between 12 and 15 km^2, housing a population in the vicinity of 150,000 – 200,000 people.[6] Cortés and his men had seen nothing like it before as they approached Tenochtitlan on 8 November 1519, as one of his officers, Diáz del Castillo, reported:

During the morning, we arrived at a broad Causeway . . . and when we saw so many cities and villages built in the water and other great towns on dry land and that straight and level Causeway going towards Tenochtitlan, we were amazed and said it was like the enchantments they tell of in the legend of Amadis, on account of the great towers and temples and buildings rising from the water, and all built of masonry. And some of our soldiers even asked whether the things we saw were not a dream . . . seeing things as we did that had never been heard of or seen before, nor even dreamed about.[7]

Montezuma treated the Spaniards most hospitably at first, lodging them in his father's palace and proudly inviting them to the summit of the Great Temple for a panoramic view of the lakes and its cities. From there, Montezuma took Cortés by the hand, writes Diáz del Castillo:

and told him to look at his great city and all the other cities that were standing in the lake, and the many other towns on the land round the lake . . . So we stood looking about us . . . we saw the three causeways which led into Tenochtitlan . . . and we saw the fresh water [aqueduct] which supplies the city, and we saw the bridges on the three causeways . . . through which the water of the lake flowed in and out from one side to the other, and we beheld on that great lake a great multitude of canoes, some coming with supplies of food and others returning loaded with cargoes of merchandise; and we saw from every house of that great city and of all the other cities that were built in the water it was impossible to pass from house to house, except by drawbridges . . . or in canoes; and we saw in those cities temples and oratories like towers and fortresses and all gleaming white, and it was a wonderful thing to behold . . .

. . . we turned to look at the great market place and the crowds of people that were in it, some buying and others selling, so that the murmur and hum of their voices and words that they used could be heard more than a league off. Some of the soldiers among us who had been in many parts of the world, in Constantinople, and all over Italy, and in Rome, said that so large a marketplace and so full of people and so well regulated and arranged, they had never beheld before.[8]

In letters to the king of Spain, Cortés wrote that Tenochtitlan was as big as Seville or Córdoba, with wide main streets and many squares – one of which was:

twice as big as that of Salamanca, with arcades all around, where more than 60,000 people come each day to buy and sell, and where every kind of merchandise produced in these lands is found; provisions as well as ornaments of gold and silver, lead, brass, copper, tin, stones, shells, bones, and feathers . . . There is a street where they sell game and birds of every species . . . They sell rabbits and hares, and stags and small gelded dogs which they breed for eating.

There are streets of herbalists . . . shops like apothecaries' . . . There is every sort of vegetable . . . and there are many sorts of fruit, among which are cherries and plums like those in Spain. They sell honey, wax, and a syrup made from maize canes, which is as sweet and syrupy as that made from the sugar cane . . . There are many sorts of spun cotton, in hanks of every colour, and it seems like the silk market at Granada, except that here there is a much greater quantity . . .[9]

The list goes on – firewood and charcoal; mats and mattresses; earthenware; leather; dyes; grain and bread; fresh, salted and cooked fish; chicken and fish pies; hen and goose eggs. Virtually anything an Aztec city-dweller could desire was available in the markets and streets of Tenochtitlan. In this respect the eye-witness reports of Cortés and Díaz del Castillo invite a conclusion concerning life in Tenochtitlan which has subsequently been confirmed by archaeological and historical evidence from other sources: the Aztecs ran a tribute economy. In other words, they required people under their control to pay for the upkeep of the empire and its capital. Like most cities, Tenochtitlan was dependent on the supplies and goods it received from outlying communities; but unlike other cities, its relationship with its suppliers was aggressively parasitic – not at all symbiotic.

The fact is that, although the basin was environmentally diverse, its productivity was limited. And as population growth in Tenochtitlan and its urban satellites had begun to outstrip available resources, the Aztecs resorted to warfare with their neighbours as a means of meeting their needs. But they were not interested in occupying or settling in the conquered territories; they simply harnessed the available resources to their own ends. The vanquished were forced to pay tribute, and the appropriation of food and other goods in this way became more and more essential as the Aztec ruling system evolved and its population expanded. In effect, warfare and tribute became fundamental to the economy of the Aztec empire.

When the Spanish arrived in 1519, they found that a total of 371 towns were paying tribute to Tenochtitlan.[10] In a single year the city imported 7,000 tons of maize, 5,000 tons of beans, and 8,000 tons of sundry other produce – which adds up to 20,000 tons of produce in all, an average of 55 tons per day. Large quantities of dried fish, chillies, cacao seeds, cotton, henequen fibres, vanilla, honey and fruits were among the many other products regularly brought into the city.[11]

The Aztecs built no grand ships, but their capital city, Tenochtitlan, was dependent on water transport for 95 per cent of its subsistence needs. For strategic reasons, the city was located on an island in the largest of the five interconnected lakes which filled much of the Basin of Mexico in Pre-Columbian times. From all around the lake, land transport throughout the Aztec-controlled regions of Mesoamerica was handled by the *tlamemes*, an occupational group (probably hereditary) of men, women and children specifically committed to a lifelong career of portage labour – carrying goods. The *tlamemes* were well organised and numerous. They operated in relay fashion, with the best porters capable of carrying a load of 23 kg up to 28 km between relay stations in a day. So the hinterland (and thus food supply and sustainable population size) of a city on the plateau area of central Mexico was effectively limited to the distance the *tlamemes* could cover in a day – 28 km.[12]

But since Tenochtitlan could be supplied by water as well as by land, its hinterland was not just a 28 km radius around the city, but actually extended 28 km inland around the entire lake shore – from which a single canoe could transport up to forty *tlameme* loads to the city in a matter of hours. Thus an advantageous combination of location and transport systems gave Tenochtitlan access to a vast economic hinterland and explains (along with Aztec political and military ambitions) the city's dominant status in Mesoamerica.[13]

Tenochtitlan was a city with up to 200,000 inhabitants when Hernán Cortés and his conquistadors arrived there in November 1519. The lake was swarming with canoes. Early Spanish accounts vary in their estimates of the total number supplying Tenochtitlan at that time, ranging from 50,000 up to 200,000; but even as late as 1580, the colonial administration reported that from 3,000 to 4,000 canoes a day were making the 10 km crossing from Mexicalzinco (on the southern shore of the main lake) to Mexico City[14] – and it may be supposed that many more were supplying the city from other parts of the lake.

The Aztec canoes were dugouts – shallow-draft, square-bow craft which must have varied in size as much as the single logs from which they were hewn. One early Spanish writer described canoes that he claimed were as big as the tower of a well-known church – 30 m long and 10 m wide; another records lengths of up to 11 m and a modern estimate puts the range at from 4 to 15 m.[15] But whatever the size, the efficiency of their operation is not in dispute. Job demarcation was strict.

The canoeists themselves were a specialised body of men, with responsibilities limited to the conveyance of goods while other fraternities dealt
with dockside matters, such as sales, storage, loading and unloading;
some workers did nothing but launch canoes. The cargoes they carried
included everything produced in central Mexico, but most were bulk
commodities, such as maize and other cereals, salt, meat, fish, fruit,
flowers and vegetables, as well as building materials – stone, timber and
sand. And supplying Tenochtitlan with its needs was aided to a considerable extent (given the quantities involved) by the current flowing
from the upper lakes to the lower lake in which Tenochtitlan was
located. Thus heavily laden canoes bound for the city were assisted by
the current, and were lightly laden on the return journey against the
current.

To preserve fresh produce, inward journeys were made at night – six
to eight hours for a typical trip – and there was always a fine balance to
be drawn between size and speed: the larger canoes carried more, but
travelled more slowly and required additional paddlers if the average
speed was to be attained, thus incurring additional costs, while a one-
man canoe could transport a substantial cargo with relative ease. Diáz del
Castillo reports seeing a single man poling a canoe loaded with over a
ton of maize:[16] the equivalent of more than forty *tlameme* loads.

Unsurprisingly, the Aztecs' dependence on a warfare and tribute
economy caused deep resentment among the subjugated groups. Cortés
was not slow to realise that this discontent could be used to his
advantage. He made alliances with those hardest hit by the Aztec's
demands for tribute, and with their help was able to take Tenochtitlan
with only a few dozen Spanish soldiers. By August 1521 he controlled
the entire Aztec empire.

Without doubt, Tenochtitlan's isolation and lack of self-sufficiency
contributed significantly to the ease with which the Spanish took
control of the Aztec empire – though more insidious agents were also at
work. The diseases that Cortés (and other groups that joined him from
Spain) brought to Mexico killed thousands throughout the Basin. A
devastating smallpox epidemic left Tenochtitlan with only 30,000
inhabitants at the beginning of its existence as a colonial city (and that
figure included Spanish settlers). One hundred years after the Conquest,
the population of the entire Basin had fallen from 1.5 million to fewer
than 100,000.[17]

With the Spanish Conquest, Tenochtitlan was renamed Mexico City.

Both transportation and agricultural practices in the Mexico Basin changed too – with far more serious effect. Many of the water supply and irrigation canals built by the Aztecs were filled in to make roads for the horses, mules, wheeled carts and wagons that the Spanish introduced to Mexico. They continued to employ the *tlamemes* and canoes, but as disease drastically reduced the size of the indigenous population, and the navigable area of the lakes was reduced by Spanish drainage schemes, their capital city became increasingly dependent on animals for transport. A seventeenth–century source states that more than 3,000 mules arrived in Mexico City every day with supplies of wheat, corn, sugar and other goods for the city.[18]

The logistical implications of relying on mules to such an extent are not insignificant – especially when compared with the functional elegance and economic advantage of maintaining a fleet of canoes. Even raising mules is a complex matter. They are sterile hybrids, produced by mating female horses with male donkeys (jacks). Thus maintaining a population of mules calls for the breeding and rearing of three other populations: donkeys for the jacks, horses for the mares, jacks and mares for the mules.

Mules are strong and have lots of stamina. They could carry the loads of four *tlameme* porters over the same distance in a day, but they could never match the efficiency of water transport. A fleet of just 250 canoes could have supplied Mexico City with as much cargo as 3,000 mules[19] – and would have left less of a mess behind.

Apart from mules, donkeys and horses, the Spanish also brought in cattle, sheep, goats and pigs. These of course were needed as a source of meat, but their introduction severely affected the environment, with ultimately disastrous consequences for the water balance of the region. The land use and character of the surrounding mountains changed dramatically, as forests were felled to provide timber for construction, and to create grazing lands for the Spanish livestock. Inevitably, stripping the mountain slopes like this caused a major increase in surface runoff, and in the amount of silt brought down into the lakes during the rainy season. Environmental conditions changed still more drastically as roads were built and obstructed the flow of surface water in and around the city. Large expanses of stagnant water were created.

In due course, these changes made the lake on which Tenochtitlan was located more prone to flooding (since it occupied the floor of a closed basin), and whereas the Aztecs had had to contend with an infrequent severe flood, the Spanish found themselves facing a constant threat. Their response was to construct a canal which would drain excess water away from the lake towards lower altitudes in the north. The Mexico Basin was closed no more.

The first canal, built in 1608, was 15 km long and served only as a spillover system, taking water from the Basin when the lakes became dangerously full; but with the construction of larger canals in the eighteenth and nineteenth centuries, drainage was more or less continuous, and the lacustrine area of the Basin began to shrink rapidly. Now the aim was not only to avert flooding but also to create more dry land, and as the long arm of the Industrial Revolution brought railroads and factories to Mexico during the late nineteenth and early twentieth centuries, urban settlement in the Basin, once regarded as a series of separate towns linked by commerce, now became a single urban unit – Mexico City.

As the lake shrank Mexico City grew. The urban population reached 50,000 by 1689 and rose to 105,000 by 1790 – a twofold increase in 100 years. By 1900, nearly four centuries after the Spanish conquest, the city had a population of 344,000. And then it raced ahead – doubling to 700,000 in the ten years to 1910 and growing more than fifty-fold during the twentieth century as a whole. By the year 2000 Mexico City had a population of over 18 million.[20] And now, with the lakes drained and so much of the Basin covered with tarmac and concrete, water is more of a problem than it ever was. A substantial proportion of the rain falling on the Basin and the surrounding watershed is now directed away from the city by the drainage system, or lost to evaporation. Only a fraction soaks down to replenish the aquifer from which Mexico City draws its water supply.

Since Aztec times, wells had supplemented the springs and aqueducts which brought water to the city. By the late twentieth century they were its principal source of supply, with the city authorities pumping a massive volume of water each day from 347 wells – some up to 200 m deep. In addition, over 3,000 officially registered private wells and anything from 5,000 to 10,000 illegal wells were also pumping water from the aquifer.[21]

And still it was not enough – in terms of neither quantity nor quality. Even though over 90 per cent of the Basin's inhabitants had direct access to water, either through a connection to the house or from standpipes in the neighbourhood, few believed the city's water supply clean enough to drink straight from the tap. They preferred to buy their drinking water from public or private tankers. And it was not cheap. In fact, this essential of life, which the developed world takes so much for granted, cost working people in Mexico City from 6 to 25 per cent of their daily earnings – and the less they earned, the more they were likely to pay. A survey conducted in 1994 found that poor people buying water from tankers were paying 500 times more than registered domestic consumers.[22]

In theory, Mexico City ought not to have a problem with its water supply. The aquifer is huge; with reserves large enough to sustain current rates of extraction for between 212 and 344 years – even though its natural recharge is little more than half the current offtake.[23] But there is a price for taking out more water than natural recharge replaces: subsidence.

With wells drawing out more than double the amount of water that flows in, the watertable under the city is dropping at a rate of about one metre each year. This has been going on for many years, of course, and as the upper levels of the aquifer have dried out, the soil has progressively compacted, shrunk and subsided. The result of this is that surface levels are sinking at a rate of 15–40 cm per year in some parts of the city. Subsidence in the central areas has stabilized at about 6 cm per year since 1954, when new wells were banned there and some old ones closed off. Even so, parts of downtown Mexico City have sunk up to 9 m during the past 100 years.[24]

The change that subsidence has brought to the city is dramatic. In 1900, the original lake bed was 3 m *below* the average level of the city centre – and still covered in water. By 1974 it was 2 m *above* – and bone dry (if not covered in tarmac). Some well-heads from which people drew water a century ago now stand several metres above ground; children mark their height on the casings to see if they are growing faster than the ground is sinking. As a result of the subsidence Mexico City is now more threatened by flooding than it has ever been, and although an expensive storm drainage system has been constructed, flooding is still a serious problem during the torrential storms which are a common feature of the Basin's rainfall pattern.[25]

But the problems do not end with water supply and flooding. Indeed, they are cyclical and mutually reinforcing: water extraction has caused the city to subside and subsidence has, in turn, caused extensive damage to the city's water supply. Pipes break as the ground subsides. In the late 1990s, Mexico City's water authority instigated a programme of routine repairs as part of their overall strategy, and soon were fixing hundreds of leaks every day. Even so, it is estimated that leakages still account for more than 30 per cent of the city's water consumption – enough to supply more than 4 million people.[26]

With Mexico City's water supply problems becoming ever more serious, the authorities resorted to a solution in the Aztec tradition (though without the warfare): in the 1970s they drew up plans to harness supplies from outside the Basin. By the late 1990s, Mexico City was receiving almost a third of its water supply from the Lerma and Cutzamala watersheds. But since some points of extraction were over 100 km away, and 1,300 m below the altitude of Mexico City, transferring the water from source to city has required the construction of eight reservoirs, a 127 km aqueduct, 21 km of tunnels, a 7.5 km canal and six pumping stations to raise the water from source to city. The scheme cost more than $1.3 billion to build, and every day costs an estimated $900,000 to run – which in the course of a year adds up to nearly eight times more than the income the water authorities receive from their customers.[27]

It will be appreciated that in a closed basin such as the Mexico valley, acquiring fresh water is only a part of the problem – there are also vast amounts of wastewater that have to be disposed of. Mexico City produces more than 2.3 million km^3 of wastewater per year, the greater part of which finds its way into the Gulf of Mexico via an extensive network of underground collectors and tunnels, treatment plants, storm tanks, pumping stations, dams, lagoons, piped rivers and open canals.[28] A not insignificant proportion, however, escapes directly into the ground from numerous subsidence-related leaks in the sewage and drainage systems. Some of this is untreated and inevitably will contaminate the aquifer – from which Mexico City must continue to draw most of its water for the foreseeable future.

Another significant proportion of the city's drainage water flows through open channels to semi-arid farmlands more than 100 km away, where it is used – untreated – for irrigation. Production yields have improved substantially since this practice began in 1912. The area has become known as the 'bread basket' of the country. Unfortunately, though, Mexico City's drainage water has also become seriously polluted over the years – with detrimental consequences for the land and its produce. So much so, in fact, that the cultivation of vegetables that are eaten raw is illegal (though how closely the law is observed remains a matter of conjecture).[29]

The Basin of Mexico became a subsidised ecosystem under the Aztecs in the fifteenth century, when they began acquiring large inputs of natural resources and energy from external sources. The Spanish continued the practice for 500 years, and in modern times the imbalance has reached immense proportions. At the beginning of the twenty-first century the situation is critical: 'few ecosystems in the world are so far from being self-sufficient as the Basin of Mexico'.[30] Indeed, Mexico City's problems are so profound that they have attracted an exceptional amount of academic attention. In a sense, the city and the basin it parasitises have become a laboratory in which the processes that control the urban environment are being tested to the limit. The studies it generates provide both morbid fascination and 'terrible insights' into what the future may hold for the megalopolises of the developing world.

As for Mexico City, well, it is the world's second largest city (after Tokyo) – but the rate of growth is slowing down. People are not migrating to the city at the same rate anymore, and some of its residents are moving to urban centres outside the Basin.[31] The slow-down is not enough to alleviate Mexico City's problems to any significant degree in the short term, but at least it offers some hope that they can be contained.

13

Turn to the Sun

Food and water are the first priorities, but cities also need energy to keep them working. Hitherto, organic and fossil fuels have seen cheap and viable options, but mounting environmental costs add urgency to the search for alternative sources of energy.

When an atomic bomb was detonated above Hiroshima on the 6 August 1945, the city was flattened and consumed in flame. Over 130,000 people lost their lives and another 200,000 were rendered homeless but – as United States military experts ruefully reported – the atomic bomb 'failed to damage seriously the war-production potential of the urban area'.[1] Of course, it has been argued that the bombing was in any case a political experience – not a strategic necessity. Japan was no longer a military threat to United States forces: incapable of mounting a counter-offensive and actually close to surrender. But no matter, the country's leaders were still behaving belligerently enough to justify a demonstration of nuclear capability which would bring a dramatic end to hostilities and – no less significantly – establish America's strategic supremacy in the Cold War that was expected to dominate world affairs after the war.[2]

Because the bomb dropped on Hiroshima was small (by modern standards of nuclear weapon potential) and detonated approximately 580 m above the ground it created maximum blast and immediate radiation, but relatively little of the long-term hazard that radioactive fallout from a ground explosion would have caused. Indeed, much of the radioactive airborne material that rose from the devastated city was blown away to the north, where it fell as 'black rain', sticky with soot and dust, in drops the size of marbles. Many who survived the initial blast later became ill and died from radiation sickness caused by this fallout, but the city was not rendered uninhabitable in the way that Chernobyl and its surroundings were by the near-meltdown of an adjacent nuclear power station in 1986. At Hiroshima, potatoes were baked in the ground by the heat of the blast, but were safe to eat.[3]

The blast, hitting the city with radiant heat of up to 4,000°C· and the force of a 35 tonne truck travelling at 1,600 kph, totally destroyed or severely damaged 91.9 per cent of the 76,327 buildings that stood within a radius of 5 km from the hypocentre.[4] The force and speed of the blast decreased with distance from the hypocentre, but was strong enough to knock over trains in a station 2 km away, and shifted the concrete roadway of a bridge 2.3 km away.[5] A few buildings (specifically designed to withstand earthquakes) were left standing – though even they were severely damaged. Otherwise, what the blast had not flattened instantaneously, the subsequent firestorm incinerated. Photographs taken in the following weeks show a scorched plain stretching in all directions, criss-crossed with empty streets, marked here and there with bare trunks of tall trees. Wooden telegraph poles had burned to ash, but numerous trees survived as charred trunks, their leaves and branches having borne the brunt of the firestorm (a dozen or so of these trees are still alive and standing in Hiroshima today).

Like the buildings, the residents and working people of Hiroshima were most densely concentrated in the targeted central area of the city, with between 57 and 61 per cent living within 2 km of the hypocentre, and 81–87 per cent within 3 km. Overall, 63 per cent of those within 2 km of the blast died, but less than 2.5 per cent of those who were more than 3 km away. Of approximately 350,000 people believed to have been in Hiroshima at the time of the bombing, between 130,000 and 150,000 died instantly, or within six months from injuries or radiation sickness.[6]

But the horrors of an atomic bomb do not end with the massive destruction caused when one is dropped; they continue to haunt and handicap individuals and communities through succeeding generations. More than 90 per cent of the 200,000 survivors were made homeless, and none can have been totally untouched by the trauma of the bombing – if not physically, psychologically or economically affected in some way themselves, it is certain that a relation or close friend will have been – and many thousands required a lifetime of medical care. The term 'survivor' came to be avoided, however, because its emphasis on being alive could imply some failing on the part of those who had died. In its place, a more neutral name was used, *hibakusha*, which literally means 'explosion-affected person'.

In the aftermath of the blast, while medical and humanitarian teams struggled to care for survivors, both the Japanese and American authorities were keen to discover exactly what the bomb had done to the city. Japanese physicists knew about nuclear fission and urgently wanted to measure levels of radiation, while the US military was anxious to assess the effects of an A-bomb detonated above a city, as compared with data from ground tests in the uninhabited deserts to which their test detonations had been restricted hitherto.

Medical teams from the Japanese army and navy were first in, arriving within hours of the bombing. Japanese scientists from Tokyo arrived in the city on 30 August and immediately began measuring levels of residual radioactivity. They found it to be only four times higher than the normal background radiation of the area (levels of at least 1,000 times would be required to cause serious effects on the human body). The Americans began their comprehensive survey of the city's destruction on 9 September – just five weeks from the day of the blast, but already the devastated city was determinedly on the road to recovery.

Hiroshima in the aftermath of the bomb (and Nagasaki too, both cities suffered horribly – concentrating on one does not imply lack of consideration for the other) is a salutary example of the human drive to restore a semblance of normality under even the most horrendous of circumstances. Those who were able quickly resumed whatever they could of their everyday lives. On the day after the bombing, for instance, the banks whose central offices had been totally destroyed opened jointly for business at an undamaged branch office of the Bank of Japan on the outskirts of the city. There was only one customer that first day, but 900 a few days later. Within ten days of the bombing, 42 per cent of those employed in the city's ten largest industrial plants had returned to work. Hiroshima's through-transport – by road, rail and sea (Hiroshima is a port) to other parts of the country – hardly stopped, and damage to the city's power-generating plants was quickly repaired; within two days electric trams were running around the central area of devastation,[7] and where buildings remained standing and inhabitable, the electricity was switched on.

No less significantly, the A-bomb had left the mains component of the city's water supply virtually intact. Prior to the blast, the system had been capable of supplying filtered water to the city at the rate of

75 million litres per day. In the region of 70,000 connections from the mains to individual buildings had been broken by the blast, but only eight major leaks occurred in the 300 km of underground cast-iron pipes (ranging from 10 to 75 cm in diameter) which comprised Hiroshima's mains water supply network (one 40 cm main running across a bridge was also broken). The main reservoirs and plant, located within 3 km of the hypocentre, were damaged but able to provide an emergency water supply even on the day of the bombing itself. By the end of October, the mains leaks had been repaired, the 70,000 broken connections had been closed off, and a functioning water-supply was available to the thousands struggling to rebuild their lives – and the city of Hiroshima.[8]

Thirty-three days after the explosion, a young clerk from the personnel department of the East Asia Tin Works, Miss Toshiko Sasaki, was taken from the temporary relief station at which the injuries she had sustained in the blast were being treated to the Red Cross Hospital in the city itself where, it was hoped, doctors would be able to hasten the healing of her badly broken and swollen leg. The office in which she had been sitting at the moment of the blast was about 1.5 km from the hypocentre, and although the devastation of the city had been described to her, this was the first chance she had had to see the ruins for herself. As John Hersey tells her story in *Hiroshima,* a moving record of the first of only two occasions on which an A-bomb has been used in war (the second was dropped on Nagasaki three days after Hiroshima had been destroyed), Miss Sasaki was shaken by what she saw. But it was not just the burned and flattened ruins of the city that affected her; in particular she noticed that the natural world was already beginning to reclaim the artificial urban environment that humanity had created – and now destroyed:

> Over everything – up through the wreckage of the city, in gutters, along the riverbanks, tangled among the tiles and tin roofing, climbing on charred tree trunks – was a blanket of fresh, vivid, lush, optimistic green; the verdancy rose even from the foundations of ruined houses. Weeds already hid the ashes, and wild flowers were in bloom among the city's bones. The bomb had not only left the underground organs of plants intact; it had stimulated them. Everywhere were bluets and Spanish bayonets, goosefoot, morning glories and day lilies, the hairy-fruited bean, purslane and clotbur and sesame and panic grass and feverfew. Especially in a circle at the center, sickle senna grew in extraordinary regeneration, not only standing among

the charred remnants of the same plant but pushing up in new places, among bricks and through cracks in the asphalt. It actually seemed as if a load of sickle-senna seed had been dropped along with the bomb.[9]

Foreign news agencies had reported that Hiroshima, contaminated by radioactivity, would be barren and uninhabitable for seventy years. Nothing would grow in the city and no one could live there, it was said. In fact, the heavy rains which fell a few weeks after the bomb brought forth a profusion of plants; fresh buds sprouted from the stumps and bare charred trunks of burned trees – gingko, camphor, eucalyptus, fig, willow, oleander, azalea and bamboo. Seedlings sprang from every patch of bare ground, as Miss Sasaki had noticed, and people returning to rebuild their lives in the city did not hesitate to plant vegetables and winter wheat. Harvests were good. While vacant and awaiting reconstruction, even the devastated areas closest to the point of explosion produced better crops of wheat, maize, millet, tomatoes, eggplant and beans than were harvested in surrounding villages. The tomatoes in particular were excellent, plentiful and unblemished by the disease and pests which had previously made them difficult to grow in the city.[10] The bomb had sterilised the soil, and the ashes had fertilised it – creating ideal conditions for urban agriculture in a wasteland and affirming that life prevailed; normality would be restored.

'Risen from the ashes' is a cliché but it accurately describes the history of Hiroshima after the war – and the history of Japan too, as the nation became the world's leading supplier of consumer goods. And Japan, the Land of the Rising Sun, is now at the forefront of efforts to develop the technology that will harvest the energy of the sun direct from space and beam it down to earth. The need for an alternative to fossil fuels becomes ever greater as the world population grows – with more and more people living in cities.

The global population is expected to increase by a third between 2000 and 2025, rising from 6 to 8 billion, but since 60 per cent will be living in urban areas by then, the global demand for electricity will double during those same twenty-five years. Unless some alternative is found, the increased production of electricity by current means will inevitably lead to increased emissions of the 'greenhouse gases' which have already been identified as the principal cause of global warming.

Since gas, coal and petroleum all come from the fossil remains of plants whose living processes were fuelled by sunlight, the energy they provide is in fact fossilised sunlight, which has been locked away in the depths of the Earth for millions of years. But the amounts of energy available via fossil fuels are only a minute fraction of the energy the sun beamed down on the living tissue – and which it continues to beam down on the Earth today. Harvesting the sun's energy directly would be much more efficient. If we could harvest just a fraction of the amount that strikes the Earth each day, it would make a significant difference to the world's energy budget.

The amount of energy hitting the Earth as sunlight is on average enough to run seven 100 W bulbs per square metre. This may not seem much, but we all know that if you leave the lights on the sums add up. And the total amount of radiant energy striking the Earth is huge. In the course of an average year, for instance, Hiroshima alone receives the equivalent of 185 times the energy of the atomic blast that devastated the city in 1945.[11] Over the whole world, the sun's energy is enough to evaporate the top metre from all the oceans and put tens of thousands of cubic kilometres of water into the atmosphere. Above the atmosphere, the amount of available energy is at least double, and it is from here that Japanese scientists are planning to harvest it.

The idea is to position a satellite in geostationary orbit about 36,000 km above the Earth, where it will gather solar energy for beaming back to Earth in the form of microwaves. With two gigantic solar panels each 3,000 m long and 1,000 m wide, the satellite should be capable of generating 1,000,000 kW per second – equal to the output of a nuclear plant. The receiving antennae, themselves several kilometres in diameter, would be set up in uninhabited regions, or at sea, and the electricity relayed from them along conventional cables. The satellite, weighing around 20,000 tonnes in all, would have to be sent up and assembled in stages. The estimated cost of the project is $17 billion, and announcements from Japan's ministry of economy, trade and industry confidently predict that the idea will be a reality by 2040.[12]

Sounds like pie in the sky? Well, in the late 1970s the United States Department of Energy and NASA spent $50 million investigating the feasibility of beaming the sun's energy down to Earth. They concluded that while technically possible, the scheme would be impossibly expensive to implement. But things have changed since then. Modern photovoltaic cells are up to eight times more efficient at converting sunlight to electricity than their predecessors; reusable launch vehicles and associated technological developments have lowered the cost of putting a satellite into orbit to one-tenth of what it was in the 1970s.

Furthermore, the need for alternative sources of energy is greater than ever. Thus NASA have dusted off the plans that were shelved and are actively pursuing the space solar power concept, sagely pointing out that with commercial interests now spending more on satellites and space technology than government-funded enterprises, it should not be long before venture capitalists begin investing in what is certain to become a global market for solar energy.[13]

One has only to think of the number of cultures with sun gods, sun temples, solstice ceremonies and so forth to appreciate that acknowledgement of the sun's supreme authority over the living world has long been a fact of human existence. And people have been looking for ways to make use of the sun's radiant energy (or avoid it) for at least as long as they have been living in cities. Sumerians, Greeks and Romans all had worked out the most advantageous designs and alignments for housing, so that they would receive maximum benefit from the sun's warmth during the winter months, when its daily trajectory was low in the sky, and minimum discomfort from its heat during the summer, when it was higher. Socrates explained the principle: 'in houses that look toward the south, the sun penetrates the portico in winter, while in summer the path of the sun is right over our heads and above the roof so that there is shade.'[14]

In Roman times, Pliny the Younger wrote that the *heliocaminus* (literally 'solar furnace') was a favourite corner of his villa on the outskirts of Rome, and the *heliocaminus* seems to have been popular enough to provoke disputes over sun-rights as the city became more densely packed, and buildings more apt to shade one another. Indeed, the right to sunlight was eventually enshrined in Roman law: 'If any object is so placed as to take away the sunshine from a *heliocaminus*, it must be affirmed that this object creates a shadow in a place where sunshine is an absolute necessity. Thus it is in violation of the *heliocaminus'* right to the sun.'[15]

The practical application of the sun's energy to human affairs for anything more than simply keeping warm took longer to develop. The ancients knew that a curved mirror can concentrate the sun's radiant energy onto an object with enough intensity to make it burst into flames within seconds, and Archimedes is alleged to have destroyed an invading Roman fleet with such a device in 212 BC (though authoritative confirmation is lacking). In the sixteenth century, Leonardo da Vinci designed a huge parabolic mirror and associated arrangements which, he said, would 'supply heat for any boiler in a dyeing factory, and with this a pool can be warmed up, because there will always be boiling water'. Leonardo left sketches and a description of the proposal in his notebooks – but nothing more. On the strength of these references, Leonardo is credited with having produced the earliest known plans for the industrial application of solar energy,[16] but it was not until the time of the Industrial Revolution that the idea of harnessing the energy of the sun was put into practice.

By then, fears were growing that supplies of fuel wood and coal could not keep up with the demands of the factories and, since the machines were powered by steam engines, determined attempts were made to use sunlight as an alternative means of boiling the water that produced the steam. In France, Augustin Mouchot developed a solar engine capable of raising over 40 kg of pressure even 'under a slightly veiled but continually shining sun', and he astounded visitors to the Universale Exposition held in Paris in 1878 by connecting the engine to the motor of a refrigerator, and thus using the sun to make ice.[17]

In America during the early 1900s, Frank Shuman proposed that solar energy could enable humanity to utilise the arid and fuel-deficient but sunny regions of the world – even to the extent of irrigating deserts and powering factories throughout the tropics. Predicting that 'ten per cent of the earth's surface will eventually depend on sun power for all mechanical operations', he attracted the investment needed to develop and build machines capable of producing over 40 kW of energy and pumping 27,000 litres of water per minute. On the strength of trials in Egypt, at which the performance of Shuman's solar engine compared favourably with that of a conventional coal-fed plant, plans were made for solar power to irrigate a 12,000 ha cotton plantation in the Sudan. The German government offered $200,000 for the installation of solar power plants in South West Africa (a German colony at the time), and with such support Shuman spoke of developing facilities in the Sahara which would provide the world in perpetuity with an amount of energy 'equal to all the fuel mined in 1909'.[18]

The First World War put an end to Shuman's schemes and the rosy future that he and like-minded enthusiasts predicted for solar energy. Not simply in that hostilities hindered the development and installation of solar engines, but rather – even more so – in that the war wedded the industrial world to the internal combustion engine and the fuel that powered it: oil. Ironically, major oil-fields were developed in precisely the arid and fuel-deficient regions that Shuman had targeted as prime locations for solar power plants, and with more and more oil available at lower and lower prices, industries and governments alike soon ceased to worry about finding new sources of energy.

Individual householders, though, were always keen to keep their fuel bills down, and while oil knocked the steam out of solar energy projects for industry and agriculture, a niche market developed for solar panels that would heat up the bath water. The market flourished for a time in the early twentieth century, and showed signs of reaching critical mass – especially in areas where sunshine was abundant and fuel scarce, such as California, Australia and Africa. But although popular in towns to begin with, solar water heating was always more suited to rural areas, where alternative options were few. Unfortunately, however, the rural market was not big enough to attract the level of interest and investment needed to improve the technology. So, once natural gas and electrification came along, making hot water and power available at the flick of a switch anywhere, day and night, solar water heating was priced out of business.

In the meantime, the potential of the photovoltaic cell was advancing by leaps and bounds. When Edmund Becquerel had noted in 1839 that the action of sunlight striking certain materials generated an electrical current, the voltage he recorded was very low indeed. But the prospect of converting sunlight directly into electricity was tantalising, a physicist's equivalent of the alchemist's stone; and 160 years of research and serendipity (the discovery of silicon's light sensitivity was a happy accident) has brought the technology to the point at which a wafer of amorphous silicon backed with stainless steel will convert a significant fraction of the light striking it into electricity. Even on a cloudy day in south-west London, for instance, the array of photovoltaic cells on the roof of a modest terrace house produces enough electricity for 350 cups of tea, 35 hours of television and 800 slices of toast (or equivalents thereof). On a good day it actually produces a surplus that is fed into the national grid – and thereby earns a modest financial return.[19]

For the time being, though, financial savings are not a prime attraction of PV power. Fitting out the average three-bedroom house costs more than fifteen years of electricity bills; but, as advocates point out, prices have been falling steadily as growing concern about emissions of greenhouse gases and global warming stimulates demand. Significantly, two of the world's leading oil producers, Shell and BP, have added their corporate weight to the development of an economically viable – and environmentally clean – alternative to the products that made them rich.

BP's Solarex company is based in the United States, and Shell has chosen to site a large new PV manufacturing plant in Germany.

So far, the United States leads the world in PV installations, already collecting 54 MW of power from the sun, and has plans to install another half-million PV roof-top units in the early years of the twenty-first century; Germany intends to have at least 110,000 installed by 2005; Japan has embarked on plans for a staggering 2.3 million installations by 2010 (in addition to its plans to beam down solar energy from a space satellite); Italy has a five-year 10,000 roof programme; in Britain, a government grant package is expected to boost PV installations tenfold by 2005; Norway and the Netherlands have longstanding programmes; India, Taiwan, China and Australia all have growing PV industries; both the United States and the European Union have announced 'million roof' programmes, with half of the European Union's plan earmarked for developing countries.[20]

Already, worldwide PV sales have been growing at more than 40 per cent per year for several years, and analysts predict that by 2010 the global market for PV products and installations will be worth £11 billion per year. Such volumes of business are expected to make the cost of solar electricity competitive with the output of conventional power stations by 2020.[21] Then, perhaps, practical expedience will take over from the environmental lobby as the force most likely to bring about a significant reduction in the emission of greenhouse gases and a halt to global warming. Once the markets believe there is more money to be made from alternative energy sources than from power stations, our cities will be powered by solar energy soon enough.

14

Eternal Problems

Waste disposal is at least as important to the life of a city as its food, energy and water supply. But waste ranks much lower in the order of obvious priorities. Out of sight, out of mind, it bursts to attention only when prevailing arrangements are inadequate or break down. Cities have always taken their waste disposal responsibilities very seriously – in the late 1800s Paris even combined it with a highly profitable market garden enterprise.

Leonardo da Vinci was twenty-seven years old and had been living in Milan for four or five years when bubonic plague struck the city in 1478. This was yet another of the terrible epidemics which had swept across Europe at irregular intervals since the Black Death killed up to one-third of the continent's population in 1347. The number of deaths caused by each epidemic had been declining since those first outbreaks, as resistance to the disease increased among the survivors and people became more adept at avoiding it. Nonetheless, the 1478 epidemic killed a total of 22,000 people in Milan (from a population of about 150,000) while in Brescia – less than 100 km away – people died at a rate of 200 per day for four months, and the city's population fell from nearly 38,000 to little more than 3,400.[1]

Leonardo makes no direct mention of the plague in his writings, but it is more than likely that an awareness of its ravages was responsible for a sudden interest in hygiene and town planning that appears in his notebooks around this time. In sketches and plans – with accompanying notes – he developed a characteristically perceptive concept of the ideal city, built along the banks of a river.[2] But this was not to be a

Renaissance city of cathedrals and palaces, in which dazzling flourishes of architectural brilliance would be employed to flaunt the power of popes and princes. Here, as in many other instances, Leonardo was more interested in the practical expediences of everyday life. In particular, he would tackle the pressing question of how an unhealthy state of affairs could be alleviated. Leonardo's ideal city was designed to eliminate all risk of the plague.

If nothing else, over a century of devastating epidemics had demonstrated the ignorance and helplessness of humanity when confronted by catastrophe on this scale. Once the plague had struck a city, most of the inhabitants could only watch and wait in fatalistic dread as the disease picked out its victims. Few could afford the treatment sardonically offered as the only guarantee of survival: 'pills made of three ingredients called *cito, longe,* and *tarde,* namely run swiftly, go far and return tardily'.[3] There was no cure for those who could not escape. Death could be horrifically painful; merciful only when it was swift.

To anyone examining the incidence of plague in cities it would have been patently obvious that the disease was most prevalent in the poorest and most crowded districts. Milan was no exception, and Leonardo had a radical proposition for dealing with the problem. Milan should be split up into ten new cities of 5,000 houses, each thus capable of accommodating up to 30,000 people. 'In this way,' he wrote, 'you will disperse the mass of people who are now herded together like a flock of goats, filling every corner with their stench and spreading pestilential death.' The new cities should be laid out around a network of canals, he proposed, which apart from facilitating the waterborne movement of goods and people would also provide the means for irrigating kitchen gardens and washing the streets (waterwheels would lift the water where necessary, and locks would control the flow of the city canals; wastewater would be dealt with separately).

Life in the new cities would be lived on two levels, Leonardo proposed, with an upper level reserved for pedestrians, and a lower level where animals and wheeled traffic was allowed and access to the canals would be provided. As for dwellings, the upper level was to be exclusively for the houses of wealthy citizens (and public buildings), while shopkeepers and artisans would have their commercial and living premises on the lower levels – along with the ordinary working people and their families who made up the greater part of the city's population.

The two-level scheme Leonardo had devised clearly represented a social as well as a practical separation of the city's communities, but he

In the early Middle Ages, religious authority called on the profits of industry and trade to create the most sublime symbols of an age – the cathedral city (Salisbury, 43). Cathedral-building kept generations of craftsmen employed (44). The scale of the enterprise inspired innovations in design and construction; horsepower was harnessed to the task with the development of a collar that did not restrict breathing (45).

43

44

45

46

47

While the harsh realities of life in the Middle Ages were tempered by religion's promise of paradise after death for the righteous, fanciful ideas of a paradise on earth also abounded. In the Land of Cockaigne and Schlaraffenland (46), no one suffered or went without. Thomas More's Utopia (47), first published in 1516, offered a more sober version.

48

Epidemic disease was rife in the medieval city; none more feared than the Black Death which killed more than one-quarter of Europe's population (48). Leonardo da Vinci's plans (49) to re-house residents of Milan's insanitary districts in spacious multi-level satellite cities were not fulfilled. A contemporary print shows that nineteenth century cities were no healthier (50).

49

50

51   52

The construction of sewage systems (51) capable of dealing with the volume of
human waste produced each day in Europe's large cities was a foremost engineering
triumph of the nineteenth century. The Paris system hosted fashionable touring
parties (52). Outlets at Gennevilliers nourished extensive and highly productive
market gardens (53).

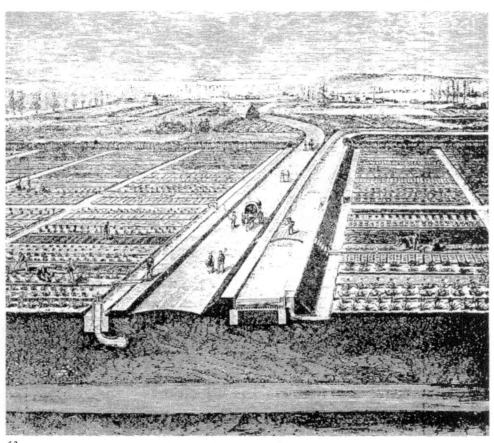

53

54   55

Wealth generated by the Industrial Revolution funded the construction of grand city thoroughfares, such as in Vienna (54), but most city workers lived in far less salubrious conditions – in jerry-built housing under polluted skies (55, 56).

56

57

While the advent of railways heralded the era of mass public transportation (58), it was the bicycle that made independent travel more generally available (57). Mass-produced, bicycles were cheaper and far less costly to run than horses.

58

60

The rapid industrial development of
Berlin in the late 19th century attracted
millions of country people to the city.
An elevated transit system opened in
1902 (59), testified to Berlin's advanced
status, but the first world war
impoverished the city and left many
Berliners dependent on soup kitchens
for survival (60). A circus elephant was
harnessed to haul coal (61).

59

61

From grand city square (62), to war-razed expanse transected by the Berlin Wall (63), to contentious development (64), Potsdamer Platz exemplifies the twentieth-century history of Berlin. Reunified and rebuilt, Berlin is again capital of Germany, and the Reichstag its parliament (65).

62

63

64

65

claimed the overall plan would 'relieve the infinite hardships' of the poor and improve conditions for everyone. Throughout the city, 'quality of life' was to be a primary consideration. The width of the streets would be determined by the height of the buildings standing along them, so that each house would get as much light as possible. A specially invented system of chimneys would disperse smoke high above roof level; there were to be pavements raised above street level and gutters which would carry rain and other wastewater to the sewers (which were underground and distinct from the canals).

Since inadequate (or unenforced) arrangements for the disposal of human waste were generally believed to be a factor contributing to the high incidence of disease in the poor and overcrowded districts, Leonardo was determined to ensure that his new cities would be free of the problem. Waste disposal was a paramount concern. For public buildings he stipulated spiral staircases, so that people could no longer relieve themselves in dark corners – as they frequently did on landings of the customary square staircases; in any case, there would be more public lavatories and, with typical foresight, he provided a design for one that would not be out of place today: 'The seat of the latrine should be able to swivel like [a] turnstile . . . and return to its initial position by the use of a counterweight,' he wrote, ' and the ceiling should have many holes in it so that one would be able to breathe.'

In the 1490s, when the city authorities at last decided that conditions in the poorest and therefore most disease-prone districts of Milan must be improved, Leonardo seized the opportunity of applying his theories to actual conditions. This could not be an entire new city such as he had described in his notebooks years before; more a 'pilot scheme', according to one authority, that would demonstrate what his concepts of town planning could do for a run-down district occupying about one-tenth of the city's land area. The notebooks record that he researched the subject (looking for maps and noting that 'a book about Milan and its churches' was available in a local bookshop), and worked out the dimensions of the city and its suburbs, its streets and canals, as the basis of a large-scale plan. One of his sketches depicts a piazza, surrounded by arcades with residential buildings on the upper level, which imposes a symmetrical pattern of streets and canals on the city plan. Leonardo intended that the square should become the commercial and civic centre of a relatively small urban unit, which would be topographically, economically and perhaps even administratively independent from the greater city of Milan.

We would call Leonardo's proposal 'decentralisation', and it seems that the ruling councils of fifteenth-century Milan were no more keen on devolving power than their counterparts today. This impressive forerunner of modern town planning concepts was not put into practice. Indeed, scholars have been unable to find any evidence of the plan's influence on architects of the day or in the years ahead.[4]

There is even some doubt as to whether the plans were submitted to the relevant authority. Leonardo worked out how the scheme could be financed, and shrewdly defined the economic, political and social advantages that would accrue to its instigators. There are draft letters, beginning with salutations 'to my most illustrious Lord Ludovico . . .' but they were left unfinished, and there is no evidence that Lord Ludovico ever saw the plans. One suspects Leonardo knew that his lordship was unlikely to have much enthusiasm for the concept of decentralisation.

Waste and rubbish are the eternal problems of human settlement. I was reminded of this when I spent some time with a band of BaMbuti pygmies in the eastern Congo's Ituri forest. After a few days their camp resembled a rubbish tip. The small domed huts – made anew of fresh saplings and a thatch of large green leaves when I arrived – were falling apart, the open spaces were a litter of fireplaces and ash, kitchen waste, fruit skins, nut shells, and sundry items of discarded personal property: a broken calabash bowl; rusty tin cans; cloths of indeterminable origin now shredded beyond all practical use. Dogs and infants had deposited small piles of excrement indiscriminately, and although adults retired to the surrounding forest to relieve themselves, the air in the clearing was ripe with the odour of humanity and its bodily functions. Yes, time to move on, Baruwani said.

Hunter-gatherers in the forests and on the savannahs, nomads herding livestock on the plains, can simply move away from the mess of their temporary settlements. But urban communities have no such option. Instead, they must develop the ways and means of moving the mess away from them. And as the process of urbanisation has accelerated through the ages, with more and more people living in bigger and bigger cities, the problem of waste disposal always seems to have been racing ahead of a city's capacity to deal with it. The recorded history of humanity is replete with complaints for more to be done. They occur in the clay-tablet texts of ancient Sumer; the Greeks and Romans wrote of the problem; Leonardo set his mind to improving waste disposal arrangements in Renaissance Italy; and yesterday's newspapers report yet another government initiative (a tax on plastic shopping bags from the supermarket).[5]

In the consumer age of the twenty-first century, it is packaging and worthless or unwanted manufactured goods that constitute the greater part of the rubbish that citizens of the developed world put out for disposal each week. We throw away relatively little organic matter, and our own biological wastes are quickly and efficiently flushed away, out of sight. In earlier centuries the reverse prevailed. Very little non-organic matter was thrown away while arrangements for the disposal of biological waste were far from perfect. Furthermore, there were always some people who brought a piece of the rural economy to the towns: they kept poultry and livestock in their homes.

Reporting on conditions in a north Italian town in September 1607, a master mason, Lorenzo Lucini, wrote: 'some reduction must be made in the number of pigs, since nearly every household has one and their sties stink to high heaven'. From the town of Laterina it was reported a few years later that:

there are many pigs . . . and these [pigs] are the cause of much dirt in the streets, squares, loggia and even in the courtroom, and there is great risk that the air will be infected and human bodies corrupted since the streets of this place are narrow and always full of rubbish and the pigs root around and cause an unimaginable stench.

Likewise:

a large number of pigs, lambs and sheep raised by the inhabitants are kept in the [town of Pontedera] and therefore one sees great quantities of filth, which cause a terrible stench; and the said inhabitants have the habit of throwing excrement, urine and other filth out of the windows and they keep heaps of muck, manure and other filth in the [town] itself; and just as it must be suspected that these were the cause of diseases which have afflicted this place in the past, so it may be believed that in the future they may have a very bad effect on public health.[6]

These are instances from 400 years ago, but the penchant for keeping pigs in cities did not disappear with the passing centuries. In a classic exposé of slum conditions in New York at the end of the nineteenth century, *How the Other Half Lives,* Jacob Riis describes how a family which offered board and lodging in a house on the city's Cedar Street provided accommodation for a family of pigs too – in the cellar, which 'contained eight or ten loads of manure'.[7]

The inhabitants of medieval London also kept pigs in the city, along with horses, cattle and poultry, but the manure was generally piled in great heaps along streets on the outskirts of the city, where it frequently encroached upon rights of way and gave rise to complaint. In the city itself, in the numerous lanes leading down to the waterfront, there were stables for the horses employed in carting merchandise to and from the wharves; here too thoroughfares could become blocked with dung, but human waste was a more intractable problem. As Ernest L. Sabine wrote in a most engaging paper on the subject:

> The streets of mediaeval London were narrow indeed, and were made to seem even more so in the congested parts of the city. There the houses, standing as a rule with their gable ends to the streets, were two, three, and sometimes four stories high, and not infrequently had each successive storey projecting from one-and-a-half to three feet beyond the one below. When such buildings happened to be tenements, the families living in the upper flats found no small inconvenience in disposing of their kitchen garbage and bedroom slops. They were therefore tempted to disregard the city regulations and to cast at least the liquid part of their filth out of the windows.[8]

The city of London had regulations concerning the disposal of rubbish, but they were not always followed or strictly enforced. In 1349 King Edward III himself wrote to the mayor of London complaining 'that filth was being thrown from the houses by day and night, so that the streets and lanes through which people had to pass were foul with human faeces, and the air of the city poisoned to the great danger of men passing . . .' He therefore ordered that the city and suburbs be cleansed of all odour and kept clean as of old.[9]

It is commonly believed that medieval cities were universally filthy, vile and obnoxious, and it is certainly true that the examples given above are among many that would support common belief. On the other hand, it is worth noting that the most authoritative examples of this deplorable state of affairs have been gleaned from court records. Some are cases of complaint brought by private individuals against a neighbour's improper or unsociable disposal of waste; others deal with infringements of existing regulations; all are taken from a breadth of time and space large enough to suggest they are exceptions rather than the general rule. And of course, just as the media today rarely bother to report good news, so the medieval court records are primarily evidence of what was going wrong in the cities of the day – not what was good about them. Some good news, though, can be inferred from the fact that complaints and infringements came before the courts in the first place; clearly, there were standards of behaviour and rules regarding the cleanliness of cities to which the majority of inhabitants adhered, and the offending minority was dealt with accordingly.

This is not to say that conditions in the medieval city approached modern standards of cleanliness and sanitation, far from it; but if judged according to their own assessment of the problems and what could be done, they are not so gravely remiss – and there is plenty of evidence to show that medieval cities took their responsibilities seriously. London records, for instance, include a wealth of regulations based on ancient custom, together with newly enacted laws, that were set down from the thirteenth century on, as the growth of the city brought recurring refuse and sanitation problems.[10]

By the fourteenth century, with a population of about 40,000, London already had an extensive organisation responsible for city cleaning – fully the equivalent of a modern urban cleansing department. Under the overall authority of the Serjeant of the channels, who was elected to ensure that the city's streets and lanes were kept free of rubbish and to fine delinquents, each of London's twenty-six wards employed a hierarchy of officials charged with the duty of maintaining the standards of cleanliness laid down in the city regulations. Surveyors of pavement – four to each ward – had to keep the pavements in good shape and 'remove all nuisances of filth, and to take distresses [goods in kind], or else four pence, from those who had placed them there, the same being removed at their cost'. Scavengers acted as overseers, supervising the work of the rakers, who actually cleaned the streets. In addition, there were the beadles, who issued warnings to the forgetful and collected fines from the wilfully negligent. Each beadle had two or more constables to assist him.

All in all – with beadles, constables, serjeants, surveyors, scavengers and rakers – medieval London's cleansing department employed a force of several hundred men (a far larger number per thousand residents than is common today), but it was of course the rakers who were in the front line of operations. Rakers were assigned to gather the filth and rubbish from the streets and lanes and cart it either to designated sites outside the city, or else to places on the banks of the Thames, from whence it would be taken by boat for dumping in the estuary. They needed to be men of stalwart constitution. Nothing was excluded from the rubbish they were obliged to collect. Kitchen garbage, the rushes that served as disposable carpets in London homes, the contents of cesspits and latrines, building rubble, carpenters' off-cuts, butchers' and tradesmen's refuse, horse dung, straw and anything left lying about – broken barrels, casks, furniture and carts – had to cleared up and taken to the assigned dumping ground. But at least the city provided the necessary cart and two horses (though with the threat of dismissal if said equipment was used for anything but official business). The city also ordered that beadles and constables should assist the rakers in collecting their quarterly dues from the residents of their respective wards, and in 1384 sought to ease the rakers' burden with an ordinance that any present-day city-dweller would appreciate: householders were forbidden to put rubbish on the street until there was a cart ready to take it away. In other words, the modern practice of putting rubbish out only on the day scheduled for collection was a point of law in London more than 600 years ago.

Though the 'filth' the rakers were obliged to clear from London streets might often include quantities of human as well as animal dung, the city's cleansing department was not responsible for the disposal of sewage. This is an area of social responsibility in which the maxim, 'out of sight, out of mind' has a pungent relevance, and some form of public–private partnership seems to have evolved as the most practical way of dealing with it. It has been claimed[11] that nothing to match the drainage and waste disposal facilities of Mesopotamia, Carthage and Rome was known before the mid nineteenth century, when European cities began their massive programmes of sewage construction, but in those civilisations (and subsequently, too) human waste was regarded as something that could be used – even sold – rather than simply flushed into the nearest river.

In the days before the invention of soap, urine was commonly used for cleaning woollen cloth; so that managing Rome's public urinals, for instance, was a valuable contract for the enterprising individuals who collected the urine for sale to fullers and laundrymen.[12] Night soil (as human excrement was called in polite circles), either neat or composted with straw and horse manure, made an excellent fertiliser, and reports of farmers in northern Italy buying cartloads of the 'solid stuff' from those who emptied the cesspits of nearby towns are examples of a widespread practice.[13] But although human waste doubtless had its practical uses there was a limit, particularly in the towns and cities of northern Europe, where the growing season was short, composting facilities were limited, and muck spreading was a demanding, unpleasant and labour-intensive endeavour. After all, if every citizen produced a modest 500 g daily on average (plus a litre or two of urine), a city the size of medieval London (with about 40,000 inhabitants), would have had 20 t of night soil to dispose of every morning – summer and winter, sun and rain.

Doubtless some of medieval London's night soil was used as fertiliser, and some was left to the rakers, but the evidence presented by Ernest Sabine in a paper[14] on the latrines and cesspools of the city certainly suggests that both private individuals and the public authorities went to considerable lengths to facilitate the disposal and removal of human waste. There were public latrines, built over running water, placed strategically around the city for the use of visitors and local householders who had no access to private latrines. London Bridge – which as early as 1358 was not only the principal river crossing but also a commercial centre with 138 shops, had several 'necessary houses or wardrobes' for the convenience of tenants and customers. Some must have been quite commodious, with at least two entrances, for court records from 1306 tell of a man who evaded a creditor by leaving the gentleman waiting at one door while he escaped from the other.

Considerable sums of money were spent on the provision of these facilities. A new latrine built at the north end of London Bridge in 1382–3 cost £11 – at a time when a skilled artisan earned seven pence per day – making it worth the equivalent of hiring ten good builders for thirty-seven days, at least £15,000 in modern terms. A mason's account books show that in 1391–2 a landlord he worked for spent £4 providing latrines for his tenants – the equivalent of more than £5,000 today; and in 1396–7 the same mason built a latrine for a private householder at a cost of £5 6s 8d – over £9,000 today.[15] Clearly, the provision of these facilities was considered to be a desirable and worthwhile investment.

It might be supposed that wherever possible latrine wastes would be flushed directly into the river – either straight into the Thames or via its tributaries, the Fleet on the west side of the city, the Walbrook to the east and other minor streams. This certainly was the case in a number of instances but, as before, the information comes mostly from court proceedings where city by-laws were broken or offence caused to neighbours; it was far from being the general rule. In fact, a proclamation issued in 1357 forbade the dumping of rubbish, dung and excrement into the Thames and the city's other waterways 'for saving the body of the river, and preserving the quays . . . and also for avoiding the filthiness that is increasing in the water and upon the banks of the Thames, to the great abomination and damage of the people.'[16]

Though latrines continued to be used for another century, the construction of new ones over the Fleet and Walbrook was banned in 1462–3, and in 1477 an ordinance was passed banning latrines from any of the city's running waters and ordering the closing down of those already in existence. Cesspits were now the preferred alternative, and ultimately they became the only officially approved receptacles for the daily deposits of London's human population.

Fortunately, deep beds of gravel underlay the Thames-side clays upon which London is built. Cesspits, dug 6 m or more deep into the gravels, and loosely lined with timber or stone, drained readily (though with questionable effect on the quality of the water drawn from the city's numerous wells) and filled slowly, but inevitably they had to be cleared and cleaned from time to time – generating good incomes for those willing to tackle the noisome task.

The account books of a London property owner in medieval times give details of the amounts paid for clearing out his privies over a period of thirty years. Henry Ivory, privy cleaner, was the principal recipient, and his services did not come cheap. Ten shillings – the cost of hiring a skilled artisan (at 7d per day) for seventeen days – was the lowest charge that Mr Sabine quotes from the records; many were for between one and two pounds and the highest was 53s 4d (worth the labour of ten men for nine days at 7d per day). The charges were determined by the amount of filth (as the reports consistently called it) removed, at the rate of between 1s 8d and 2s 4d per pipe (a cask holding over 470 litres), so that even the most modest charge of 10s involved the removal of about 2,000 litres of 'filth', and for the last princely sum, 53s 4d, Mr Ivory's team cleared out over 13,500 litres of the stuff.

Where on earth did they put it all? Well, there were official 'laystalls' beyond the city limits for the disposal of filth, and also facilities at the river for its transfer to dung boats, which then carried it away for dumping in the estuary. Here was another source of income for enter-prising individuals – though not without its dangers. The Coroners' Rolls for 1322 reveal that a certain John Thorp and his wife drowned when their heavily laden dungboat foundered in a storm.[17]

Though these paragraphs support the contention that the residents of medieval London were concerned about the cleanliness of their city, and did as much as they could to ensure that rubbish and filth were effectively disposed of (at least to the extent that available technology permitted), there can be no denying that, by modern standards, London must have been a very dirty and smelly place. And it remained so until after 1834, when at last the city authorities began to install a system of underground sewers. Even then private cesspools remained in use; no householders were compelled to make alternative arrangements, nor were they allowed to drain even the overflow of their cesspits into the city sewers except in return for a sizeable fee.[18] Presumably cleaning and disposal of cesspool contents continued in the time-honoured fashion that Henry Ivory had exemplified.

Meanwhile, though, in both Britain and France advocates of the 'sanitary idea' were calling for the application of science and technology to the sewage collection and disposal problems of the rapidly growing industrial cities. In Britain, the barrister-turned-sanitarian Edwin Chadwick (1800–1890) was the prime mover.[19] Investigations conducted when he was a member of the commission which published the Poor Law Report in 1834 had convinced Chadwick that poor health – and even social unrest – in cities were directly attributable to poor housing and deplorable sanitation. His *Report on the Sanitary Conditions of the Labouring Population of Great Britain,* published in 1842 (and a bestseller), focused attention on the ravages of poverty and the dismal state of the industrial cities. By way of remedy Chadwick adopted a belt-and-braces approach, proposing nothing less than a complete and entirely new system of waterborne sewage, requiring both a massive input of clean water and an extensive network of large underground sewers through which the wastes would be flushed from the city into the tidal reaches of the Thames, and thence to the estuary and the North Sea.

London's Metropolitan Sewage Commission was established under Chadwick in 1849, and it says much for both Chadwick's determination and the urgency of the problems confronting the Commission that enough sewers were completed by 1852 for the scheme to be evaluated. The results were not encouraging; mainly because Chadwick refused to see the need for separate sanitary and storm water sewers, as others were advocating. He believed that rain and natural water flows would always be sufficient to flush sanitary wastes into the Thames, and that the river and tidal flows of the Thames would always be voluminous and powerful enough to carry everything away to the estuary. He was wrong, and the Great Stink of 1858 proved the point. Hot weather and the flushings of London's lavatories (the water closet was becoming popular) had left thousands of tonnes of putrefying sewage to accumulate in the Thames as the river level fell. Boatmen suffered from headaches and nausea. Parliamentary sessions were bearable only when sheets soaked in chloride of lime were hung from the windows. As one contemporary observer reported, Londoners were living in a sewer:

> For the first time in the history of man, the sewage of nearly three millions of people had been brought to seethe and ferment under a burning sun, in one vast open cloaca lying in their midst. The result we all know. Stench so foul, we may well believe, had never before ascended to pollute this lower air. Never before, at least, had a stink risen to the height of an historic event.[20]

The point was made. Chadwick's scheme was abandoned. Working to the plans of an up-and-coming civil engineer, the 28-year-old Joseph William Bazalgette, a series of main intercepting sewers were constructed to catch discharges before they reached the Thames, and redirect them to outfalls far down river from the city. The main drainage system was virtually complete by 1865; within twenty years over 130 km of sewers were laid, draining more than 250 km^2 of the city.

But of course, the sewage of nearly three millions was still going into the river – albeit beyond the sensitivity of London noses. A waste in every sense of the word, Chadwick might have remarked, for he was a keen proponent of the idea that human sewage should be used to manure the lands that feed the cities. Chadwick's vision was a system that not only cleansed the city but also helped to restore the organic balance between the urban and rural environments that the industrial revolution was destroying. He wanted to see fresh water brought from the countryside into the cities, and human waste evacuated to the countryside for use as fertiliser to grow more food for the cities. In this way, he wrote in 1845, 'we complete the circle and realize the Egyptian type of eternity by bringing as it were the serpent's tail into the serpent's mouth'.[21]

The germ of this idea was planted during Chadwick's research for the 1842 *Report*. In Edinburgh, where the authorities were eager to gain support for a campaign against unsanitary practices, he was taken to see the place where sewers carrying wastes from the city's streets and lavatories gushed into a stream known locally as the Foul Burn. What caught Chadwick's attention, however, was not the sight and smell of the place so much as the farmers who were labouriously diverting the Foul Burn onto their fields. While admitting this was the cause of the foul odours that drifted back to the city, the farmers pointed to the astonishing fertility of the fields, and resolutely refused to abandon the practice. Instead of condemning the farmers as his hosts had expected, Chadwick saw their ingenuity as a solution to the problem of human waste disposal.

The German chemist Justus Liebig had by then demonstrated that liquified sewage sludge preserved the valuable nitrogen that escaped when human waste was dried for use as fertiliser. Nitrogenous smells are a product of the drying process, and thus 'may be said to indicate loss of money', Chadwick declared. But if liquified sewage could be transported to the fields in enclosed pipes, smells would be minimised and fertiliser input maximised. In this way, using liquified human sewage for agriculture could even finance the operations of the sewage system itself. And this, Chadwick believed, would do more than anything else to hasten the introduction of running water and flush toilets in cities. So obvious, so simple. But it was not to be. Flush toilets, yes, but as long as sewage outflows could be located far enough from the cities, on rivers powerful enough to carry the wastes out to sea, the idea of using sewage as fertiliser in Britain was dismissed.

But not in France, where a system along the lines of Chadwick's proposal helped the Seine to deal with the ever-increasing volumes of sewage that Paris was pouring into the river.

When Napoleon III approved Baron Georges Haussmann's plans to give Paris a major facelift in the 1850s, his motives were as much military as aesthetic. Never mind the beautiful buildings and monuments that were to be constructed – the reorganisation of city districts, together with the widening and redirecting of thoroughfares, would also facilitate the rapid deployment of troops in the event of civil unrest. Haussmann, however, saw a more vital opportunity as well. With a nod to the revolutionary mood of the moment, he noted that while rebuilding the city above ground, a new sewage system for Paris could be constructed underground, one that was free of blocked arteries and foul orifices, and would clear out the sluggish intestines of the old *régime*:

> The underground galleries, organs of the large city, would function like those of the human body, without revealing themselves to the light of day. Pure and fresh water, light, and heat would circulate

there like the diverse fluids whose movement and maintenance support life. Secretions would take place there mysteriously and would maintain public health without troubling the good order of the city and without spoiling its exterior beauty.[22]

Haussmann was as good as his word. While the total length of city streets in Paris doubled from 424 km to 850 km under his schemes, the sewage system expanded more than fivefold from 143 km to 773 km. Each street had one sewer; large thoroughfares had two or even more. Old sewers were rebuilt to new standards: large enough for men to walk through, and laid at a gradient of 3 cm per metre – shallow enough to ensure that sewermen did not slip, but steep enough to permit cleansing sands to be swept through. Crucially, the new sewers were not round, but egg-shaped in plan, with the sharp end at the bottom, thus concentrating the flushing action even when the volumes of water flowing through were relatively small.[23]

The principal outflow of the new system was on the Seine, beyond the city limits at Clichy and Saint-Denis. By 1874, 450,000 kg of raw sewage per day were being pumped into the river, and the Seine simply could not cope – not least because it was an exceptionally slow-flowing river (the volume and speed of the Seine through Paris is less than in any of twenty-two European cities sited on rivers, according to one survey). Consequently, as the sewage gushed into the Seine below the city the solid content coagulated. Stinking masses of sewage drifted sluggishly downstream, like huge vile rafts of lumpy chocolate mousse, not mixing with the river flow, hugging the banks. 'The water is entirely black. For close to a kilometre, it leaves mud shoals which renew themselves continually, despite constant dredging. Immense bubbles of gas [up to one metre in diameter during the summer] escape from this rotting matter and break through the water's surface.'[24]

But there was relief at hand, harking back to Chadwick's suggestion that if human sewage were to be liquified, it could be used profitably as an agricultural fertiliser. While Chadwick's ideas fell on barren ground in Britain, French scientists had been experimenting with the use of liquified manure on a tract of city-owned land in Gennevilliers, then a sparsely inhabited farming district near Paris with porous soils which had never been very productive. A system of pipes and pumps had been set up to irrigate 6 ha of plots with liquified manure, and forty volunteer farmers were invited to raise crops on it for free. The results astonished farmers, engineers and visitors alike. In July 1870, another 165 farmers petitioned Paris for an extension of the system. Word spread, scepticism evaporated. Napoleon III made an 'incognito' inspection, and left with an abundance of fine vegetables for his table.[25]

And while consumers marvelled at the fine vegetables that could be grown at Gennevilliers on poor land irrigated with liquified sewage, sanitary engineers had discovered that the fine sandy soil was capable of filtering and purifying the sewage water too. Each day for a month they had poured 10 litres of liquified sewage into a 2 m deep cistern filled with sand and soil from near Gennevilliers, and drawn a stream of clear water from the bottom. Not only clear, but found in comparative tests to be purer even than water which had been chemically treated.

With the discovery that filtration was the simplest and best method of purification, plans went ahead for the extension of sewage farming at Gennevilliers – though from the sanitary engineers' point of view agriculture was a secondary consideration; they saw the irrigated land as a series of filtration beds and devised a system which would feed the liquified sewage into the soil at plant root level and draw off the filtered water some metres below ground.

From the Clichy collector the sewage was pumped to Gennevilliers via pipes fixed underneath bridges over the Seine. It arrived at an elevation of 3.5 m, at a rate of 800 litres per second. Gravity distributed the sewage through an extensive network of pipes and ducts, soaking the soil but never coming into direct contact with stems and leaves. Drainpipes, laid 4 m underground, collected the filtered water and directed it back to the Seine.

By the late 1890s Paris was irrigating some 5,000 ha at Gennevilliers. Each hectare received about 40,000 m^3 of sewage per day and was capable of producing up to 40,000 cabbages, 60,000 artichokes or 100 t of sugar beet. Spinach, beans, peas, celery, onions, asparagus, lettuce, onions, strawberries – virtually everything flourished. The best hotels in Paris clamoured for vegetables from Gennevilliers. The town flourished too, its population rising from 2,100 in 1870 to 7,400 in 1896. More and larger units were established elsewhere around the capital, and the Gennevilliers system of sewage irrigation and filtration was adopted elsewhere in Europe. Berlin, for instance, abandoned chemical purification in its favour and by the early 1900s had 6,800 ha devoted to sewage farming. But the system was ultimately overwhelmed by the growth of the cities it served. As land values soared and pumping sewage to more distant sites proved technically demanding, sewage irrigation as a means of filtration and disposal became increasingly uneconomic. Furthermore, biological agents had been introduced to supplement filtration and refine the purification process. Nonetheless, 2,000 hectares of sewage farms were still producing vegetables for Paris in the 1980s – though they used only about 5 per cent of the sewage from just one of the several plants handling the sewage from Paris and its suburbs.[26]

It was a long haul from the problems of waste disposal in medieval London to the antiseptic cleanliness of modern cities in the developed world, but progress has not been as rapid or as universally thorough as might be supposed. New York City, for instance, was still pouring 750 million litres of raw sewage daily into the Hudson River just south of the George Washington Bridge in 1986. By 1996, treatment plants were removing 90 per cent of the organic matter from the sewage prior to discharge.[27] Meanwhile, a 1997 report reveals that less than 10 per cent of sewage in China receives any treatment at all before it is discharged onto the land as fertiliser.[28]

15

The Greatness of Princes

The crowded environment of the ancient city was the breeding ground of sickness. Virtually all infectious diseases have evolved since people began living together in large numbers. Understanding was limited, treatment primitive. Keeping people alive when an epidemic struck the city was more of a management than a medical issue. The world's first extensive public health service began in northern Italy in the fourteenth century – a response to the plague.

Until comparatively recent times, cities had a reputation for being dangerously unhealthy places where many babies died and visitors fell ill. With good reason. In his *Essay on the Principle of Population,* published in 1803, Thomas Malthus gave figures showing that half the children born in Manchester and Norwich died before they were five years old; in London half died before the age of three, and urban conditions were even worse in Vienna and Stockholm, where half died before they were even two years old. In his commentary on these statistics Malthus wrote:

> There certainly seems to be something in great towns, and even in moderate towns, peculiarly unfavourable to the very early stages of life: and the part of the community on which the mortality principally falls, seems to indicate that it arises more from the closeness and foulness of the air, which may be supposed to be unfavourable to the tender lungs of children . . .[1]

No wonder demographers and historians write of the 'urban graveyard effect'. Deaths exceeded births in all great cities. Indeed, it was not until the beginning of the twentieth century that urban populations became reproductively self-sustaining – when, in other words, the number of births in a city began to exceed the number of deaths recorded each year. Before then, cities needed a constant flow of migrants from the countryside simply to maintain their population size – let alone provide for the astonishing growth that many of them experienced.

As noted on pages 137–8, London's population history between 1551 and 1801[2], for instance, shows that the city's death rate[3] was consistently higher than its birth rate throughout those two and a half centuries. Left to its own reproductive capacity, London would have died out. And yet the city's population grew more than tenfold during that same period, rising from 80,000 to 865,000. To maintain such a rate of growth, while also compensating for the city's excess of deaths over births, London needed an average inflow of nearly 4,800 migrants from the countryside each and every year. Just as well, then, that in rural England birth rates were consistently higher than death rates.

But even though cities were risky places to be born in, those who survived birth and early childhood in a city stood an improved chance of enjoying good health thereafter. This was a cruel paradox of city life observed when armies were being recruited for the campaigns Napoleon I waged across Europe between 1796 and his defeat at Waterloo in 1815. Officers quickly learned that scrawny ill-fed men born in urban districts were tougher and better suited to the conditions of military life than muscular and well-fed recruits from the countryside. The country boys appeared to be robust and in glowing good health when they enlisted, just what the army needed, but once in the ranks many of them became repeatedly – and often fatally – ill.[4]

The fact is that although cities have been the economic, social and cultural powerhouses of human endeavour, they are a bad idea in biological terms. The risks of disease proliferate in crowded conditions, and our aversion to squalor and unpleasant smells is a measure of the depth to which an innate acknowledgement of this is set in our evolutionary history. For our earliest ancestors on the savannahs of Africa, though, it was not so much disease as the danger of attracting the attention of predators that would have kept them from occupying camps long enough to generate squalor and smells. This is not to say that those nomadic foragers did not suffer from disease. They probably experienced the same – or similar – afflictions as our closest living relatives, the African great apes. Infestations of parasites such as round-worm, hookworm, lice and ticks are likely to have been the most common. Hepatitis, *salmonella,* trypanosomiasis (sleeping sickness) and yellow fever may have been around too, but the small size and scattered distribution of foraging groups limited the ability of infections to become established in the population, or capable of killing or seriously debilitating generation after generation.[5]

Only when people began to congregate in large settled communities could infectious diseases become endemic. Indeed, the bacterial and viral diseases that pass directly from person to person with no intermediate hosts are nothing less than the diseases of civilisation. They are the price humanity has paid for the decision to live in large, complex and densely populated urban centres – in cities. Virtually all the familiar infectious diseases – measles, mumps, whooping cough, smallpox, and the rest – have evolved only since the advent of agriculture, permanent settlement and the growth of cities. Most and probably all were transferred to humans from animals – especially the domesticated animals. Measles, for instance, is related to rinderpest in cattle; influenza came from pigs; smallpox is closely connected with cowpox. According to a standard text, humans today share a total of 296 diseases with domestic animals (many shared with more than one species), including forty-six that came from sheep and goats, sixty-five from dogs, twenty-six from poultry and thirty-two from rats and mice, and so forth.[6]

So, with agriculture and the domestication of livestock having begun only about 10,000 years ago, and large urban communities having developed only in the last 5,000 years, person-to-person, 'civilised' types of infectious disease are rank newcomers in terms of biological evolution. They could not have established themselves in human populations much before 5,000 years ago when, as it happens, the population of Sumer – the heartland of cities and civilisation – probably was around half a million.[7] Thereafter, disease and pestilence are the recurring horror of recorded history.

There are tales of illness in the Sumerian texts, and the Bible is replete with instances of death-dealing disease which, though undoubtedly a record of oral history rather than eyewitness accounts, make it clear that by the time the Old Testament was written down in its present form between 3,000 and 2,500 years ago, the people of the Middle East had suffered more than one episode of terrifying epidemic disease. In the Book of Exodus, for instance, the scourges that Moses brought down upon Egypt included 'sores that break into pustules on man and beast'. In a single night, an unspecified affliction on Egypt's first-born left 'not a house where there was not someone dead'. David's sins were said to have been responsible for the sudden death of 70,000 able-bodied men in Israel and Judah, but disease was the more likely culprit. Likewise, the 'fatal visitation' which slew the Assyrian army of 185,000 men overnight, thereby persuading King Sennacherib to abandon his plans for the capture of Jerusalem, was probably an epidemic disease.[8]

From classical times, Procopius, the Greek historian, has left a vivid account of an epidemic that began in Egypt in AD 541 and swept rapidly through Asia Minor, Africa and Europe before arriving in Constantinople, the capital of the Byzantine Empire, in the late spring of 542.[9] Merchant ships and troops then carried it through the known Western world, where it flared up repeatedly over the next fifty years, causing huge mortality. Procopius reports that in Constantinople the plague raged for months, claiming from 5,000 to 10,000 victims each day. People were terrified, knowing they could be struck without warning. The emperor Justinian fell ill and recovered, but 300,000 of his subjects were said to have died in the city (though some scholars believe these figures are greatly exaggerated). The authorities were completely overwhelmed by the task of disposing of the dead.[10]

Ancient accounts of widespread death-dealing epidemics customarily have the word 'plague' attached, even though they could have been any one of the infectious diseases to which crowded cities are prone. This is especially true of biblical accounts, and not surprisingly, since the familiar versions of the scriptures were translated or transcribed during the Middle Ages, when Europe endured several catastrophic visitations of bubonic plague. Medieval writers called it the Great Dying, the Great Pestilence and, later, the Black Death. They had no rational explanation for its arrival; no cure for its horrible symptoms. Millions died, and among surviving generations nothing can have so convinced public consciousness of the power that disease has over human affairs. And not just plague has afflicted humanity in this way.

In cities around the world, at one time or another, epidemics of smallpox, typhus, measles, yellow fever, influenza, typhoid, cholera, whooping cough and scarlet fever as well as plague have caused death and panic.[11] Each stage of Western civilisation has suffered its own extraordinary devastating scourge of disease. In the Dark Ages it was leprosy; in the Middle Ages, plague; tuberculosis was the disease of the Industrial Age, and AIDS is the current example of these unheralded afflictions. And each time, prophylactic and preventative measures could do no more than apply lessons learned from previous experience, while the ingenious microbes made a devil's playground in other areas of human biology that the crowded and unhygienic cities had left exposed.

This is not to say that no efforts had been made to understand the causes of ill-health and prescribe remedies. Herbalists and apothecaries had been doing just that since earliest times. Hippocrates is said to have established a school of medicine in Athens (and elsewhere) in the fifth century BC, and the Greek physician Claudius Galen set down a systematic record of medical knowledge in the second century AD, based on the supposition that everything was determined by the will of God. Galen's approach tended to discourage fresh investigation, but his influence lasted more than 1,000 years.

Arabian medicine drew upon translations of the works of Hippocrates and Galen as the basis of its procedures, and was notably advanced in the care of patients – if a contemporary account[12] from thirteenth-century Cairo is to be believed. The hospital being described sounds as though it would not be out of place in the twenty-first century. The founder is reported to have said:

> . . . this institution [is] for my equals and for those beneath me, it is intended for rulers and subjects, for soldiers and for the emir, for great and small, freemen and slaves, men and women.

And the commentary continues:

> He ordered medicaments, physicians and everything else that could be required by anyone in any form of sickness; placed male and female attendants at the disposal of the patients, determined their pay, provided beds for patients and supplied them with every kind of covering that could be required in any complaint. Every class of patient was accorded separate accommodation: the four halls of the hospital were set apart for those with fever and similar complaints; one part of the building was reserved for eye-patients, one for the wounded, one for those suffering from diarrhoea, one for women; a room for convalescents was divided into two parts, one for men and one for women. Water was laid on to all these departments. One room was set apart for cooking food, preparing medicine and cooking syrups, another for the compounding of confections, balsams, eye-salves, etc. The head-physician had an apartment to himself wherein he delivered medical lectures. The number of patients was unlimited, every sick or poor person who came found admittance, nor was the

duration of his stay restricted, and even those who were sick at home were supplied with every necessity.

That was Cairo, in the Muslim world, where the religious prohibition on dissection restricted the investigation of human anatomy and physiology, and hindered the advance of diagnostic practices. Meanwhile, although religion also hindered medical investigations in Europe, the study of the human body and treatment of its afflictions moved into a more scientific mode with the establishment of universities during the thirteenth and fourteenth centuries. Medical schools were opened, and the medical profession accorded a degree of status and respect – especially in northern Italy. Documents show that Venice already had a guild of physicians and surgeons by 1258; Florence had a guild of physicians and apothecaries long before 1296, and Pisa's College of Physicians was established between 1286 and 1318. No other country had comparable facilities for medical training. Indeed, when Thomas Linacre introduced the idea of a college of physicians to England in the early sixteenth century, they had been operating in Italy for about 300 years.[13]

In truth, though, the medical profession of medieval times could never offer more than a palliative for serious illness. Discerning doctors recommended that good health was assured more by 'an orderly life and a wise behaviour' than by medicine, and many doctors had no patience for 'the beautifully long, complicated recipes that some physicians pompously prescribe for the benefit not of the patient but of the apothecary, and that are so revolting they would bother even a stomach made of marble'.[14]

For centuries, the understanding of life-threatening diseases and their cause hardly moved beyond a deep-rooted belief in the malignant potency of miasmas, bad air (hence malaria, *mal aire*) and divine retribution. Ailments and minor sicknesses were treated very effectively with herbal remedies and good sense, but when terrifying disease began killing people in large numbers the horror of its arrival was compounded by ignorance of its nature and cause. At the time of the medieval plagues, for instance, medical practitioners knew nothing of bacteria and viruses; they had no concept of the microscopic living organisms which could carry disease from one person to another, either directly (in the case of contagious diseases) or via an intermediary insect, contaminated food or water (the infectious diseases).

Nebulous 'humours and miasmas' were believed to be responsible for the plague. People spoke of an ill-defined but universally recognised 'corruption and infection of the air', which degenerated into highly poisonous 'sticky' miasmas. They believed that the initial corruption and infection of the air could have been caused by vapours rising from marshy waters, by foul and filthy surroundings, by the putrid odours of decomposing human wastes, by volcanic eruptions, or simply by an inauspicious conjunction of the stars.[15] And however the corruption had arrived, people were convinced that its poisons could be absorbed by simply breathing the infected air, or touching anything it had come into contact with. Hence the frenzied zeal with which the authorities set about burning the clothes, furniture and bedding of deceased victims, and disinfecting their dwellings with sulphur, vinegar and lime. Some even insisted upon the extermination of domestic dogs and cats, in the hapless belief that all hairy things were a potential source of contagion – but of course this measure merely made life easier for the rats that carried the fleas which spread the plague.[16]

Avoiding contact and attempting disinfection were sensible measures derived from the aversion for squalor and bad smells that became an important aspect of humanity's survival strategies at an early stage in our evolutionary history. But cities and civilisation made it difficult for people to follow the simple rules of basic instinct. The pills made of '*cito, longe,* and *tarde*', (run swiftly, go far and return tardily, see page 202) were luxuries that few could afford. Most had to take their chance in the cities.

'The greatness of princes lies in having populous cities and a populous dominion, and they may be called poor who rule over untitled and unpeopled lands,' the governor of Bergamo proclaimed.[17] The plague, arriving unheralded, travelling unseen except for the horrible deaths and half-empty towns that marked its route, was a harsh and mysterious affliction that impoverished many princes as its lethal scythe repeatedly cut swathes through the population of Europe. Princes and populace alike learned a harsh lesson; namely, that while hard work and good behaviour earned the comforting security of home and a laden table, even the most deserving beneficiaries could be cut down indiscriminately, without warning, any day, by a force of nature that lay beyond the power of human control.

But as cities and great princes grew rich on the profits of burgeoning medieval economies, they began assuming some responsibility for the health of the populations upon whom their prosperity and future depended. By the thirteenth century, doctors paid from public funds were a common feature of the social scene in Italy. Milan, for instance, had a population of about 60,000 in 1288, and three surgeons paid by the city whose specific charge was to treat 'all the poor needing surgical care'. Similarly, in 1324, Venice employed thirteen physicians and eighteen surgeons (in addition to an unknown number of private practitioners) for its population of 100,000 – a ratio of three doctors for every 10,000 citizens.[18] Such then were the facilities available when the plague struck northern Italy for the first time in 1347.

Bubonic plague is believed to have originated among marmots, the large rodents native to Central Asia which were trapped for their fur. Along with their skins (and their fleas) traders introduced the disease to the Mediterranean and Europe via the Silk Road. Constantinople, Egypt, Sicily and northern Italy had all been infected by 1347, and most of Europe was affected before the epidemic finally subsided five years later. Europe, North Africa and the Levant had a combined population of around 100 million in 1346. Within a few years, a quarter had died and the population growth which had fuelled the establishment of cities and marked the evolution of medieval society was brought to an abrupt halt.[19]

At the individual level, first symptoms of the disease were a mild fever, followed a few days later by swellings of the lymph nodes, especially those in the groin or armpit. Once the swellings – known as buboes – appeared, the victim either went into a deep coma, or became violently delirious, paranoid or suicidal. Anyone with buboes that filled with pus had a chance of recovery, but black blisters presaged immediate death. Most victims died within days. As individuals succumbed in their thousands, every aspect of life – from the economy to politics and religion – was affected. Health in the cities rapidly became a matter of public rather than just individual concern, and a management rather than a medical issue.

On 30 March 1348, with the plague erupting near and far, the city council of Venice appointed a committee of three men specifically and urgently 'to consider diligently all possible ways to preserve public health and avoid the corruption of environment'. This committee of Venetians was among the first of Italy's Public Health Boards.[20] Established initially as a means of coordinating a city's response to the threat of the plague, they rapidly became a feature of urban administration throughout northern Italy. By the second half of the sixteenth century there was a permanent Public Health Board in every major Italian city – exchanging information, coordinating strategy for the treatment of patients and compiling statistics – which in effect makes them the world's first public health service. Certainly the regions adjacent to the cities of Venice, Milan, Genoa and Florence had by far the most developed health service organisation in Europe or further afield at that time.

The historian Carlo Cipolla gives an account of the efficiency with which the Public Health Boards operated in the early seventeenth century. News of an outbreak of plague in the northern part of Lake Como reached Milan on 21 October 1629, he reports. Five days later, most towns in northern and central Italy were on alert and began taking protective measures. On 27 October, for instance, Venice decreed that neither people nor merchandise could travel to or from the territories of Lecco, Risano and Chiuso (the cities nearest the outbreak). Verona followed suit on the 29th; Bologna on the 31st; Modena and Florence on 8 November. Meanwhile, however, plague had broken out in Milan itself, causing the other cities to extend their bans to the entire state of Milan.

But bans and decrees could not keep out the plague – no matter how swiftly and efficiently they were put into operation. Within weeks, Venice, Verona, Bologna, Modena, Florence and other major cities fell prey to the epidemic and by August 1630 most cities, towns and villages in northern Italy were suffering the horrors of the plague. Milan had a population of about 130,000 when the plague arrived; nearly half died.[21]

Once the first defence of closing off a city had been breached, and plague broke out among the inhabitants, isolation and quarantine were all the Health Boards could offer. Some cities built lazarettos, or pest-houses, for the confinement of people with plague or thought to be incubating it. Other cities simply sealed up the houses of infected families, opening them only to hand in supplies of food and water – or take out the dead. Whether in a lazaretto or at home, confinement was at worst a death sentence; at best a terrifying experience – though staying at home may have been a marginally better option. Conditions in the lazarettos were appalling. The women's section of the Florence lazaretto had 82 beds – and 412 female patients to share them during the plague of 1630. The men were hardly any better off, with 93 beds for 312 patients.[22] Cipolla quotes a report on conditions in the Bologna lazaretto that same year:

Here you see people lament, others cry, others strip themselves to the skin, others die, others become black and deformed, others lose their minds. Here you are overwhelmed by intolerable smells. Here you cannot walk but among corpses. Here you feel naught but the constant horror of death. This is a faithful replica of hell since here there is no order and only horror prevails.[23]

With isolation and quarantine apparently offering so little protection once plague had broken out in a city, some people questioned whether official intervention was of any benefit at all. A case in point: three-quarters of Genoa's 73,000 inhabitants died during the epidemic of 1656–7, despite the city's intervention. 'If no measures had been taken to rid the city of the epidemic,' a commentator asked, 'would Genoa have suffered greater losses?'[24]

But whatever the effectiveness of plague control measures, the suffering of plague victims could not be ignored, or left unalleviated. In cities under siege the threat of death was common to all; a sense of self-preservation ensured that what could be done was done. But the costs were high – not simply in the toll of human life, but also in hard cash. Running the Health Boards was expensive at the best of times; during an epidemic expenditure soared. The boards had to hire extra personnel – from physicians to gravediggers; additional guards were needed at the borders of the territory and at the gates of the city; arrangements had to be made for the isolation of infected people and their contacts; food had to be provided for impoverished people quarantined either in their homes or in pesthouses; disinfections and fumigations had to be paid for; and people had to be reimbursed for all the household items which were burned.

Cipolla reports that during the 1576 epidemic, an operation to disinfect 1,563 buildings (in which 4,066 families were crowded into 8,953 rooms) with vinegar, sulphur and lime cost Milan's Health Board the equivalent of 50 kg of gold – worth more than $500,000 dollars at today's prices.[25] Simply feeding people in quarantine completely exhausted available civic funds in four days, and the city had to finance its subsequent expenditure by taking on high-interest loans and imposing extra taxes.

Bologna was forced to adopt similar tactics in 1630, when its Health Board spent the value of about 5 kg of gold on disinfecting 1,260 houses.[26] A doctor working in Sicily during the 1576 plague chose for his motto the words: *ignis, furca, aurum* . . . – fire to destroy infected items, the gallows to punish those who violated the health regulations and gold for the expense of the operation. In towns stricken by plague, sinister bonfires of infected goods were always burning.[27]

The direct expenses of dealing with an epidemic of plague were a huge burden on civic finances; declining revenues imposed another, and these deficiencies of the balance sheet combined to ensure that the human tragedy of the plague left economic disaster in its wake. Local merchants and craftsmen suffered from a calamitous decline in both customers and goods to sell, while commercial enterprises dependent upon external markets were ruined by health regulations prohibiting trade and communication beyond the city limits. When the plague struck Busto Arsizio in 1630, for example, a chronicler noted that the locally produced cotton cloth was banned from every part of Italy 'just as the devil is banned from Paradise'. Silk exports from Genoa fell 96 per cent during the 1657 epidemic.[28]

Throughout the affected regions, skilled artisans who survived the plague found themselves out of work and their families faced with starvation as a consequence of the blockade. There was little help for them. Charitable institutions were hard-pressed, and the city authorities stretched to the limit. When Verona's textile industry was closed down by the plague, a city representative pleaded with higher authorities in Venice for a suspension of the ban. Many people had died of starvation, he said, and the unemployed could not seek help elsewhere because they were imprisoned in a city under quarantine.[29] No reprieve was forthcoming.

Meanwhile, though, some people were doing extremely well. In a very real sense, the plague turned the existing social order upside down. Wealthy and respectable citizens became increasingly dependent upon the unworthy dregs of society to whom they would not previously have given the time of day. Vagrants and criminals willing to take the risk of brushing against death were recruited to perform essential services. Though only at a price. To get enough recruits, cities had to offer generous incentives, high wages – and payment in advance.

Undertakers, fumigators, cleaners and clearers of plague-stricken houses profited handsomely from the city's misfortune, and in some quarters were characterised as scavenging birds for their avarice: the 'kites' of Florence, and the 'crows' of France.[30] Thus scholars perceive 'mild forms' of social revolution arising in the wake of the plague. There was a redistribution of wealth, and a tendency for survivors to behave as a privileged group (regardless of their previous status) insolently certain of their invulnerability. In the aftermath of the epidemic that devastated both the population and the economy of Bergamo in 1630, a doctor reported that:

> Priests and friars who have survived the plague, and persons of low condition who have recovered from it, are both grown very rich, the first by burying, administering the sacraments, and helping the sick, and the second by physicking and serving infected persons – for people in these extreme needs were forced to spend lavishly and without restraint . . . The fumigators, bearers of the dead, police constables, quacks, thieves and other such people did very well for themselves.[31]

It could be argued that the epidemics of plague that swept through medieval Europe created the fertile social, economic and geographical environments from which the achievements of the Renaissance emerged. Maybe so, but above all the plague demonstrated very clearly that human social and cultural structures are always subject to the greater authority of biology. When people began domesticating animals they provided the opportunity for numerous infectious diseases to jump species; when people began living in densely packed cities they enabled infectious diseases to become endemic among human populations; and once those diseases had become endemic, migration and trade gave them the potential for wider distribution.

To the extent that they were able, afflicted cities accepted the social responsibilities that the plague thrust upon them; but even the most resourceful was hampered by an inadequate understanding of the disease. They were fighting an enemy they had not identified and whose strategies they did not comprehend. In this unequal battle they were also misled by erroneous theories. Exterminating cats and dogs is one example, insofar as these animals limited the spread of rats to some extent. Even clearing the streets of rubbish was misguided in that more rats (and their fleas) moved into the houses as a result. People were careful, though, and in one revealing instance their precautionary measures actually gave a clue to the cause of the plague – but the significance was misinterpreted. It happened thus:

Early in the seventeenth century some French doctors adopted the practice of wearing an all-enclosing robe coated with a hard lacquer of wax and aromatics when they visited patients. The uniform was topped off with a cowl and hat to protect the neck and head, glasses to protect the eyes and a beak-like nose that enabled the doctor to breathe through a filter soaked with perfume and disinfectants. An uncomfortable and sinister garb (still worn by revellers at the Venice carnival), but justified, the doctors believed, because miasmic poisons could not stick to its smooth shiny surface and thus could not be transferred from place to place. It seemed to work. Doctors wearing a robe survived, and in the nature of circular arguments, this seemed to confirm prevailing theories about the role of miasmas in the spread of disease. But an energetic young friar caring for plague victims in Genoa during the epidemic of 1657 was sceptical. Father Antero Maria da San Bonaventura had no faith in either current theory or practice, and was certain that shiny waxed robes did nothing to prevent people catching the plague. 'The waxed robe . . . is good only to protect one from the fleas which cannot nest in it,' he declared.[32]

If only Father Antero had realised that protection from fleas was also protection from plague. But of course fleas were a commonplace aspect of medieval life, annoying but innocent animals – which the plague most definitely was not. How could anyone imagine that fleas carried the disease and infected the people they bit? Everyone knew that the plague was especially prevalent among those who dealt with wool, cotton, hemp, carpets, flax, bags of grain and such like, but this was attributed to the hairiness – the stickiness – of the materials, not to the fact that they harboured fleas. Conversely, hard smooth and slippery materials were safe because the poisonous miasmas could not stick to them. Nor could fleas.

It was not until the 1890s that the role of fleas in spreading the plague was properly understood, and the discovery stemmed directly from the invention of a microscope with compound lenses (rather than single lenses as before). The greater magnification and resolution of the new instrument, combined with improved techniques for preparing specimens, enabled scientists to delve deeper and deeper into the mysteries of life processes. Medical historians speak of the second half of the nineteenth century as 'the golden age of bacteriology', during which dozens of diseases were incontrovertibly attributed to the activity of an identified microbe – hookworm, dysentery, leprosy, malaria, typhoid fever, tuberculosis, cholera, diphtheria – and the plague.[33]

A French bacteriologist, Alexander Yersin, identified the bacterium responsible for bubonic plague in 1894 (hence the scientific name: *Yersinia pestis*), but the role of the flea in the spread of the disease was not revealed until a few years later, during a terrible outbreak of plague in Bombay. Several teams of investigators, sponsored by their national governments, 'hastened to the affected city, charged with the task of studying the disease. Probably never before or since has such an imposing array of epidemiological talent assembled in one place for research into a specific disease', an account reports.[34] The situation was grim. The plague killed over 354,000 people in Bombay alone between 1896 and 1900, and over 8 million in India as a whole before the epidemic spluttered to an end in 1914. Efforts to control the spread of the disease provoked fierce resistance, riots, mob attacks on Europeans and even the assassination of British officials, but amidst the deaths and panic the investigators discovered much of what is now known about bubonic plague.[35]

Officials charged with the Herculean task of controlling the spread of the disease based their strategies on the entrenched belief that the plague was caused by a miasma and caught by coming into contact with an infected individual or environment. Despite the advances made in the understanding of disease during the nineteenth century, this 'miasmatico-contagious point of view' was still favoured by many writers on plague in the late 1890s; even in the 1920s there was 'a vigorous reaction on the part of an influential group of British epidemiologists against current conceptions of the role of microbes in the causation of disease'.[36] Entrenched beliefs died hard, but the contradictory evidence was accumulating.

First it was discovered that the *Yersinia pestis* bacterium died very quickly once its host was dead; and could not survive for long outside a living body. Indeed, living bacteria were rarely, if ever, found in any of the places where the 'miasmatico-contagious point of view' required them to be. They did not infest the foodstuffs and water that people were consuming in infected areas; they were not in the soil or street rubbish that people walked through, nor were they lurking in the clothing, bedding, furniture and floors that the inhabitants of infected houses regularly came into contact with. But if people were not picking up the bacteria in any of these places, by contact, how were they being infected? It was another French bacteriologist, P. L. Simond, who completed the puzzle.[37]

It was already known that plague infected rats – the elimination of such vermin was the only benefit that plague could be said to have brought to afflicted cities. Simond took a closer look at the disease in rats and, in the course of his investigations, found plague bacteria in the guts of fleas feeding on infected animals. From that observation only a conceptual leap to the truth was required: when a rat died of plague the fleas feeding on its infected blood quickly moved on to another host, taking a dose of plague bacteria with them. In 1898, Simond published the breakthrough paper showing that the plague was spread through urban communities by rats, and transferred to humans via the blood-feeding predilections of those familiar, annoying, but far from innocent animals – fleas.

But identification and attribution were not cures. People continued to die from the diseases of civilisation. While the plague was killing 8 million people in India between 1896 and 1914, for instance, tuber-culosis and malaria killed more than twice as many; the global influenza epidemic of 1918–19 killed at least 16 million in barely four months; smallpox and cholera accounted for millions more.[38]

The fact is that while bacteriology was forging ahead, medical science made few advances in the direction of actually curing epidemic disease. The practice of vaccination developed from Edward Jenner's obser-vation (published in 1798) that milkmaids were protected from smallpox by the mild doses of cowpox they caught in the cowshed was a notable contribution, and the discovery that quinine kept malaria at bay was among other helpful developments – but these were prophylactic, not curative treatments.

Medicines capable of killing offending bacteria before they killed the infected patient – and without harming said patient – have proved difficult to formulate. And even the development of antibiotics since the mid twentieth century has proved to be less of a knock-out blow than was hoped as resistant strains of bacteria evolved. Tuberculosis, influenza and enteritis are still potential killers; outbreaks of cholera still occur – even plague is not unknown at the beginning of the twenty-first century – and although a worldwide vaccination programme effectively eradicated the scourge of smallpox from human concern, the virus still exists; an outbreak would kill millions before it could be brought under control. Meanwhile, large segments of modern society have developed an unnerving willingness to believe in the ability of doctors, hospitals and the pharmaceutical industry to find a cure for whatever ails them.

Biology has not finished with humanity yet. Fear of heart disease and cancer lurks in the mind of every inhabitant of cities in the developed world – medical statistics indicate that one-third of us will die from one or the other of them, while Alzheimer's and Parkinson's are likely to strike with indiscriminate cruelty among people in their later years. AIDS arrived on the scene as though from nowhere in the 1980s, like a plague. Obesity is approaching epidemic proportions on the global health scale, affecting 60 per cent of adults in the United States (and 42 per cent of school children in one US survey).[39] Diseases related to air pollution are on the increase, with 10–12 million people suffering from asthma in the United States and asthma-related deaths rising by 40 per cent in the ten years to 1991. In Great Britain asthma was affecting one child in seven by the late 1990s.[40]

Meanwhile, a rising demand for infertility services in post-industrial cities suggests that biology may be applying its ultimate sanction on humanity's headlong rush towards megapolis and a predominantly urban society. Could it be that environmental pollution, economic pressure and the psychosocial stresses of urban life are reducing sperm counts, adversely affecting ovarian function and generally making it more difficult for people in cities to have children?[41]

Birth and death rates, longevity, general well-being – however we choose to measure the distance that civilisation and medical science have brought us from the horrors of the medieval plague, there are still human frailties that can haunt us. In the times of the plague, great princes led prayers to God for deliverance. Today we put our faith in doctors and the pharmaceutical industry. Hospitals are the cathedrals of the twenty-first century.

16

Capturing the Horizon

Convenient access to essential goods and services might be expected to encourage a sedentary way of life, but people in cities travel more than their rural counterparts ever did. Paradoxically, cities awakened an urge to be somewhere else, stimulating the growth of a transport industry that facilitated travel within and between cities and enabled the world's wealthiest urban communities to acquire goods from around the globe.

In the late 1940s, BBC radio's Home Service featured a weekly programme called *Country Magazine*, in which Ralph Wightman would present a cameo of country life in a part of England he had recently visited. The transcript of a programme he made in 1948 on Cranbourne Chase in Wiltshire lies among more celebrated historical documents preserved in the archives of the Salisbury Museum. Just a few pages of undistinguished typescript on the face of it, but also an untarnished record of English country life in the years immediately following the Second World War and, courtesy of the villagers Wightman interviewed, of conditions during the decades preceding the First World War. Commentary and conversation speak directly from the page of vanished eras that span a century, when circumstances of birth limited the horizon of a villager's prospects to the encircling landscape, and the idea of actually living in a city was a preposterous ambition that any sensible adult would abandon with the irresponsibilities of childhood.

Cranbourne Chase is a 2,050 km² tract of chalk downland on the southern flank of Salisbury Plain. Wightman describes it as a dry country without any really reliable source of water; he speaks of clay soils full of flint overlying the chalk – the home of beech and ash, of evergreens and hazel. Buffer Lucas tells him that the autumn harvest of hazel nuts was a real godsend for the villagers, bringing in enough money to pay for clothes for a year. Buffer knew the hazel woods well. Making sheep hurdles from their long, straight and pliable young growth was the mainstay of his livelihood. He would buy cutting rights to a hazel copse at so much a lug – 10 strides wide and 10 strides long is four lugs, he explained – and needed about three or four acres of copse for a year's work. The wood was cut by the end of March and all out for working by June. Buffer admitted that he wasn't above supplementing his income from hurdles by poaching the odd pheasant on his way through the woods to church on a Sunday morning, and even confessed to taking deer during hard winters – though their size was always a problem. 'Trouble is with deer, he's terribly bulky. You can't just pop him in your big pocket like a pheasant. Used to have to hide him. Sometimes in a tomb. When you're hungry you do get a bit artful.'

Old Ted Coombs joins the conversation, telling how when he was a lad (in the 1880s and '90s) there were so many rabbits that nobody was bothered if you took one for the pot; and you could always get a bob for holding some wealthy gent's horse . . . The words seem designed to evoke familiar images of a rustic paradise. One awaits the neat cottage gardens and jolly Morris dancers. But just as suspicions that his story is more wish-fulfilment than accurate recollection begin to stir, Ted delivers his judgement on where things went wrong, and why the village became paradise lost. The sparse typewritten text emphasises the vehemence of his opinion on the subject. 'What ruined the village,' he announces, 'was the coming of the bicycle! Chaps went off to the towns on their bikes . . .'

It is an abiding paradox that even when people are comfortably settled in one place, many of them will develop an irrepressible urge to be somewhere else. It was of course this impulse to expand the local horizons that led humanity from its African birthplace into every inhabitable niche the world has to offer. And we walked there, on two legs. The human gait is unique, possibly because it is a very inefficient mode of locomotion. In terms of the energy required to move pro-portionately equal units of body mass over given distances, people are not much more efficient than penguins. Mice, squirrels, horses and gazelles are significantly more efficient – dogs even more so.[1] But humanity was more adventurous than any of them.

With a cognitive brain to override instinctive fears of the unknown, they pressed on. Turn left after crossing the Isthmus of Suez for Europe and right for Asia. From the extremity of Asia it was not too hard to get to North America across the Bering Straits when sea levels were down, and North America was conveniently joined to South America. Even Australia was accessible via the stepping stones of south-east Asia and some short sea voyages. People reached New Zealand, the last remaining sizeable piece of uninhabited land fit to live in, about 700 years ago.

The journey from our origins in East Africa to New Zealand had taken perhaps 200,000 years in all, say 10,000 evolving generations, more than enough for the urge to seek broader horizons to have become a deeply ingrained genetic trait of the species. And, after all, it has only been during the latter stages of our evolutionary and colonising history that people began to live in large settled communities.

Satisfying humanity's irrepressible urge to seek new horizons while at the same time providing permanent accommodation at fixed points in the landscape has made transportation an extremely important factor in the form and character of cities – not just living and working space has to be provided, but also the room and facilities for people and goods to move around. Indeed, ever since people began building cities a primary thrust of human ingenuity has been applied to the problems of enabling them to go somewhere else.

The sheer number of giant articulated trucks streaming constantly into every city might suggest that the movement of essential goods and services is the primary transportation issue of urban living – with thousands of tonnes of food and materials required daily – but transporting people is actually a much larger and more demanding fact of city life. Both the total mass and the number of individual units are far greater, and while goods and services operate to and from a relatively limited number of fixed points, each person's journey is a unique affair, with any number of different beginnings and endings and routes in between to choose from.

Christopher Alexander, an authority on city planning, encapsulates the social imperatives of transportation in the modern world with the phrase: 'your friends live not next door, but far away . . .'[2] He explains that in traditional communities such as Buffer Lucas and Ted Coombs were familiar with, if someone was asked to name their best friends and each of those in turn was asked to name their best friends, they would all name each other – so forming a closed group. But today's social structure is utterly different. If a modern city-dweller is asked to name his or her best friends and then each of those is asked to name their best friends, they would probably all name different people, many of them unknown to the first person; and these people would again name others, and so on outwards.

There are virtually no closed groups of people in modern society, Alexander concludes. There are networks instead, growing and facilitated by the advances that technological developments bring to the means of transportation. And there is no end in sight. The demand for travel is insatiable. Just as building new highways does not eradicate congestion, but gradually draws still more traffic into the network, so every new development has served to increase the amount of travel, not just satisfy immediate demand. When a journey meant going on foot or at best on horseback, the options were limited – both in terms of how far a person could travel and who could afford it, but since the Industrial Revolution mobility has become universally available: on better roads, by bicycle, train and steamship; most recently by bus, private car and airliner.

The huge scale of industrial development since then, and the tremendous economic growth generated by the process of industrialisation around the world has made mechanised travel widely available and affordable. And most travel is either between or within cities. Indian Railways sell 4.5 billion tickets a year to the country's population of a billion people. In the developed and developing world there are hundreds of millions who think nothing of commuting long distances to work every day, while among citizens of the richer countries there are millions more who take their vacations hundreds or thousands of kilometres from home. In a world of 6 billion people the IATA airlines alone sell 1.5 billion tickets each year.[3]

But while a massive travel industry, and a tourist industry, have developed to serve humanity's insatiable urge to move around, it is worth remembering that every advance in the provision of transport has succeeded primarily because it served the needs of the individual. The bicycles that Ted Coombs complained about were made and bought in huge numbers, but carried just one person apiece; the steam locomotive and railways were developed initially to facilitate the transport of coal from the mines, but achieved economic viability only when they began providing a means of transport for large numbers of individuals – becoming cheaper (and more profitable) as the networks expanded. Already in 1838, just thirteen years after the world's first commercial railway line had opened between Stockton and Darlington (a distance of

40 km) in north-east England, Britain's railways were carrying 5.4 million passengers a year; by 1862 that figure had risen to 170 million.[4]

A similar scale of economic transition occurred with the development of the motor car. It began life as an expensive recreational vehicle for the prosperous gadabout, but came of age with the mass production assembly lines pioneered by Henry Ford. By 1914, Model T Fords were rolling off the assembly line at a rate of one every ninety minutes. One million were built in 1921. Two million in 1922. During the nineteen years (1909–28) that the Model T Ford was in production, more than 15 million were built. And this was a tough vehicle that could go virtually anywhere, perfectly suited to the travel needs of individuals and their families – indeed, they called it 'the family horse'.[5]

Meanwhile, cities were growing along with the manufacturing plants which had been built to meet the demand for transport. Detroit was founded on the success of its motor industry. Los Angeles (which already had two cars for every three residents by 1930[6]) gave an early demonstration of things to come, as the city expanded by bringing small surrounding towns under its administrative umbrella and lacing them together with freeways. Coventry evolved from cathedral town to industrial city as its bicycle manufacturers became world leaders – coincidentally stimulating industrial and economic development in other regions at the same time: in Japan, for example.

Bicycles were extremely popular in Japanese cities at the end of the nineteenth century, when the import of goods that Japanese manufacturers could not compete with on price – or could not make at all – was damaging the national economy. Clearly, if bicycles could be made in Japan, both the massive demand for an individual means of transport and the national economy would be served at the same time. As Jane Jacobs points out in her book *The Economy of Cities*,[7] Japan could have responded to this challenge by inviting foreign manufacturers to establish plants in the country – though this would have brought little profit to the Japanese themselves. Or they could have built a factory of their own – which would have required large investments in specialised machinery and the training of a skilled labour force. The Japanese followed neither of these options. Instead they exploited an indigenous talent for 'economic borrowing' – or imitation, as non-specialists would call it. It worked like this:

Not long after the importation of bicycles had begun, large numbers of one- and two-man repair shops sprang up in the cities. Since imported spare parts were expensive and broken bicycles too valuable to cannibalise, many repair shops found it worthwhile to make replacement parts themselves – not difficult if each of the shops specialised in making only one or two specific parts, as many did. In this way, groups of bicycle repair shops were in effect manufacturing entire bicycles before too long, and it required only an enterprising individual to begin buying parts on contract from the repairmen for Japan to have the beginnings of a home-grown bicycle manufacturing industry.

So, far from being costly to develop, bicycle manufacturing in Japan paid for itself at every stage of its development. And the Japanese got much more than a bicycle industry from the exercise. They had also acquired a model for many of their other industrial achievements: imitation and a system of reducing complex manufacturing work to a number of relatively simple operations which could be done in small autonomous workshops. The pattern was applied to the production of many other goods, and underwrote the soaring economic success of Japan during the twentieth century. Sony began life at the end of the Second World War as a small shop making tubes on contract for radio assemblers. The first Nikon cameras were exact copies of the Zeiss Contax; Canon copied the Leica; Toyota Landcruisers were powered by copies of the Chrysler straight-six engine.

The attraction of the bicycle is that it multiplies the distance travelled per unit of energy – a thrust on the pedals carries the rider much further than a stride on the ground – and until the advent of this mechanical wizardry in the late nineteenth century the only way of going further or faster than by foot was courtesy of an animal or by boat. And the boat, being inanimate and requiring minimal care, was the preferred choice wherever a suitable watercourse existed. Indeed, all the earliest known cities were located precisely where the advantages of river transport could best serve the travel and commercial affairs of their inhabitants; and there have been few major cities since then which did not exploit the potential of boats, ships or canoes at some stage in their history.

Eridu, Uruk and Babylon were served by the Euphrates and its tributaries. Plato remarked that the Greek city-states were clustered about the shores of the Mediterranean 'like frogs on a pond'; Athens, Corinth, Syracuse, Miletus and so on. The benefits were obvious. To quote just one reported instance: a merchant could consign two or three thousand jars of oil, weighing 50 kg apiece, to distant markets in a single ship of only moderate size – whereas he would have needed an endless file of donkeys or oxcarts to carry them overland.[8]

More than 2,000 years ago, voyages regularly encompassed the entire

Mediterranean and extended to the far north of Scotland – possibly even to Iceland. Clearly, navigation skills and shipbuilding technology were well-advanced by then. In fact, Roman shipbuilders in the first century AD were capable of building vessels larger than any ship that sailed for the British navy until 1861, when the last of its wooden ships were launched (thereafter iron construction became the norm).[9] It was in this tradition that Columbus carried Europe's expanding influence to the New World – in ships that both the Romans and the British navy would have known how to sail.

When Christopher Columbus set sail in 1492 on the voyage that was to bring Spain the wealth of an empire, he was the vanguard of a movement which had been recapturing and consolidating the horizons of Spanish influence for nearly 700 years, as its Christian forces had driven Islamic invaders from the Iberian Peninsula. A plundering band of Arabs and Berbers from North Africa had invaded Spanish territory in 710, and within fifty years the Moors – as they became known – controlled all but the northern sector of the entire Iberian Peninsula. But their rule was never uncontested. Indeed, even as the Moors established territorial supremacy, their grip began to loosen. Century by century, remorselessly, the forces of Iberia's independent regional powers – Portugal, Leon, Navarre, Aragon, Barcelona and Castile, all united in their determination to be rid of foreign rule – drove the occupying Moors southward, back towards the Mediterranean.

By auspicious coincidence, the year during which the Moors were expelled from Granada, their last stronghold on the peninsula, was also the year in which Columbus sailed from Seville and into the Atlantic – 1492. (Less auspiciously, some 170,000 Jews were also expelled from Spain in 1492, an act of intolerance that deprived the country of its most astute businessmen just when their experience could have been employed to the nation's benefit in the financing and organisation of complex 'new world' ventures. In their absence, Spain was obliged to use the services of less obliging Italian and German financiers, with the result that an unnecessarily high proportion of the wealth its empire would generate was mortgaged in advance.[10])

With the Moors gone, the nominally united Spanish regions returned to the pursuit of separate and differing interests. Portugal maintained its autonomy in the west, Navarre in the north had connections over the Pyrenees, and Aragon looked eastwards into the Mediterranean – all of which left Castile in control of the main central and south-western regions, from which came the majority of the New World *conquistadors*.

'From its first emergence,' a commentator writes, 'Castile was a frontier kingdom, whose people, prompted by pugnacity, land hunger and religious zeal, looked to expansive war and conquest for the satisfaction of their ambitions.[11] Where its frontiers touched the Mediterranean, Castile had also acquired a level of maritime expertise to match its military prowess, so that by 1492, with the Moors expelled from Granada and Castilian knights looking for fresh fields to conquer, Spain was well-equipped to exploit the promising new horizons which Columbus would find across the Atlantic.

The challenges of establishing an empire, with the associated prospects of a share in its profitable enterprises, reached beyond regional differences to become a common cause under the control of Castile. Recognising that the government of newly unified Spain should be based in a location which would offend none of the jealously competitive regional cities, Castile's rulers selected a town close to the geographic centre of the Iberian Peninsula – Madrid. On 8 May 1561 Philip II decreed that Madrid was to be the capital of Spain – thus making it the earliest of modern capital cities founded to ensure that entrenched local political interests would not influence national issues. Others include Washington DC, founded in 1792; Ottawa, 1858; Canberra, 1908; and Brasilia, 1960.

Whatever the political advantages of establishing Spain's national capital at the very centre of the Iberian Peninsula, Madrid's location created enormous supply and transportation problems. Indeed, a leading authority on the subject states bluntly that 'Lack of an adequate transportation system in the Spanish interior was a primary cause of the political and economic stagnation of the country in the nineteenth century.'[12] And it is clear that from the beginning Madrid was destined to become an economic liability – only the wealth of an empire and absolutist rule such as was described in chapter 8 sustained it. The primary problems were, of course, distance and transportation.

Madrid was at least 350 km, and in some directions 600 km, from the sea and important peripheral cities – and accessible only by land. Though the lower reaches of the Guadalquivir and Ebro rivers are permanently navigable, the greater part of the Iberian land mass is devoid of navigable waterways. In fact, Madrid is perhaps the largest city without access to water transport in European history.[13] Anything the city had to import from afar was transported most of the way by road –

over difficult terrain: there are few places in Spain where it is possible to travel more than 80 km without having to climb a mountain.

Madrid's transportation problems would not have been so great if the city had been able to call upon the bounty of a fertile, well-populated and prosperous hinterland. In that case a new capital city could have generated substantial economic exchange between the urban and rural communities of the interior, stimulating the economy and development of the region as a whole. But in fact the Spanish interior was thinly populated; and its soils were infertile, giving some of the lowest grain yields in Europe. With the exception of wool, the region produced nothing that could bear the cost of transport to the coast and still be profitable.

The rural population was self-supporting in terms of food, and had produced surpluses large enough to support the 20,000 people living in Madrid before the city became capital of Spain, but struggled to feed the growing city. The population of Madrid doubled in the decades immediately after 1561, reached 65,000 before the end of the 1500s and had soared to 175,000 by 1630[14] – still not an excessively large city, smaller even than Tenochtitlan at the time of the Spanish conquest but fraught with the same difficulties the colonial city had experienced as it had become dependent upon land rather than water transport.

As the authority which had made Madrid the capital of Spain, it was the royal government rather than the existing city administration that bore responsibility for ensuring the capital was adequately supplied with food and fuel.[15] By the 1780s nearly one-third of the Crown's net revenues was being spent on Madrid[16] – a substantial proportion of which doubtless was allocated to the acquisition of basic supplies and transporting them to the city. Pack animals and ox-wagons by the thousand were kept busy supplying Madrid on a daily basis. From an early stage, favoured elements of the transport industry had been granted government subsidies, concessions and protection – even the equivalent of 'legal aid' for cases in which carters were prosecuted for mis-demeanours committed in the course of their work.[17] But no royal privilege could eliminate the fundamental problems of using mules, donkeys and ox-carts to haul vast quantities of food, materials and manufactured goods across the length and breadth of Spain.

Not only distance and the terrain, but the seasons also conspired against the smooth and regular operation of an efficient transport system. The winter months were cold and rainy, the high passes were often blocked by snow, and even lowland routes were muddy and difficult.

Routes were easier in spring and autumn, but then many transporters found working the land more important than plying the roads. During the hot and dry summer months the problem was that grazing for the haulage animals along the routes could be sparse and hard to come by.

Nothing was ever easy, but the provision of wayside grazing (and water) was the most intractable of the difficulties facing the transporters and the royal council responsible for the provisioning of Madrid – particularly in respect of the preferred means of conveyance: ox-wagons. The point here is that while a pair of oxen could haul a substantial load, they worked best to a fixed routine. Mules and donkeys were fairly accommodating – manageable by day or night, grazing on the hoof, and content to have their intake topped up with a bag of oats. Oxen, by contrast, not only had to rest all night, preferably in open pasture, but also needed to be unyoked for about three hours around the middle of the day in order to graze and – since they are ruminants – to give them a chance to lie down and chew the cud.

To facilitate the immutable requirements of oxen, the royal council had granted carters the right of unhindered access to all common pasture in Castile – that is all the open grazing land that was customarily reserved for the use of people living in the immediate neighbourhood. In all farming communities that have cattle, an area of common pasture is vital, providing somewhere for cattle to graze when their owner's other land is being cultivated, and a reserve of grazing for when conditions are bad. But the capacity of any common land to sustain livestock is limited. Hence, though common, its use has always been strictly reserved for the people who were most concerned to maintain its viability – the local farmers. Now the carters were to have unrestricted access – and were even granted the right to use of the commons for their overnight stays. Furthermore, the royal council decreed that where common land was insufficient, carters were entitled to use any private pasture on payment of a nominal daily fee – with the additional condition that once carters had claimed the right to rent a piece of land it could not be used for anything else, until they formally relinquished the right to rent it.

The carters took full advantage of the rights they had been granted, diligently picking their routes through the network of wagon roads that joined villages and towns throughout Spain not simply according to the distances involved, but primarily according to the extent and quality of available grazing. And as though to acknowledge that their rights went beyond what could be reasonably expected, these privileged agents of the crown were empowered to prosecute any community which failed to keep local roads open and passable for their traffic, and to forestall any feigned ignorance on the part of uncooperative communities, the carters carried printed copies of their authorisation – with the royal council's seal prominently attached.[18]

It must have been clear to any objective observer that the royal council's arrangements for the provisioning of Madrid were short-sighted and unsustainable. As David Ringrose points out in the account of Spain's transportation problems upon which these paragraphs are based,[19] the carter's privileges were in effect a tax on the rural communities that was being used to support the government and its unproductive, parasitic capital city – a hidden tax the already impoverished countryside could ill afford and which undoubtedly retarded regional development. Furthermore, the carters not only collected the tax fully and methodically – their demands were greatest precisely when the countryside was least able to meet them. If the rains failed and harvests throughout Spain were inadequate, for instance, the government was forced to import supplies by sea. With little or no local grain available, supplying Madrid then became a predominantly long-distance operation which put more carts on the road for longer periods. But, of course, a drought that kills the crops also kills the wayside grazing – thus intensifying the crisis.

With a steadily growing population, and local harvests suffering the effects of recurrent drought, Madrid had to be supplied with imported grain repeatedly during the 1700s. There were times when 70 per cent of Castile's carting capacity and 50 per cent of its pack animals were hauling vital foodstuffs and fuel to the capital. It was a precarious situation, even in favourable circumstances; when war disrupted the delicate balance of supply and transportation during the winter and spring of 1811–12, 20,000 people died of starvation in Madrid.[20]

It would be wrong to imply that the members of the royal council were unaware of the inadequacies of the supply and transportation system upon which their capital city depended – they knew its failing well, and did make some attempt to improve matters. Major schemes of transport innovation were planned and commenced. Unfortunately they came too late – and were too grandiose – to make any difference.

During the latter half of the seventeenth century, construction work began on a system of royal highways which would connect Madrid to all Spain's important peripheral cities. As David Ringrose reports, these royal highways equalled anything in Europe for size, capacity, cost – and slow construction. Laid on a carefully built limestone foundation, their domed surface of cut stone was from 10 to 20 m wide, and flanked by extensive retaining walls. They took the most direct routes, often going through mountains and across swamps at great expense that could have been skirted more cheaply. Progress was frequently delayed by the construction of a bridge or causeway deemed necessary to keep the road level, where a mild gradient would have perfectly acceptable. Indeed, a contemporary traveller reported that the engineers' tendency to emphasise straightness and levelness made progress so slow 'that the first sections of a road are already falling into decay before the road itself is finished'.[21]

Slow construction, lack of maintenance and the devastation of the Napoleonic Wars left significant parts of the royal highway system still incomplete a century after building had commenced. Furthermore, only a small part of the radial network that was finished actually eased the problem of supplying Madrid. The money, effort and time could have been more usefully spent on improving the existing network of wagon roads – not least because although the new straight and paved royal highways enabled ox-wagons to travel faster, their design and routing virtually ensured that wayside grazing would be even more scarce than on traditional roads.

Perhaps realising that a radial system of royal highways could never be an adequate long-term solution to Madrid's – and Spain's – transportation problems, the government embarked upon an even more grandiose scheme, 'one of the great unfinished projects in Spanish history':[22] canals. The essence of the scheme was twofold: first to extend the navigable lower reaches of the Ebro river across north-eastern Spain, into the Cantabrian mountains and down to the Bay of Biscay, thus producing a waterway across the neck of the peninsula from which tributary canals would give Spain's interior – and especially Madrid – access to both the Atlantic and the Mediterranean; and second to extend the Guadalquivir river into Andalucia and thence north to Madrid, thus giving the capital direct and rapid access to Córdoba, Seville, the Gulf of Cadiz and the ocean beyond.

There can be no doubt that a canal system would have served Madrid and the Spanish interior far better than the royal highways, but the scheme suffered even more from the difficulties of transforming grandiose vision into reality. The master plan for the canals specified a depth of near 3 m throughout, a bottom width of 6 m and a top width of 17 m. Canals on such a scale required extensive aqueducts, embankments and cuttings – especially if they were to cross several hundred kilometres of Spain's rugged and arid landscape.

The Ebro canal, for instance, would have to climb nearly 1,000 m in its roughly 400 km journey from the Mediterranean to the ridge of the Cantabrian mountains, and then descend the same amount in a short 80 km journey to the Atlantic on the other side. But despite construction difficulties and huge expense, by the end of the 1780s major building work was underway at strategic points in the proposed system. Over 300 km of canals were eventually built – a massive achievement in many respects, but also a total waste, since none of the crucial connections were ever completed. As David Ringrose puts it: the canals 'began nowhere and ended nowhere'.[23]

In the final outcome, railways were the solution to Spain's transportation problems, and subsequently the internal combustion engine, but they came too late for Spain to invest the wealth of a global empire in a mechanised transport system at home. By the time railways and trucks became an option, Spain had suffered the catastrophic upheavals of war, lost an empire, and squandered a significant proportion of its fabulous fortune on an ill-chosen capital city – Madrid. Spanish fleets had encircled the globe, captured distant horizons and brought back the greatest volume of material riches ever seen – and what happened? It was squandered on the extravagances of Madrid, and the narrow horizons of a trundling transport system, which in turn strangled economic development in Spain and created 'a degree of stagnation and backwardness unmatched in Western Europe'.[24]

Meanwhile, railways were expanding the horizons of individuals and commerce wherever they were built. As mentioned on page 237, Britain's railways alone were carrying 170 million passengers a year by 1862 – and enjoying the added benefit of freight traffic revenues which were at last beginning to exceed the income from passengers. A similar rush to rail was occurring in Europe north of the Pyrenees – Belgium began planning a national railway system to by-pass Dutch-controlled waterways and ports within months of achieving independence from the Netherlands in 1830, and by 1875 had built the most dense rail network in the world – one kilometre of railway for every 85 km^2 of area. Rail networks were expanding across Germany, France, Switzerland, Austria and through the Alps to Italy by the 1870s – even Spain had made a start – but the most prodigious progress was made in North America. As settlers moved west, the challenge of capturing an expanding horizon – both commercial and territorial – stirred industries to towering heights of innovation and productivity, laced the continent with railroads, enticed millions of immigrants across the Atlantic, and transformed wayside stations into cities.

Mobility. Transportation in one form or another has always been an essential factor in the prosperity of national economies and the growth of cities, but efficiency – not distance – is the defining measure of its worth. The gold and riches that Spanish ships brought back from a global empire in the sixteenth and seventeenth centuries, for instance, did little for a national economy whose transportation system was limited to the capacity of mule trains and ox-wagons, while the rail network Britain's colonial government built in India during the nineteenth century not only united the entire sub-continent together as never before, but also extended the horizons of British commerce to all parts of India, capturing markets – as well as resources – for the benefit and selfish prosperity of the British economy. Likewise, the 'lunatic line' linking Uganda to the East African port of Mombasa, and other railways or road links that similarly facilitated the movement of resources from – and manufactured goods to – the interior of colonial possessions around the world, functioned as important contributors to the prosperity and growth of cities at home.

The colonial powers inflicted enormous damage on the territories they exploited, and have been soundly condemned for it, but a potentially no less damaging style of colonialism is active today: the mega-city. The great cities of the modern world have captured even the most distant horizons; in effect they have colonised the entire globe and are exploiting its resources to an unprecedented and accelerating degree. With half of humanity already living in cities (and much of the other half dependent on urban markets for their existence), mega-cities are by far the most disruptive feature of humanity's presence on earth, and their demand for food, energy and consumer goods has profoundly altered our relationships with the planet and its ecosystems.

The parasitic aspect of a city's existence has always been self-evident. Even as far back as 1300, London – then a city with 100,000 inhabitants – called upon a surrounding hinterland of over 10,000 km^2 for its grain supply.[26] A proportion of London's grain reached the city by water from farms with access to the upper reaches of the Thames, but most of the supply was transported overland. In any event, the size and survival of fourteenth-century London was limited by the efficiency of the transportation system serving it. The same is true of every city – then and since. But increasingly, and with astonishing acceleration, mechanisation has expanded the hinterland of cities in every direction. Nowadays the sky is the limit – literally. London exploits a global market – importing fish from the Pacific, beans from Africa, onions from South America, or even cherries from Madrid if the price is right.

17

'The city here, complete'[1]

There has never been a shortage of people with bold ideas of
what would constitute the perfect city. Some have even had
the opportunity to put their ideas into practice. The results
have been mixed. Plans for what would be perfect today are
often invalidated by the changing imperatives of tomorrow.
No one thing, but only the nurturing of diversity serves best.

Urban planning has always been fertile ground for argument between
the dreaming idealists of society, the perceptive realists and the hard-
nosed pragmatists who believed that when it came to founding a new
city (or rebuilding an old one), cost and expedience were the factors to
which prime consideration should be given. There were always some
individuals who sincerely wanted to create cities that were planned and
arranged primarily for the greatest convenience of their inhabitants, and
a few who were keen to apply the best of all available talent to the aim
of creating urban environments that were attractive places to live in, but
issues of cost and practical expedience generally prevailed. Edward I of
England, for instance, tried several times in 1296 and 1297 to convene
meetings at which experts would discuss how to build the ideal city,[2] but
no constructive developments were forthcoming.

Aristotle, no less, declared that 'the art of planning cities' was
'invented' in the fifth century BC by the Greek architect Hippodamus
(actually, modern archaeological investigations have shown that the
ancient cities of the Indus basin – Mohenjo-daro, Dholavira and
Harappa, for instance – had also been constructed to a set plan 2,000
years before Hippodamus, but Aristotle could not have known that, nor
could Hippodamus – from their point of view his plans were original).

248

Hippodamus' claim to fame rests on his master plan for Miletus, the Ionian Greek city which had been captured, sacked and destroyed by Persian forces in 494 BC, and recaptured by the Greeks some fifteen years later. Determined to re-establish Miletus as a major centre for commercial and military power, the authorities called upon a coterie of architects, led by Hippodamus, to plan 'an entirely new and modern city',[3] with all its component parts – the central area, housing districts, commercial, cultural and leisure facilities, and defensive wall – arranged to create a wholly integrated urban entity.

The returning survivors might have been expected to start rebuilding on a small scale, reinstating the random layout of the old city which had coalesced, and evolved organically from a pre-existing pattern of settlement on the rocky and indented peninsula. But no, they took a grander and more far-sighted approach, adopting plans which not only served their immediate needs but would also facilitate future expansion. Indeed, the plans for Miletus covered the entire peninsula from the start, and were so well conceived that the city's greatly mounting importance and growing population were accommodated without loss of form or the demolition of existing buildings.[4] It was a robust yet eminently adaptable scheme that remained applicable even as Miletus grew from an urban community of perhaps not more than a few thousand when re-building began in 479 BC, into a city of 80,000–100,000 inhabitants under the Romans over 500 years later.

The fundamental characteristic of the Miletus city plan was that most expedient of urban planning schemes – the gridiron: a geometrically ordered grid of streets which divided any designated area into square or rectangular blocks, some of which could be set aside for specific buildings or purposes, and the rest further divided into separate plots as required.[5] The great advantage of the gridiron from the planners' point of view was a rigid orderliness that ignored topographical features – in other words, it could be easily applied, anywhere (in theory, at least). While the layout of a prospering village would follow the natural contours of the landscape as it grew into a town and then a city, mould-ing itself around a hill, along a riverbank, and doubtless postponing the use of prime agricultural land as long as possible, the planners' gridiron immediately reduced any irregularities of the landscape, or qualitative distinctions, to a geometric pattern of squared off, rectangular blocks and plots – the size (and value) of which could be precisely determined in advance. No wonder it appealed to those who were keen to establish an urban presence in otherwise unoccupied regions, or who wished to impose a controlling sense of order on a hitherto randomly constructed urban environment.

After Hippodamus, the gridiron became a regular feature of the Greeks' planned cities. The Romans also used it as the basis of their urban planning. The thousands of fortified legionary bases constructed throughout the Roman empire, for instance, were invariably laid out according to the gridiron, within a predetermined rectilinear defensive perimeter. Though established primarily for military expedience and as administrative centres, some of these forts grew into towns whose Roman origins survived even the fall of the Empire. Intimations of the original Roman gridiron are to be found in the layout of cities throughout Europe and north Africa – from Carlisle to Alexandria – and are especially apparent at the heart of modern Zaragoza, where the unusual extent of an underlying Roman grid form in the present-day street plan stands as evidence of uninterrupted – or not seriously affected – urban status from the end of the Empire to the present-day.[6]

Medieval monarchs were also keen on the gridiron basis of city planning. Indeed, the Laws of the Indies as laid down by the kings of Spain during the sixteenth and seventeenth centuries in effect made the gridiron layout mandatory for new cities established in the Spanish colonies. Phillip II, who in 1561 had declared that Madrid should be the capital city of Spain, in 1573 issued a royal ordinance governing the founding and physical planning of new towns throughout the Empire.[7] Since most of Spain's first settlements in the Caribbean and the Americas were already in place by then, the ordinance was to some extent retrospective, serving to reiterate imperial standing orders and refine existing practices. The gridiron layout, for instance, was already evident in the layout of Santa Domingo (now capital of the Dominican Republic), which had been founded in 1502; in Havana (founded 1515); San Juan (1521); Cartagena (1533); and other urban centres.

So, although a gridiron street layout is not specified as such in the Laws of the Indies, there can be little doubt that it was the framework within which the instructions and specifications of the royal ordinance were to be followed. One of the document's first clauses, for example, states that 'the plan of the place, with its squares, streets and building lots is to be outlined by means of measuring by cord and ruler, beginning with the main square from which streets are to run to the gates and principal roads, and leaving sufficient open space so that even if the town grows it can always spread in a symmetrical manner'.[8]

Symmetry is of course the essence of gridiron planning – and something the United States applied on a national scale with its Great American Grid, as formulated in the Land Ordinance of 1785. This was (and is still) by far the largest example in rural or urban history of a pre-determined plan for land apportioning and allocation. It was also an example of practical expedience at its most incisive – especially in New York, where, as immigrants and industry quickened the pace of economic development in the United States, the gridiron plans drawn up for the city in 1811 served the demands of land exploitation, utility and profitability with scant regard for the niceties of city planning. It was a brutal scheme. Creating an urban environment that would be a congenial place in which to live was far from the planners' minds. Practical expedience was all – and the striking similarities between the plans of Miletus and Manhattan when they are compared side by side,[9] with a grid layout covering both the peninsula of the former and the island of the latter, reveal the power and persistence of expedience as a motivating force through more than 2,000 years of city planning.

New York was originally a collection of randomly constructed homes, stores and warehouses established on the southern tip of Manhattan Island by Dutch settlers in 1624. By the early 1800s, the settlement had grown into a city which occupied virtually the entire southern tip of the island up to what is now Washington Square. In anticipation of further rapid growth, the state of New York appointed commissioners in 1807 to produce plans for the extension of the city into the undeveloped tracts of the island to the north of Washington Square. Motivated mainly, it is said,[10] by considerations of economic gain, the commissioners' plans covered the island completely with a uniform grid: twelve 100-foot-wide (30 m) avenues running north to south, and 155 streets, each 60 feet wide (18.3 m) crossing the island from east to west. Manhattan Island was to be covered from shore to shore with buildings, avenues and streets. The rocky topography of the island was ignored; minimum attention was given to the need for public amenities; no waterfront esplanades, parks or adequate open spaces were proposed. Indeed, the commissioners themselves declared that the principal aim of the plan was to provide the most convenient and cheapest housing – just as Hippodamus had done for Miletus, in Aristotle's opinion.[11]

Only as the blocks on the commissioners' grid began to fill up with buildings, and New Yorkers began to clamour for relief from the ruthlessly expedient design of their city, did concerted attention focus on the need for some major public open space. A campaign for a park was launched in 1844. Predictably, it aroused the fierce opposition of real estate interests, but by the late 1850s these masters of expedience had abandoned their protest and accepted nearly $8 million for some fifty blocks of prime real estate lying along the spine of the island between Fifth and Eighth Avenues, from 59th St up to 110th St. This tract of land became Central Park, now unquestionably an essential oasis of relief from the hard urban realities of Manhattan.

Beyond New York and the already well-populated states of New England, the Great American Grid provided a practical means of selling land promptly – sight unseen – to the mounting numbers of people then wanting to move west, or buy a stake in the territorial expansion of America. The Grid ignored topographical features of the landscape completely (with some anomalous results), but by dividing the sprawling territories lying between the eastern states and the Pacific Ocean into a neat pattern of squares and sections, it enabled people to locate their purchases in the wilderness with relative ease, and reduced the likelihood of border disputes.

On paper at least, the Grid transformed the regions of America which hitherto had been inhabited by groups of indigenous hunters and farmers into a civilised collection of townships, six miles (9.6 km) square, with each township further divided into thirty-six one-square-mile (266 ha) sections. The Land Ordinance stipulated that half the land should be sold in units of one township or more, and the other half by the section. And thus, a commentator writes:

> today, as one flies over the last mountain ridges from the east, one sees stretching ahead to the horizon a vast chequer board of fields and roads. With military precision, modified only on occasion by some severe topographic break or some earlier system of land distribution, this rectangular grid persists to the shores of the Pacific.[12]

The story of Cleveland, Ohio, is a good example of how a great many cities in the United States were founded from scratch on principles that the Great American Grid enshrined.

Cleveland was not named after its counterpart in the north of England as might be supposed. Reflecting the more businesslike ethic of land as saleable property it was named after Moses Cleaveland, a New England resident and director of the Connecticut Land Company which bought 3 million acres (4,000 km²) of land on the southern shore of Lake Erie from the state in 1795 – sight unseen. Cleaveland was also the leader of a surveying party which laid out the original site of the city in the spring of 1796, having first persuaded the resident Mohawk and Seneca Indians to move out (they had previously signed a treaty relinquishing their rights to the land) with a payment of '500 pounds New York currency, two beef cattle, and 100 gallons [375 litres]of whiskey'.

The town that Cleaveland and his party laid out on a bluff over the eastern bank of the Cuyahoga river, which flows into the lake at that point, was neat, regular and precisely measured – as might be expected of speculators more interested in promoting the sale of land than in facilitating its use – but settlers were slow to arrive. Not least because the site was virgin territory, more than 400 miles (640 km) from the Atlantic coast and the inhabited states of New England. Prospective settlers knew full well that although the map showed a neat plan of 222 two- and four-acre plots (0.8 and 1.6 ha) laid out like a New England town in a grid of streets with an expansive 10-acre (4 ha) public square at its centre, the reality was a pattern of surveying pegs linking some rough clearings in the midst of a dense hardwood forest. 'The soil is pretty good and the water extraordinarily good and plenty', reported one of Cleaveland's party. 'The timber is beech, elm, ash, maple, walnut, chestnut, oak, whitewood, butternut . . . There are grapevines at this place loaded with their first fruit . . .'

Two traders set up shop in a two-storey log cabin they and their families had built on the banks of the Cuyahoga in 1797, offering 'a meal and a bed, and a drink of New England rum' to travellers, and operating a ferry service for the convenience of anyone wishing to trade with the Indians across the river. In 1798 a blacksmith arrived, and when the Company reduced the price of plots and offered extended terms, a number of other settlers followed. A primitive distillery was the first manufacturing business to be established in the settlement, producing raw alcohol ostensibly for medicinal purposes but mainly as a trade item valued for its 'calming influence on unruly Indians'.

Thirty-two residents – twelve women and twenty men – gathered at the traders' riverfront cabin on 4 July 1801 to celebrate the twenty-fifth anniversary of American independence, and although the population of the region had swollen to 1500 by the time the thirty-fifth anniversary was celebrated ten years later, there were still only fifty-seven people living in the town. And the town hardly merited that title. An early settler later recalled:

... when I rode behind my father on horseback to Cleveland ... there were many large stumps in the Square, and clumps of bushes which extended to the lake, and all along the bank of the lake, from the summit to the beach, the trees were all standing ... [F]rom the Square ... was woods, except some four or five spaces adjoining the street for as many houses and gardens ... west, south and east, the forest stood in its native grandeur.[13]

By 1815, while tree stumps still hindered traffic along the only two streets that had been cleared, and bushes still flourished on undeveloped plots, several more traders and craftsmen had been attracted to Cleveland. The town had lost the 'a' of Cleaveland (no one seems to know why) but now had 150 permanent residents and although most of the thirty-four houses then standing were of unsawn log construction, windowless and with earthen floors, three fine frame-built residences stood on prominent corner sites, and a two-storey courthouse (complete with jail) had been erected on the Public Square. The town's first lawyer had hung up his shingle, a judge had been appointed, and an Indian had been tried, found guilty and publicly executed for the murder of two fur-trappers.

When the British finally abandoned attempts to extend their Canadian territories across to the southern and western shores of Lake Erie after 1812, Cleveland found itself most fortuitously sited on the transcontinental route that gave access via the Great Lakes and overland to the Great Plains and the vast economic potential of the north-western United States. The city's fortunes were enhanced still further in 1827, with the opening of a 57.6 km canal (dug mainly by German and Irish immigrants) linking Cleveland and the lakes to the Ohio river, Pittsburgh and the continental interior. Within a year, coal from distant mines was being shipped up the Ohio and along the canal to fuel steamboats on Lake Erie. Even more auspiciously – with coal now available to replace charcoal, the number of iron foundries sited on the flat open estuary of the Cuyahoga river quickly multiplied. Cleveland's iron industry had began in a small way, casting pillars, plate metal and decorative iron-work from a low-grade ore found locally, but with the discovery of vast reserves of high-grade ore in upper Michigan state during the 1840s, and the construction of canals and facilities to ship ore through the lakes during the 1850s, Cleveland's iron and steel industry became the most advantageously situated in north America. People flocked to Cleveland. In 1853 the city directory referred proudly to a population of '30,000 souls'.[14]

The railway had reached Cleveland in 1851, securing the city's share of the massive investment in the iron and steel industry that was to lift United States production of rails alone from 141,000 tons in 1856 to over 335,000 tons a year by 1864, and again to more than 775,000 tons by 1871. And rails were not the only product that Cleveland's expanding iron and steel industry was supplying to an expanding nation. Steel plate, castings, locomotives and ships, wheelbarrows, shovels, sewer pipes and drainpipes, barbed wire and nails – the demand mounted year by year and each decade brought further innovations and inventions which opened new markets and provoked still more demand. The introduction of the telegraph, for example, boosted cable output from 250,000 tons in 1875, the year before Bell's invention was publicly demonstrated, to 1.2 million tons in 1898, when it had become the indispensable medium of business communication. The electrically operated elevator followed the invention of travelling cranes and in turn facilitated the construction of the first skyscraper – a ten-storey insurance office building erected in Chicago in 1885.

Until then the height of buildings had been constrained by the sheer weight of stone, and by the greater width of the base required to support any increase in height. But skyscrapers are built around frames of steel, with curtain walls hung from each floor and Harvey Corbett, a pioneer of New York's skyscraper architecture, expressed the significance of this perfectly in 1926:

> The transition of steel, from merely strengthening stone to carrying the masonry load at each floor, was the most momentous step in the history of architecture since the days of Rome. In a single bound architecture was freed from the shackles of stone-weight and made flexible beyond belief. Suddenly architecture gained a new dimension. Height.[15]

Once in motion, the steel-based industrial economy soon showed signs of becoming self-perpetuating – with each new invention prompting new demands which in turn inspired further invention, each stage adding momentum to the growth of the economy. And as industry sought the finance for its expanding operations, the prerogatives of production shifted from the factory floor to the boardroom and the bank. Production decisions – what to make, how much of it, and for whom – needed the approval of people motivated primarily by the imperatives of the financial markets: profit or security – and preferably both. Financiers liked to congregate in regional and national cities, close to the ear of governments that controlled public finance, where legislative control of economic and social affairs was exercised and might be lobbied. With the banks and the insurance companies came the headquarters of large industrial companies, the media and the marketing agencies.

Banking, accounting, management, law, journalism, advertising – by the beginning of the twentieth century a new form of specialised urban human activity was firmly established – the white-collar city office worker. Reasonably affluent and with the security of a regular income, these new citizens outnumbered both the very rich and the very poor sections of city communities. In fact, they were an entirely new class of society: the middle class – with a correspondingly new set of needs and wishes. They bought accommodation, food and services, clothing and entertainment in ever-increasing quantities, and were inclined to buy for style and fashion, rather than for value and utility. The needs and wishes of the middle class promised to become so vast, so ephemeral, that only an entirely new industry could satisfy them: the consumer industry.

For the first time in history, a huge mass market was inclined to buy goods more on the basis of their immediate appeal than on their lasting value. The accompanying development of mass-production manufacturing techniques duly enshrined the concept of obsolescence and made a virtue of persuasive marketing. Increasingly, manufacturers aimed to produce what people might want, rather than what they were known to need. Thus goods were produced speculatively, and advertising was called upon to create demand. And because the system was driven by the financial market's expectations of a return on its investments, the consumer industry had to grow continuously. New demands had to be created and exploited, new horizons captured: that's capitalism.

The emergence of the modern city as a centre of political and financial influence, encapsulated within a massive consumer industry, is a feature of every industrial nation, but its characteristics are especially visible in the United States, where no large city is more than two centuries old and all are therefore undisguised by the heritage of pre-industrial merchant and princely design that still dominates many Old World cities. Modern America is very clearly the product of a drive to accumulate and manipulate wealth. The grid network that distinguishes road maps of the United States, for instance, shows how large chunks of the nation were bought by speculators and then sectioned off for sale. Likewise in the cities, where a grid pattern of streets simplified the business of selling plots – and reduced the potential for variety in the groundplans of city landscape.

Few cities were better placed than Cleveland to capitalise on the coalescence of economic and social developments that the Industrial Revolution brought to North America. Timber, coal and iron ore; river, canal, lake, road and rail transportation; massive financial investment and an eager pool of immigrant labour – all had helped to put Cleveland in the front rank of America's up-and-coming industrial cities by the early 1860s, when the fortuity of its location made it a centre for what was to become the leading source of wealth and influence in the modern world – oil.

In the Allegheny mountains to the east of Cleveland, crude petroleum oil had been seeping from rocks and floating out on the surface of streams for millennia. It had its uses locally, but its wider potential was recognised only after 1859, when Edwin Drake drilled the world's first oil well and showed that crude oil could be produced in quantity. In those days, before the invention of the petrol engine, the foremost potential of crude oil was as an alternative source of kerosene, then only obtainable from coal by an extraction process that made it too expensive to sell as a fuel for household lamps (a huge market then dominated by whale oil). In 1860, three Cleveland entrepreneurs, convinced that kerosene would replace whale oil as a lamp fuel once it was cheap enough, bought ten barrels of crude oil from Drake's well, and experimented with it until they succeeded in producing kerosene at a fraction of the cost of extracting it from coal, and cheaper even than whale oil.

The oil refining and supply industry that sprang from the first production of kerosene in Cleveland soon developed a sturdy momentum of its own, while the finance, technology and steel requirements that the oil exploration and drilling industry called into being gave yet another boost to Cleveland's fortunes. The city's population rose steadily. Foreign immigrant workers constituted most of the influx, but it also included bankers, builders, hoteliers, traders and large numbers of independent souls in search of their personal fortunes. Among the most determined of the latter category was a young man who, having invested $40 in a business studies course at a Cleveland commercial college in the summer of 1855, launched himself onto the city's job market in the autumn of that year at the age of seventeen, and went on to earn the title of the world's wealthiest man: John D. Rockefeller.

Rockefeller and Cleveland could stand as a defining example of talent and location coming together at precisely the most mutually advantageous moment in time. Rockefeller's business talents had already earned him a fortune by 1863 when, with a partner, he went into the kerosene business, establishing the Excelsior Works refinery on 1.2 ha of land conveniently close to the rail terminal on the Cuyahoga flats. John D. bought out his partner in 1865, by which time crude oil was flowing from the Allegheny wells at a rate of 10,000 barrels a day. Rockefeller saw his future in oil. A large part of Cleveland's future was tied up with Rockefeller's vision too, as it turned out, along with a good part of the economic future of New York, North America and the world, for Rockefeller built the Excelsior Works into Standard Oil – Esso – the first of the world's huge multinational companies.

By 1872, Cleveland was the oil centre of the United States. Kerosene, for lighting, heating and cooking, was the mainstay of the business, but by-products such as petroleum jelly, lubricants, paraffin waxes and gas – everything from chewing gum to Vaseline, Rockefeller boasted – also contributed substantial profits, while control of freight services, railroads and a near-monopoly of pipeline and storage facilities poured still more money into the Standard Oil coffers. And needless to say, with the development of the petrol engine, automotive power and aeroplanes, the prospects of profit were virtually limitless – but never out of Rockefeller's sight. John D. was the Marco Datini of his day – a careful man who always took a close and personal interest in how things stood. Everything was on record; the bottom line of his 1912 personal ledger, for instance, recorded a net worth of $302,713,419 and 83 cents.

In 1912 the population of Cleveland was over 560,000, of whom probably 75 per cent were either foreign-born or the children of foreign parents. By 1930 the continuing flood of immigrants had swollen the population to over 900,000, making Cleveland the nation's sixth largest city, after New York, Chicago, Philadelphia, Detroit and Los Angeles. Throughout the latter part of the nineteenth century and into the twentieth, foreign immigrants had flocked to prosperous Cleveland in search of the 'American Dream', but found a city wallowing as much in filth as in riches under a pungent cloud of smoke. Caring citizens had been complaining about the deteriorating state of the Cleveland environment for decades. A newspaper editorial suggested in 1855:

> It is yearly becoming a thing more necessary to the comfort of our citizens, that the smoke rolling in such volume out of the chimneys

of our large manufactories should be entirely consumed. We have now in and about our city scores of chimney stacks, that pour out clouds of smoke and soot, producing a great amount of discomfort.[16]

Some legislation to control pollution was passed, but never achieved much effect when answered by the fulminations of the industrialists. The indictment of a railroad iron mill company for smoke nuisance in 1860 produced a typical response: '. . . the idea of striking a blow at the industry and prosperity of the infant iron manufactories of Cleveland . . . is an act that should and will be reprobated by the whole community.' Even attempts to control the disgorging of industrial wastes, 'slops, filth etc., in the Cuyahoga River within the city limits' were opposed in the belief that the river's current was strong enough to wash offending matter out into Lake Erie. Stinking air and a polluted river were simply a by-product of successful industry which had to be endured. Restrictions would retard the growth and prosperity of the city, and prosperity was deemed far more important than a congenial environment.

The immigrants had no choice but to endure smoke and grime as they laboured for a share of the new prosperity but, needless to say, the industrialists and businessmen could enjoy both prosperity and a congenial environment. As the inner city was degraded, its wealthiest residents built successive waves of large splendid houses at increasing distances from the smell and dirt of the city centre. Down the length of Euclid Avenue, its very name a memorial to the geometry of classical civilisation, they built houses of such opulence that John D. Rockefeller's mansion, three floors with mansard roof and arched windows in ecclesiastical style, and one of the first on the avenue, soon seemed restrained and conservative in comparison. Brick, stone and ironwork, French style, Oriental, Italian, Palladian, Grecian, all that money could buy – even cupola and turnip dome, lavishly ornamented, sumptuously appointed . . . they stood, these piles of domestic ostentation, as symbols of individual acquisitiveness, to be measured one against the other.

Before long, though, the stink of industry from the Cuyahoga flats was so intense that it reached down the length of Euclid Avenue. Those that could afford it moved further afield – the pattern of their dispersal broadened by their growing numbers, serviced by enterprising land and building speculations, facilitated by the provision of a municipal transportation system and, ultimately, individualised by the private motor car.

Meanwhile, the industrial pollution continued in one form or another into the twentieth century until, on 22 June 1969, Cleveland achieved yet another record of distinction in its remarkable career: the Cuyahoga river actually burst into flames. This extraordinary event was caused by the spontaneous combustion of flammable industrial wastes floating in the river. That a river could catch fire made news around the world, and at home brought Cleveland's environmental policies to the critical attention of the United States Environment Protection Agency. A major programme to clean up the river was ordered. At last, the city set about the task of doubling its sewage treatment capacity; steel-works were obliged to spend millions of dollars on water treatment plants, and the chemical giant, Du Pont, established controls which, even ten years after the conflagration, were still removing over 430 kg of heavy metals from the Cuyahoga river every day.

But this heightened concern for the environment could also be seen as a reflection of changing priorities. By the end of the twentieth century industry had abandoned Cleveland, and its citizens shared the plight of many urban communities in the United States and the developed world, as the latest twist in human economic organisation turned them away from any need to be directly involved in heavy industry. Finance, information technology, business managment, health care, real estate, advertising, entertainment – these were the activities that offered the best options for reviving the fortunes of Cleveland at the beginning of the twenty-first century, and they have populated the city with a new wave of wealth-motive devotees. They live in lush suburbs, some in houses as opulent in the modern idiom as any that a previous generation built on Euclid Avenue. They spend thousands of dollars each year on the lawns that run smooth and unfenced down to the roadside. They raise the Stars and Stripes from balconies over their pillared porticoes, and luxuriate around cool pools during the sweltering heat of summer. The style is informal, but there is a brittle quality to Cleveland's burgeoning prosperity. It is riven with fears of the impoverished, jealous and disorderly factions that have surfaced among the citizens of Cleveland – and many other cities – who were left without a job or future prospects when industry moved on.

Each day, the new custodians of Cleveland's economic future drive speedily through a 5 km band of derelict and decaying properties to the north and south of Euclid Avenue. The area has become the home of blacks, the unemployed and the impoverished, for whom the once exclusive inner city is now a cheap place to live – and has been especially so since riots in the 1960s and '70s reduced substantial tracts of it to rubble. The inner city was a depressed and depressing place, and the majority of Cleveland's new high-flyers are more likely to be tuned in to early market reports than to the plight of inner-city residents as they drive through. It is physically dangerous to stop or venture down the side streets. The people there are washed up, they say – the flotsam of society, stranded, left high and dry by the wayward tides of economic prosperity.

Opportunities to plan the layout of a large urban area in its entirety are rare, and surely deserve that the most talented of eligible practitioners should be given the task. It is often said that London, for instance, would be a much better place today if it had been rebuilt after the Great Fire of 1666 according to plans that Christopher Wren had submitted. Lewis Mumford, in his book *The City in History,* declared that but for the 'tenacious mercantile habits and jealous property rights' of vested interests, Wren would have bestowed upon London all the baroque glories of city planning then popular with the kings and princes of Europe.[17] The rejection of Wren's plans was 'the greatest missed opportunity in urban history' according to some sources.[18] But was it? And were the plans upon which the rebuilding programme actually proceeded anything less than appropriate for what was then one of the world's largest cities (with about 350,000 inhabitants), and rapidly becoming Europe's leading commercial centre?

The fire certainly cleared the ground for redevelopment. It had started in a baker's premises in Pudding Lane in the early hours of Sunday, 2 September. After an unusually hot August the neighbouring thatch and timber buildings were dry as tinder, already half-burned, so that the fire found friendly territory,[19] and was further aided by a strong south-east wind, which quickly sent the flames blazing through the narrow meandering streets and lanes of a city that was still largely medieval in character and configuration. Those in a position to do so took to the Thames, loading boats and barges with such possessions as they could save. The diarist Samuel Pepys, whose house on Seething Lane stood dangerously close to the fire's point of origin, was also on the river, and wrote of being 'almost burned with a shower of fire drops' before retreating to the safety of an ale-house on the southern bank. From there he 'saw the fire grow . . . in corners, and upon steeples, and between churches and houses, as far as we could see up the hill of the City, in a most horrid, malicious bloody flame . . .'[20]

The fire raged uncontrolled for four days; at its height the medieval St Paul's – which by ill-chance was at the time surrounded by the wooden scaffolding of renovation contractors – succumbed to 'the noise and cracking and thunder of the impetuous flames'; streams of molten lead from its roof ran through the streets, 'glowing with fiery redness, so as no horse or man was able to tread on them'. People leaving the city journeyed for hours under a cloud of thick smoke which, it was said, could be seen from Oxford, 80 km away. On the fifth day, a number of houses standing in the path of the fire in the northern and eastern quarters of the City were blown up with gunpowder to create a firebreak, and the consuming fury of the blaze was at last halted.

A smouldering landscape remained, a ruin of charred black timbers and stone burned brilliant white, punctuated by clouds of steam and dark smoke belching from 'subterranean cellars, wells and dungeons'. Fully five-sixths of the City had been totally destroyed, covering fifteen of the City's twenty-six wards. Over 13,000 houses, on 460 streets, had been burned to the ground. Apart from St Paul's, eighty-nine churches had been reduced to ashes. The buildings of virtually all London's major institutions had gone – the Royal Exchange, the Custom House, the halls of forty-four City companies, Guildhall and nearly all the City's administrative buildings. About 80,000 people were made homeless by the fire. According to official records only six people were killed, though in the absence of any reports on the evacuation of institutions such as hospitals and especially the City gaols, with their many subterranean cells, the true figure may have been much higher. Were the incarcerated released? Did they escape as the bars melted, or did they die in their cells as a result of official negligence?[21]

Homelessness and deaths aside, the fire had severely affected the commercial life of the City. The destruction of workshops, warehouses and shops had put a large proportion of London's merchants and craftsmen out of business. Also, the City itself had suffered a severe loss of rental income, as well as administrative disruption, from the destruction of its property. The need to begin rebuilding was urgent. The opportunity for planners to create a new city was unparalleled – and not one that eligible practitioners were likely to miss.

Christopher Wren must have set to work on his plans for a new city just as soon as it became clear that the old one was about to be totally destroyed. On 11 September, nine days after the fire began and before it was even fully extinguished, he submitted a radical redevelopment plan for the City, complete with written commentary. But Wren was only the first. Within days, John Evelyn, Valentine Knight, Robert Hooke and others who felt qualified to undertake the task of rebuilding London had also submitted proposals. The recipient of these proposals was the king, Charles II, who while not in absolute control of London affairs, could make representations to parliament and impose taxes to help the City with rebuilding costs, as well as exercise some influence over the City authorities.

Not being a Londoner by birth or inclination, Charles II took a thoroughly objective view of the City. Its 'disadvantages were not dimmed for him by the kindly veil of familiarity', as one commentator has put it.[22] When critics had presented details of the City's short-comings five years before, he encouraged them to press on and find remedies. He already knew that fire was a constant hazard in the old City; and that wider streets were needed for London's growing trade and traffic. The king, in short, was sympathetic to the concept of a completely replanned City of London. At the same time, though, 'he was at one with the City', in recognising the need to start rebuilding with a minimum of delay.[23]

The plans submitted for the king's consideration in the immediate aftermath of the Great Fire were all distinguished by their determination to impose a radically new layout of streets and blocks upon the devastated area of the City. While of necessity respecting the location of the River Thames and its tributaries – the Fleet and the Walbrook – they gave scant regard to topography, existing street networks or property ownership boundaries; only the city wall and the sites of St Paul's and the Royal Exchange were inviolate.

Robert Hooke, a mathematician and a founding member of the Royal Society renowned for his pioneering work in microscopy, proposed a plan strikingly similar to the drawing of cells which illustrates his treatise on the microscopic structure of vegetable matter published in 1665.[24] There were to be about 100 blocks, all more or less square and of identical size, with four open civic spaces (as well as St Paul's and the Royal Exchange) set in a grid of six streets running from east to west, crossed by twenty streets running from the north down to the Thames – all of equal width.

Valentine Knight, an army officer, devised what the urban historian A. E. J. Morris describes[25] as a 'super-grid' of main and secondary streets dividing the city into a series of regular blocks, 500 feet by 70 feet (152.5 by 21.4 m), rather in the manner chosen by the New York com-missioners for Manhattan, 150 years later.

John Evelyn's plans (he submitted three) were the work of 'a typically wealthy, well-educated nobleman, who could live entirely for his hobbies and who divided his time equally between aesthetic and practical subjects',[26] though his plans for London hardly merited inclusion in either category. To one commentator: 'Evelyn's new city resembled a giant chessboard dominated by twelve squares or piazzas.'[27]

Wren's proposal was more carefully conceived and presented than any of the others.

Christopher Wren was thirty-four years of age at the time of the Great Fire, a Professor of Astronomy at Oxford and a gifted member of the Royal Society who already had numerous original works on astronomy, physics and engineering to his name. Clearly a young man with energy and ambition to match his talent, architecture was his driving interest. As yet, though, he had designed only two buildings – the Sheldonian Theatre, in Oxford, and the Chapel of Pembroke College at Cambridge – which Nikolaus Pevsner, the architectural historian, rather sniffily dismissed as 'evidently the work of a man with little designing experience'.[28] But Wren had friends in high places who were prepared to promote talent before experience. A royal commission set up in 1663 to advise on the restoration of St Paul's had already called upon his services. Indeed, Wren had submitted a report and suggestions for work on the church just weeks before it was destroyed in the Great Fire.

But perhaps the most significant conjunction of events in all this was the fact that from July 1665 to March 1666 Wren had been in France, studying architecture. This was a time when the baroque ideas of town planning were gaining favour among the princes and prelates of Europe whose wealth enabled them to think of extending the grandiose pretensions of their absolute power to plans for palaces and cities:

> The baroque towns, as they began to be planned in the sixteenth century in Italy and developed over much of Europe in the seventeenth and eighteenth, became part of the deliberately dramatic and theatrical appeal of absolutist monarchy . . . the baroque city became a huge theatrical setting for the display of the court, the princes of the church, the nobility and other rich and powerful persons.[29]

Above all, the baroque city was intended to impress: with monumental buildings, magnificent palaces and perspective used to focus attention on majestic views along broad, straight avenues. Symmetry, with a classical sense of balance and regularity, was a defining characteristic.

Although the most flamboyant expressions of the baroque movement were built later – at Versailles, for example, Karlsruhe and St Petersburg – its principles were firmly established at the time of Wren's study tour in France, and an intention to impress is certainly evident in the plan for rebuilding London that Wren submitted to Charles II.

The plan essentially divided London into two parts: a western section consisting of rectangular blocks, and an eastern section of polygonal squares joined by streets radiating from each. These broadly disparate parts were linked by two grand thoroughfares angled across the plan to meet in the form of an arrowhead at the site of St Paul's. There were several piazzas, merchant shipping quays, and also a Grand Terrace along the Thames with adjacent public halls.[30]

On paper, Wren's plan for London offered an impressive city – fit for a king even though it lacked a palace. But he must have known the scheme was irrelevant to the needs of the City. A. E. J. Morris describes it as 'an overnight exercise based on a superficial use of continental Renaissance planmotifs', which is perhaps a little unkind, though it bolsters Morris's suggestion that the plan may not have been seriously intended at all, but was simply a pre-emptive strike on the part of an ambitious though untried architect who was keen to establish his claim to a major share of the rebuilding work. If so, the overnight exercise certainly paid off. Wren became a member of the six-man commission formed to advise and oversee the rebuilding programme; he was appointed Surveyor-General in 1669, given the commission to design the new St Paul's and sixty-six other City churches, as well as almost all the worthwhile architectural work of the period.[31]

Whatever its conceptual attributes, Wren's plan failed from a practical point of view in its total disregard for the topography of London. His new city was designed as though it occupied a flat plain, whereas in fact the site undulates considerably (even more so then than now), with hills on either side of both the Fleet and the Walbrook tributaries of the Thames. The rise and fall of these hills would have obliterated the magnificent perspective vistas that the plan promised, as well as distorting the proposed arrangement of neat blocks, tidy squares and radiating streets. Wren's baroque vision could never have existed in reality. In point of fact there was never much chance that it would.

Quite apart from the practical difficulties of wrapping a two dimensional plan over a three-dimensional landscape, Wren's scheme also called for an almost total rearrangement of streets and buildings within the City. Many property owners would have been obliged to build to a different ground plan, or on a different site, and no one had the authority to insist upon that – especially not the king, given how successful London had been at limiting royal involvement with City affairs (see page 122–3). Wren had submitted his plan to the king, but Charles could not take it further without the unanimous agreement of parliament and all London's landowners and institutions. Such a consensus would be hard to achieve on even the most innocuous of issues; impossible when all parties simply wanted to get on with the urgent task of rebuilding their lives and livelihoods – London would fail or prosper accordingly.

But the king was in any case 'at one with the City'. On 13 September he issued a royal proclamation on desirable rebuilding procedures, undertook to rebuild the Custom House promptly and to relinquish Crown property in the City wherever it would be of common benefit. By the end of September, there was general agreement that the existing street lines and property boundaries must be accepted, and at the beginning of October six commissioners were appointed to supervise and effectively to control all technical aspects of the rebuilding work. Three were nominated by the king, and three by the City. Wren was one of the king's nominees, Hooke was one of the City's.

With a severe winter having forestalled pressure for an immediate commencement of rebuilding, the commissioners' preliminary recommendations and the royal proclamation were incorporated into a Rebuilding Act passed by Parliament in February 1667. Certain streets were to be widened, and street widths standardised, with a new coal tax paying for land acquisitions. The new houses were to be built exclusively of brick or stone, and there would be four classes 'for better regulation, uniformity and gracefulness'. Those on the principal streets (only six were classified as such) were to be four storeys high; in the streets and lanes of note three storeys was the rule; in by-lanes two storeys were prescribed.

By the spring of 1667 the City had been cleared, the streets and property lines demarcated. Around the country, the call went out for 'all persons who are willing to serve and furnish this City with timber, brick, lime, stone, glass, slates and other materials for building'. Within two years of the Fire 1,200 houses had been completed, and another 1,600 the following year. Thousands of new people had been drawn to the City: craftsmen, suppliers, transporters, builders and property speculators

— not to mention the hundreds of hawkers and traders serving a city which had lost half of its markets and most of its shops. The social order and distribution of London's population was changing – but in a way that was not in any way related to what the planners might have envisaged, or thought to be ideal. This was a classic example of how the flow of economy, society and culture can contradict – even invalidate – the ideas and theories that planners have advocated.

Even before the Fire, the crowded and unhealthy state of the City – culminating in a serious outbreak of plague in 1665 – had persuaded a number of noble and wealthy families to leave and move to the country immediately west of London, within easy carriage distance of the capital. In the aftermath of the Fire what had been an individual whim became a social trend. At first, the pattern was a scattering of mansions and large houses and service buildings within their own spacious parks and gardens, but these gradually filled out to become a distinct urban entity. As Steen Rasmussen describes the development in a definitive work on London:

> Beside London, the town of producers, the capital of world-trade and industry, there arose another London, the town of consumers, the town of the court, of the nobility, of the retired capitalists. . . . [and] when an earl or a duke did turn his property to account, he wanted to determine what neighbours he got. The great landlord and the speculative builder found each other, and together they created the London square with its character of unity, surrounded as it is by dignified houses, all alike.[33]

On land owned by the Earl of Southampton, the Dukes of Westminster, Portland and Bedford, Viscount Portman, the Marquis of Northampton and other wealthy citizens, more than two dozen squares were built in the 200 years before 1827, including Covent Garden and Leicester Square (1630 and 1635), Grosvenor Square and Bedford Square (1695 and 1775), and Belgrave Square (1825).[34] Thus London expanded during this period on the basis of clearly defined social-class districts. Upper-class and middle-class families established the genteel social environment of the West End, a relatively short carriage ride from the commercial City of London in the east, and from the social attractions of the Court and the City of Westminster to the south. The north and east of the City, given over to the commercial and industrial activities of the capital, and generally spoken of as the East

End, became the principal and densely crowded home of London's working class.

The working class. Out of sight in the East End, or below stairs in the West End, but never entirely out of mind in any prosperous city as the dynamics of the Industrial Revolution widened the divide between rich and poor. By 1801 London had a population of 1,117,000 – 12 per cent of all the people then living in England and Wales – and by far the greater proportion of them were working class, and impoverished. They were vital components of the capitalist economy, but obliged to live in circumstances determined principally by the profit motive, rather than by the basic requirements of a decent life. Low wages, dismal, insanitary and overcrowded living conditions were their lot. At an average of nine people per house, London's occupancy rate in 1800 seems reasonable, when compared with Paris at twenty per house, and Vienna with forty-seven. And things were no better a century later in Vienna, where tenement blocks occupied by several hundred people were the norm, thanks to speculators and property developers:

> Apartments consisting of one room and a kitchen gave on to long galleries with communal lavatories and water-taps. Barred windows often added to the gloom of already dreary kitchens. The façades, sparsely decorated with historic motifs, generally concealed the sorry spectacle of a humanity crammed together like sardines in a tin. Since few could afford to pay the exorbitant rents, sub-letting – not only of living space, but of actual beds – became the rule in what were already overcrowded apartments. By 1890, 'bed-hirers' constituted about one-tenth of the working-class population in the outer districts . . .[35]

And this the capital of the Austro-Hungarian Empire, a hub of European culture, the birthplace of modern classical music, the city of Haydn, Mozart, Beethoven and Schubert. A city which at the instigation of Emperor Franz Josef had undergone thirty years of major refurbishment in the late nineteenth century.[36] Wide thoroughfares, magnificent vistas, and a swathe of majestic new buildings: opera house, town hall, national archive, library, museums and galleries, and a new wing for the palace – all of the baroque tendency. This massive programme of urban renewal cost a total of 102,329,686 Gulden, but the city received revenues of 112,525,831 Gulden from the sale of plots, buildings and demolition materials to speculators, property developers and builders, thus making a tidy 10 per cent profit.[37] Meanwhile, a seven-day, seventy-hour week was standard for Vienna's working population in the 1880s (though children were given one day a week off from 1883),[38] and the rent for minimal living space might equal one quarter of a working man's meagre wage.

For those enjoying life in the upper echelons of society during this period of massive city expansion in Europe, the only aspect of urban poverty likely to affect them personally was their conscience, and crime. There was a lot of crime, and most criminals came from the poverty-stricken urban hordes. In London, a *Treatise on the Police of the Metropolis* reported in the late eighteenth century that '115,000 persons . . . were regularly engaged in criminal pursuits' – about one-seventh of the population – despite there being over 350 offences for which a man or woman could be hanged at the time.[39] The death penalty for over a hundred offences was abolished in 1823, and the effect on crime seems to have been a 105 per cent increase in the average number of convictions each year. Which in turn put more pressure on London's prisons.

With society generally agreed that the best thing to do with criminals was to lock them up, assign them to hard labour or ship them to Australia, the provision and management of custodial facilities had become a growth industry. In 1812, architects throughout England were invited to compete for the prize of designing a new prison for London, and the winning Millbank Penitentiary which was completed in 1822 immediately joined the ranks of the most expensive public buildings in England[40] – and filled to capacity almost as quickly.

Pentonville Prison, which opened forty years later, was not only hugely expensive (each cell cost as much as a decent artisan's cottage, and the prison's running costs could have built more than 100 such dwellings every year), it was also the most advanced building of its time. With hot and cold running water and a lavatory in each of its 520 cells, a newly invented heating and ventilation system, and mechanised meal distribution arrangements that fed the entire prison in less than ten minutes, only the Reform Club and the new Houses of Parliament could match the mechanical sophistication of the custodial premises on Pentonville Road. Indeed, the prison had no sooner filled with convicts than it became something of a national monument. Prince Albert inspected its technological marvels; so did the king of Prussia, the king of Saxony, Grand Duke Michael of Russia, Prince Alexander of the Netherlands, the Archduke of Austria and the commissioners for a dozen or so European governments. The king of Prussia declared on the spot that he would rebuild the prisons of his own country on the new plan.[41]

The idea that it might be more advantageous to spend money on building decent artisans' cottages rather than on prisons was a long time coming. The enlightened argued that relieving poverty and improving the living conditions of the poor would also lessen the likelihood of them resorting to crime, but society as a whole was far from ready to assume responsibility for the expense and social changes this would involve. In an era of rampaging capitalism that revered private enterprise, people were expected to be content with the best living conditions they could afford – and that was that. Land, after all, was an asset and landowners had a perfect right to expect market-value returns from their properties.

In this measure of things, development meant increasing the value of the asset, and thus the return – which was not something that the improvement of living conditions for the working classes could guarantee. Indeed, in every prospering city there were expanses of insanitary and poorly built working-class housing which in itself was seen as a hindrance to development – valuable real estate that could be put to more profitable use, and certainly ought not to stand in the way of city improvement. And it was here, where working-class deprivation directly confronted – and thwarted – capitalist ambition, that a new emblem of social justice was forged: publicly financed housing schemes.

18

Accommodating Politics

Nineteenth century European cities thrived as marketplaces in which everything had its price – including accommodation. With thousands forced to live in the cheapest they could find, governments and cities began accepting responsibility for the provision of decent, affordable housing. Birmingham led the way. The expansion of post-war Stockholm pursued socially democratic ideals.

That something had to be done about the appalling conditions under which many people lived in the industrial cities of the nineteenth century was patently obvious – and repeatedly stated. 'Heaps of dung, building rubble . . . one-storey houses whose ill-fitting planks and broken windows suggest a last refuge between poverty and death . . . below some a row of cellars, [with] 12 to 15 human beings crowded into each repulsive hole . . .' This was the French liberal politician Alexis de Tocqueville writing in 1835 of Manchester, a city of half-daylight, as he put it, smothered by black smoke.[1] But 'from this foul drain', he continued: '. . . the greatest stream of human industry flows out to fertilise the whole world, from this filthy sewer pure gold flows'.

It was a grim paradox – such poverty, producing such wealth. Manchester was the first of the world's great industrial cities, grown fat on cotton, sustained by the stunning efficiency of its immense textile mills. To many, Manchester was the future, the kind of city that would make all others old-fashioned – if not obsolete. Even those who were appalled by its sordid living conditions, as Alexis de Tocqueville was, and those who deplored the ominous gulf that lay between the few wealthy mill-owners and their impoverished mass of workers, as Marx and Engels did, even they believed Manchester was a portent of the future in a capitalist world. But what could be done to improve conditions for the workers? Marx and Engels of course were for tearing apart the entire edifice of capitalism and replacing it with something more egalitarian. That would take time and a great deal of political manoeuvring. Meanwhile, it was Britain's second industrial city that showed the way: in the 1870s Birmingham took on the responsibility of housing at least some of the thousands who could not afford to house themselves.

Cities had been initiating publicly funded schemes aimed at improving the well-being of their inhabitants for centuries. But most of these were of a prestigious nature – more concerned with winning hearts and minds than keeping body and soul together. Museums, art galleries, imposing municipal buildings and so on would, it was hoped, engender a civic spirit, and make people proud of the greatness of their city, no matter where in it they lived. And often it worked. When the Brooklyn Bridge was opened, for example, a proud local shopkeeper adorned his window with a display announcing: 'Babylon had her hanging garden, Egypt her pyramid, Athens her Acropolis, Rome her Athenaeum; so Brooklyn has her Bridge.'[2]

But Birmingham was breaking new ground, with municipal action which was intended to 'distribute amongst the great mass of our poorer citizens, advantages and benefits and blessings which would otherwise be the exclusive privilege of a few'. This enlightened declaration of municipal public service achieved its fullest expression in the city corporation's 'municipal gospel', which was implemented under the leadership of Joseph Chamberlain in the 1870s. Writing of this scheme at a later date, Chamberlain claimed that his improvement programme had 'created a new sense of the responsibility of citizenship, and had given fresh incentive to public spirit and private munificence'. His allies saw the scheme's influence extending well beyond Birmingham and Britain's shores, boasting that municipal reformers thereafter looked to Birmingham in the same way 'as the eyes of the faithful are turned to Mecca'.[3]

Fine words, but the reality of moving public spirit and private munificence in the direction of improving living conditions for the poor in Birmingham was going to take more than fine words. There was a lot of persuading to be done, and some of it was going to require tangible rewards. Inevitably, the idea that a city should assume responsibility for housing its citizens did not meet with universal approval. Property-owners were especially outraged. Doubly so, in that the city would be charging minimal rents and thus undercutting their market and, furthermore, the public housing schemes would be financed from taxes the city levied on its more wealthy citizens – property-owners foremost among them. Only by incorporating some trade-off between the conflicting issues of public interest and private enterprise could the scheme be made to work.

Birmingham's 1875 Improvement Scheme was a political gem – open to interpretation that fulfilled the expectations of both public housing advocates and private enterprise. In the first instance it offered brand new modern housing for 9,000 people who were currently living in the city's most abject slums. In the second, the scheme was an integral part of a plan to create a new commercial district for Birmingham by running 'a great street as broad as a Parisian boulevard' through the centre of the city and lining it with commercial premises earning 'such improved rents as they will bear'.[4]

But there was a flaw, a loophole, a catch, or an intentional vagueness in the wording of the scheme which ensured that property-owners derived far more benefit from it than did those in need of public housing. The area through which the street as broad as a Parisian boulevard would run was precisely where the 9,000 people to be rehoused were currently living. The slums were appalling and rents were correspondingly low. Thus the area was in any case a source of very little income for the people who actually owned property there. These landlords were only too happy to hand over their housing obligations to the civic authorities in return for a commercial development earning 'such improved rents as they will bear'. The problem was that while they believed the city would provide new housing for the displaced 9,000, the city believed this was the responsibility of the developers. And although the Birmingham Improvement Scheme had legal authority, its wording was not robust enough to enable either public housing advocates or developers to enforce their will. But it did permit the developers to proceed with impunity. Their 9,000 slumland tenants were simply evicted as and when work on the development required.

Compulsory land purchases were completed by 1881. In the first stages of work on Corporation Street (as the thoroughfare was called in honour of the City Corporation's initiative) 650 working-class dwellings were demolished, but by 1888 not one new house had been built to replace them. Even worse, almost 200 houses which an 1875 survey had labelled as 'back slums' to be demolished were still standing in 1914 – and occupied by working people who paid rent to the Corporation.[5]

At first the Corporation insisted that its responsibilities ended with the demolition of insanitary housing as the new streets were laid out. 'We are not going to build a single house', the leader of the Corporation declared. And an 1884 Royal Commission taking evidence from Birmingham on the issue of Housing for the Working Classes generally was told that 'the re-construction and re-housing of the poor may be safely left to private enterprise'.[6] But private enterprise did not agree. While work proceeded apace on the fine buildings that graced Corporation Street, no houses were built for the area's ousted residents. Birmingham's failure to provide housing became a topic of fierce political debate, provoking a chorus of accusations that Birmingham, 'the first provincial municipality who obtained powers to improve Slum-Land', had done less than any great city to resolve its housing problems. While Birmingham dithered, the provision of public housing was going ahead in London, Liverpool, Glasgow, Edinburgh and Germany.

Birmingham was eventually, reluctantly, goaded into action. The Corporation built some terrace houses and flats in the late 1880s and '90s – twenty-two here, eighty-one there – specifically for renting to low-paid working people. But not enough, and fierce political in-fighting, polarised by the stand-off between public interest and private enterprise on the housing issue, eventually brought progress to a complete halt. Meanwhile, the entire length of Corporation Street was opened in 1904, and within a few years was earning the city an annual income of such proportions that even a former sceptical councillor was inspired to declare that it was 'a magnificent asset' to the city. No further municipal housing was built in Birmingham until after the First World War.[8] Meanwhile, Birmingham's population had doubled between 1875 and 1914[9] as the city's booming economy became a magnet for immigration. These people had to be housed. Attitudes had to change, but it took a war to change them.

The First World War, with its expectation that working men by the million should be willing to fight and die for their country, and that people everywhere should endure the privations of war, helped to transform the issue of publicly financed housing from a troublesome municipal obligation into a civic virtue that offered political rewards. There was widespread feeling that, after so much suffering, the governments of Europe had a large social debt to repay. Cities must be rebuilt, and communities rehoused. Among politicians, those in tune with public sentiment saw there were votes to be harvested here. Social awareness, and championing the causes that mattered deeply to millions of ordinary people – housing, health, education, jobs – could get them elected. Germany's odious National Socialist government took the principle to extremes in the 1930s. Elsewhere, the link between social provision and political power was more democratic, establishing a trend that ultimately put public housing near the top of political agendas during the 1930s. The Second World War, during which so many more houses were destroyed than in the First, intensified demand. Here again, there were debts to be repaid, but this time they were underwritten by a more widely shared sense of social obligation.

However, although war and its aftermath had convinced a majority in many afflicted countries that the state must accept more responsibility for its citizens in respect of everything from housing to health care and unemployment benefits, the most determined attempt to create the complete welfare state and ideal city in a capitalist economy evolved in a country that did not participate in either of the twentieth century's world wars: Sweden. Here, in the course of the twentieth century the vision of a state providing all basic needs for its citizens was pursued to the limit – and a step beyond.

Sweden was a late starter in terms of its economic and social development, with a poor and substantially rural-based population virtually to the end of the nineteenth century. But while lagging behind in the progress that the industrialised nations had made, Sweden was establishing a sound economic base for its future with the export of iron, timber and wood pulp. Indeed, here was its road to industrialisation. Having become wealthy enough to import the very latest in manufactured goods and technology, Sweden was poised to leap ahead with innovations and entirely new products of its own, as was also the case in Japan (see pages 237–8). Lars Magnus-Ericsson invented the first table telephone; Sven Wingquist perfected the modern ball-bearing; Alexander Lagerman made a machine for the mass production of matches; Alfred Nobel patented dynamite; Baltzar von Platen invented the gas-powered refrigerator; Gustaf de Laval developed the milk separator. Thus Sweden's manufacturing industry was specialised and sophisticated from the start, and rapidly developed a reputation for high-quality products that the modern world appreciated, ranging from office machines, medical equipment and furniture to ships, automobiles and steam turbines. Other industries grew out of traditional homecrafts, notably the textile industry.

Sweden's growth in manufacturing output was prodigious, increasing fivefold in just over thirty years to 1871; then tenfold to 1900, and then making a massive 24-fold increase during the fifty years to 1950. No less significantly, 40 per cent of Sweden's industrial output was exported, giving its economy a wide income base. Furthermore, Sweden's economic growth was sustained, maintaining an average annual rise in per capita income of 2.1 per cent for the 100 years up to 1970 – way ahead of every other industrial nation except Japan and putting Sweden's per capita income some 40 per cent above the average for western Europe.[10]

As with industrial development, so the process of urbanisation in Sweden also benefited from a late start. Nine out of ten Swedes lived on the land in 1800, and even by 1900 the population was still 80 per cent rural. But the trend to urban living was firmly set, and in the case of Stockholm the advisability of planning in advance for the city's anticipated growth was particularly obvious. Sweden's capital city had been founded in the thirteenth century on a small island in the channel linking the country's extensive natural waterway system with the Baltic. Stockholm had already spread beyond the confines of the island by the seventeenth century, onto both the north and south shores of the channel. But with the city itself owning the land, and the government insisting that the city should be laid out and built to a regular plan, the winding street network of the medieval period was gradually replaced by a layout of straight streets crossing each other at right angles and, so far as topography permitted, regular blocks.[11] No majestic buildings, or perspective-enhanced views down broad avenues. Merely a sensible utilitarian response to an identified need – practical expedience again. The man principally responsible for the city plans and their implementation was Anders Torstensson, who was appointed town engineer in 1636 and set a precedent for professional urban planning in Sweden.

The population of Stockholm was a little under 100,000 in the 1850s. Industrial development was gaining momentum; the railway was coming and city services were being improved with a gas supply and a new mains water system. Crucially, the planning committee formed to plan for the future development of the city overall predicted that its population would grow from 126,000 in 1865 to 200,000 in 1890 and to 300,000 in 1915. (This forecast proved to be remarkably accurate: the actual figures were 246,000 and 364,000 respectively). The committee regarded this growth as unfortunate but impossible to prevent, and planned accordingly. Efficient traffic control, wide streets planted with trees, and a large number of parks were deemed essential remedies against 'all the wretched consequences in our towns, which undermine the health of the body and pollute and exhaust the mind'. The committee estimated that implementation of the plan would take sixty-three years, although in fact most of it was completed in less than forty years[12] – by which time pressure was mounting for still more expansion.

Looking ahead as ever, the city of Stockholm had been buying large tracts of land towards the city limits and further afield from as early as 1904, initially for water supplies and waste disposal, but also with the idea that it could be used for housing at a later date. Subsequently, a series of annexations extended the city limits to include large areas which had been outside the city when purchased. There were accusations of wasting money, commentators report,[13] but the city kept on buying land, until Stockholm eventually owned 70 per cent of all the land within its own boundaries (and still more that lay beyond).

Meanwhile, as the realities of population growth were directing the policies of Stockholm's city planning department, the country at large was embracing a political philosophy with soaring visions of social idealism. It had begun in the 1930s, when Sweden's political leaders, business elite and bureaucrats united under the banner of the Social Democratic party with the declared intention of creating a new kind of society, no less. A society that neither followed the unpredictable course of rampant capitalism, nor adopted the stultifying centralized control policies of communism, but would take what they called the Middle Way. Based on the conviction that a modern civilised society could – and should – make a binding social contract that would bring equality and prosperity to all, this was to be a complete welfare state. Care from cradle to grave was the aim, with everyone housed in the latest version of a decent artisan's cottage; all without abandoning the capitalist system.

There was opposition to these ideas, from both the left and the right of the political spectrum, but in the post-war years, when humanity was not only struggling to rebuild the physical structures of the civilised world, but also needed to regain its sense of self-esteem, socialist ideals struck a responsive chord in democracies everywhere. And Sweden, which had been a neutral observer of the war's terrible events rather than an active participant, was especially sensitive to the trend. Furthermore, Sweden possessed both the resources and the political will to make a reality of the socialist vision. Thus, in the post-war decade the Social Democrats were given a mandate to lead Sweden along the

Middle Way on a national programme of social reconstruction – with Stockholm as its showpiece.

In June 1947 the Social Democratic government declared that each municipality in Sweden must provide housing for every one of its inhabitants. In the same year, the city of Stockholm purchased one of the country's major property development and management companies, turning it into a publicly owned instrument of the city's development plans. Work on a master plan for Stockholm had actually begun in 1945 and the final version, hammered out over seven years of intense debate and modification, was published in 1952. By then the population of the city was around the one million mark and predicted to reach 2 million by the end of the century.[14] Thus the city had to make provision for housing an additional million inhabitants. This was an immense challenge in itself, but since a significant proportion of the additional inhabitants were expected to find employment in the city's central business district, moving them between the workplace and home was a no less formidable task.

Committed to the ethic of providing public facilities, and doubtless wary of the problems created by the private motor car in Los Angeles and elsewhere, a public transport system – a subway – linking the new suburbs to the city centre was fundamental to the 1952 General Plan for Stockholm. A series of new suburban districts, each accommodating from 10,000 to 15,000 inhabitants, 'would be strung like beads', as Peter Hall puts it, along the line of the new subway. Within each suburb, most residents were to be housed in apartment blocks – none of which would be more than 500 m from a subway stop.

Some 10–15 per cent of the housing units in the Stockholm suburbs were to be single-family houses, which could be up to 1,000 m from a subway stop – but no further. The suburbs were of course themselves linked together by the subway, and the distribution of facilities and services among them ensured that within a group of suburban districts, serving from 50,000 to 100,000 residents in total, virtually all the urban services that anyone might expect to find in a medium-sized town would be provided: business offices, medical centres, schools, cinemas, libraries, theatres, restaurants. Thus there was to be a hierarchy of facilities and services: area centres for 50,000 to 100,000 people, district centres for 8,000 to 25,000, and neigbourhood centres for 4,000 to 7,000.[15]

And they did it. By the 1960s Stockholm could proudly claim to have built a model of what the ideal city should be. With its reconstructed city centre, modern urban transport system, suburbs resplendent with functionally appropriate domestic accommodation grouped conveniently close to subway stations, with services and facilities efficiently supplied, shopping centres and parks impeccably laid out and landscaped, by then Stockholm was widely acknowledged as the physical expression of a social philosophy – a 'social democratic Utopia'[16] – attracting the interest and often the veneration of like-minded architects and city-planners from around the world. But then the world moved on.

In Sweden, the consensus which had promoted the ideals of social democracy from conception to realisation began to weaken. And in Stockholm, the vision of social unity which had seemed desirable in the 1930s, achievable in the 1950s, wonderful in the 1960s and '70s, had become an anachronism by the 1990s. The emphasis of Sweden's social imperatives had shifted to the right. The issues now were not the benefits of unity so much as the restrictions of conformity, not the need for equality but the attractions of individuality. And it is ironic that the primary focus of disaffection was precisely the issue which had been fundamental to the 1952 General Plan for Stockholm: accommodation. Time had shown that the citizens of Stockholm were not so much in favour of all things communal as the planners had supposed.

In fact, even in 1945 a survey of young Stockholm families had found that less than half wanted to live in the suburbs at all. And of the minority that did want to live in the suburbs, nearly nine out of ten wanted a detached house. Overall, very few selected a high-rise apartment as first choice. Yet the 1952 General Plan specified that in each suburban district the available accommodation would consist primarily of apartments. Sixty-two per cent was the proportion stipulated in the General Plan, but several suburbs were built with apartments accounting for between 86 and 96.5 per cent of the housing stock.

And even while the plan was so definitively contradicting the clearly expressed preferences of its intended beneficaries, construction delays heightened public ire. Sweden succeeded in building over 1.7 million dwellings in the twenty years from 1956 – a remarkable achievement by international standards, but one that received little credit at home. The urban housing shortage remained acute throughout that period. There were 120,000 on Stockholm's waiting list in the mid-1960s, with a waiting period of ten years. People joked ruefully about a young man postponing marriage until he and his fiancée were given an apartment.

Why not move in with his parents in the meantime? 'Because they are still living with my grandparents,'[17] he replied.

Social democracy had failed to fulfill a key promise on its journey down the Middle Way, and after thirty years of national support its successors lost control of the political arena. Swedes remained devoutly attached to the welfare state in respect of health and social security, but wanted a better deal on housing. In response, restrictions on the allocation of municipal land, housing subsidies, mortgage interest relief and so forth were amended, thus allowing more Swedes to buy or even to build their own homes. In 1970 more than 70 per cent of all new dwellings in Sweden had been for rental; just seven years later the proportions were reversed, with only 28 per cent for rental, while an astonishing 72 per cent of completions were for private ownership.

And as the balance tipped sharply towards owner-occupiership, so the Swedes revealed their underlying preference for single-family homes. Here too the proportions were reversed, with a majority of completions in the mid-1980s being single-family houses. In the matter of a decade or so, the nature of housing in the suburbs of Stockholm and cities throughout the country changed completely, from tightly planned landscapes of public housing to a thoroughly utilitarian use of available land and resources by private enterprise. The result was often visually unattractive, 'with closely packed houses in unimaginative uniform rows, reminiscent of the worst kind of American suburbia,' Peter Hall reports,[18] 'but the demand was huge and they sold easily.' Expedience was again in control of events – in the service of reality rather than vision.

19

Visions and Opportunities

Cities contain some of the world's most valuable real estate. There are huge profits to be made from the expansion of cities and the redevelopment of existing properties. The recent history of London and the rebuilding of Berlin as capital of Germany after reunification exemplify the tensions generated as issues of public concern are subjected to the pressure of commercial interests.

Social democracy may have gone out of fashion in Sweden and elsewhere as the twentieth century drew to a close, but the power of vision as a political force certainly had not. In Britain, for instance, the Prime Minister Margaret Thatcher's vision of a free-market Utopia rode high on the wave of disenchantment with socialist ideology that swept the country during the 1980s and '90s. 'There is no such thing as society,' she declared. The welfare state was dubbed the 'nanny state'. Ministers urged the growing millions of unemployed to 'get on their bikes' and look for jobs beyond their immediate neighbourhood. The Greater London Council was abolished, and the reins on the acquisitive instincts of speculators and property developers were loosened, all with the enthusiastic support of the government – especially when 2,000 ha of disused docklands to the east of the city was made available for development.

The Docklands site offered the greatest opportunity for development in London since 1666, but this time it was a very different kind of upheaval that determined the course of events. Not a Great Fire, but a Big Bang, which hit the City's financial operations with the deregulation of the London Stock Exchange in October 1986. From the frenzy of financial free-marketeering that the Big Bang released, two factors emerged to focus attention on the Docklands development: one was the huge amounts of capital available for speculative investment, and the other was a desperate shortage of office space in the City itself. In tandem, these factors took development of the Docklands site to the extremes of the capitalist vision, its progress characterised by financial waywardness, political sleight-of-hand, and administrative shortcomings.

The *pièce de résistance* of the Docklands development unquestionably was Canary Wharf – an office complex of more than 800,000 m^2 built where the ships bringing sugarcane from the West Indies and bananas from the Canary Islands had once docked. Canary Wharf was a massive development – the largest in Europe – but despite widespread con-sternation about its proposed size and purpose, demands for a public inquiry were rejected. Indeed, one insider memorably noted that the plans were approved with less scrutiny than might be given to 'a planning application for an illuminated sign on a fish and chip shop in the East India Dock Road'. But then it was known – and is recorded in the minutes of the deliberations – that 'political considerations' favoured the scheme.[1]

One of Britain's pre-eminent architects, Richard Rogers, called the Docklands development scheme 'a fiasco'. Speaking about the state of urban planning in Britain at a symposium in October 1990, he presented a picture of London as 'a politically paralysed city which appears to be almost completely in the hands of the developers':[2]

After the war there was a very enthusiastic, even idealistic attitude in relation to reconstruction, with programmes for housing, schools, hospitals etc. Architects approached the councils with their proposals and decisions were taken as part of a democratic process. Nowadays there is an inverse situation. No one wants to work for the council if it is possible. The Greater London Council no longer exists. Due to government policy the individual councils are mainly concerned with increasing their tax revenue . . . As far as building is concerned all that's important is maximum return on investments. If we suggest a project to an investor he immediately asks: 'why do you need trees, why arcades'? Developers are only interested in office space. If you cannot guarantee that the building will amortise within ten years at the outside then there's no point in approaching them at all . . . I am telling you this as a warning . . . What you basically need is an institution which will protect public space.[3]

Richard Rogers was speaking in Berlin. The Wall had fallen less than a year before. He was one of the international architects and urban planners whom the City Council of Berlin had brought together for a two-day brain-storming session on the city's planning options now that Berlin was destined to become the capital of a reunited Germany. Berlin was buzzing with anticipation. After fifty years of existence as an outpost of Western democracy marooned in communist East Germany, cocking a snook at Moscow, the improbable vision had become reality. Few – if any – West Berliners had dared to believe they would live to see the collapse of the Soviet Union and their city in one piece again. They kept in touch with family and friends on the other side of the Wall, and talked nostalgically of the old days, but their unquestioning assumption that West Berlin would never be surrendered to the communists was not matched by any hope of seeing the severed halves of their city reunited. They would shrug, gesture metaphorically towards the Wall and invite consideration of just how improbable it was that things could change. Berlin reunited? Wonderful idea, they implied, but impossible.

My own ideas about Berlin date back to the barrage balloons and shrapnel of a wartime childhood, when to my mind the city was just a den of ogres that our planes should be bombing even harder than theirs were bombing London. In the stark clarity of childhood certainties, it was all very simple: Berlin was the enemy's capital and therefore deserved to be obliterated. We cheered when the newsreels showed film of Soviet troops capturing the defeated and devastated city. A few years later, with little or no grasp of what was really going on, we cheered again and puffed up with the pride of a victor's magnanimity as the newsreels showed pictures of the Berlin airlift. It was dramatic stuff, with lots of nighttime scenes of Dakotas landing, loading and taking off again without even (this could be a mistaken memory) cutting their engines. The purpose, I believed at the time, was simply to feed a defeated enemy, but the scale of the operation was beyond my comprehension. Flying in food I could understand, but delivering coal by aeroplane – when ours came by horse and cart?

The prejudices of wartime experience, the concentration camps, and the stereotypes of war and Germans which became standard ingredients of popular entertainment – all helped to suffuse Britain with at best indifference and at worst an aggressively negative attitude towards Germany after the war. I was familiar with that, but believe my view of the issues was at least a little broader by the time I first visited Berlin in 1972. Recent personal experience had certainly deepened my sensitivities. My wife had been born during an air raid on Berlin in March 1943. Her father had been last heard of on the eastern front in March 1945. I was introduced to an extended family of women – mother, grandmother, aunts, great-aunts and cousins – who had lived in Berlin through wars that had killed grandfathers, fathers, uncles, brothers and nephews. Some, including an eighty-year-old grandmother, lived on the wrong side of the Wall. None believed the situation would change in their lifetimes.

But the history of Berlin might have kept a spark of hope alive in the hearts of anyone given to fanciful musings, for the city had shown a remarkable capacity for renewal during the 800 years of its existence.

The First World War and defeat had brought Germany to its knees, but the country was up and active again in a remarkably short space of time – thanks in no small measure to the American-inspired Dawes Plan which took effect from 1924. The principal benefits of the plan were twofold: first it reduced the crippling load of reparations imposed at Versailles to a more manageable scale of annual payments, and second it facilitated the provision of short-term foreign loans. Within months of the plan's introduction, inflation had cleared industry's debts and foreign loans were pouring in. Production was soon back to pre-war levels and went on to put Germany at second place (behind America) in the world ranking of exporters (of commodities as well as manufactured products), and world leader in the export of manufactured products. It was, as a commentator reports, 'one of the most spectacular recoveries in the world's entire economic history'.[4]

Berlin was a major beneficiary of Germany's economic and political rehabilitation. Indeed, the city earned an international reputation as capital of the 'Golden Twenties', awash with easy money, confident of continuing prosperity and imbued with an optimism that stands now in stark contrast to terrible events that lay ahead. But at the time, perhaps the only cloud on the Berlin horizon was the city's rapidly growing population: experts were predicting that Berlin would be the home of more than 4 million people in a decade or so. In fact the population reached 4.2 million in 1933, making Berlin the world's third-largest urban community after London and New York. By then, though, Berlin was already the world's biggest city in terms of area.

In 1920 the city had extended its boundaries to include the surrounding network of loosely linked towns and communities which had always been informally known as part of Berlin but whose regional differences had often frustrated the city's plans for growth and development. Eight towns, fifty-nine parishes and twenty-seven rural estates joined the central districts of old Berlin to create a city which grew more than twelvefold in the process: from 65 to 820 km^2. Of that area a third (273 km^2) was forest and natural landscape; furthermore, the legislation which had created Greater Berlin guaranteed that a large proportion should stay that way.[5] Today, 43 per cent of Berlin consists of forest, lakes, parks and agricultural land – an area of 382 km^2 in total, nearly seven times the size of Manhattan Island (57 km^2). Twenty per cent of this open space is protected land – that's 76.4 km^2 to be exact, one and a third times the size of Manhattan Island.[6]

With the additional tax revenues (as well as territory) of its extended boundaries, the Berlin planning authorities of the 1920s could afford to implement their vision of a modern city and infrastructure capable of accommodating, employing and serving the every need of up to 4 million people. They built the massive power stations which in turn enabled the central industrial area to expand, and financed housing schemes which attracted worldwide attention. These were the heady days of modernist fantasy – Le Corbusier, Bauhaus and all that – when architects truly believed they could influence the form and nature of society simply by reshaping the places in which people lived. Gropius and Mies van der Rohe worked in Berlin. Bruno Taut and Martin Wagner designed the massive Hufeisen (horseshoe) residential estate, and received wide acclaim for its innovative layout and features.

There were many other schemes – all providing comfortable rooms, central heating and hot water, community centres, lavish gardens, light, open space . . . there was even piped-in radio.[7]

Berlin in the 1920s, said Heinrich Mann, was a '*Menschwerkstatt*' – a workshop for the creation of a new kind of human being. Unhappily, the people who during the 1930s finagled their way into control of the workshop – and Germany – diverted its output towards the creation of the Third Reich, a perverted vision of ethnic supremacy and territorial expansion that led to world war. By 1945 their attempts to make a reality of the vision had reduced Germany – and Berlin – to a state of even greater ruin than in 1918. Then came the blockade that marooned Berlin in Soviet-controlled East Germany, followed in 1961 by the ignominy of a Wall slicing the city in two and encircling all of West Berlin.

The reason for the Wall is not difficult to understand: people had been fleeing from East Germany to the West in their thousands for more than a decade. Just under 60,000 in 1949, over 330,000 in 1953 (the year of violent demonstrations against communist rule in East Berlin); nearly 280,000 in 1956 (the year of the Hungarian Uprising). Life became increasingly dire for those who remained behind. Hospital wards were forced to close because so many nurses had left. Factories stood empty and the departure of many bus and train drivers brought public transport to a standstill in parts of East Berlin. The departure of many professional people was no less damaging. By 1961, over 5,000 doctors and dentists had fled to the West; 2,000 scientists (most of them under forty-five); hundreds of academics (including the entire Law Faculty of the University of Leipzig) – even Soviet soldiers were defecting in significant numbers, Alexandra Richie reports.[9]

By 1961 it was clear that East Germany was facing collapse, and the rush to escape accelerated accordingly, with 30,415 people crossing to West Berlin during July alone, followed by another 21,828 in the first week of August. It was now widely expected that the East Germans would reinstate some sort of blockade, but no one – not even the CIA or the Allied military intelligence services – had the slightest hint of what was to happen in the early hours of Sunday, 13 August. By evening the East Germans encircled West Berlin with 115 km of concrete blocks and barbed wire. In all, 3 million East Germans had crossed and registered with the West Berlin authorities by then, and another 430,000 are believed to have escaped without registering.

Joining the two halves of the city together again to create a unified whole after the collapse of communism and the final breaching of the Wall in November 1989 presented Berlin with visions and opportunities such as no city in history had seen – a city reborn, a new capital in the vanguard of a new world order. But making a reality of the vision presented challenges of huge and hitherto unencountered proportions. After forty years of physical separation, East and West Berlin were divided by more than just the hard cicatrised scar of the Wall. The crudely severed halves had grown into two distinct urban communities by then – two cities, in effect: independent, self-sustaining and fundamentally different in their governing philosophies. A completely separate network of civic structures, services and support systems had developed on either side of the divide, and few if any of them were directly compatible. Removing the Wall was only the first and most dramatic stage of the reunification process. After that came the complex problems of not simply joining the separate systems together but actually combining them to work as a single, smoothly functioning entity – one united city.

They began with the most obvious part of a city's infrastructure: the road network.[10] In a remarkably short space of time 189 roads which had previously linked East and West Berlin were reconnected and in service again. In several places, where the Spree river had served as the border between the two Berlins, reconnecting the roads also meant reconstructing bridges and even building some new ones. In all, seven major river crossings were either reconstructed or newly built. Reconnecting the road network was an expensive business – costing roughly $35 million in 1994 alone – but for every dollar spent above ground, more than two were spent on attending to the thousands of tubes, pipes, sewers, cables and canals that ran beneath the streets. Water and waste disposal systems, electricity and gas supply lines all had to be reconnected where appropriate, repaired where necessary and newly installed where required.

Then, on separate budgets, there were the railways – both above and below ground – which were reconnected to serve the whole city again. And the trams: though here it was not so much a matter of reconnection as an impressive example of collaboration and mutual benefit, with re-creation on one side of the city and renewal on the other. In West Berlin the tramway system had been removed completely in the 1960s; in the East, the antiquated track and rolling stock had been kept running – the network was even extended to serve residents of large new estates on the city's eastern outskirts. Since reunification the decrepit East Berlin system and its outdated trains have been ungraded with the very latest technology, while the system was successively reintroduced to the western half of the city.

Of all the systems which had to be reconnected, upgraded, repaired or newly laid before Berlin could begin to think of itself as a whole and wholly integrated modern city again, it is in the example of the humble telephone that the dimensions of the gulf – social and physical – between East and West are most tellingly revealed, from a human perspective. Much of East Berlin's telecommunications equipment dated back to 1926. Party lines for two or more users were the rule, and even then not many people had a phone in the home – the East Berlin telephone directory was the size of a slim paperback. There were just 72 lines connecting East to West, and 460 running in the other direction. The ordinary citizens of East and West Berlin – families cut apart by the Wall – could never talk to one another by simply picking up the phone whenever they chose.

Reunification has changed all that. Deutsche Telekom invested nearly $10 billion in Berlin's telecommunications system between 1990 and 2000, putting the city at the forefront of world progress in the field. In the first three years of the installation programme, 320,000 new connections were made in East Berlin, and now the telephone directory for reunified Berlin fills three fat volumes which together weigh more than the directories for Munich, Stuttgart, Frankfurt and two or three small towns combined. Not that telephone directories will be relevant for much longer in the era of the Internet – especially as Deutsche Telekom installs a glass fibre network to replace the city's old copper cables, beginning with a 14 km^2 area of central Berlin, where it will give the Federal and State government, ministries, embassies, business organisations and thousands of individuals immediate access to high-speed broadband technology.

And living space in the new Berlin? Population growth projections showed that with reunification and the city's new status as capital of Germany, Berlin could expect to have up to 300,000 additional residents by 2010 – and this in a city that was already short of accommodation for its 3.5 million inhabitants in 1990. To meet existing shortages and projected requirements the city approved plans for the provision of 400,000 new residential units by 2010, and for another 150,000 residential units on lower priority. With 43 per cent of its surface area consisting of forest, lakes, parks and agricultural land (only 20 per cent of which was protected), Berlin was not short of land for new housing. In fact, though, the plan stipulated that 90 per cent of the extra accommodation should be created by increasing the density of existing residential areas and structures: by building on vacant lots; by increasing the density of more open construction styles; by extending the ground plan of existing buildings or putting on an extra floor; by converting attics and roof spaces. In the first ten years after reunification new residential units approved by the planning authorities impinged upon only 3,864 ha of Berlin's open space.[11]

It was fortunate – and something of a paradox, given the city's broad expanses of open space – that apartments rather than single-family units have always been the accepted and seemingly preferred type of accommodation in Berlin. Of course the city had a long history of providing such accommodation, dating back to a housing law passed by Frederick the Great in 1747 which allowed property speculators to build 'ideal' three-storey apartment blocks in central Berlin[12] and taken to extremes with the plans that James Hobrecht devised for the city (see pages 147–8).

During the twentieth century the city authorities had taken on primary responsibility for providing accommodation. In 1930s Berlin, and again in West Berlin after the Second World War, the city housing department entered into partnerships with property owners and developers, providing low-interest finance for building and reconstruction in return for an undertaking that an agreed proportion of the units would be made available to low-income earners at regulated rents which, it was stipulated, should be substantially below the market rate. Many such agreements are still in force – underpinning the fact that 90 per cent of Berliners live in rented property today, most of them in apartments.

In East Berlin it was of course a tenet of communist ideology that the state would provide accommodation and services for everyone at subsidised rates from cradle to grave. But although the responsible authorities were adept at putting up huge Stalinist apartment blocks in the city, and building satellite towns on its boundaries – each housing more than 100,000 people – they were less competent at building to standards which would ensure that the apartments outlasted even the life span of people occupying them. A survey of all Berlin's residential accommodation conducted after reunification found that 1.7 million apartments in the former East Berlin required extensive work to bring them up to European Union standards: new roofs, new kitchens, new bathrooms, new windows, new electric wiring, up-graded gas supply, structural repairs, waterproofing, insulation and many gallons of paint – inside and out. Through the late 1990s and into the twenty-first century, this work was proceeding on schedule at a rate of 100,000 renovations per year.

The meeting Richard Rogers addressed as mentioned on page 282 was among the first of many thousands convened during the 1990s to discuss ideas and formulate plans for the new Berlin. Poised on the cusp of a new millennium, with 800 years of urban history to look back on, access to global expertise and the latest environmental monitoring and assessment technology at its disposal, the city was understandably anxious to consult fully and proceed on the basis of unanimity wherever possible. Berlin's pioneering Stadtforum – City Forum – was established in 1991, as the core element of what has been termed a 'participation-planning' strategy. The basic idea was to provide a platform for discussion and the interchange of views between users and providers on plans for the reconstruction and development of the city. 'Consent-oriented dialogue and rational negotiation' was a declared aim.

For the first two years the Stadtforum met twice a month for two days – Friday and Saturday. Berliners were invited to attend and comment on presentations from a cross-section of experts – city planners, architects, urban developers, zoning authorities, environmentalists, businessmen, lawyers and so forth. The Stadtforum was an earnest and thoroughly commendable effort to involve the Berlin community as a whole in the task of defining what the city should become. Doubtless some good came of it, but from an objective perspective it was distinguished primarily by its inability to do anything very much about the issues that troubled people most – the development of the inner city, where the public wanted elegant architecture and open space, and developers wanted to throw up a cluster of big money-spinning buildings.

In the event, as in countless cities throughout the ages, expediency ruled. With debts mounting to $30 billion by 1995, and interest payments running at around $2.3 billion per year,[13] Berlin was strapped for cash. Vast areas of central-city real estate became available for development after reunification – especially in the former East Berlin – all of it highly valuable and most of it owned by the city. Major German and international companies, financiers and developers were lining up to invest in the rejuvenation of the city. They wanted to build the corporate office complexes, swanky high-rise apartment towers, and high-brow shopping districts that would make Berlin a modern world city to stand alongside New York, Paris and London. They were less keen on the subsidised housing and mix of commercial and residential premises which were not only a characteristic feature of the city but were also prescribed by district building regulations.

At the Stadtforum, Berliners had repeatedly called for the preservation of existing buildings, the extension of public housing developments, and for the curtailment of office construction. But these views found little favour with the developers – or even with the city leaders. In some cases, property-owners even persuaded the Berlin *Senat* to overturn unfavourable planning decisions, and in a particularly retrogressive move the *Senat* stripped all significant authority from the districts responsible for such major projects as Potsdamer Platz and Alexanderplatz[14] – two of the most prestigious locations which became available for development in the new Berlin. Indeed, it has been alleged that Sony and an American partner 'more or less blackmailed and overran the city' with their plans for development on Potsdamer Platz. All the elaborate rules about height and public space were ignored. The result is that today the Sony Center dominates Potsdamer Platz with an edifice of steel and glass 'so strident and repelling that you'd feel unwelcome even if you could find a way in', the *New Yorker*[15] reported.

So commercial expediency replaced the heady idealism of plans that reunification had at first seemed to make possible for Berlin – inevitably perhaps, given that costs had soared far beyond even the most extravagant expectations. Even for Europe's largest and most robust capitalist economy, taking over and assimilating its former socialist neighbour was proving to be 'a heavy lunch'. The official figure for the first ten years' expenditure was a little under DM500 billion (about $330 billion), though unofficial estimates put it at double that amount.[16] In some quarters the German government was reported to have spent $800 billion on reunification to 2000 – which worked out to $12,000 in taxes for every west German man, woman and child.[17] No wonder the visions dimmed as financial realities became clear. The Federal Government cut its plans for new buildings to more affordable dimensions, and state financing for social housing and rent subsidies in Berlin were drastically reduced.

Berlin was not destined to become Utopia after all. Still, even though financial expediency prevailed, the city avoided the worst of the dire scenario that Richard Rogers had presented at the meeting he addressed in 1990. Public space was respected – by and large. With some notable exceptions (which, sadly, must include Rogers's own contribution to the Potsdamer Platz fiasco), architectural standards among the many thousands of new buildings and renovations were consistently high – in a few cases outstandingly so. Daniel Liebeskind's Jewish Museum is a hugely impressive and heart-stopping creation which has received unanimous acclaim from around the world. Sir Norman Foster's renovation of the old Reichstag building, crowned with a glass dome from the interior of which encircling ramps give visitors a panoramic view of the new Berlin, is another brilliant and widely admired piece of work.

The move of the Federal German parliament (the Bundestag) from Bonn to Berlin, with the Reichstag building as its home and a debating chamber bathed in light from the transparent dome above, was the culmination of the reunification process. The Bundestag formally took possession of their beautifully renovated parliament building in a ceremony held on 7 September 1999 – a day of special significance for the entire country, since it was also the fiftieth birthday of the Federal Republic of Germany. Very much, then, another moment of rebirth in a tradition that Berlin seems to have made its own – 1450, 1701, 1871, 1920, 1945, 1961, 1989, and in 1999 the capital of a reunified Germany.

But the city was far from finished. It was still the biggest building site in Europe. Visiting journalists wrote of 700 cranes towering above construction sites on which 130,000 officially registered workers (and many more unregistered foreigners) were rebuilding the city to plans drawn up by a battalion of over 5,600 architects working under the administrative direction of more than 6,000 city officials. Even the Spree river had been temporarily diverted while a hole the size of Regent's Park was dug for the tunnels, stations, track and highways of a major road and rail interchange at the heart of the city. Work was held up for a while when excavators hit the foundations of a triumphal arch which Hitler had ordered for Berlin as capital of the Third Reich. The foundations were the size of a battleship. Hitler's arch would have made the Arc de Triomphe look like a keyhole. The Second World War ensured that it was never completed.

Berlin has experienced more cataclysmic upheavals than most major cities, each leaving its mark on the city in some way. There was the Brandenburg castle around which the city was founded; the Prussian capital of imperial ambition; the territorial expansion of 1920; the colossal emblems of Nazi aggrandisement; the mutually antagonistic East–West consolidations of the Cold War; and now the amazing phenomenon of reunification. Though the nature of each stage was dictated by the circumstances of the moment, the measure of its wisdom and viability has always been determined by subsequent events. So how will the new Berlin fare?

On the face of it, welding together and renovating the two parts of a split city, and declaring Berlin capital of the country, seems more of an idealistic gesture than a sensible pragmatic reaction to the collapse of communist East Germany – especially when that city was precariously perched on Europe's eastern margin. Certainly the business community has not shown much inclination to follow the Bundestag to Berlin. Sony and Daimler-Benz took the plunge and moved their entire European operations to Berlin, but most German companies and many multi-nationals adopted a wait-and-see attitude, limiting their commitment to the establishment of figurehead offices close to the city centre. Even Siemens – though founded in Berlin – was not persuaded to move back. And Lufthansa, Germany's flagship carrier, operates only shorthaul international flights from Berlin; travellers to the Americas, Africa, and the Middle or Far East must fly via Frankfurt.

But if Berlin cannot persuade the multinationals and large German companies of past and current eras to come back, it may have more success with the new business enterprises of the twenty-first century. For them the city has a number of world-beating assets in its favour: up-to-the-minute infrastructure, plenty of space and congenial surroundings, the world's most advanced urban policies on environmental management and renewable energy and – most important of all – a location with the potential to make Berlin the *de facto* capital of Europe.

Since the fall of the Soviet Union, eight east European nations have revitalised their economies to the point of becoming eligible for membership of the European Union. Poland, Hungary, the Czech Republic, Estonia, Latvia, Lithuania, Slovenia and Slovakia (plus Cyprus and Malta) applied and became members in 2004 – which almost doubles the membership from fifteen to twenty-five states. This is 'a Europe no one has seen before and that people have dreamed of since the 15th century'.[18]

The advent of a united and economically integrated continent of Europe just fifteen years after the fall of the Berlin Wall is a tremendous political achievement with a potential of huge and far-reaching benefits: social, cultural and economic. With its new members, the population of the EU will leap overnight from 370 to 480 million, all trading in a single market, mostly with the same currency. The EU will be 30 per cent larger, and even cautious academics estimate that the economic benefits of enlargement will amount to €33 billion per annum for the EU as a whole – more than two-thirds of which will be generated by the economies of the new members.[19] In this scenario, Europe's centre of gravity will shift eastward. By 2020 it could be Brussels, Madrid, London and Paris that are perched on the fringes of the continent, while Berlin is its very heart – the capital of Europe.

German Railways clearly had this prospect in mind when they invested more than £7 billion in new rail transport facilities for the city. The two great trans-European rail routes – from Paris to Moscow and from Stockholm to Vienna now cross precisely in the centre of Berlin, at the sparkling new twenty-first century Lehrter Bahnhof, with its 430 m glass concourse, fifty-eight escalators, thirty-seven lifts and easy access to the Reichstag, government ministries, foreign embassies and legations.

The last word on Berlin surely belongs to Karl Scheffler: 'Berlin is a city that never is, but is always in the process of becoming.'[20] Berlin has become and been many things since those words were written 1910. Like London and every other great city, it will be a wonderful place when it's finished.

20

We Tread too Heavily

Cities are the defining artifacts of civilisation, but they are also dangerous parasites, with a capacity to harm regions far beyond their own boundaries. The ecological impact of cities on the global environment is out of all proportion to their size. Soon, most of humanity will be living in cities. The ecological imbalance will have to be rectified.

Berlin or London? Venice, Vancouver, Abijan, Tehran or Tokyo? Given the choice, how would you decide which city to live in? For economic migrants the answer is of course stark and simple: whichever city you can get to that offers some chance of finding a job. But at a less basic level, for someone with talent or skills that will be snapped up anywhere (and setting aside questions of language), how would you choose? Is it purely a matter of personal comfort and the standard of available services, or is the physical structure and environmental context of a city just as important? And what about the cultural ethos – the quality of newspapers, radio and television; sporting life and facilities; galleries, concert halls and museums? The social ethos is important too. Indeed, some might be inclined to believe that one's attitude towards a city is likely to be deeply and permanently influenced by personal encounters during the first few hours of being in it. Smiles win hearts, growls do not make friends.

The nub of the matter is 'quality of life', a multi-faceted concept that one of the world's leading human resources consultancies presents as a survey and quantitative measure of the factors which make one city more, or less, attractive than another.[1] Ranking 215 of the world's major cities in terms of the quality of life they offer, the annual surveys are primarily intended to help governments and international companies determine appropriate salaries and allowances for the personnel they are posting abroad. And since these quality-of-life assessments are made by a key component of the commercial sector – namely, human resource consultants – and since international commerce is an increasingly significant factor in global affairs as the time approaches when the majority of the world's population will be living in cities, the surveys are also open to interpretation as evidence of the ideas and trends which could influence city development and management now and in the future.

The survey assesses and evaluates thirty-nine key 'quality of life' determinants, ranging from the state of the economic, political, socio-cultural and natural environments, to climate, housing, public services, transportation, medical and health facilities, schools, crime, censorship, the availability of consumer goods, and the general standard of restaurants, leisure activities and so forth.

With New York as the benchmark, rated 100, cities are given scores above or below that baseline. It is no surprise to find that none of the forty-one African and Indian Ocean cities in the survey appears in the top fifty – indeed, the highest ranking of these is Cape Town, which comes in at 80th, and Johannesburg at 85th, with 84.5 and 83.5 points respectively. Nor is it surprising that nineteen African cities feature among the world's worst twenty-five, and that Brazzaville and Pointe Noire in Congo, Bangui in the Central African Republic, and Khartoum in Sudan (with an average score of 33.75 points each) are four of the world's five least appealing cities. Worst of all is Baghdad, where concerns regarding security and the city's precarious infrastructure brought its score down from 30.5 in 2003 to 14.5 in 2004.

The fact that European, Australasian and North American cities dominate the table is equally predictable, with Zurich in top place, followed by Geneva, Vancouver, Vienna and Auckland, (averaging 106 points). The benchmark city, New York, comes in at 40th, equal with Madrid and Kobe in Japan. And the cities mentioned at the beginning of this chapter? Berlin is 15th; London, 35th; Abijan, 173rd; Tehran, 167th; and Tokyo, 33rd. Venice was not among the cities surveyed.

With only 4.5 points separating Zurich at the top of the overall ranking (with 106.5 points) from Brisbane at 25th place (102 points), anyone looking for a more incisive measure of differences between the top cities must turn to their rankings in specific aspects of the quality of life assessment, and it is revealing – even heartening – that in 2002 the survey chose to emphasise the primary importance of environmental issues. Here it was levels of air pollution, the efficiency of waste disposal and sewage systems, transportation and general cleanliness that counted, and at a stroke Zurich dropped from top to 10th place, equal with Tsukuba in Japan, which did not even make the top fifty in overall rankings. Likewise, Vienna (2nd overall) dropped to 39th, Vancouver (3rd overall) to 17th and Sydney, a proud 4th overall in 2002, dropped right out of the top fifty environmental rankings.

Calgary was top of the 2002 environmental rankings, up from 39th overall, followed by Honolulu (22nd overall). Severe air pollution made Mexico City the world's most unattractive city from an environmental point of view, and Athens was the worst in Europe, coming in at 196th − only twenty places ahead of Mexico City. London, with its public transportation problems, severe congestion and over-stretched waste disposal system, was ranked 102nd; Rome and Paris, similarly afflicted, ranked 98th and 84th respectively. Indeed, European cities generally did very badly in the environmental rankings, with only thirteen making the top-fifty; and eight of those in either Switzerland or Scandinavia − both regions with a reputation for heightened environmental awareness. Helsinki was Europe's most environmentally favoured city, ranking 3rd behind Calgary and Honolulu, and throughout the top rankings it is clear that good air quality, space and a general lack of congestion are the qualities that make a city most attractive. Berlin is a special case, expected to leap up the environmental ratings once the structural work of reunification is completed.

Of course, there may be diplomats or business executives who find the lower rankings most attractive − for that is where remuneration and allowances will be most generous − but for anyone concerned about the future of the world's cities, there is a glimmer of hope in the fact that one of the world's largest human resource consultancies − surely the oracles of modern corporate enterprise − puts the environment at the forefront of factors determining the quality of life that a city has to offer.

In the developed world at least, environmental issues are of increasing importance, gaining a relevance to city-dwellers that extends from the headline-grabbing stunts of eco-activists to supermarket shelves stacked with organic produce, European Union regulations banning the use of environmentally damaging substances, and governments thereby committed to meet standards that directly affect the quality of life. The drive to establish enforceable environmental standards is scarcely more than a few decades old, but its effects are already apparent. Europe now has cleaner cities, cleaner air, cleaner rivers and beaches than at any time since before the Industrial Revolution. And in some cases the country-side appears to be moving into the cities, challenging the antagonisms that have for so long characterised the urban–rural dichotomy.

London, for instance, has become so heavily wooded that in 2002 the UK Forestry Commission saw fit to appoint the city's first-ever Forestry Conservator. London thus became Britain's newest officially recognised forest.[2] Implausible though it may seem, fully one-fifth of the entire land area of Greater London is covered with trees growing densely enough to be described as woodland – and not just in respect of Epping and Waltham forests, the heavily wooded Richmond Park, Bushey Park or even Hyde Park. In fact there are some 65,000 woodlands and stands of trees in the city – covering an area of 7,000 ha in total, of which nearly 5,000 ha is made up of woods at least 10 ha in extent. Furthermore, two-thirds of London's forest is registered as ancient woodland, suggesting that it is a remnant of the forest which originally covered all Britain.

London's new Forestry Conservator is charged with the task of encouraging the recreational use of existing woodlands, and directing the establishment of new ones on the capital's wastelands and 'urban deserts'. The official philosophy behind this declares that forestry in the twenty-first century is more about people than trees. In the past, the Forestry Commission was widely believed to concern itself principally with planting vast forests of conifers as a source of commercial timber. The Commission still does that, but also plans to 'bring the forests down from the hills to towns and cities'. There is clear scientific evidence, it says, that people feel better simply for being in woodlands. Within minutes of stepping into the green dappled shade of a wood, measurable improvements in pulse rate and muscle tension are evident. Thus woods can help reduce levels of stress in a city, and London is not the only beneficiary of the new thinking. Millions of pounds are being spent on the creation of Community Forests in other parts of Britain too, most especially in the Greater Manchester and Merseyside regions, where they will directly help to heal a century's environmental damage by traditional industries.[3] Where slag heaps and derelict factories moulder, forests will grow.

Though the facts are presented clearly enough in the official documents, and the money is already being spent, there is an air of the fanciful about these schemes to make sylvan retreats of blighted urban landscapes. It just seems so improbable. But such scepticism overlooks the tremendous fecundity of the natural world. Just think of how grass takes root in the cracks of a neglected tarmac road, and imagine how quickly a city could be smothered in vegetation if left to its own devices. If I for one had not pulled out the dozens of sprouting acorns and horse-chestnuts that squirrels had buried (and presumably forgotten about) in my allotment over the past twenty years, I'd be tending a splendid twelve-rod patch of woodland by now.

Trees in particular are virtually irrepressible – climax vegetation is how botanists describe them – and will inevitably become a forest where and whenever circumstances permit. Furthermore, evidence from New York City indicates that trees actually grow better – bigger and faster – in cities than in the adjacent countryside.

In a three-year project, scientists tracked the growth of eastern cottonwoods grown from cuttings and planted at various locations in the city centre, and at suburban and rural sites on Long Island and in the Hudson Valley about 100 km away.[4] Most people would suppose that soil and air pollution would stunt the growth of the city-grown trees; but in fact, the city trees grew twice as fast as their rural counterparts. At first the researchers thought this was because city centres tend to be warmer than the suburbs, and because polluted city air contains more carbon dioxide (which stimulates photosynthesis) and nitrogen oxides (potential plant nutrients). But further investigation showed that it was not the city's advantages which had made the difference – it was the disadvantages of the rural environment. High levels of ozone pollution had stunted the growth of the trees in rural locations. Ozone is a highly damaging plant pollutant.

The findings sound counter-intuitive. The countryside is where trees and all vegetation should grow best. Ozone is supposed to be a good thing, filtering out the UV radiation that heightens the risk of skin cancer. Diminishing levels of ozone in the stratosphere are a cause of concern. How come there is more of it in the countryside than in city centres? In fact, although ozone is generated wherever sunlight reacts with pollutants such as car exhausts, it is so reactive that it soon breaks down again wherever pollution levels are sufficiently high. In New York City they are very high, and even as ozone is generated there are enough pollutants left over to mop it up, scrubbing the city clean and reducing ozone levels to below those recorded under the South Pole's ozone hole. Ironically, it is in the less polluted suburbs and beyond that ozone concentrations build up to levels that stunt growth and prevent flowering.

Another study found the New York City environment could also

Twenty million Europeans emigrated to the United States between 1880 and 1920, the majority of them passing through Ellis Island (66). They powered North America's industrial development and fuelled the growth of cities such as New York (67). All no doubt had hoped for a better life, but many found little or no improvement (68).

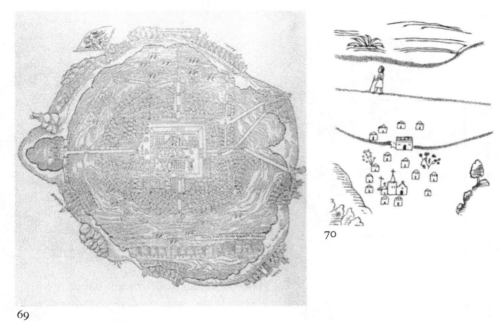

70

69

Mexico City was founded in the 16th century by Spanish conquisadores on the site of the Aztec capital, Tenochtitlan. Contemporary Spanish woodcuts (69 & 70) and modern archaeological surveys (71) show that Tenochtitlan occupied an island in a large lake, at the heart of a landscape dotted with hundreds of small settlements.

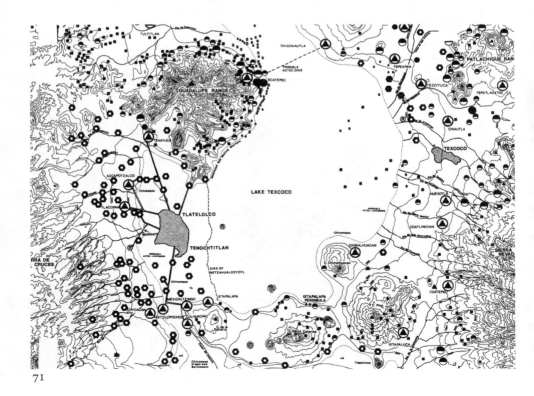

72

With 18.5 million people, Mexico City (72) is now the world's second largest city (after Tokyo). The ruins of Tenochtitlan lie beneath the modern city, and the lake that once surrounded the Aztec capital has dried out, causing severe subsidence. The cathedral was sinking into its foundations (73) and in danger of collapse until a programme of stabilisation was instigated.

In Calcutta, a mother and child make a temporary home of sewer and storm drains (74). In Nairobi, families occupy makeshift shacks on open land in prosperous residential areas (75). The living conditions are appalling, the inequality shameful, but cities are the last and only hope of people who have nothing else.

74

75

76   77

City parks and allotments were an important source of homegrown food for Britain during the Second World War (76). In Havana (77), Lomé, Togo (78) and many other third world countries, such 'urban farming' has achieved agro-industrial status and is a vital source of food and income for many citizens.

78

80

Founded in 1796, Cleveland, Ohio (79, 80), grew rich on its access to resources that powered America's industrial development. Individual enterprise underwrote the city's economic progress. Individual home-ownership characterises its suburban expansion (81).

79

81

82

While it was the principles of social democracy that determined the form and character of Stockholm's suburban development (82), with the city committed to providing accommodation for all, the expansion of cities such as La Paz (83) has been almost entirely uncontrolled; people put up houses wherever there was space, whether or not adequate water, sanitation and other services were available.

Cities are destined to become humanity's principal home: two of every three people on Earth will be living in a city by 2030. Cities appear to contradict the natural order, in that rural environments, brimming with the potential for growth, seem natural in a way that cities such as Tokyo (84), with their constant need of maintenance, do not. But cities can still surprise us. Researchers have found that trees in New York's Central Park (85) grow better than their rural counterparts.

84

attract and sustain a greater variety of tree species than more 'natural' environments – without the involvement of people.[5] This too contradicts expectations, but city park records indisputedly reveal that an 18 ha patch in the New York Botanical Gardens which in the 1930s had been a forest of hemlock had become a mixed bag of species by the 1980s. Norway maple, black cherry and Asian cork were among the trees which had replaced the hemlock. Without any direct human intervention, the forest had been completely transformed in less than fifty years.

Obviously, the new vegetation had grown from seeds spread by wind or wildlife from the surrounding city, where cork trees and other species are planted in streets and gardens. But how did they manage to establish themselves in territory as foreign as a long-established hemlock forest? Ecologists are looking for answers. A factor which has already emerged is that decomposition rates are much faster in the city than in the countryside – mainly because the city forest soils have thriving populations of earthworms and rural forest soils do not. Clearly, there is much that is still to be understood regarding city environments and their relationship with surrounding rural areas.

City environments, city forests, quality-of-life assessments made by international human resource consultants . . . these are not issues that will be hotly discussed (or mentioned at all) among the majority of the world's city-dwellers – they live in the less-developed world, where poverty and a lack of basic facilities are the primary concern. To repeat some figures given in chapter 11 (see page 162): the urban population of the less-developed world is already twice the size of the developed world's, and growing nearly six times as fast. In Africa, the world's most impoverished continent, the number of city-dwellers multiplied nearly tenfold between 1950 and 2000, rising from 32.7 million to 309.6 million, and is expected to double again by 2025, when more than half of Africa's entire population (predicted to reach nearly 1.5 billion by then) will be living in cities. Many of these people moved to the cities because they had no other hope of survival. They do not expect to enjoy the quality of life that Zurich, Vancouver and other top-ranking cities offer their inhabitants, but they do yearn for some improvement. Clean water, congenial housing, electricity. What chance is there of them ever getting it?

Not much while world trade and the distribution of wealth is so skewed in favour of the developed Western economies.[6] At present, the poorest countries, with 40 per cent of the global population, produce just 3 per cent of world exports. Meanwhile, Western countries with only 14 per cent of the global population account for 75 per cent of world exports. This disparity carries through to the way in which the available money is spent. The poorest countries have very little choice, but the West can afford to spend $350 billion each year on agricultural subsidies alone. $350 billion! Just to keep farmers producing cheap food (which is not cheap at all, since the subsidies are paid out of taxation). One scandalous result of this is that Europe's cows are better off than half the world's human population. The average cow in Europe receives $2.20 a day in subsidies and other aid, while 2.8 billion people in developing countries around the world live on less than $2 a day.

The shame of this imbalance is that so much could be done with just one year's agricultural subsidies. Three hundred and fifty billion dollars would go a long, long way towards improving the quality of life for city-dwellers in the world's poorest countries: $170 billion would be enough to provide clean water and a safe sewage system for the entire world; $30 billion would give everyone access to energy over twenty years; $13 billion would provide basic health and nutrition for all – and there would still be billions left over for education, fighting HIV/AIDS, malaria and TB, improving and maintaining infrastructure, building affordable housing . . . all from the subsidies that the West gives its farmers in just one year.

Clearly, the world has the resources and the means to raise standards of living to acceptable standards everywhere. Only the determination to do something about it is lacking. From an historical point of view, you could say the disparity that exists today between rich and poor countries, between the quality of life in Addis Ababa at one end of the scale and Zurich at the other, is analogous to the disparities which prevailed in Europe and North America in the nineteenth century. The Industrial Revolution made some people very rich and forced many more to live in penury, creating a volatile social environment: unhealthy, insecure (and not without the threat of violent revolution) and of direct concern to all sections of society – not just the poor. The people at the top and middle levels of the economic ladder were particularly sensitive to the danger of allowing the lower rungs to decay and collapse beneath them. Perhaps they even had a vision of how much would be gained by improving conditions for those below. Thus, along with altruism and charity, self-interest played a crucial role in the raising of living standards from the late nineteenth and into the twentieth century. Self-interest is a compelling incentive. When people are aware of serious danger ahead, all but the very foolish will look for alternative routes and strategies. Something of the sort is happening now. In developed nations that have the power to affect change, people are increasingly aware of the unsustainable demands that our quality of life imperatives impose on global resources. We tread too heavily on the Earth – especially in respect of our cities.

Cities have always been the engines of economic growth and the brightest stars in the constellation of human achievement, but today more than ever they also resemble black holes, drawing in and consuming the output of regions vastly larger than themselves – and putting very little back into the system. In fact, though cities today occupy only 2 per cent of the world's land surface, they use over 75 per cent of the world's resources. This is a sobering statistic, and a concept developed by environmental scientists during the 1990s gives a powerful illustration of its implications for the global ecosystem. They call it the *ecological footprint* – a simple yet comprehensive tool which measures the flow of energy and material in and out of any city, region or economy and calculates the total areas of productive land and water required to support those flows.[7]

'What is 120 times the size of London?' asks a 1995 report prepared for Britain's Department of the Environment. Answer: 'the land area required to supply London's needs.' This is London's *ecological footprint*. Having analysed the working of the city as though it were a giant machine, consuming large quantities of resources and emitting substantial amounts of solid, liquid and gaseous wastes, researchers found that although the city itself occupies an area of only about 1,500 km^2, London actually requires up to roughly 20 million square kilometres of territory for its supplies and waste disposal. The city is home to just 12 per cent of Britain's population, but in effect it uses the equivalent of all Britain's productive land. In reality, of course, the horizons that fulfil London's needs extend beyond the British Isles to such far-flung places as the wheat prairies of Kansas, the soybeans fields of the Mato Grosso, the forests of Canada, Scandinavia and the Amazon, and the tea estates of Assam and Mount Kenya.[8]

And London is not the only city to have had the dimensions of its backyard assessed in this way. It has also been shown that Vancouver, one of the world's top-ranking quality of life cities, needs an area of roughly 20,000 km^2 to support the half a million or so people living within its 114 km^2 of land. This means that the city's inhabitants use the productive output of a land area nearly 180 times larger than the city itself to maintain their quality of life. And if the use of marine resources is added to that figure, the total becomes 24,000 km^2, or over 200 times the size of the city.[9]

A group of Scandinavian researchers limited their investigations to a selection of resource inputs and waste outputs, but even then found that the twenty-nine largest cities in the Baltic Sea drainage basin appropriate an area of forest, agricultural, marine and wetland ecosystems that is at least 565 times larger than the area of the cities themselves. Furthermore, an extrapolation of their findings showed that carbon dioxide emissions by the world's 744 largest cities (those with more than 250,000 inhabitants) exceed the absorption capacity of all the world's forests put together by more than 10 per cent.[10]

Overall, these studies not only define the ecological footprints of cities, they also give a measure of the enormous differences in resource appropriation that have opened up between the world's developed and developing regions.[11] Expressed in terms of the area appropriated by each individual, for instance, the figures show that every citizen of North America (roughly 300 million in all) actually uses up the resources of an area of the Earth's surface amounting to 4.7 ha – which is the equivalent of almost ten football pitches. Meanwhile, the one billion inhabitants of India manage with an average of just 0.4 ha each – about half the size of the centre court at Wimbledon. And this disparity becomes even more sobering when you consider that 80 per cent of North Americans live in a city – many of them without even a window-box, never mind a working garden the size of ten football pitches. In India only 30 per cent of people live in cities; the remainder live directly off their half of a tennis court.

Clearly, the accelerating pace of mechanisation and the consumer demand during the past two centuries have increased the city's dependence on the natural world, not lessened it. Although cities, trade, technology and transportation have severed the direct connection between urban-dwellers and the land, the ties that bind them together have never been stronger. High-income urban communities need a constant input of material and energy from the natural world not only to feed themselves, but also to build and maintain everything that modern city life provides – accommodation, services, consumer goods, entertainment and, of course, transportation. Popular illusion and misconception notwithstanding, the inhabitants of today's large cities are more utterly dependent on the services of nature than at any previous time in history. Furthermore, the inputs needed to sustain the cities and consumer lifestyles are drawn from land and ecosystems around the globe, and the implications are serious – simply because global resources are finite. As the human population has risen to over 6 billion, and cities have grown to accommodate more and more people, the ecologically productive land 'available' to each person on Earth has steadily decreased from about 5.6 ha per person in 1900 to 3 ha in 1950, and down to no more than 1.5 ha at the beginning of the twenty-first century (and this last figure includes wilderness areas that probably should not be used for any other purpose). Meanwhile, the land area 'appropriated' by the cities and citizens of richer countries has steadily increased, so that the ecological footprint of a typical North American today (4.7 ha) is more than three times his or her fair share of the Earth's bounty. Which means that if everyone on Earth lived as comfortably as the average citizen of North America we would need not just one, but three planets to provide for them all.[12]

Clearly, the present state of affairs cannot be sustained. With current trends set to ensure that around two-thirds of all humanity will be living in cities by 2030, the ecological balance between urban and rural regions must be redressed. How? Harnessing the resources of neighbouring planets is not a viable option, and it is too easy to say that we must mend our ways, show more respect for the environment, make do with less . . . Of course we must do all this – and more – but persuading sufficient numbers to take sufficient action is going to be an uphill task at every level: national, regional, communual and individual. While three-quarters of humanity struggle to get a toe on the 'quality of life' ladder, and the rest jostle for position on the higher rungs, only a minority are ever likely to show much enthusiasm for adopting and promoting the policies that might make a difference.

Meanwhile, the doomsayers and their gloomy prophecies challenge the hopes of even the most ecologically enlightened. The problem is that although the media excel at uncovering the iniquities of everyday affairs, their unrelenting emphasis on the negative aspects of environmental issues creates a sense of helpless inertia. What is the point of doing anything, when the situation is already so bad? Once the facts of resource depletion, environmental degradation, global warming and climate change have been established, every confirmatory piece of evidence is just another nail in the coffin. We are constantly bombarded with bad news and dismal predictions: rising sea levels are going to flood thousands of towns and cities; GM crops are going to change the plant world for ever; forests are vanishing; fish stocks are declining; animals, birds and insect species are becoming extinct; soils are poisoned; rivers are polluted; the air itself is hardly fit to breathe; and, as the ozone layer thins, even sunlight is a killer.

There is a long-established tradition of blaming cities for the failings of humanity. The Bible's description of Babylon – 'the mother of harlots and abominations of the Earth'[13] set the tone. Then and ever since, the human propensity for picking out what is wrong with a situation has ensured that a discomforting sense of cities as a source of human failing taints even the most reasoned accounts of them. Lewis Mumford's classic *The City in History*, for instance, examines the origins, transformations and prospects of the city in exhaustive detail, and regularly blames the city for facilitating the unfortunate or wilfully unhelpful decisions of its inhabitants. The ancient Greek city stifled the understanding of human development as a key to urban form, he writes.[14] Venice, though 'perhaps the most beautiful example of municipal architecture in the world', engendered violence and secrecy as its rulers' instruments of control.[15]

Referring to modern times, Mumford suggests that 'if the civic virtues of Venice had been understood and imitated, later cities would have been better planned.'[16] Here Mumford reveals his attachment to the common belief that solutions to the problems of the modern city lie somewhere in the past. But cities are transitory markers in the progress of civilisation, not permanent fixtures. We can conserve some of the artifacts whose creation they fostered. We may even cherish some of the social ethics they promulgated, but tend to forget we have discarded or rejected a great deal – mostly for good reasons. We cannot go back in any constructive sense. Indeed, if we are going to take history into account, it would be as well to recall how the city turned out for historical figures who tried to determine its future. They, like us, confronted a fundamental truth: even the most enlightened visionaries cannot see beyond the limits of contemporary knowledge. Plans for the future may accord well with current perceptions of needs and growth, but they cannot take into account the consequences of spontaneous adaptation, creative renewal and technical innovation.

Plato limited the size of his ideal city to the number of citizens who could be addressed by a single voice – unaware, perhaps, of the megaphone, let alone the microphone, the telephone, radio and television, which today can bring a single voice to the ears of millions. Thomas

More's plans for Amaurote, capital city of his Utopia, were remarkably sensitive to both environmental and social factors, but even such insights could not foresee the impact that the steam engine and railways would have on society and the city. Similarly, no early-nineteenth-century visionary could have designed a city that specifically made adequate provision for the motor car. Ironically, however, the eighteenth- and nineteenth-century cities that were designed as grandiose monuments to the civic ideal, with broad avenues linking public buildings and urban vistas, have proved to be better equipped for the onslaught of twentieth-century motorised transport than could have been envisaged: Paris and Buenos Aires, for instance, and especially Washington DC.

And so we find that this grand and wonderful defining artifact of civilisation is at best a glorious muddle in which each generation attempts to function efficiently with the product of ideas that were up to date a century before, but could have become obsolete or downright obstructive in the meantime. And, as if that were not enough, there are always some parts of the city's past that are deemed worthy of preserving for the future.

In an age that puts so much faith in statistics, polls, graphs and predictions of probability, the evidence currently available is enough to persuade any rational person that humanity has little chance of surviving more than a few generations more. The research has been thorough, the analysis rigorous, and the predictive methodologies well tested – the outcome seems inevitable. So why bother? Why not just carry on merrily to the end? But perhaps our faith in statistics and prediction is misplaced. Not because the evidence could be wrong, but because it engenders a degree of foreboding that completely overwhelms the significance of our evolutionary history and achievements.

As a species, humanity exists today because evolution endowed our ancestors with the capacity to think and consider, invent and create. The brain is our survival tool, and it has served us very well, enabling us to occupy virtually every ecological niche the Earth has to offer. Where we could not adapt to suit the environment, we adapted the environment to suit us. The process has been accumulative, driven by conscious perception and invention. The Stone Age did not end because the world ran out of stone, but because someone discovered how to make bronze.

I am not suggesting we should therefore ignore the doomsayers and await salvation by as yet unheralded geniuses; I simply want to point out that a fatalistic acceptance of gloomy predictions is likely to become a self-fulfilling prophecy. Rather more positive thinking is required. The bad news needs to be leavened with a fuller appreciation of all that humanity has achieved so far, and more faith in our capacity to identify and tackle the problems confronting us. Bronze doubtless solved many problems of the Stone Age, and unanticipated discoveries likewise emblazon the progress of humanity – and the growth of cities – through the ages to the present day. Unarguably, the world is far from perfect. But for most people, cities are the solution, not the problem.

Notes

1 First Impressions

1. Norwich, 2001, pp. 1–2.
2. From Montanari and Muscara, 1995.
3. *Guardian*, 6 February 2004, Reuters news report, p. 20.
4. Follain 2002, and from Montanari and Muscara, 1995.
5. Yoffe and Cowgill, 1988, p. 2.
6. Vance, 1990, p. 4. Churchill's words as quoted are: 'we shape our houses, then they shape us.'

2 How Did It begin?

1. Chang, 1988, p. 309, cited in Modelski, 1997.
2. Jonathan Haas, interviewed in BBC TV programme, 'The lost pyramids of Caral', *Horizon* 31 January 2002.
3. Pozorski, 1987.
4. Solis, Haas and Creamer.
5. 89 ha equal fifty blocks – see chapter 4, p. 35.
6. Pringle, 2001.
7. Solis, Haas and Creamer, 2001, p. 723.
8. Haaland, 1992, p. 48.
9. See, among others, Maisels, 1990.
10. The scenario as presented here draws upon the ideas of several authors, most especially: Childe, 1950; Soja, 2000; and Jacobs, 1970.
11. Leick, 2001, pp. 6, 9–10.
12. Van de Mieroop, 1997, p. 177.
13. Nissen, 1988, p. 45, cited in Van de Mieroop, 1997, p. 177.
14. Mellaart, 1967, p. 216.
15. Ian Hodder, quoted in Balter, p. 1443.

16. Mellaart, 1967, p. 30.
17. ibid., p. 15.
18. Shane and Küçük, 1998.
19. Mark Patton, quoted in Balter, 1998, p. 1443.
20. Mellaart, 1967, p. 80.
21. Balter, 1998, p. 1443.
22. See the Çatal Hüyük website: http://catal.arch.cam.ac.uk/catal/catal.html
23. Deacon, 1989, pp. 557–8.
24. Pringle, 1998.
25. Balter, 1998, p. 1445.
26. Mellaart, 1967, pp. 131–2.
27. ibid., pp. 131, 209.
28. Soja, 2000, pp. 30–31.
29. Mellaart, 1967, plates 59, 60.
30. Ian Hodder, quoted in Balter, 1998, p. 1445.
31. Mellaart, 1967, p. 104.
32. *Çatal Hüyük Site Guide Book* (n.d.), p. 22.
33. ibid., p. 24.
34. The scenario as presented here draws upon the ideas of several authors, most especially: Childe, 1950; Soja, 2000; and Jacobs, 1970.
35. See, among others, Maisels, 1990.
36. Adams, 1981, p. 141.

3 Where Did It Begin?

1. Adams, 1981, p. 250.
2. Leick, 2001, p. xviii.
3. Postgate, 1992, p. 6.
4. Heidel, 1951, p. 51. Lines taken from version quoted in Leick, pp. 1–2.
5. Adams, 1981, p. 54.
6. ibid., p. 17.
7. ibid., p. 148, and base map of intensively surveyed region on the central Euphrates floodplain, inside-rear-cover.
8. ibid., general site catalog, chapter 7.
9. Childe, 1950.
10. Details on slavery in this and following paragraphs are from Postgate, 1992, p. 107.
11. Adams, 1981. pp. 69–70.
12. ibid., p. 244.

13. ibid., pp. 85–6, 146.
14. Renger, 1991, pp. 201–2.
15. Adams, 1981, p. 86.
16. Ibid., p. 12.
17. Electronic Text Corpus of Sumerian Literature.
18. Postgate, 1992, p. 167.
19. Andrew George, 28 September 2001, in Channel 4 TV documentary *Mesopotamia*.
20. Van de Mieroop, 1997, pp. 151–2, 154.
21. Grayson, 1991, pp. 292–3, quoted in Van de Mieroop, 1997, p. 155.

4 Common Threads

1. Bottéro, 1995.
2. Woolley, 1982, pp. 51–103.
3. Kramer, Noah Samuel, 1963, p. 251.
4. Woolley, 1982, pp. 141, 182.
5. Morris, 1994, p. 7.
6. Woolley, 1982, pp. 192–3.
7. See Van de Mieroop, 1997, p. 220.
8. Kramer, Noah Samuel, 1963, p. 230.
9. Kramer, Noah Samuel, 1961, p. 45.
10. ibid., pp. 56–7.
11. Postgate, 1992, p. 112.
12. Modelski, 1997.
13. Van de Mieroop, 1997, pp. 37, 75.
14. Nissen, 1988, p. 72, cited in Van de Mieroop, 1997, p. 37.
15. Quoted in Postgate, 1992, p. 74.
16. ibid., p. 218.
17. Woolley, 1982, pp. 203–4.
18. Kramer, Noah Samuel, 1963, p. 93.
19. Adams, 1981, p. 138.
20. Caroline Knight, 2003. Personal communication, Richmond, 10 November 2003.
21. Quoted in Postgate, 1992, p. 232.
22. Van de Mieroop, 1997, pp. 180–85.
23. ibid., p. 178.
24. Adams, 1981, p. 148.
25. Quoted in Van de Mieroop, 1997, p. 187.
26. ibid., p. 180.

27. Loftus, 1857, quoted in Pollack, 1999, p. 28.
28. Jacobsen and Adams, 1958.
29. Cited in Kilmer, 1972, p. 166.
30. ibid., p. 171.
31. ibid., p. 172.
32. Pollack, 1999, p. 37.
33. Jacobsen and Adams, 1958.
34. Adams, 1981, p. 152.
35. Postgate, 1992, p. 181.
36. Jacobsen, 1982, pp. 11–12.
37. Powell, Marvin, A., 1985.
38. Postgate, 1992, p. 318, n. 289.
39. Kovacs, Maureen (trans.), 1989, p. 65, tablet 7, quoted in Pollack, 1999, p. 196.

5 War, Greece and Rome

1. McNeill, 1979, p. 20.
2. See references in Reader, 1997, 142–3.
3. Gabriel and Metz, 1991, pp. 2–9.
4. Postgate, 1992, p. 241.
5. Gabriel and Metz, 1991, p. 4.
6. Letter from the King of Aleppo to the King of Der, quoted in Postgate, 1992, p. 251.
7. Gabriel and Metz, 1991, p. 5.
8. Ste Croix, 1981, p. 227.
9. Jones, A.H.M., 1957, p. 108; cf. pp. 77–8 and 93–4. Cited in Rickman, 1980, p. 27.
10. Quoted in Rickman, 1980, p. 27.
11. ibid., p. 257.
12. ibid., pp. 24–5.
13. ibid., p. 52.
14. Brunt, 1971, p. 380, cited in Rickman, 1980, p. 174.
15. Rickman, 1980, p. 170.
16. Quoted in Rickman, 1980, p. 2.
17. Rickman, 1980, pp. 178–9, 197.
18. ibid., p. 173.
19. ibid., p. 11.
20. ibid., pp. 8–10 and xiii. Rickman gives 40 million *modii*, which at 6.82 kg per *modii* (see Rickman, p. xiii) equals 272,800 t per year; 5,246 per week.

21. Rickman, 1980, pp. 134–5.
22. Rickman, 1971, pp. 189–90, cited in Rickman, 1980, p. 122.
23. Rickman, 1980, p. 17.
24. ibid., pp. 55–6.
25. Acts 27–8.
26. Acts 27:20.
27. Seneca's letters to Lucilius, 1932, Vol. 1, letter xxxvii, pp. 288–9.
28. Quoted in Meiggs, 1973, pp. 51–2.
29. ibid., pp. 31–2 and 52.
30. ibid., p. 53.
31. ibid., p. 54.
32. Rickman, 1980, p. 18.
33. Tacitus, *Annals* 15. 18. 3. Cited in Meiggs, 1973, p. 55.
34. Meiggs, 1973, p. 162.
35. Rickman, 1980, pp. 18–20.
36. Quoted in Kagan, 1992.

6 The Works of Giants Mouldereth Away

1. Chandler and Fox, 1974, pp 362–4.
2. Modelski, 1997.
3. Postgate, 1992, p. 112.
4. United Nations, Population Division 1998, pp 21–2.
5. References for this paragraph at http://www.jhuccp.org/pr/urbanpre.stm
6. Morris, A.E.J., 1994, pp. 30 and 397.
7. Jacobs, 1970, p. 141.
8. ibid.
9. ibid., p. 144.
10. Morris, A.E.J., 1994, pp. 12–14 for discussion and references on these points.
11. Boyd, 1962, p. 5.
12. Rodzinski, 1988, p. 43.
13. Quoted in Steinhardt, 1990, p. 53.
14. ibid., p. 54. NB *li* is a Chinese measure of distance equal to about 0.6 km.
15. Boyd, 1962, p. 49.
16. Steinhardt, 1990, pp. 12 and 10.
17. Wheatley, 1971, p. 430.
18. Steinhardt, 1990, p. 33.
19. Polo, Marco (trans. Ronald Latham), 1958, pp. 213–31.

20. Steinhardt, 1990, pp. 144–7.
21. Boyd, 1962, pp. 14–15, quoting Needham, 1954, vol. 1.
22. Tertullian, 30, 3, quoted in Pounds, 1973, p. 95.
23. Quoted in Pounds, 1973, p. 97.
24. Pounds, 1973, pp. 65–6.
25. ibid., fig. 3.15 and p. 162.
26. ibid., p. 97.
27. ibid., fig. 3.6 and pp. 121, 123.
28. Cook and Tinker, 1926, pp. 56–7, quoted in Pounds, 1973, p. 190.
29. Pounds, 1973, pp. 159 and 113.
30. Britnell, 1993, p. 30.
31. Quoted in Pounds, 1973, p. 268.
32. Hohenburg and Lees, 1995, p. 55.
33. ibid., p. 21.
34. Nicholas, 1997, p. 5.
35. Vance, 1990, p. 90.
36. Gimpel, 1983, p. 7.
37. Pounds, 1973, table 6.5, p. 358.
38. Cited in Hohenburg and Lees, 1995, p. 109.
39. Pounds, 1979, pp. 28 and 26.

7 In the Name of God and for Profit

1. The story of Francesco di Marco Datini told in these paragraphs is drawn from: Origo, 1957.
2. Quoted in Origo, 1957, p. 225.
3. ibid., p. 119.
4. ibid., p. 221. 'The *Ceppo* of Francesco di Marco – Merchant of Christ's Poor'; the word *ceppo* – literally, log – came from the hollow log into which members of a Franciscan fraternity, in the thirteenth century, dropped in their alms for the poor.
5. Vance, 1990, p. 115.
6. Hunt, 1994.
7. Origo, 1957.
8. Dr Simonetta Cavasciocchi, 2004. Personal communication, Istituto Datini, Prato, 5 December 2003.
9. Deuteronomy, 16. 19, quoted in Origo, 1957, p. 119.
10. Hohenburg Lees, 1995, p. 101.
11. Quoted in Mumford, 1961, p. 469.
12. Cited in Origo, 1957, p. 32.
13. ibid.

14. ibid., p. 106.
15. ibid., p. 83.
16. ibid., pp. 75–6 and 111–12.
17. Quoted in ibid., p. 146.
18. Brucker, 1962, pp. 16–17, cited in Hunt, 1994, p. 38.
19. Goethe, 1795–6, 1.10, quoted in Lee, Bishop and Parker (eds.), 1996, p. 20
20. Lee, Bishop and Parker (eds.), pp. 11–12.
21. De Roover, 1956, p. 174.
22. Pacioli, (trans. Gebsattel), 1994.
23. Taylor, 1956, p. 180.
24. De Roover, 1956, p. 166.
25. Macve, 1996, p. 24.
26. De Roover, 1956, p. 141.
27. Origo, 1957, p. 53.
28. ibid., p. 171.
29. Partner, 1976, p. 5, quoted in Hohenburg and Lees, 1995, p. 137.

8 Prince's Capital and Merchants' City

1. Origo, 1957, p. 80.
2. ibid., p. 144.
3. ibid., pp. 58 and 144.
4. Morris, 1910, cited in Britnell, 1993, p. 6.
5. Fisher, 1999, p. 58.
6. Paterson, 1998, pp. 154–5.
7. Berdan, 1999, p. 263.
8. Sabine, 1933, p. 336.
9. McNeill, 1979, p. 311.
10. Jacobs, 1970, p. 137.
11. Braudel, 1982, p. 315.
12. Black, 2001, pp. 73–4.
13. Origo, 1957, p. 62.
14. Kowaleski, 1995, p. 181.
15. Origo, 1957, p. 254.
16. Kowaleski, 1995, p. 95.
17. ibid., pp. 96, 101 and 104.
18. ibid., pp. 4, 10 and 88.
19. Black, 2001, pp. 63 and 218–20.
20. ibid., p. 32.
21. Quotes from Black, 2001, p. 65.

22. ibid., p. 157.
23. ibid., p. 130.
24. ibid., p. 136.
25. Braudel, 1982, p. 470.
26. ibid., p. 467.
27. Quoted in Vance, 1990, p. 133.
28. Origo, 1957, p. 307.
29. Martines, 1972, p. 349.
30. Burckhardt, 1865, pp. 432 and 437, quoted in Gundersheimer, 1972, p. 107.
31. Black, 2001, pp. 188 and 190.
32. Herlihy, 1972.
33. ibid., pp. 130, 143–6 and 149–50.
34. Vance, 1990, p. 133.
35. Black, 2001, p. 108.
36. Vance, 1990, p. 134.
37. http://whc.unesco.org/sites/550.htm and http://www.gamberorosso.it/e/sangimignano/sangimignano.asp
38. Vance, 1990, p. 135.
39. Black, 2001, pp. 32 and 35.
40. ibid., pp. 32–3.
41. Vance, 1990, pp. 143–4.
42. Ackroyd, 2000, p. 92.
43. Rasmussen, 1937, pp. 67–70, quoted in Vance, 1990, p. 240.
44. Quoted in De Long and Shleifer, 1993, p. 673.
45. Quoted in De Long and Shleifer, 1993, p. 671.
46. De Long and Shleifer, 1993.
47. ibid., pp. 674 and 700.
48. ibid., pp. 695, 689.

9 By What Complicated Wheels?

1. Anon., 1854.
2. Cobbett, 1823, 28 June, vol. 45, col. 781.
3. ibid., 22 February 1823, vol. 45, cols. 481–2.
4. Quoted in Morris, Christopher, 1984, p. 8.
5. Quoted in Morris, Christopher, 1984, p. 186.
6. Bayliss-Smith, 1982, p. 108.
7. Cobbett, 1821, 7 April 1821, vol. 39, cols. 10–11.
8. Cobbett, 1823, 29 March 1823, vol. 45, col. 796.
9. Cobbett, 1830, 4 September 1823.

10. Cobbett, 1823, 5 May 1823, vol. 46, cols. 377–8.
11. Woods, 1989, p. 89.
12. Burchill, Julie, 2001, p. 3.
13. Quoted in Morris, Christopher, 1984, p. 7.
14. Schaer, Claeys and Sargent (eds.), 2000, pp. 38 and 74.
15. ibid.
16. ibid., p. 83.
17. ibid., p. 67.
18. Hector and Hooper, 2002.
19. More, 1516, p. 56.
20. ibid., p. 60.
21. ibid. pp. 64 and 76.
22. ibid., pp. 79, 61 and 57.
23. Morris, William, 1890, p. 142.

10 The City Found Wanting

1. Pounds, 1996, p. 13.
2. The First Reich was the empire found by Charlemagne in AD 800, which subsequently was known as the Holy Roman Empire and essentially lasted until 1806, when it was abolished in response to threats from Napoleon.
3. Rickman, 1980, p. 2.
4. Richie, 1998, p. 248.
5. Hall, Peter, 1998, p. 384.
6. Richie, 1998, p. 148.
7. ibid., 1998, pp. 159–161.
8. Quoted in Hall, Thomas, 1997, p. 197.
9. Quataert, 1996, p. 100.
10. Davis, 2000, p. 12, n. 16.
11. Pounds, 1996, p. 29.
12. Quataert, 1996, p. 105.
13. Davis, 2000, p. 19.
14. ibid., 2000, p. 22.
15. Aldenhoff, 1996, p. 34.
16. ibid., 1996, p. 35.
17. Vincent, 1985, p. 36.
18. ibid., 1985, pp. 115 and 50, quoting Keynes, 1949, p. 24; Asquith, 1923, pp. 138–9; and Great Britain, Foreign Office, 1918, pp. 455–7.
19. Craig, 1978, p. 354, quoted in Vincent, 1985, p. 18.

20. Robert, 1997, p. 49.
21. Vincent, 1985, p. 81.
22. Chickering, 1998, p. 41.
23. Bonzon and Davis, 1997, p. 310.
24. Chickering, 1998, p. 41.
25. ibid., p. 42.
26. ibid., p. 43.
27. Allen, 1998, p. 373.
28. ibid.
29. ibid., p. 374.
30. Vincent, 1985, p. 125.
31. Bonzon and Davis, 1997, p. 337.
32. Gläser, 1929, pp. 327 and 329, quoted in Vincent, 1985, pp. 21–2.
33. Blücher, 1920, p. 158.
34. Chickering, 1998, p. 45.
35. Vincent, 1985, pp. 124 and 151, n. 1.
36. Schriener, 1918, p. 329, quoted in Vincent, 1985, p. 45.
37. Davis, 2000, p. 21.
38. Bonzon and Davis, 1997, pp. 318–19 and 330.
39. Vincent, 1985, p. 49.
40. ibid., pp. 137–40.
41. Quoted in Allen, 1998, p. 381.
42. Blücher, 1920, pp. 144 and 146.
43. ibid., p. 127
44. Chickering, 1998, p. 45.
45. Blücher, 1920, p. 184.
46. Chickering, 1998, p. 45.
47. Blücher, 1920, p. 184, and Allen, 1998, p. 373.
48. http://www.nv.cc.va.us/home/cevans/Versailles/greatwar/casualties.html
49. Quoted in Vincent, 1985, p. 49.
50. ibid., p. 45.
51. ibid., p. 50.
52. Bonzon and Davis, 1997, p. 339.

11 The Impact of Numbers
1. Extrapolated from Broek and Webb, 1978, table 16.3, p. 395.
2. United Nations, 1998, p. 146.
3. Chandler and Fox, 1974, pp. 364 and 369.
4. Broek and Webb, 1978, pp. 429–30.

5. Chandler and Fox, 1974, pp. 329 and 335.
6. Drakakis-Smith, 2000, p. 112.
7. Population growth in the developed world 1875–1925 extrapolated from European culture area figures in Broek and Webb, 1978, table 16.3, p. 395. Other statistics from United Nations, Population Divisions pp. 96–7 and 120–21.
8. ibid.
9. Habitat International Coalition, 1998, p. 2.
10. United Nations, 1995, p. 76.
11. Drakakis-Smith, 2000, p. 134.
12. ibid.
13. Hugo, 1996, p. 173.
14. Smith, 1999. p. 36.
15. Calculated from UK government survey figures at http://www.statistics.gov.uk/pdfdir/fams0204.pdf
16. Hopkins, 1973, p. 244, and Jones, W.O., 1972, p. 18.
17. *New Scientist*, 1996, p. 11.
18. Smit, Ratta and Nasr, 1996.
19. ibid., pp. 25–7.
20. Garnett, 2000, pp. 478 and 488.
21. ibid., p. 25, and citing Heimlich (ed.) 1989.
22. Smit, Ratta and Nasr, 1996, p. 27.
23. Deelstra and Giradet, 2000, p. 48.
24. Quoted in Garnett, 1996, p. 17.
25. ibid.
26. ibid.
27. The paragraphs on urban agriculture in Cuba drawn upon Novo and Murphy, 2000, and Schwartz, 2000.
28. United Nations, 1998, p. 140.
29. Foeken and Mwangi, 2000, p. 304.
30. Drakakis-Smith, 2000, p. 125.
31. Marcuse, 1980, p. 27.
32. *Garden City*, 1907, vol. 2, p. 15, quoted in King, 1980, p. 203.
33. Quoted in King, 1980, p. 221, n. 14.
34. Hansen, 1997, p. 23.
35. Quoted in Collins, 1980, p. 228.
36. Quoted in Miller, 1971, p. 413.
37. Churchill, 1908 (1972), p. 16.
38. White, Silberman and Anderson, 1948, p. 43.
39. ibid., pp. 1 and 49.

40. ibid., existing residential density zoning, map between pp. 56 and 57.
41. ibid., p. 45.
42. ibid., p. 42.
43. ibid., p. 54.
44. Freeman, 1991, p. 33.
45. United Nations, 1998, p. 148,
46. Foeken and Mwangi, 2000, p. 312.
47. Freeman, 1991, pp. 62, 93 and 105.
48. ibid., p. 43.
49. ibid., p. 44.

12 Cities Built on Water

1. http://www.waterinschools.com/challenge/ringmain.htm
2. National Research Council, 1995, chapter 4.
3. United Nations, 1998, p. 148.
4. Of the several different spellings found in the literature, this is the most familiar.
5. Ezcurra, Mazari-Hiriart, Pisanty and Aguilar, 1999, p. 34.
6. Calnek, 1976, p. 288.
7. Díaz del Castillo, 1996, pp. 190–91.
8. ibid., p. 218.
9. Cortés, 1972, p. 104.
10. Matos Moctezuma, 1988, p. 55.
11. Ezcurra and Mazari-Hiriart, 1996, p. 9.
12. Hassig, 1985, pp. 57, 30 and 64.
13. ibid., p. 66.
14. ibid., p. 62, with distance from maps on pp. 58–9 and 140.
15. ibid., p. 62.
16. ibid.
17. United Nations, 1995, p. 165, and Ezcurra et al, 1999, p. 35.
18. Ezcurra et al, 1999, p. 243.
19. ibid., p. 217.
20. United Nations, 1995, p. 165.
21. Uitto and Biswas, 2000, pp. 117–19.
22. ibid.
23. National Research Council, 1995, chapter 3.
24. Ezcurra and Mazari-Hiriart, 1996, p. 13.
25. World Resources Institute, 1996, p. 64.
26. ibid. and Uitto and Biswas, 2000, p. 120.

27. Ezcurra and Mazari-Hiriart, 1996, p. 28, and Uitto and Biswas, 2000, pp. 123–5.
28. Uitto and Biswas, 2000, p. 127.
29. ibid., pp. 129–30.
30. Ezcurra and Mazari-Hiriart, 1996, p. 27.
31. ibid., p. 31.

13 Turn to the Sun

1. United States Strategic Bombing Survey, Urban Areas Division, 1947, No. 60, p. 33.
2. Ishikawa and Swain (trans.), 1981, p. 335.
3. Hersey, 1946, 1985, p. 40.
4. Hiroshima Peace Memorial Museum, 1998, p. 15.
5. Hersey, 1946, 1985, p. 81.
6. Ishikawa and Swain (trans.), 1981, p. 347, and Hiroshima Peace Memorial Museum, 1998, p. 39.
7. United States Strategic Bombing Survey, Urban Areas Division, 1947, No. 60, p. 32.
8. United States Strategic Bombing Survey, Physical Damage Division, 1947, No. 92, pp. 226, 245–6 and 267.
9. Hersey, 1946, 1985, pp. 69–70.
10. Ishikawa and Swain (trans.), 1981, pp. 83–6.
11. Croze and Reader, 2001, p. 27 (4 km^2 equals Hiroshima blast; city area 741 km^2).
12. http://www.meti.go.jp
13. Mankins, 1997.
14. Butti and Perlin, 1980, p.5.
15. ibid., p. 27.
16. ibid., p. 32–3.
17. ibid., p. 72.
18. ibid., chapter 9.
19. Radford, 1999.
20. Sinha and Vidal, 1999.
21. ibid.

14 Eternal Problems

1. Scott and Duncan, 2001, pp. 305, 312.
2. These paragraphs on Leonardo's city are derived from: Bramly, 1992, pp. 193–6, wherein are given references to original sources.
3. Cited in Cipolla, 1973, p. 23.

4. Bramly, 1992, p. 192.
5. *Guardian*, 20 May 2002, 'Meacher's plan'.
6. Quotations from Cipolla, 1992, pp. 19–20.
7. Riis, 1957 (originally published 1890), p. 8, quoted in Melosi, 1980, p. ii.
8. Sabine, 1937, pp. 20–21.
9. ibid., p. 27.
10. Details of medieval London's street-cleaning arrangements in the following paragraphs are taken from Sabine, 1937.
11. Melosi, 2000, p. 39.
12. Robinson, 1994 (originally published 1922), p. 121–2.
13. Cipolla, 1992, p. 21.
14. Sabine, 1934.
15. ibid., pp. 307 and 315.
16. Quoted in Sabine, 1937, p. 37.
17. ibid., p. 24.
18. Sabine, 1934, p. 318.
19. These paragraphs on Chadwick etc. draw on Melosi, 2000, chapter 2, and other sources as cited.
20. Quoted in Melosi, 2000, p. 53.
21. Quoted in Reid, 1991, p. 56.
22. ibid., p. 29.
23. ibid., p. 30.
24. ibid., pp. 57–8.
25. Information on the Gennevilliers scheme in the following paragraphs comes from Reid, 1991, pp. 58–65.
26. ibid., p. 69.
27. *New York Times*, 1996, quoted in Hardin, 1998, p. 15.
28. Peters 1999, p. 167.

15 The Greatness of Princes

1. Quoted in Woods, 1989, p. 80.
2. ibid., pp. 86–9.
3. The paper cited uses the terms 'crude death rate' and 'crude birth rate', which have specific technical meaning; for the purely illustrative purposes intended here the word 'crude' is omitted.
4. Dobson and Carter, 1996, p. 121, citing McNeill, 1977, p. 59.
5. Dobson, 1992, p. 411.
6. McNeill, 1977, pp. 50–52.
7. ibid., pp. 50 and 62.

8. ibid., pp. 79–80.
9. Scott and Duncan, 2001, pp. 5–6.
10. ibid.
11. Cliff, Haggett and Smallman-Raynor, 1998, p. 16 and table 1.4.
12. Quoted in Neuburger, 1925, p. 378.
13. Cipolla, 1976, p. 6.
14. ibid., p. 110.
15. Cipolla, 1992, p. 4
16. Cipolla, 1976, pp. 60–61.
17. Quoted in Pullan, 1992, p. 119.
18. ibid., p. 88.
19. Cliff, Haggett and Smallman-Raynor, 1998, p. 14.
20. ibid., p. 11.
21. Cipolla, 1973, pp. 20–21.
22. ibid., p. 26.
23. ibid., p. 27.
24. Quoted in Cipolla, 1976, p. 57.
25. 18 September 2002. New York spot price $316.80 per ounce. One ounce equals 28 g
26. Quoted in Cipolla, 1976, pp. 58–9.
27. Cipolla, 1973, pp. 89–90.
28. Cipolla, 1992, p. 78.
29. ibid.
30. Pullan, 1992, p. 117.
31. ibid., p. 118.
32. Cipolla, 1981, pp. 9–12.
33. See Cliff, Haggett and Smallman-Raynor, 1998, pp. 16–17.
34. Hirst, 1953, p. 105, quoted in Chandavarkar, 1992, pp. 203–40, in Ranger and Slack (eds.), 1992, 215.
35. Chandavarkar, 1992, pp. 203–4.
36. Hirst, 1953, p. 89, quoted in Chandavarkar, 1992, p. 214, n. 49.
37. Chandavarkar, 1992, pp. 215–16.
38. ibid., pp. 203–4.
39. Radford, 2002.
40. Schell and Stark, 1999, p. 148.
41. Ellison, 1999.

16 Capturing the Horizon

1. Alexander, 1992, p. 84.
2. Alexander, 1965.
3. *Economist*, 31 December 1999, p. 49.
4. Vance, 1986, p. 216.
5. ibid., p. 501.
6. Hall, Peter, 1998, p. 813.
7. Jacobs, 1970, pp. 63–5.
8. Casson, 1974, p. 65.
9. Vance, 1986, p. 425, and Albion, p. 410.
10. Morris, A.E.J., 1994, pp. 144 and 293.
11. Parry, 1977, p. 293.
12. Ringrose, 1970, p. xix.
13. Ringrose, 1983, p. 310.
14. Ringrose, 1983, p. 170.
15. Ringrose, 1970, p. 37.
16. Ringrose, 1983, p. 317.
17. Ringrose, 1970, p. 105.
18. ibid., p. 104.
19. ibid., p. 119.
20. ibid., pp. 90 and 127.
21. ibid., pp. 14–15.
22. ibid., pp. 15–16.
23. ibid., p. 17.
24. ibid., p. 133.
25. Vance, 1986, p. 228.
26. Campbell, Galloway, Keene and Murphy, 1993, p. 77.

17 'The city here, complete'

1. From Thom (Gunn), 1961 'A Map of the City', in *My Sad Captains and Other Poems*, London, Faber and Faber.
2. Davies and Hall (eds.), 1978, p. 126, quoted in Hall, Thomas, 1997, p. 13.
3. Wycherley, 1962, p. 43.
4. Morris, A.E.J., 1994, pp. 43–4.
5. These paragraphs on the gridiron layout of cities draw extensively on coverage of the subject in Morris, A.E.J., 1994.
6. ibid., pp. 57 and 79.
7. Hanke, 1967, quoted in Morris, A.E.J., 1994, pp. 305–6.
8. Quoted in Morris, A.E.J., 1994, p. 306.

9. Hall, Thomas, 1997, pp. 10–11.
10. Reps, 1965, quoted in Morris, A.E.J., 1994, p. 344.
11. Hall, Thomas, 1997, p. 11.
12. Reps, 1965, quoted in Morris, A.E.J., 1994, p. 335.
13. Quoted in Chapman, 1981, p. 10.
14. Chapman, 1981, p. 38.
15. Quoted in Stern, Gilmartin and Mellins, 1987, p. 507. Cited in Hall, Peter, 1998, p. 772.
16. Chapman, 1981, p. 116.
17. Mumford, 1961, pp. 441–2.
18. Reddaway, 1951. Appendix A deals thoroughly with sources of the myth that Wren's plan was first accepted and then rejected as a result of commercial pressures, says Morris, A.E.J., 1994, p. 257, n. 48.
19. Ackroyd, 2000, pp. 221–2.
20. ibid., p. 222.
21. Morris, A.E.J., 1994, p. 255, and Ackroyd, 2000, pp. 223 and 239.
22. Reddaway, 1951, quoted in Morris, A.E.J., 1994, p. 255.
23. ibid., p. 256.
24. Reader, 1986, pp. 14 and 17.
25. Morris, A.E.J., 1994, p. 259.
26. ibid., p. 256, caption to figures 8.8 and 8.9.
27. Ackroyd, 2000, p. 238.
28. Pevsner, 1973, quoted in Morris, A.E.J., 1994, p. 257.
29. Koenigsberger, and Mosse, quoted in Morris, A.E.J., 1994, p. 160.
30. Hall, Thomas, 1997, p. 33.
31. Morris, A.E.J., 1994, pp. 258–9.
32. Ackroyd, 2000, p. 240.
33. Rasmussen, 1937, and quoted in Morris, A.E.J., 1994, pp. 262–3.
34. Mumford, 1961, p. 454.
35. Hall, Peter, 1998, p. 176.
36. Hall, Thomas, 1997, pp. 168–86.
37. ibid., p. 177.
38. Hall, Peter, 1998, p. 177.
39. Ackroyd, 2000, p. 268.
40. Hall, Peter, 1998, p. 668.
41. ibid., pp. 670–72.

18 Accommodating Politics

1. Quoted in the *Economist*, 31 December 1999, p. 32.
2. Mayne, 1993, p. 21.

3. ibid., p. 22.
4. ibid, p. 63.
5. ibid., p. 57.
6. ibid., p. 74.
7. ibid., p. 80.
8. ibid., pp. 57–9, 85–6, 57–9.
9. ibid., p. 19, 440,000–880,000, averaging the figures given in table 2.1.
10. Scott, 1977, pp. 452–3, 455, 465 and 516–17; and Lindbeck, 1975, pp. 1–2 and 7; both quoted in Hall, Peter, 1998, pp. 844–5.
11. Hall, Thomas, 1997, p. 201.
12. ibid., pp. 210 and 214.
13. Quoted in Hall, Peter, 1998, p. 858.
14. Hall, Peter, 1998, pp. 861–3.
15. ibid.
16. ibid., p. 842.
17. ibid., pp. 878–9 and 857.
18. ibid., pp. 875–6.

19 Visions and Opportunities

1. Hall, Peter, 1998, p. 921.
2. In Blomeyer and Milzkott (eds.), 1990, editors' comment introducing Rogers.
3. ibid., pp. 34–5.
4. Angell, James W., quoted without date or source reference in Richie, 1998, p. 329.
5. Schwierzina, 1990, p. 14.
6. Federal State of the City of Berlin, 1998.
7. Richie, 1998, p. 336.
8. Quoted in Hall, Peter, 1998, p. 243.
9. Richie, 1998, pp. 715–16.
10. This and the following paragraphs are primarily derived from Stimmann, 1997.
11. Berlin Digital Environment Atlas, 2002.
12. Richie, 1998, pp. 161–2.
13. Strom and Mayer, 1998.
14. ibid.
15. Kramer, Jane, 1999.
16. Milner, 2000.
17. Wallace, 1999, p. 38.

18. Anders Fogh Rasmussen, the Danish Prime Minister, speaking as Denmark began its six-month presidency of the European Union in July 2002.
19. Baldwin, François and Portes, 1997.
20. Quoted in Richie, 1998, p. 1.

20 We Tread Too Heavily

1. Mercer Human Resource Consulting, 2002/4.
2. Forestry Commission, 2002.
3. Forestry Commission, 2000.
4. Gregg, Jones and Dawson, 2003, pp. 183–7.
5. Hamilton, 1999.
6. The statistics quoted in this and the following paragraph are taken from *Earth: Health Check for a Planet and Its People under Pressure.*
7. Wackernagel and Rees, 1996, p. 3.
8. International Institute for Environment and Development, 1995, quoted in Wackernagel and Rees, 1996, p. 91; Girardet, n.d.; Chambers, Simmons and Wackernagel, 2000, p. 134.
9. Rees, n.d.
10. Folke, Jansson, Larsson and Costanza, 1997.
11. London: Chambers, Simmons and Wackernagel, 2000, p. 134. North America (averaged) and India ecological footprints from Wackernagel and Rees, 1996, p. 85. Urban population percentages from United Nations, 1998, table A.2.
12. Wackernagel and Rees, 1996, pp. 13–14.
13. Revelations 17, 5.
14. Mumford, 1961, p. 220.
15. ibid., p. 372.
16. ibid., caption to plate 22.

Bibliography

Ackroyd, Peter, 2000. *London: The Biography*, London, Chatto and Windus

Adams, Robert McCormick, 1981. *Heartland of Cities: Surveys of Ancient Settlement and Land Use on the Central Floodplain of the Euphrates*, Chicago and London, University of Chicago Press

Albion, Robert Greenhalgh, 1926. *Forests and Sea Power: The Timber Problem of the Royal Navy 1652–1862*, Cambridge, Mass., Harvard University Press

Aldenhoff, Rita, 1996. 'Agriculture', in Chickering (ed.), 1996, pp. 32–61

Alexander, Christopher, 1965. 'A city is not a tree', pt 1, *Architectural Forum*, vol. 122, no. 1., 58–62

Alexander, R. McNeill, 1992. 'Human locomotion', pp. 80–85 in *Cambridge Encyclopedia of Human Evolution*

Allen, Keith, 1998. 'Sharing scarcity: bread rationing and the First World War in Berlin 1914–1923', *Journal of Social History*, vol. 32, pp. 371–93

Anon., 1854. 'The London Commissariat', *The Quarterly Review*, vol. 95, September 1854, no. CXC, pp. 271–308

Asquith, Herbert Henry, 1923. *The Genesis of War*, New York, George H. Doran

Bakker, Nico et al (eds.), 2000. *Growing Cities, Growing Food: Urban Agriculture on the Policy Agenda*, Feldafing, Deutsche Stiftung für internationale Entwicklung (DSE)

Baldwin, R., J. F. François and R. Portes, 1997. 'The costs and benefits of Eastern enlargement', *Economic Policy*, no. 24, quoted at http://europa.eu.int/comm/enlargement/arguments/index.htm

Balter, Michael, 1998. 'Why settle down? The mystery of communities', *Science*, vol. 282, pp. 1442–5.

Bauwelt Berlin Annual, 1997. *Chronology of Building Events 1996 to 2001: 1996*, Berlin, Berhäuser Verlag

Bayliss-Smith, T.P., 1982. *The Ecology of Agricultural Systems*, Cambridge, Cambridge University Press

Berdan, Frances F., 1999. 'Crime and control in Aztec society', in Hopwood (ed.), 1999, pp. 255–69

Berlin Digital Environment Atlas, 2002 06.03 *Green and Open Space Development*, Berlin, Senate Department of Urban Development, at http://www.stadtentwicklung.berlin.de/umwelt/umweltatlas/ed603 _01.htm

Black, Christopher, 2001. *Early Modern Italy: A Social History*, London and New York, Routledge

Blomeyer, Gerald R., and Rainer Milzkott (eds.), 1990. *Zentrum:Berlin – Scenarios of Development. Working Material for the Symposium Berlin:Centre organized by the City Council (Magistrat) of Berlin*, Berlin, Nicolaische Verlagsbuchandlung

Blücher, Evelyn, 1920. *An English Wife in Berlin*, London, Constable

Bonzon, Thierry, and Belinda Davis, 1997. 'Feeding the cities', in Winter and Robert, 1997, pp. 305–41

Bottéro, Jean, 1995. 'The most ancient recipes of all', in Wilkins, Harvey and Dobson (eds.), 1995, pp. 248–55

Boyd, Andrew, 1962. *Chinese Architecture and Town Planning 1500 B.C. – A.D. 1911*, London, Alec Tiranti.

Bramly, Serge, 1992. *Leonardo: The Artist and the Man*, London, Michael Joseph

Braudel, Fernand, 1982. *Civilization and Capitalism 15th–18th Century. Vol. 2. The Wheels of Commerce*, London, Collins

Bridges, Gary, and Sophie Watson (eds.), 2000. *Companion to the City*, Oxford, Blackwell

Britnell, R.H., 1993. *The Commercialisation of English Society 1000–1500*, Cambridge, Cambridge University Press

Broek, Jan O.M., and John W. Webb, 1978. *A Geography of Mankind*, London, McGraw-Hill

Brucker, Gene A., 1962. *Florentine Politics and Society, 1343–1378*, Princeton, Princeton University Press

Brunt, P.A., 1971. *Italian Manpower*, Oxford

Burchill, Julie, 2001. *Weekend Guardian*, 6 January 2001, p.3

Burckhardt, Jacob, 1865 (trans. by S.G.C. Middlemore 1958). *The*

Civilization of the Renaissance in Italy, vol. II, New York

Butti, Ken, and John Perlin, 1980. *A Golden Thread: 2500 Years of Solar Architecture and Technology*, London, Marion Boyars

Calnek, Edward E., 1976. 'The internal structure of Tenochtitlan'. In Wolf (ed.), 1976, pp. 287–302

Cambridge Encyclopedia of Human Evolution, 1992, eds. Jones, Steve, Robert Martin and David Pilbeam, Cambridge, Cambridge University Press

Campbell, Bruce M.S., James A. Galloway, Derek Keene and Margaret Murphy, 1993. *A Medieval Capital and Its Grain Supply: Agrarian Production and Distribution in the London Region c. 1300*, Research Paper Series, no. 30, London, Historical Geography Research Group

Casson, Lionel, 1974. *Travel in the Ancient World*, Baltimore and London, Johns Hopkins University Press

Çatal Hüyük Site Guide Book, n.d.

Chambers, Nicky, Craig Simmons and Mathis Wackernagel, 2000. *Sharing Nature's Interest: Ecological Footprints as an Indicator of Sustainability*, London, Earthscan

Chadavarkar, Rajnarayan, 1992. 'Plague panic and epidemic politics in India, 1896–1914', in Ranger and Slack (eds.), 1992, pp. 203–40.

Chandler, Tertius, and Gerald Fox, 1974 (2nd edn 1984). *3000 Years of Urban Growth*, New York and London, Academic Press

Chang, Kwang-chih, 1988. *Archaeology of Ancient China*, New Haven, Yale University Press

Chapman, Edmund H., 1981. *Cleveland: Village to Metropolis*, Cleveland, The Western Reserve Historical Society

Cherry, Gordon (ed.), 1980. *Shaping an Urban World*, London, Mansell

Chickering, Roger, 1998. *Imperial Germany and the Great War*, Cambridge, Cambridge University Press

Chickering, Roger (ed.) 1996. *Imperial Germany: A Historiographical Companion*, Westport and London, Greenwood Press

Childe, V. Gordon, 1950. 'The urban revolution', *Town Planning Review*, vol. 21, pp. 3–17

Churchill, Winston Spencer, 1908 (1972). *My African Journey*, London, New English Library

Cipolla, Carlo M., 1973. *Cristofano and the Plague: A Study in the History of Public Health in the Age of Galileo*, London, Collins.

—, 1976. *Public Health and the Medical Profession in the Renaissance*, Cambridge, Cambridge University Press

—, 1981, *Fighting the Plague in Seventeenth-Century Italy*, Madison,

University of Wisconsin Press

—, 1992. *Miasmas and Disease: Public Health and the Environment in the Pre-Industrial Age*, New Haven and London, Yale University Press

Cliff, Andrew, Peter Haggett and Matthew Smallman-Raynor, 1998. *Deciphering Global Epidemics: Analytical Approaches to the Disease Records of World Cities, 1888–1912*, Cambridge, Cambridge University Press

Cobbett, William, 1821. *Cobbett's Weekly Register*, London

—, 1823. *Cobbett's Weekly Register*, London

—, 1830. *Rural Rides*, London

Collins, John, 1980. 'Lusaka: urban planning in a British colony, 1931–64', in Cherry (ed.), 1980, pp. 227–41

Cook, Albert S., and Chauncery B. Tinker, 1926 (rev. edn). *Select Translations from Old English Poetry*, Boston and New York, Ginn and Company

Cortés, Hernán (trans. A.R. Pagden), 1972. *Letters from Mexico*, London, Oxford University Press

Craig, Gordon, 1978. *Germany, 1866–1945*, New York, Oxford University Press

Croze, Harvey, and John Reader, 2001. *Pyramids of Life*, London, Harvill

Davies, Ross and Peter Hall (eds.), 1978. *Issues in Urban Society*, Harmondsworth, Penguin Books

Davis, Belinda J., 2000. *Home Fires Burning: Food, Politics, and Everyday Life in World War I Berlin*, Chapel Hill and London, University of North Carolina Press

De Long, J. Bradford, and Andrei Shleifer, 1993. 'Prince and merchants: European city growth before the Industrial Revolution, *Journal of Law and Economics*, vol. 36, October 1993, pp. 671–702

De Roover, Raymond, 1956. 'The development of accounting prior to Luca Pacioli according to the account-books of medieval merchants', in Littleton and Yamey (eds.), 1956, pp. 114–74

Deacon, H. J., 1989. 'Late Pleistocene palaeoecology and archaeology in the southern Cape, South Africa', in Mellars and Stringer (eds.), 1989, pp. 547–64

Deelstra, Tjeerd, and Herbert Giradet, 2000: 'Urban agriculture and sustainable cities', in Bakker et al (eds.), 2000, pp. 43–66

Díaz del Castillo, Bernal, 1996. *The Discovery and Conquest of Mexico 1517–1521*, New York, Da Capo Press

Dobson, A., 1992, 'People and disease', in *Cambridge Encyclopedia of Human Evolution*, 1992, pp. 411–20

Dobson, Andrew, P., and E. Robin Carter, 1996. 'Infectious diseases and human population history', *BioScience*, vol. 46, no. 2, pp. 115–126

Drakakis-Smith, David, 2000. *Third World Cities* (2nd edn), London and New York, Routledge

Earth: Health Check for a Planet, published by the *Guardian* in association with Actionaid, August 2002

Economist, 31 December 1999

Electronic Text Corpus of Sumerian Literature: www.etcsl. orient.ox.ac.uk/section5/tr563.htm

Ellison, P.T., 1999. 'Fecundity and ovarian function in urban environments', in Schell and Ulijaszek (eds.), 1999, pp. 111–35

Ezcurra, Exequiel, and Marisa Mazari-Hiriart, 1996. 'Are megacities viable? A cautionary tale from Mexico City', *Environment*, vol. 38, no. 1, pp. 6–35.

Ezcurra, Exequiel, Marisa Mazari-Hiriart, Irene Pisanty and Adrián Guillermo Aguilar, 1999. *The Basin of Mexico: Critical Environmental Issues and Sustainability*, New York, United Nations University Press

Federal State of the City of Berlin, 1998. *The ENVIBASE-Project Documentation/Online Handbook*, Berlin, Ministry of Urban Planning, Environmental Protection and Technology, at http://www.stadtentwicklung.berlin.de/archiv_sensut/umwelt/uisonline/envibase/handbook/berlinpartner.htm

Fisher, Nick, 1999. '"Workshop of Villains" – Was there much organised crime in classical Athens?', in Hopwood (ed.), 1999, pp. 53–96

Foeken, Dick, and Alice Mboganie Mwangi, 2000. 'Increasing food security through urban farming in Nairobi', in Bakker et al (eds.), 2000, pp. 303–28

Folke, Carl, Asa Jansson, Jonas Larsson and Robert Constanza, 1997. 'Ecosystem appropriation by cities', *Ambio*, vol. 26, May 1997, pp. 167–72

Follain, John, 2002. 'Tourist clogged Venice . . .', *Sunday Times*, 13 January 2002, p. 26

Forestry Commission, 2000. News Release No. 2866

Forestry Commission, 2002. Reported in the *Independent*, 31 March 2002

Freeman, Donald B., 1991. *A City of Farmers: Informal Urban Agriculture in the Open Spaces of Nairobi, Kenya*, Montreal and London, McGill-Queen's University Press

Gabriel, Richard A., and Karen S. Metz, 1991. *From Sumer to Rome: The Military Capabilities of Ancient Armies*, New York and London, Greenwood Press

Garden City, 1907, vol. 2, p. 15

Garnett, Tara, 2000. 'Urban agriculture in London: rethinking our food economy', in Bakker et al (eds.), 2000, pp. 477–500

George, Andrew, 28 September 2001, in Channel 4 TV documentary, *Mesopotamia*

Gimpel, Jean, 1983. *The Cathedral Builders*, London, Michael Russell

Girardet, Herbert, n.d., *Cities and the Culture of Sustainability*, IEA SHC Task 30 Solar City, at http://www.solarcity.org/solarcity/resresurgencecities.htm

Gläser, Ernst, 1929. *Class of 1902*, New York, Viking

Goethe, J.W. von, *Wilhelm Meisters Lehrjahre*, 1795–6

Grayson, A. Kirk, 1991. 'Assyrian rulers of the early first millennium BC (1114–859 BC)', in *The Royal Inscriptions of Mesopotamia. Assyrian Period 2*, Toronto, Buffalo and London, University of Toronto Press

Great Britain, Foreign Office, 1918. *Foreign Relations, 1918, Suppl.I*, 1, pp. 455–7

Gregg, Jillian W., Clive G. Jones and Todd E. Dawson, 2003. 'Urbanization effects on tree growth in the vicinity of New York City', *Nature*, vol. 424, pp. 183–7

Grossman, David, Leo Van Den Berg and Hyacinth I. Ajaegbu (eds.), 1999. *Urban and Peri-urban Agriculture in Africa*, Aldershot, Ashgate

Guardian, 20 May 2002, 'Meacher's plan'

Guardian, 6 February 2004, Reuter's news report, p. 20

Gugler, Josef (ed.) 1996. The Urban Transformation of the Developing World. Oxford, Oxford University Press,

Gundersheimer, Werner, L., 1972. 'Crime and punishment in Ferrara, 1440–1500', in Martines (ed.), 1972, pp. 104–28

Haaland, R., 1992. 'Fish, pots and grain: early and Mid-Holocene adaptations in the Central Sudan', *Afr. Archaeol. Rev.*, vol. 10, pp. 43–64

Haas, J., S. Pozorski and T. Pozorski (eds.), 1987. *The Origins and Development of the Andean State*, New Directions in Archaeology, Cambridge, Cambridge University Press

Haas, Jonathan, 31 January 2002, interview in BBC TV programme, 'The lost pyramids of Caral', *Horizon*

Habitat International Coalition, 1998. 'Urban community waste management: a sub-Saharan study', http://www.enda.sn/rup/hec/Studies/anglophafarica.htm#titre

Hall, Peter, 1989. 'The rise and fall of great cities: economic forces and population responses', in Lawton (ed.), 1989

—, 1998. *Cities in Civilization: Culture, Innovation and Urban Order*, London, Weidenfeld and Nicolson

Hall, Thomas, 1997. *Planning Europe's Capital Cities: Aspects of Nineteenth-Century Urban Development*, London, E. and F.N. Spon

Hamilton, Gary, 1999. 'Urban jungle', *New Scientist*, vol. 161, no. 2178, pp. 38–42

Hanke, L., 1967 (1973). 'Spanish ordinances for the layout of new towns, 1573', in Hanke (ed.), 1973.

Hanke, L. (ed.), 1967 (2nd edn 1973). *The History of Latin American Civilisation, Vol. 1. The Colonial Experience*, Boston, Little, Brown

Hansen, Karen Tranberg, 1997. *Keeping House in Lusaka*, New York, Columbia University Press

Hardin, Russell, 1998. 'Garbage out, garbage in.' *Social Research*, vol. 65, no. 1

Hassig, Ross, 1985. *Trade, Tribute and Transportation: The Sixteenth-Century Political Economy of the Valley of Mexico*, Norman, University of Oklahoma Press

Hector, Andy, and Rowan Hooper, 2002. 'Darwin and the first ecological experiment', *Science*, vol. 295, 25 January 2002, pp. 639–40

Heidel, A., 1951. *A Babylonian Genesis*, Chicago, University of Chicago Press

Heimlich, Ralph E. (ed.), 1989. *Land Use Transition in Urbanizing Areas: Research and Information Needs*, Washington DC, The Farm Foundation in cooperation with the US Department of Agriculture, Economic Research Service

Herlihy, David, 1972. 'Some psychological and social roots of violence in the Tuscan cities', in Martines (ed.), 1972, pp. 129–54

Hersey, John, 1946, 1985. *Hiroshima*, New York, Vintage Books

Hiroshima Peace Memorial Museum, 1998. *The Outline of Atomic Bomb Damage in Hiroshima*

Hirst, L. Fabian, 1953. *The Conquest of Plague: A Study of the Evolution of Epidemiology*, Oxford, Oxford University Press

Hohenburg, Paul M., and Lynn Hollen Lees, 1995. *The Making of Urban Europe 1000–1994*, Cambridge, Mass., and London, Harvard University Press

Hopkins, A.G., 1973. *An Economic History of West Africa*, Harlow and New York, Longman

Hopwood, Keith (ed.), 1999. *Organised Crime in Antiquity*, London, Duckworth

Hrouda, B., 1991. *Der alte Orient: Verlorene Schätze, vergangene Kulturen zwischen Euphrat und Tigris*, Munich, Verlag Bassermann

Hugo, Graeme, 1996. 'Urbanization in Indonesia: city and countryside linked', in Gugler (ed.), 1996, pp. 133–84

Hunt, Edwin S., 1994. *The Medieval Super-Companies: A Study of the Peruzzi Company of Florence*, Cambridge, Cambridge University Press

International Institute for Environment and Development, 1995. *Citizen Action to Lighten Britain's Ecological Footprints*, London, IIED

Ishikawa, Eisei, and David L. Swain (trans.), 1981. *Hiroshima and Nagasaki: The Physical, Medical, and Social Effects of the Atomic Bombings*, London, Hutchinson

Jacobs, Jane, 1970. *The Economy of Cities*, London, Jonathan Cape

Jacobsen, Thorkild, 1982. *Salinity and Irrigation Agriculture in Antiquity*, Bibliotheca Mesapotamica 14, Undena Publications

Jacobsen, Thorkild, and Robert McAdams, 1958. 'Salt and silt in ancient Mesopotamian agriculture'. *Science*, vol. 128, no. 3334, pp. 1251–8

Jones, A.H.M., 1957. *Athenian Democracy*, Oxford, Blackwell

Jones, W.O., 1972. *Marketing Staple Foods in Tropical Africa*, Ithaca, Cornell University Press

Kagan, Donald (ed.), 1992. *The End of the Roman Empire: Decline or Transformation?*, Lexington, Mass., D.C. Heath

Keynes, John Maynard, 1949. *Two Memoirs*, London, Hart-Davis

Kilmer, A.D., 1972. 'The Mesopotamian concept of overpopulation and its solution as reflected in the mythology', *Orientalia (Nova Series)*, vol. 41. pp. 160–77

King, A.D., 1980. 'Exporting planning: the colonial and neo-colonial experience', in Cherry (ed.), 1980, pp. 203–26

Koenigsberger, H.G., and G. L. Mosse, 1968. *Europe in the Sixteenth Century*, London, Longman

Kovacs, Maureen (trans.), 1989. *The Epic of Gilgamesh*. Stanford, Stanford University Press

Kowaleski, Maryanne, 1995. *Local Markets and Regional Trade in Medieval Exeter*, Cambridge, Cambridge University Press

Kramer, Jane, 1999. 'Living with Berlin', *New Yorker*, 5 July, 1999, pp. 60–61

Kramer, Noah Samuel, 1961. *History begins at Sumer*, London, Thames and Hudson

— 1963. *The Sumerians: Their History, Culture and Character*. Chicago, University of Chicago Press

Lawton, Richard (ed.), 1989. *The Rise and Fall of Great Cities: Aspects of Urbanisation in the Western World*, London and New York, Belhaven Press

Lee, T.A., A. Bishop and R. H. Parker (eds.), 1996. *Accounting History from the Renaissance to the Present*, New York and London, Garland Publishing

Leick, Gwendolyn, 2001. *Mesopotamia: The Invention of the City*, London, Allen Lane

Lindbeck, A., 1975. *Swedish Economic Policy*, London, Macmillan

Littleton, A.C., and B.S. Yamey (eds.), 1956. *Studies in the History of Accounting*, London, Sweet and Maxwell

Loftus, William Kennett, 1857. *Travels and Researches in Chaldaea and Susiana; with an Account of Excavations at Warka, the 'Erech' of Nimrod, and Súsh, 'Shushan the Palace of Esther', in 1849–52*, London, James Nisbet

Macve, Richard H. 1996. *Pacioli's Legacy*, in Lee, Bishop and Parker (eds.), 1996, pp. 3–30

Maisels, Charles Keith, 1990. *The Emergence of Civilization: From Hunting and Gathering to Agriculture, Cities and the State in the Near East*, London and New York, Routledge

Mankins, John C., 1997. 'Solar power from space.' Statement before the Subcommittee on Space and Aeronautics, Committee on Science, House of Representatives, October 24, 1997. www.prospace.org/issues/spss/jmankin-test.htm

Marcuse, Peter, 1980. 'Housing policy and city planning: the puzzling split in the United States, 1893–1931', in Cherry (ed.), 1980, pp. 23–58

Martines, Lauro, 1972. 'Political violence in the thirteenth century', in Martines (ed.), 1972, pp. 331–53

Martines, Lauro (ed.), 1972. *Violence and Civil Disorder in Italian Cities 1200–1500*, Berkeley and London, University of California Press

Matos Moctezuma, Eduardo, 1988. *The Great Temple of the Aztecs: Treasures of Tenochtitlan*, London, Thames and Hudson

Mayne, Alan, 1993. *The Imagined Slum: Newspaper Representation in Three Cities, 1870–1914*, Leicester and New York, Leicester University Press

McNeill, William H., 1977. *Plagues and Peoples*, Oxford, Blackwell

—, 1979. *A World History*, Oxford, Oxford University Press

Meiggs, Russell, 1973. *Roman Ostia*. Oxford, Clarendon Press

Mellaart, James, 1967. *Çatal Hüyük: A Neolithic Town in Anatolia*, London, Thames and Hudson

Mellars, Paul, and Chris Stringer (eds.), 1989. *The Human Revolution: Behavioural and Biological Perspectives on the Origins of Modern Humans*, Edinburgh, Edinburgh University Press

Melosi, Martin V., 1980. 'Environmental crisis in the city', in Melosi (ed.), 1980 pp. 3–31

—, 2000. *The Sanitary City: Urban Infrastructure in America from Colonial Times to the Present*, Baltimore and London, Johns Hopkins University Press

Melosi, Martin V. (ed.), 1980. *Pollution and Reform in American Cities, 1870–1930*, Austin and London, University of Texas Press

Mercer Human Resource Consulting, 2002/4. 'World-wide quality of life survey', www.mercerhr.com/qol

Miller, Charles, 1971. *The Lunatic Express*, New York, Ballantine Books

Milner, Mark, 2000. 'Germans learn that two into one won't go', *Guardian*, 3 October 2000

Modelski, George, 1997. 'Early world cities: extending the census to the fourth millennium', at http://www.etext.org/Politics/World.Systems/papers/modelski/geocit.htm

Montanari, A., and C. Muscara, 1995. 'Evaluating tourists flows in historic cities: the case of Venice', *Tijdschrift voor Economische en Sociale Geografie*, vol. 86, no. 1, pp. 80–87, as quoted at: http://www.egt.geog.uu.nl/L_UG_2.html

More, Thomas, 1516, *Utopia*, Everyman, 1994. J.M. Dent, London

Morris, A. E. J, 1994. *History of Urban Form: Before the Industrial Revolutions* (3rd edn), Harlow, Longman

Morris, Christopher, 1984. *William Cobbett's Illustrated Rural Rides 1821–1832*, Exeter, Webb and Bower

Morris, William, 1890. *News from Nowhere*, in *Stories in Prose, etc.*, Centenary Edition, 1944, Nonesuch Press, London

Morris, William Alfred, 1910. *The Frankpledge System*, London, Longman

Mumford, Lewis, 1961. *The City in History: Its Origins, Its Transformations and Its Prospects*, Harmondsworth, Penguin Books

National Research Council, 1995. *Mexico City's Water Supply – Improving the Outlook for Sustainability*, Washington DC, National Academy Press

Needham, Joseph, 1954. *Science and Civilisation in China, Vol. 1*, Cambridge, Cambridge University Press

Neuburger, Max, 1925. *History of Medicine*, 2 vols. Oxford, Oxford Medical Publications

New Scientist, 1996. 'Farming comes to feed the world', *New Scientist*, vol. 150, no. 2034, 15 June 1996, p. 11

New York Times, 9 June 1996, sec. 1., p. 46

Nicholas, David, 1997. *The Later Medieval City 1300–1500*, London and New York, Longman

Nissen, Hans J., 1988. *The Early History of the Ancient Near East, 9000–2000 B.C* (trans. Elizabeth Lutzeier), Chicago and London, University of Chicago Press

Norwich, John Julius, 2001. 'The Religion of Empire', review of *Venice: Lion City* by Garry Wills, in *Los Angeles Times Book Review*, September 30, 2001

Novo, Mario Gonzalez, and Catherine Murphy, 2000. 'Urban agriculture in the city of Havana: a popular response to a crisis'. In Bakker et al (eds.), 2000, pp. 329–47

Origo, Iris, 1957. *The Merchant of Prato: Francesco di Marco Datini*, London, Jonathan Cape

Pacioli, Luca, *Exposition of Double-Entry Bookkeeping, Venice 1494.* (trans. Antonia von Gebsattel, introduction and commentary by Basil Yamey), 1994, Venice, Albrizzi Editore

Parkins, Helen, and Christopher Smith (eds.), 1998. *Trade, Traders and the Ancient City*, London and New York, Routledge

Parry, J. H., 1977. *The Spanish Seaborne Empire*, London, Hutchinson

Partner, P. 1976. *Renaissance Rome, 1500–1559: A Portrait of a Society*, Berkeley, University of California Press

Paterson, Jeremy, 1998. 'Trade and traders in the Roman world: scale, structure and organisation', in Parkins and Smith (eds.), 1998, pp. 149–67

Peters, J. 1999. 'Urbanism and health in industrialised Asia', in Schell and Ulijaszek (eds.), 1999, pp. 158–74

Pevsner, Nikolaus, 1973. *An Outline of European Architecture*, London, Allen Lane

Pollack, Susan, 1999. *Ancient Mesopotamia: The Eden That Never Was*, Cambridge, Cambridge University Press

Polo, Marco (trans. Ronald Latham), 1958. *The Travels of Marco Polo*, Harmondsworth, Penguin Books

Postgate, J. N., 1992. *Early Mesopotamia: Society and Economy at the Dawn of History*, London and New York, Routledge

Pounds, Norman J.G., 1973. *An Historical Geography of Europe 450*

B.C.–A.D. 1330, Cambridge, Cambridge University Press

—, 1979. *An Historical Geography of Europe 1550–1840*, Cambridge, Cambridge University Press

—, 1996. 'Historical geography', in Chickering, Roger (ed.), 1996, pp. 13–32

Powell, Marvin A., 1985. 'Salt, seed and yields in Sumerian agriculture: a critique of the theory of progressive salinisation', *Zeitschrift für Assyriologie*, vol. 75, pp. 7–38

Pozorski, S., 1987. 'Theocracy vs. militarism: the significance of the Casma valley in understanding early state formation', in Haas, Pozorski and Pozorski (eds.), 1987, pp. 15–30

Pringle, Heather, 1998. 'The original blended economies', *Science*, vol. 282, p. 1447

—, 2001. 'The first urban center in the Americas', *Science*, vol. 292, 27 April 2001, pp. 621–2.

Pullan, Brian, 1992. 'Plague and perceptions of the poor in early modern Italy', in Ranger and Slack (eds.), 1992, pp. 101–23

Quataert, Jean, 1996. 'Demographic and social change', in Chickering (ed.), 1996, pp. 97–130

Radford, Tim, 1999. 'Sunshine superman,' *Guardian* science section, 12 August 1999, p. 8

Radford, Tim, 2002. 'World health "threatened by obesity"' [report on American Association of the Advancement of Science meetings 2002, Boston, Mass.], *Guardian* 18 February 2002, p. 8

Ranger, Terence, and Paul Slack (eds.), 1992. *Epidemics and Ideas. Essays on the Historical Perception of Pestilence*, Cambridge, Cambridge University Press

Rasmussen, Steen Eiler, 1937. *London: The Unique City*, New York and London, Macmillan

Reader, John, 1986. *The Rise of Life: The First 3.5 Billion Years*, London, Collins

—, 1997. *Africa: A Biography of the Continent*, London, Hamish Hamilton

Reddaway, T.F., 1951. *The Rebuilding of London after the Great Fire*, London, Edward Arnold

Rees, William E., n.d. *Ecological Footprints: Making Tracks towards Sustainable Cities. Virtual Policy Dialog*, at http://www.iisd.ca/linkages/consume/brfoot.html

Reid, Donald, 1991. *Paris Sewers and Sewermen: Realities and Representations*, Cambridge, Mass., and London, Harvard University Press

Renger, Johannes, 1991. 'Wirtschaft und Gesellschaft', in Hrouda, 1991, pp. 187–215

Reps, J.W., 1965. *The Making of Urban America*, Princeton University Press

Richie, Alexandra, 1998. *Faust's Metropolis: A History of Berlin*, New York, Carroll and Graf, Inc.

Rickman, Geoffrey E., 1971. *Roman Granaries and Store Buildings*, Cambridge, Cambridge University Press

—, 1980. *The Corn Supply of Ancient Rome*. Oxford, Clarendon Press

Riis, Jacob, A., 1996 (originally published 1890). *How the Other Half Lives: Studies among the Tenements of New York*, Boston, Bedford Books, St. Martin's Press

Ringrose, David R., 1970. *Transportation and Economic Stagnation in Spain, 1750–1850*, Durham, NC, Duke University Press

—, 1983. *Madrid and the Spanish Economy, 1560–1850*, Berkeley, University of California Press

Robert, Jean-Louis, 1997. 'Paris, London, Berlin on the eve of the war', in Winter and Robert, 1997, pp. 25–53

Robinson, O.F., 1994 (originally published 1922). *Ancient Rome: City Planning and Administration*, London and New York, Routledge

Rodzinski, Witold, 1988. *The Walled Kingdom: A History of China from 2000 BC to the Present*, London, Fontana

Sabine, Ernest L., 1933. 'Butchering in medieval London', *Speculum*, vol. 8, pp. 335–53

—, 1934. *Latrines and Cesspools of Medieval London*, *Speculum*, vol. 9, pp. 303–21

—, 1937. *City Cleaning in Medieval London*, *Speculum*, vol. 12, pp. 19–43

Schaer, Roland, Gregory Claeys and Linda Tower Sargent (eds.), 2000. *Utopia: The Search for the Ideal Society in the Western World*, New York and Oxford, New York Public Library/Oxford University Press

Schell, L. M., and A. D. Stark, 1999. 'Pollution and child health', in Schell and Ulijaszek (eds.), 1999, pp. 136–57

Schell, L. M., and S. J. Ulijaszek (eds.), 1999. *Urbanism, Health and Human Biology in Industralised Countries*, Cambridge, Cambridge University Press

Schreiner, George E., 1918. *The Iron Ration*, London, John Murray

Schwartz, Walter, 2000. 'Havana harvest', in *Guardian* Society suppl. pp. 8–9, *Guardian*, 16 January 2002

Schwierzina, Tino, 1990. 'Welcoming address', in Blomeyer and Milzkott (eds.), 1990

Scott, F.D. 1977. *Sweden: The Nation's History*, Minneapolis, University of Minnesota Press

Scott, Susan, and Christopher J. Duncan, 2001. *Biology of Plagues: Evidence from Historical Populations*, Cambridge, Cambridge University Press

Seneca's letters to Lucilius (trans. Barker, E. Phillips), 1932, 2 vols., Oxford, Clarendon Press

Shane III, O.C., and M. Küçük, 1998. 'The world's first city', *Archaeology* vol. 51, no. 2, March/April 1998, pp. 43–7

Sinha, Ashok, and John Vidal, 1999. 'Solar day dawning', *Guardian* Society suppl., pp. 4–5, *Guardian*, 23 June 1999

Smit, Jac, Annu Ratta and Joe Nasr, 1996. *Urban Agriculture: Food, Jobs and Sustainable Cities*, Habitat II Series, New York, UNDP

Smith, David, 1999. 'Urban agriculture in Harare: socio-economic dimensions of a survival strategy', in Grossman, Van Den Berg and Ajaegbu (eds.), 1999, pp. 9–40

Soja, Edward W., 2000. 'Putting cities first: remapping the origins of urbanism', in Bridges and Watson (eds.), 2000, pp. 26–34

Solis, Ruth Shady, Jonathan Haas and Winifred Creamer, 2001. 'Dating Caral, a Preceramic site in the Supe Valley on the coastal plain of Peru', *Science*, vol. 292, 27 April 2001, pp. 723–6

Ste Croix, G.E.M. de, 1981. *The Class Struggle in the Ancient Greek World*. London, Duckworth

Steinhardt, Nancy Shatzman, 1990. *Chinese Imperial City Planning*, Honolulu, University of Hawaii Press

Stern, R.A.M., G. Gilmartin and T. Mellins, 1987. *New York 1930: Architecture and Urbanism between the Two World Wars*, New York, Rizzoli

Stimmann, Hans, 1997. 'Invisible urban development', pp. 88–101 in *Bauwelt Berlin Annual*, 1997

Strom, Elizabeth, and Margit Mayer, 1998. 'The new Berlin', *German Politics and Society*, vol. 16, pt. 4, pp. 122–39, at http://userpage.fu-berlin.de/~mayer/mm/pubs/newberlin.htm

Taylor, R. Emmett, 1956. *Luca Pacioli*, in Littleton and Yamey (eds.), 1956, pp. 175–84

Tertullian, Quint: Septimi Florentis Tertulliani De Anima (ed. J.H. Waszink), 1947. Amsterdam, J.M. Meulenhoft

Uitto, Juha I., and Asit K. Biswas, 2000. *Water for Urban Areas: Challenges and Perspectives*, New York, United Nations University Press

United Nations, 1995. *The Challenge of Urbanization: The World's Largest Cities*, New York, United Nations

United Nations, Population Division 1998. *World Urbanization Prospects, 1996 revision*, New York.

United States Strategic Bombing Survey, Urban Areas Division, 1947. No. 60: *The Effects of Air Attack on the City of Hiroshima*, Washington DC, US Government Printing Office

United States Strategic Bombing Survey, Physical Damage Division, 1947. No. 92: *Effects of the Atomic Bomb on Hiroshima, Japan, Vol. III, pt 2*, Washington DC, US Government Printing Office

Van de Mieroop, Marc, 1997. *The Ancient Mesopotamian City*, Oxford, Clarendon Press

Vance, James E. Jr, 1986. *Capturing the Horizon: The Historical Geography of Transportation since the Transportation Revolution of the Sixteenth Century*, New York, Harper and Row

—, 1990. *The Continuing City: Urban Morphology in Western Civilization*, Baltimore and London, Johns Hopkins University Press

Vincent, C. Paul, 1985. *The Politics of War*, Athens, Ohio, and London, Ohio University Press

Wackernagel, Mathis, and William E. Rees, 1996. *Our Ecological Footprint: Reducing Human Impact on the Earth*, Gabriola Island, BC, New Society Publishers

Wallace, Charles P., 1999. Across the Great Divide. TIME International vol. 154 no. 20, November 15 1999, p. 38

Wheatley, Paul, 1971. *Pivot of the Four Quarters*, Edinburgh, Edinburgh University Press

White, L.W. Thornton, L. Silberman and P. R. Anderson, 1948. *Nairobi: Master Plan for a Colonial Capital*, London, HMSO

Wilkins, John, David Harvey and Mike Dobson (eds.), 1995. *Food in Antiquity*, Exeter, University of Exeter Press

Wills, Garry, 2001. *Venice: Lion City*, New York, Simon and Schuster

Winter, Jay, and Jean-Louis Robert, 1997. *Capital Cities at War: Paris, London, Berlin 1914–1919*, Cambridge, Cambridge University Press

Wolf, Eric R. (ed.), 1976. *The Valley of Mexico: Studies in Pre-Hispanic Ecology and Society*, Albuquerque, University of Mexico Press

Woods, R. 1989. 'What would we need to know to solve the "natural population decrease problem" in early-modern cities?' in Lawton (ed.), 1989, pp. 81–95

Woolley, Sir Charles Leonard, 1982. *Ur 'of the Chaldees'*, London, The Herbert Press

World Resources Institute, 1996. *World Resources 1996–97*, New York, Oxford University Press

Wycherley, R.E., 1962. *How the Greeks Built Cities*, London, Macmillan

Yoffe, Norman and George Cowgill (eds.), 1988. *The Collapse of Ancient States and Civilisations*, Tucson, University of Arizona Press

Index

University 146; tenement buildings in 148; urban plans for 289–93; vision for 285; Wall built 285–6; wartime food rationing in 152–5; wartime memories 283–4; waste disposal in 215, *see also* Germany

bicycles 234, 236, 237–8

Birmingham, housing schemes in 272–4; population of 274

Black, Christopher 116, 118

Black Death 91, 93, 201, 220

Black Sea 54, 56

Blantyre 174

Blücher, Evelyn 154, 156–7, 158

Bologna 120; illness and health in 225, 226

Bombay (Mumbai) 72, 229–30

Book of Good Manners (Certaldo) 118

Bourbon family 124, 126

Boyd, Andrew 79

BP (British Petroleum) 199

Brandenburg 144–5

Brasilia 124

Braudel, Fernand 117

Brazil 164

Brazzaville 295

Bremen 62, 149

Brescia 201

Brighton 136–7, 138

Brisbane 295

Brooklyn Bridge 272

Brueghel the Elder 140

Bruges 87, 102

Brussels 293

Buenos Aires 305

Bulawayo 174

Burchill, Julie 138

Burckhardt, Jacob 118

Caesar, Julius 58, 65, 145

Cairo 69, 71, 73, 221–2

Calgary 296

California 199

Cambridge 264

Campania 63

Canada 168

canals *see* rivers and canals

Canberra 124

Cape Town 3–4, 295

Caral (Peru) 11–12, 13, 18

Cartagena 250

Carthage 61, 62; waste disposal in 208

Casma (Peru) 11

Castile 243

Castillo, Diáz del 181

Çatal Hüyük 27, 74; artworks at 19–21; burials at 21–2; craftsmen at 16, 20–1, 22–4; domestication of the wild at 18–19, 21; and exploitation of surrounding environment 18–19; layout of 17–18; occupation/desertion of 17; pottery at 15–16; social/ economic arrangements at 15–16; uniqueness of 17; as world's first city 16

Catalonia 103

cathedrals and monasteries 86, 88–9, 90

Cato the Elder 62

cave paintings 19, 20

Central African Republic 295

Central America 10

Ceppo di Francesco di Marcho foundation 96, 97

Certaldo, Paolo da 118

Chadwick, Edwin 211–14

354

apprenticeships 42; beliefs 27; canal system 27, 51–2; cities of 24, 25, 26–7; clay tablets 40; collapse of cities 68, 69; epics 53; food recipe 32–3; illness 219; location of cities in 72; ordinary life 33, 35–50; pottery 15–16; royal tombs 34; slaves 28–9; and solar energy 197; and warfare 51–3; waste disposal 204, see also Mesopotamia; Ur; Uruk

Sweden, economic base 275; industrial development in 275–6; manufacturing in 276; nature of housing in 280; social democracy in 277–80, 281; urbanisation in 276, see also Stockholm

Switzerland 296
Sydney 124
Syracuse 238
Syria 39

Tacitus 66
Taiwan 166, 200
Tang dynasty 70
Tanzania 124, 166
Taut, Bruno 285
Tehran 295
Tenochtitlan 180; canoes 184–5; dependence on water 184; food for 183–5; history of 181; isolation and self-sufficiency 185; lake and canal system 186–7; population of 181, 184, 185; renamed Mexico City 185; size of 181–3; Spanish arrival in 181–3; tribute paid to 183–4; water supplies for 184, 186, see

also Mexico City
Terracina 65
Thatcher, Margaret 281
Thebes 54
Third Reich 285, 292
Thorp, John 210
Tiber river 60, 62, 64–7
Tiberius, Emperor 58, 145
Tigris river 25, 46, 53, 72
Tocqueville, Alexis de 271
Tokyo 73, 190, 294, 295; population of 71, 72
Tomorrow: A Peaceful Path to Real Reform (Howard) 173
Tours 89
trade and commerce, and the Church 95, 96, 101; counterfeit goods 121; and customer outrage 44; and double-entry bookkeeping 104–5; effect of hostilities on 102–3; Greek 54; Mesopotamian 39, 44; in Middle Ages 87–8; nefarious dealings 112–14; northern European ascendance 121; Roman 60; Sumerian business records 40–1, 44; and use of money alternatives 103–4; variety of 100–3, see also Datini, Francesco di Marco; grain trade, merchant class
Trajan, Emperor 66
transport see travel and transport
travel and transport 302; Aztec 184–5, 186; and bicycles 234, 236, 237–8; crossing the Alps 105–6; growth in 236; and Hiroshima 193; in Middle Ages 87, 102; and the motor car 237; and the railways 236–7, 245–6;